THE BIG RED
BOOK OF
SPANISH GRAMMAR

THE BIG RED BOOK OF SPANISH GRAMMAR

Dora del Carmen Vargas, Ph.D.

New York   Chicago   San Francisco   Lisbon   London   Madrid   Mexico City
Milan   New Delhi   San Juan   Seoul   Singapore   Sydney   Toronto

1 2 3 4 5 6 7 8 9 10 11 12 13 14 15 16 17 18 19 20 21 22   FGR/FGR   0 9 8

ISBN 978-0-07-154758-1 (book and CD-ROM set)
MHID   0-07-154758-4 (book and CD-ROM set)

ISBN 978-0-07-154759-8 (book for set)
MHID   0-07-154759-2 (book for set)
Library of Congress Control Number: 2007934608

Interior design by Monica Baziuk

McGraw-Hill books are available at special quantity discounts to use as premiums and sales promotions or for use in corporate training programs. To contact a representative, please visit the Contact Us pages at www.mhprofessional.com.

CD-ROM for Windows
To install: Insert the CD-ROM into your CD-ROM drive. The CD-ROM will start automatically. If it does not, double-click on MY COMPUTER; find and open your CD-ROM disk drive, then double-click on the install.exe icon.

Minimum System Requirements:
Computer: Windows 2000, XP, Vista
Pentium III (450 MHz recommended), or better
256 MB RAM
14″ color monitor
8X or better CD-ROM
Sound card
Installation: Necessary free hard-drive space: 150 MB
Settings: 800 x 600 screen resolution
256 (16-bit) colors (minimum)
Thousands (24- or 32-bit) of colors (preferred)

CD-ROM for Mac
To install: Insert the CD-ROM into your CD-ROM drive. A window will open with the contents of the CD. Drag the program icon to your Application folder. For easy access, create an alias of the program on your desktop or your dock.

Minimum System Requirements:
Computer: Mac OS X 10.3.x, 10.4.x, 10.5.x
Power PC (G3 recommended), or better; any Intel processor
256 MB RAM

Call 1-800-722-4726 if the CD-ROM is missing from this book.
For technical support go to http://www.mhprofessional.com/support/technical/contact.php

This book is printed on acid-free paper.

Contents

Articles

Articles are words used before nouns, or before words that function as nouns, to indicate their gender and number. They also indicate whether the noun is known to the reader or the listener (*definite* article) or if it is unknown (*indefinite* article). In Spanish there is also a *neuter* article, **lo**, which refers to abstract nouns and does not point to gender or number.

Definite Article Forms

The English definite article *the* has four equivalent forms in Spanish: *el*, *la*, *los*, and *las*.

Singular			Plural		
masculine: *el barco*	the boat		masculine: *los barcos*	the boats	
feminine: *la sierra*	the hill		feminine: *las sierras*	the hills	

Article-Noun Agreement

A. **The definite article agrees in gender and number with the noun to which it refers:**

Los autos japoneses son muy populares.	Japanese cars are very popular.
Quiero visitar las ruinas de Machu Picchu.	I want to visit the ruins of Machu Picchu.

However, there are some exceptions when the noun is singular but has a plural form:

el paraguas	the umbrella	*los paraguas*	the umbrellas
el botones	the bellboy	*los botones*	the bellboys

B. The definite article does not agree in gender with singular feminine nouns that begin with a stressed *a* or *ha*, for the sake of euphony:

*el **á**guila*	eagle	*el **a**gua*	water	*el **ha**mbre*	hunger
*el **a**lma*	soul	*el **a**rpa*	harp	*el **a**ula*	classroom

If the *a* or *ha* is unstressed, the feminine definite article must be used:

la araña	spider	*la amapola*	poppy	*la aduana*	customs

NOTES:

(1) This apparent masculine article is actually a modification of the old form of the feminine definite article, *ela*, blending the pronunciation of the letter *a* with the first vowel of the noun.

(2) The adjectives that modify the preceding nouns follow the normal rules of agreement. Since the noun is feminine, the adjective needs to be in the feminine form:

El arpa vieja estaba guardada en el sótano.	The old harp was stored in the basement.
Los niños ocuparon el aula grande y espaciosa.	The children occupied the large and spacious classroom.

(3) The apparent gender change does not affect the plural form of the definite article:

las águilas	*las aguas*	*las hambres*
las almas	*las arpas*	*las aulas*

(4) To name the letters *a* and *h,* the feminine definite article is still used, although the *a* sound is stressed:

La "a" es la primera letra del abecedario.	"A" is the first letter of the alphabet.
La "hache" no se pronuncia en español, a menos que esté precedida de "c".	"H" is not pronounced in Spanish unless it is preceded by "c."

(5) If an adjective beginning with stressed *a* is placed between the definite article and the noun, the feminine form of the definite article is maintained:

*la **á**cida manzana*	the sour apple
*la **a**mplia habitación*	the spacious room

(6) In a familiar style, the feminine definite article is also used before a feminine name that begins with stressed *a*:

*la **A**na*	*la **Á**gueda*	*la **Á**ngela*

Uses of the Definite Article

A. The definite article with geographical names

1. The definite article agrees with the noun in gender and number:

el Mediterráneo	la Antártida
el Peñón de Gibraltar	la América Latina
el Río de la Plata	la Patagonia
el lago Titicaca	la Isla de Pascua

2. Before names of countries and large areas or regions, the definite article is usually omitted, although it is frequently used in cases such as the following:

el África	la China	el Paraguay
la Argentina	el Ecuador	el Perú
el Asia	los Estados Unidos	la Siberia
el Brasil	el Japón	el Uruguay

3. The definite article is used when the names of cities and countries are modified by a complement:

el México moderno	**la** Roma de los Césares
la España de Franco	**la** Rusia de los Zares

4. Naturally, the definite article is used when it is part of the name:

Las Vegas	La Habana	La Paz

B. The definite article with names of streets, avenues, and parks

The definite article is used when the word *calle* (*street*), *avenida* (*avenue*), or *parque* (*park*) appears as part of the address:

la Avenida 9 de Julio	**el** Parque Centenario
la Quinta Avenida	**el** Parque Central
la Calle 14	**el** Parque Lezama

Otherwise, it is not used:

Vivo en **Larrea** 120.	I live at 120 Larrea Street.
Corrientes corta la Avenida 9 de Julio.	Corrientes Street intersects July 9th Avenue.

C. The definite article with names of people

1. The definite article is used when a name is preceded by a title:

la señora Juana	*el doctor Fernández*
el profesor Pérez	*la abogada García*
el Papa Pablo VI	*el general Franco*

El señor García es muy bueno.	Mr. García is very nice.

The definite article is used in indirect speech, when talking about a person:

Vi a la profesora Gómez ayer.	I saw Professor Gómez yesterday.

NOTES:

However, the definite article is not used:

(1) in direct address:

Buenas tardes, profesor Pérez.	Good afternoon, Professor Pérez.
Doctor Fernández, escríbalo, por favor.	Dr. Fernández, write it, please.

(2) with *doña* or *don*, as in *doña Juana* or *don Carlos*. (The feminine *la doña*, used without the name of the person, as in *Juan vio a la doña*, has a contemptuous or humorous connotation.)

(3) with religious titles such as *San Antonio, Santa Catalina, Fray Luis de León, Sor Juana Inés de la Cruz, Santo Tomás*.

(4) with titles that include either a cardinal or an ordinal number, such as *Pío Doce* (Pius XII) or *Felipe Segundo* (Philip II).

2. The definite article is used when a name is preceded by an adjective:

el pobre Sancho (poor Sancho)	*la vieja Celestina* (old Celestina)

3. The definite article is used when a name represents the title of a book, a play, or an opera:

el Hamlet	*la Aída*	*el Martín Fierro*

NOTES:

The definite article is not used, however, if

(1) The title does not include the name of a person, as in

Me gustó mucho Rebelde sin causa.	I liked *Rebel Without a Cause* very much.

(2) The title already has a definite article:

*Leímos un comentario sobre **El** hablador.*   We read a commentary on *El hablador.*

4. The definite article is used when a name denotes someone's character:

   *Su amigo se creía **el** Lorca del club literario.*   His friend considered himself the Lorca of the literary club.

5. The definite article is used when a name is followed by an epithet:

   *Juana **la** Loca*   Juana the Mad
   *Lorenzo **el** Magnífico*   Lawrence the Magnificent

6. The definite article is used when a feminine name is part of a sentence written in familiar or figurative speech:

   *Miguel se lo dio a **la** Dora.*   Michael gave it to Dora.
   *¿Oíste el discurso de **la** Hillary?*   Did you hear Hillary's speech?
   *Tuve una clase con **la** Tortello.*   I had a class with Mrs. Tortello.

7. The definite article is used when a feminine name is used in legal or journalistic style:

   ***La** Fernández declaró no haberlo conocido.*   Fernández declared that she had not met him.
   ***La** Serrano probó que ya había salido del trabajo.*   Serrano proved that she had already left work.

8. The definite article is used in the masculine plural with a family name.

   The definite article is used in the masculine plural form with the family name (last name) to refer to a married couple or to a family including all its members:

   ***Los** García no han llegado todavía.*   The Garcías have not arrived yet.
   ***Los** Morales están en la sala.*   The Morales are in the living room.

9. The definite article is not generally used with names of relatives.

   (a) In direct or indirect speech, the name never follows *papá* or *mamá*, and the definite article is omitted:

   Papá, aquí está el café.   Dad, here's the coffee.
   Mamá, acompáñame a la tienda.   Mom, come with me to the store.
   Dile a papá que venga.   Tell Dad to come.

(b) Sometimes a father-in-law or mother-in-law is addressed as *papá* or *mamá*, with the name added for clarification. Although this is not generally done in English, a literal translation follows:

Dáselo a Papá Esteban.	Give it to Dad Esteban.
Le escribió una carta a mamá María.	He wrote a letter to Mom María.

(c) If the relative is *tío(a)*, the definite article is omitted in direct speech but may be used in indirect speech:

Tía Carmen, ven pronto.	Aunt Carmen, come soon.
*Le dije **a la** tía Carmen que viniera pronto.*	I told Aunt Carmen to come soon.

(d) If the relative is *abuelo(a)*, the definite article is omitted in direct speech but is generally used in indirect speech:

Abuela Ana, tráeme los anteojos.	Grandma Ana, bring me the glasses.
*Dale los anteojos a **la** abuela Ana.*	Give the glasses to Grandma Ana.

D. **The definite article in the masculine form with a phrase or a sentence that functions as a noun:**

*No me importa **el** <u>qué dirán</u>.*	I don't care about their opinion.
*Le satisface **el** <u>que le hayamos dicho la verdad</u>.*	It satisfies him that we have told him the truth.
***El** <u>que lo haya dicho</u>, no indica que sepa lo que está pasando.*	The fact that he has said it does not indicate that he knows what is going on.

NOTES:

(1) When there is an adjective that functions as a noun, the definite article agrees with the adjective:

***Los** <u>interesados</u> vinieron a la reunión.*	The interested (parties) came to the meeting.
***La** <u>elegida</u> era muy bonita.*	The chosen one was very pretty.

(2) If a noun is left out, the definite article agrees with the gender and number of the implied noun (second example sentence below).

La <u>señora</u> de enfrente es rusa.	The lady across the street is Russian.
La de enfrente es rusa.	The one across the street is Russian.

E. **The definite article in the masculine form with infinitives that function as nouns**

When the infinitive functions as a noun and is in the position of the subject, it is preceded by the masculine singular form of the definite article:

El ir y venir de la gente era insoportable.	The coming and going of the people was unbearable.
El comer tarde no es bueno para la salud.	Eating late is not good for one's health.
El no contestar mis cartas me dice que ella no está interesada.	Her not answering (The fact that she doesn't answer) my letters tells me that she is not interested.

F. The definite article with parts of the body

The definite article is used in Spanish with parts of the body instead of the possessive adjective:

Me lastimé la muñeca.	I hurt my wrist.
Juan se ha golpeado el codo.	Juan has hurt his elbow.
Tiene los pies hinchados.	She has swollen feet.

NOTE:

However, in order to emphasize a particular part of the body or to avoid ambiguity, the possessive adjective is generally used.

Todavía recuerdo los matices de su pelo.	I still remember the shades of her hair.
Mis manos temblaban.	My hands were trembling.

G. The definite article with a noun used in apposition with another noun to give emphasis or for clarification:

Juan, el hijo de Carlos, terminó sus estudios.	Juan, Carlos's son, finished his studies.
Ana, la maestra de secundaria, no gana mucho.	Ana, the high school teacher, does not make much money.

NOTE:

In some cases, the use of the definite article indicates individuality:

Carlos, electricista de la firma, es mi hermano.	Carlos, an electrician in the firm, is my brother. (Carlos is not necessarily the only electrician there.)
Carlos, el electricista de la firma, es mi hermano.	Carlos, the electrician of the firm, is my brother. (Carlos is the only electrician in the company.)

H. The definite article with a noun used after the conjunction *o* (*or*) to indicate an alternative:

Quiero comprar **la** falda o **la** blusa.	I want to buy the skirt or the blouse.

> **NOTE:**
>
> However, it is omitted when the noun after *o* is used as a clarification of the noun before it:
>
> | | |
> |---|---|
> | El inspector **o** encargado de la investigación dio una explicación sobre el material desaparecido. | The inspector, or head of the investigation, explained about the material that had disappeared. |

I. The definite article with superlative forms:

La jirafa, **el** animal más alto, come hojas.	The giraffe, the tallest animal, eats leaves.

J. The definite article with pieces of clothing

In Spanish, the definite article is used when the possessive adjective would be used in English:

Delia se puso **el** vestido nuevo para la fiesta.	Delia put on her new dress for the party.
Tienes **los** zapatos bien lustrados.	Your shoes are well polished.

K. The definite article with days of the week

1. The masculine form of the definite article is used with days of the week. Also, the definite article is used in Spanish when the preposition *on* would be used in English:

Llegaremos **el** lunes.	We will arrive on Monday.
Tengo clases **los** martes.	I have classes on Tuesdays.
El jueves es un buen día para mí.	Thursday is a good day for me.

2. The definite article is used after *hasta* and *para*:

¡Hasta **el** martes!	See you on Tuesday!
Esto es para **el** sábado.	This is for Saturday.

3. The definite article follows the word *todos* (*every*):

*Visita a su madre todos **los** martes.*　　　　He visits his mother every Tuesday.

4. The definite article is omitted when the day of the week follows the verb *ser* to identify the day:

Hoy es viernes.　　　　Today is Friday.
Ayer fue lunes.　　　　Yesterday was Monday.

5. The definite article is omitted with the expression *de ... a* to indicate *from . . . to*:

Juan trabaja de miércoles a domingo.　　　　Juan works from Wednesday to Sunday.

L. The feminine definite article with the hours of the day:

*Es **la** una y media de la tarde.*　　　　It is 1:30 P.M.
*Son **las** cuatro y veinte.*　　　　It is 4:20.
*Son **las** veintiuna en punto.*　　　　It is exactly nine o'clock P.M.

M. The definite article with meals

1. The definite article is used when the noun describes a specific meal:

El desayuno es a las ocho.　　　　Breakfast is at eight.
*Reservamos una mesa para **el** almuerzo.*　　　　We reserved a table for lunch.
*Ellos vendrán para **el** té.*　　　　They will come for five o'clock tea.
*Los chicos toman **la** merienda a las cinco.*　　　　The kids have a snack at five.
*Hay muchos invitados para **la** cena.*　　　　There are many guests for supper.

2. The definite article is generally used after *para (for)*:

*No hay nada para **el** desayuno.*　　　　There's nothing for breakfast.
*Para **el** almuerzo tenemos pollo.*　　　　For lunch we have chicken.
*Para **la** cena hay arroz y también verduras.*　　　　For supper there is rice and also vegetables.
*Para **la** merienda tenemos queso y jamón.*　　　　For a snack we have cheese and ham.

NOTE:
The definite article always follows *para* when referring to teatime.

*No hay mermelada para **el** té.*　　　　There's no marmalade for teatime.

3. The definite article always follows *hasta (until)*:

*Esperaremos hasta **la** cena.*　　　　We'll wait until supper.

*Trabajé hasta **el** almuerzo.*　　　　I worked until lunch.

4. The definite article is omitted after *de*:

No hay nada <u>de desayuno</u>.　　　　There's nothing for breakfast.

<u>De cena</u> tenemos arroz y verduras.　　We have rice and vegetables for supper.

<u>De merienda</u> tenemos queso y jamón.　　We have cheese and ham for a snack.

<u>De almuerzo</u> tenemos pollo.　　　　We have chicken for lunch.

> **NOTE:**
>
> This construction is not used with teatime; *para el té* is used instead:
>
> *<u>Para el té</u> tenemos torta.*　　　　We have cake for teatime.

N. **The definite article with *madrugada*, *mañana*, *tarde*, and *noche* as expressions of specific times of the day**

1. The definite article is not used after *de*:

Vino <u>de madrugada</u>.　　　　He came at dawn.

Llegamos <u>de tarde</u>.　　　　We arrived in the afternoon.

> **NOTE:**
>
> However, it is used after *de* to indicate a specific hour:
>
> *Llamaste a las ocho de **la** noche.*　　You called at 8:00 P.M.
>
> *Me desperté a las cuatro de **la** madrugada.*　I woke up at 4:00 A.M.

2. The definite article is used after *a*:

*Vino a **la** mañana.*　　　　She came in the morning.

*Llegamos a **la** noche.*　　　　We arrived at night.

O. **The definite article (optional) with *mediodía* and *medianoche***

The definite article may be omitted after *a, antes de,* and *después de*:

*Estudiamos **a(l)** mediodía.*　　　　We studied at noon.

*Comió **antes de(l)** mediodía.*　　　　He ate before noon.

*Llamó por teléfono **después de (la)** medianoche.*　　She called on the phone after midnight.

Salió *a (la) medianoche.*	He left at midnight.
Después de (la) medianoche saldremos de viaje.	We'll leave on a trip after midnight.

P. The definite article with numbers used to indicate *at a certain age*:

*Vino a los Estados Unidos a **los** veinte años.*	He came to the United States when he was twenty years old.
*Escribió su última novela a **los** ochenta.*	He wrote his last novel when he was eighty.

Q. The definite article with seasons of the year

The definite article is used when the seasons are the subject of the sentence, including constructions with the verbs *gustar* and *preferir*:

***El** verano es muy caluroso en Florida.*	Summer is very hot in Florida.
*Me gusta **la** primavera.*	I like spring.
*Preferimos **el** otoño porque no hace frío.*	We prefer the fall because it is not cold.

NOTE:

The definite article may be dropped in other cases:

*Me gusta nadar en primavera (en **la** primavera).*	I like to swim in the spring.
*Vamos a esquiar en invierno (en **el** invierno).*	We go skiing in the winter.

R. The masculine definite article with dates:

*Vinieron **el** 25 de diciembre.*	They came on December 25th.
*Me llamó **el** 7 de mayo.*	She called me on May 7th.
*Llega **el** primero de junio.*	He arrives on June 1st.

NOTES:

However, the definite article is omitted:

(1) When dating a letter:

Nueva York, 25 de mayo de 1962
2 de enero de 2005

(2) After the expression *estamos a ...* (another form of indicating today's date):

Estamos a 17 de agosto.	Today is August 17. (Literally: We are at . . .)

S. The definite article with months of the year

The definite article is used only if the name of the month is modified:

Octubre es uno de los meses más lindos del año.	October is one of the nicest months of the year.
El cálido octubre invitaba a hacer caminatas.	The warm October was an invitation for long walks.

T. The definite article with names of languages

1. The masculine form of the definite article is used with names of languages:

El inglés se habla en casi todo el mundo.	English is spoken in almost the whole world.
El ruso es un idioma muy difícil.	Russian is a very difficult language.

2. The definite article is not used after the prepositions *en* and *de*:

*Las instrucciones están escritas **en** italiano.*	The instructions are written in Italian.
*Vamos a la clase **de** español.*	We are going to the Spanish class.

Note that, when nationality rather than language is being expressed, the definite article is used after *de*:

*El libro **del** español es mejor.*	The book by the Spanish writer is better.

3. The use of the definite article is optional after verbs such as *aprender, comprender, conocer, enseñar, entender, escribir, estudiar, hablar, leer,* and *saber*:

*Queremos aprender **(el)** japonés.*	We want to learn Japanese.
*Todos los paraguayos saben **(el)** guaraní.*	Every Paraguayan knows Guarani.
*Me gustaría hablar **(el)** portugués.*	I would like to speak Portuguese.

> **NOTE:**
> If an adverb is placed between the verb and the name of the language, the definite article must be used:
>
> | | |
> |---|---|
> | *Queremos aprender <u>bien</u> **el** japonés.* | We want to learn Japanese well. |

U. The definite article with expressions of possession

1. The definite article may be omitted with possessive pronouns:

Esta cartera es (la) mía.	This purse is mine.
Los libros que están aquí son (los) nuestros.	The books that are here are ours.

> **NOTE:**
>
> The use of the definite article may imply an identification, more than merely possession.
>
> | | |
> |---|---|
> | *Esta cartera es **la** mía.* | This purse (and not the other one) is mine. |

2. The definite article is used when possession is indicated with *de*, with or without the noun:

***Los** libros de Carlos están sobre la mesa.*	Carlos's books are on the table.
***Los** de Fernando están sobre el sofá.*	Fernando's are on the sofa.

V. No definite article in exclamations or in the vocative case (when calling someone):

¡Madre mía!	Good heavens!
¡Dios mío!	Dear Lord!
¡Estudiantes!	Students!

W. The definite article with a noun used in a general sense

1. With a noun used in a general sense, the definite article is used in the singular or plural form, as needed:

***El** gato tiene uñas largas.*	Cats (in general) have long nails.
***Los** aviones han influenciado el progreso.*	Planes (all planes) have influenced progress.

> **NOTE:**
>
> This usage can also indicate specific nouns, as in:
>
> | | |
> |---|---|
> | ***El** gato de Juan tiene uñas largas.* | Juan's cat has long nails. |
> | ***Los** aviones alemanes han influenciado el progreso.* | German planes have influenced progress. |

2. If a limiting adjective modifies a noun used in a general sense, the definite article is omitted:

Juan come comidas <u>grasosas</u>.	Juan eats fatty meals.
Tengo <u>poco</u> dinero en mi cuenta.	I have little money in my account.

To identify the noun, the definite article is used:

*Juan come **las** comidas grasosas que hace su mamá.*	Juan eats the fatty meals made by his mother.
*En mi cuenta tengo **el** poco dinero que me diste.*	In my account I have the little money that you gave me.

X. The definite article with abstract ideas:

***La** sinceridad es algo que lo caracteriza.*	Sincerity is something that makes him stand out.
***El** amor es la más sublime de todas las cualidades humanas.*	Love is the most sublime of all human qualities.

Y. The definite article with the words *todo/a, todos/as*

1. To indicate a class as a whole, the definite article is used:

*Toda **la** leche se vende a los mercados.*	All milk is sold to the markets.
*Todo **el** centro está recargado de tránsito.*	All downtown is heavy with traffic.
*Todos **los** estudiantes toman un examen de ingreso.*	All students take an entrance examination.
*Todas **las** valijas son revisadas en la aduana.*	All bags are checked at the customs office.

2. To indicate *each one* or *every one* in the group, the definite article is omitted:

<u>*Toda leche*</u> *debe ser pasteurizada.*	Every milk bottle must be pasteurized.
<u>*Toda valija*</u> *que llega a la aduana será abierta.*	Every bag that arrives at customs will be opened.
<u>*Todo barrio*</u> *es parte vital de las ciudades.*	Every neighborhood is a vital part of the cities.
<u>*Todo estudiante*</u> *deberá tomar un examen.*	Every student will have to take an exam.

Z. No definite article when referring to a part of a whole concept

Whenever *some* or *any* is used in English, the definite article is omitted in Spanish:

Me dio aceite y vinagre para la ensalada.	She gave me some oil and vinegar for the salad.
Hay que ponerle pimienta a la salsa.	We need to put some pepper in the sauce.

AA. The definite article with units of weight, units of measure, or rates

When English uses *per, the,* or *a/an* to establish a unit of weight, measure, or a rate, the definite article is used in Spanish:

Las bananas están a un dólar el medio kilo.	Bananas cost a dollar per pound.
La alfombra cuesta diez pesos el metro.	The carpet costs ten dollars the yard.
Las frutillas están a dos pesos la caja.	The strawberries are at two dollars a box.
Mi hermano gana seis pesos la hora. (or *por hora*)	My brother makes six dollars an hour. (per hour)

BB. The definite article to indicate a unit of time

When English uses *next* (**próximo**) or *last* (**pasado**) to indicate a unit of time, the definite article is used in Spanish:

*Vamos a Orlando **el** próximo jueves.*	We go to Orlando next Thursday.
***El** año pasado terminé los cursos de la universidad.*	Last year I finished the university courses.

CC. The definite article with idiomatic expressions, set expressions, and proverbs

The definite article may or may not be used with idiomatic expressions and proverbs. Since many of these expressions do not have an exact equivalent in English, it will be necessary to consult a list of the most common expressions in order to use them properly. Some examples are:

Más largo que esperanza de pobre.	(Regarding distance:) As unreachable as the hopes of a poor person.
Sin duda Alberto vendrá mañana.	Without a doubt (No doubt) Alberto will come tomorrow.
No creo en la renguera del perro ni en lágrimas de mujer.	Literally: I don't believe in a dog's limping nor in a woman's tears. (I don't believe what you are saying).
La paciencia es la madre de la ciencia.	Literally: Patience is the mother of science (wisdom).

DD. No definite article with nouns used to establish a relationship:

Pelean como perro y gato.	They fight like cats and dogs.
Los declaro marido y mujer.	I pronounce you husband and wife.
Juana e Isabel son carne y uña.	Juana and Isabel are very close friends. (Literally: flesh and nail).

1. When the masculine singular definite article *el* follows the preposition *a* or *de,* it is contracted (losing the *e*):

Iremos [a + el] teatro para ver una ópera.	We'll go to the theater to see an opera.
Iremos al teatro para ver una ópera.	
Éste es el libro [de + el] profesor.	This is the professor's book.
Éste es el libro del profesor.	

NOTES:

The contraction of definite article and preposition does not take place in the following cases:

(1) With masculine plural or with feminine forms:

El jefe lee el informe a los empleados.	The boss reads the report to the employees.
Este libro es de los estudiantes.	This book belongs to the students.
El estudiante entrega el cuaderno a la(s) maestra(s).	The student turns in the notebook to the teacher(s).
Los lápices son de la(s) niña(s).	The pencils belong to the girl(s).

(2) When the definite article is part of a title:

Ya leí la mitad de El sombrero de tres picos.	I've already read half of *El sombrero de tres picos.*

2. After the prepositions *a, de,* and *en* in expressions with **casa**, when **casa** means *home,* the definite article is not used:

Juan viene a casa todos los jueves.	Juan comes home every Thursday.
Lucía salió de casa a las ocho.	Lucía left home at eight.
Los niños se quedaron en casa.	The children stayed home.
But: *Los niños se quedaron en la casa* (not necessarily their home).	

3. The use of the definite article is optional after *a, de,* and *en* with **clase** (*class*) and **misa** (*Catholic mass*):

Vamos a (la) clase de 8 a 10.	We go to class from 8:00 to 10:00.
Salimos de (la) clase a las 11.	We leave class at 11:00.
Los alumnos están en (la) clase.	The students are in class.

*Aída acostumbra ir a (**la**) misa los domingos.*	Aída usually goes to mass on Sundays.
*Lo veo cuando regresa de (**la**) misa.*	I see him when he returns from mass.
*Está serio como si estuviera en (**la**) misa.*	He is as quiet as if he were at mass. (popular proverb)

FF. The definite article in phrases that replace proper names and common nouns:

la *ciudad eterna*	Rome
la *ciudad santa*	Jerusalem
la *reina del Plata*	Buenos Aires
el *Mártir del Gólgota*	Jesus Christ
el *astro rey*	the sun
la *casa de Dios*	the church
la *última morada*	the cemetery
el *manco de Lepanto*	Miguel de Cervantes
el *rey de los animales*	the lion
la *ciudad de la música*	Nashville, TN

GG. The definite article with nouns in a series

1. If the nouns are closely related, the definite article precedes only the first one:

*Recuerdo **las** tristezas y desilusiones de mi niñez.*	I remember the sad moments and disillusions of my childhood.
*Se refirió **al** gobierno y control de los súbditos.*	He referred to the government and control of the subjects.

> **NOTE:**
> In the following exceptions, either each noun must be preceded by the definite article, or else each noun must stand by itself:
>
> | | |
> |---|---|
> | ***El*** *padre y **la** hija de Juan viven en la misma ciudad.* | Juan's father and daughter live in the same city. |
> | *Madre e hijo se llevan bien.* | Mother and son get along fine. |

2. The definite article is used only once when more than one noun refers to the same individual:

La *secretaria y encargada de las compras gana poco.*	The secretary and purchasing clerk doesn't make much money. (same person)

Compare the following example, where there is more than one individual:

La secretaria y la encargada de las compras no han recibido el informe. The secretary and the purchasing clerk have not received the report. (two different people)

Other examples include:

la maestra de inglés y física the teacher of English and physics (one person)

la maestra de inglés y la de física the English teacher and the physics teacher (two people)

el décimo y último día de vacaciones the tenth and last vacation day (same day)

el décimo y el último día de vacaciones the tenth and the last vacation days (two days)

HH. The definite article with subjects of study

The following rules apply:

1. When referring to a subject in general, the definite article is usually omitted:

   Mi hermana estudia geografía y matemáticas. My sister studies geography and mathematics.

   (La) física es un tema que me interesa. Physics is a subject that interests me.

2. The definite article must be used if there is a modifier:

   La física del siglo XX produjo resultados esperados. Twentieth-century physics produced expected results.

II. No definite article to indicate material or contents

The definite article is not used with a noun that indicates either the material of which an item is made or the contents of an item.

una pulsera de plata	a silver bracelet
el tenedor de plástico	the plastic fork
la casa de madera	the wooden house
una taza de té	a cup of tea
la botella de vino	the bottle of wine
la caja de aspirinas	the box of aspirin

Indefinite Article Forms

The English articles *a, an,* and the plural form *some* (*several, a few*) have four equivalent forms in Spanish: *un, una, unos,* and *unas.*

Singular		Plural	
masculine: *un niño*	a boy	masculine: *unos niños*	some boys
feminine: *una camisa*	a shirt	feminine: *unas camisas*	some shirts

Article-Noun Agreement

A. **The indefinite article agrees in gender and number with the noun to which it refers:**

Un árbol adorna la entrada del jardín.	A tree decorates the entrance to the garden.
Unas niñas venían corriendo por la calle.	Some girls came running down the street.

B. **The indefinite article with singular feminine nouns beginning with stressed *a* or *ha***

The indefinite article does not agree in gender with singular feminine nouns that begin with stressed *a* or *ha*, although forms such as *una águila, una ánfora,* and *una habla* are not considered incorrect, but are very seldom used.

un águila	eagle	*un agua*	water	*un hambre*	hunger
un alma	soul	*un arpa*	harp	*un aula*	classroom

NOTE:

The adjectives that follow these nouns maintain the normal rules of agreement (i.e., feminine adjective for a feminine noun):

Corría un agua cristalina y pura sobre las rocas.	A crystalline and pure water was flowing over the rocks.
Enseño en un aula amplia en la esquina del edificio.	I teach in a big classroom in the corner of the building.

C. **The indefinite article before an adjective beginning with a stressed *a***

If an adjective beginning with a stressed *a* is placed between the article and the noun, the feminine article is maintained:

Estudiamos en una amplia aula que da al jardín.	We study in a big classroom that overlooks the garden.

Uses of the Indefinite Article

A. **The indefinite article used to refer to nouns that are not specified:**

Tengo **un** libro de gramática española.	I have a Spanish grammar book.

In this sentence, the article refers to any Spanish grammar book, without specifying which one. In order to indicate a book that is well known to both the speaker and the reader, the definite article *el* should be used:

Tengo **el** libro de gramática española.	I have the Spanish grammar book.

B. **The indefinite article as a numeral**

The singular forms of the article (**un/una**) are used to indicate the number **one**, which also has a feminine form in Spanish. If necessary, meaning may be clarified in context or by pronouncing the particular word more emphatically when it refers to the numeral.

Hay **un** caballo en el establo.	There is a horse in the stable.
Hay **un** caballo en el establo.	There is one horse in the stable.
Tengo **una** lámpara en la cocina.	I have a lamp in the kitchen.
Tengo **una** lámpara en la cocina.	I have one lamp in the kitchen.

C. **The indefinite article used to show availability, existence, or lack of something**

When there is no indication of number, especially after verbs such as *buscar, encontrar, haber, llevar, querer, tener,* and *usar,* and also in negative sentences, the following rules apply:

1. The indefinite article is omitted before plural nouns:

Tienen hijos e hijas.	They have sons and daughters.
No tienen hijos.	They do not have children.
Hay barrios residenciales en esta ciudad.	There are residential areas in this city.

2. The indefinite article may be omitted before singular nouns:

Quieren (**una**) casa con terreno.	They want a house with a yard.
No quieren (**una**) casa con terreno.	They don't want a house with a yard.
Busco (**una**) secretaria que venga de lunes a viernes.	I'm looking for a secretary who will work Monday through Friday.

Buscan (**un**) plomero con experiencia.	They're looking for a plumber with experience.
Encontramos (**un**) lápiz y (**un**) papel.	We found pencil and paper.
Tenía (**una**) bufanda.	He had a scarf on.

NOTES:

(1) If number or emphasis is required, the indefinite article must be used.

Se durmió sin **una** queja.	She fell asleep without a complaint.
Tenía **una** bufanda preciosa.	She had a beautiful scarf.
¡Tiene **una** gracia para bailar!	He has such grace in dancing! (He is such a graceful dancer!)
Tiene **un** miedo horrible.	She is terribly afraid.

(2) In negative sentences with *tener*, the indefinite article is not used.

No tienen perro.	They do not have a dog.
No tenía dolor de muelas.	He did not have a toothache.

3. The indefinite article is generally omitted with *llevar, usar*, and other verbs that indicate customary action:

Las chicas de esa escuela usan zapatos negros como parte del uniforme.	The girls in that school wear black shoes as part of their uniform.
Siempre lleva sombrero cuando llueve.	He always wears a hat when it rains.
Escribe cartas a sus amigos.	She writes letters to her friends.

4. With forms of *haber* (*there is/there are*), the following rules apply.

(a) If *un (una)* acts as an indefinite article (and not the number *one*), it is not used after *haber* in negative sentences:

No hay pánico.	There is no panic.
No había respeto.	There was no respect.
Dijo que no hay problemas.	She said there are no problems.

(b) If the noun is modified in such a sentence, however, the indefinite article may be used:

No hay **un** pánico <u>aparente</u>.	There is no apparent panic.
No había **un** respeto <u>incondicional</u> hacia las autoridades.	There was no unconditional respect for the authorities.

D. The indefinite article used to indicate nationality, professions, or affiliation

1. The indefinite article is normally omitted with nationality, professions, or affiliation:

Carlos es boliviano.	Carlos is (a) Bolivian.
Mi padre es médico.	My father is a doctor.
Él es demócrata.	He is a Democrat.
Juana es metodista.	Juana is (a) Methodist.

2. The indefinite article is needed, however, when an adjective is added:

*Jaime es **un** <u>buen</u> venezolano.*	Jaime is a good Venezuelan.
*Mi padre es **un** <u>excelente</u> médico.*	My father is an excellent doctor.
*Él es **un** demócrata <u>empedernido</u>.*	He is a fanatical Democrat.
*Juana es **una** metodista <u>devota</u>.*	Juana is a devout Methodist.

NOTE:

The indefinite article may be omitted when the noun and the corresponding adjective are widely used together:

Jaime es cantante famoso.	Jaime is a famous singer.
Mi padre es excelente médico.	My father is an excellent doctor.
Su esposa es buena compañera.	His wife is a good companion.
Pedro es buen alumno.	Pedro is a good student.

3. The indefinite article is used with some set expressions:

*¡Jaime es **un** bandido!*	Jaime is a rascal!
*¡Pedro es **un** nene de mamá!*	Pedro is a Mama's boy!
*Julia es **una** cosita linda.*	Julia is a cute little thing.

E. The indefinite article with prepositions and *como*

1. After the preposition *con*, when *con* only expresses existence or availability, the indefinite article is not used.

Se vino con sombrero.	He came with a hat. / He had a hat on.
Haré el trabajo con cuidado.	I'll do the job carefully.

NOTE:

If number or emphasis needs to be indicated, the indefinite article is used:

*Se vino con **un** sombrero <u>viejo</u>.*	He came with an old hat.
*Haré el trabajo con **un** cuidado <u>tremendo</u>.*	I will do the job with extreme care.

2. After *como*, when showing a comparison, the following rules apply:

(a) The indefinite article is omitted in some popular sayings:

Salió como escupida de músico.	She left as fast as the spitting of a musician.
Se fue como alma que lleva el diablo.	He left like a soul being carried off by the devil.

(b) In other cases of comparison after *como*, especially in idiomatic expressions, the indefinite article may be omitted:

*Es flaco como (**una**) rata de iglesia.*	He's as skinny as a church rat.
*Estaba triste como (**una**) tarde de domingo.*	She was as sad as a Sunday afternoon.

(c) The indefinite article is also omitted when *como* is used in other combinations that require the indefinite article in English, such as the following:

como medida preventiva	as a preventive measure
como resultado de	as a result of
como consecuencia de	as a consequence of
como corolario	as a corollary
Como profesor, él es...	As a professor, he is . . .
Sirvió como medio para...	It served as a means to . . .

3. After the preposition *de*, the indefinite article is omitted whenever *de* has the meaning of *as* in English:

Trabajaron de enfermeras.	They worked as nurses.
Tiene un puesto de asistente.	He works as an assistant.

4. After the preposition *para*, the indefinite article is not omitted when *para* means *for* in English.

Para un principiante, Juan es muy habilidoso.	For a beginner, Juan is very skillful.
Para una madre soltera, Pepa se da maña para sobrevivir.	For a single mother, Pepa is managing to survive.

5. After the preposition *sin*, whenever *sin* expresses the lack of an item or nonexistence, the indefinite article is omitted:

Me fui a trabajar sin dinero.	I went to work without money.
Lo dijo sin remordimientos.	She said it without remorse.

> **NOTE:**
>
> If number or emphasis needs to be indicated, the indefinite article is used. If the noun is plural, it must be changed to singular after the indefinite article.
>
> | | |
> |---|---|
> | *Me fui a trabajar sin (siquiera) **una** moneda.* | I went to work without (even) a quarter. |
> | *Lo dijo sin **un** remordimiento.* | She said it without (any) remorse. |

F. **The indefinite article with two nouns in apposition**

1. The indefinite article is omitted if no adjective is used:

Viven con Luis, chico adoptado por sus padres.	They live with Luis, a boy adopted by their parents.

2. The indefinite article is used if the noun is modified:

*Viven con Luis, **un** buen chico adoptado por sus padres.*	They live with Luis, a good boy adopted by their parents.

G. **The indefinite article with words such as *cien, ciento* (hundred); *cierto/a* (certain); *medio/a* (half); *mil* (thousand); *otro/a* (other); ¡Qué ... ! (What…!); *tal* (such); and *semejante* (such):**

1. The indefinite article is omitted when *cien(to)* expresses an exact amount:

Gano <u>cien</u> dólares por semana.	I earn a hundred dollars a week.
Miguel puso <u>ciento</u> veinte pesos en su cuenta de ahorros.	Miguel put a hundred and twenty pesos into his savings account.

> **NOTES:**
>
> (1) If *ciento* (rather than *cien*) is used to indicate exactly one hundred, it must be preceded by the indefinite article and followed by *de*:
>
> | | |
> |---|---|
> | *Había **un** ciento **de** personas en la plaza.* | There were one hundred people in the public square. |

(2) The indefinite article is used in the plural form to give the idea of *about, approximately*:

*Había **unas** cien personas en la plaza.*	There were about a hundred people in the public square.
*Él gana **unos** cien dólares por semana.*	He makes about a hundred dollars a week.
Juana pesa unos sesenta kilos.	Juana weighs about a hundred and twenty pounds.

(3) When the plural form *cientos* is used to indicate a large and indefinite amount, the indefinite article is omitted and the preposition *de* precedes the noun:

*Ganó cientos **de** dólares en la lotería.*	He won hundreds of dollars in the lottery.

2. The indefinite article is omitted when *cierto* or *cierta* does not refer to anything specific:

***Cierto** día se vino con su familia.*	On a certain day, she came with her family.
*Tenemos que reunirnos a **cierta** hora.*	We need to get together at a certain time.

NOTE:

To indicate a more specific event or item, the indefinite article is used:

***Un** cierto día llegó a visitarnos.*	On a certain day, he came to visit us.
*Debemos reunirnos a **una** cierta hora todos los días.*	We need to get together at a certain time every day.

3. The indefinite article is omitted when *medio* or *media* indicates *half*:

Quiero comer medio durazno.	I want to eat half a peach.
Me dio media manzana.	He gave me half an apple.
Se quedó media hora.	She stayed half an hour.

NOTE:

The indefinite article is used to indicate *approximately, about*:

*Quiero comer **un** medio durazno.*	I want to eat about half a peach.
*Se quedó por **una** media hora.*	She stayed for about half an hour.

4. The indefinite article is omitted when *mil* (*thousand*) is intended to express an exact amount:

*Tiene **mil** dólares en el banco.*	He has a thousand dollars in the bank.

(1) To indicate an indefinite large amount, the plural form *miles* (*thousands*) and the preposition *de* are used:

*La tía le dejó **miles de** dólares.*   His aunt left him thousands of dollars.
                                          (many dollars)

(2) However, a more limiting idea may be indicated by using the indefinite article in the plural form:

*La tía le dejó **unos miles** de dólares.*   His aunt left him a few thousand. (not
                                               as many)

5. The indefinite article is omitted before *otro*:

   *Quiero ver **otro** vestido.*   I want to see another dress.
   *Quiero ver **otro**.*   I want to see another one.
   *Me gustaría vivir en **otra** casa.*   I would like to live in another house.
   *Me gustaría vivir en **otra**.*   I would like to live in another one.

   NOTE:

   A similar construction uses the word *alguno/a*, with the same meaning of *another one* in English:

   *Quiero ver **algún otro** vestido.*   I want to see another dress.
   *Quiero ver **algún otro**.*   I want to see another one.
   *Me gustaría vivir en **alguna otra** casa.* I would like to live in another house.
   *Me gustaría vivir en **alguna otra**.*   I would like to live in another one.

6. The indefinite article is omitted after *¡Qué ... !* (What...!):

   *¡**Qué** lugar maravilloso!*   What a wonderful place!
   *¡**Qué** hombre más inteligente!*   What an intelligent man he is!

7. The indefinite article is omitted after *tal* when it means *such a*:

   *Nunca había estado en **tal** lugar.*   I had never been in such a place.
   *No quiero hablar con **tal** persona.*   I don't want to talk to such a person.

   NOTES:

   (1) When *tal* indicates an unknown person, the indefinite article is used. This expression has a pejorative connotation, however. The word *fulana* or *fulano* is also used instead of *tal* in this case.

*Ayer lo vi con **una tal** en el parque.*	Yesterday I saw him with some woman in the park.
*Ayer la vi con **un fulano*** en el aeropuerto.*	Yesterday I saw her with some guy at the airport.

(2) When *tal* refers to a person who is unknown, even though identified by name, the indefinite article is used:

*Ayer te llamó **un** tal Pérez. (or, **una** tal Luisa)*	Someone by the name of Pérez (or Luisa) called you yesterday.

(3) When *semejante* means *such a* (and not *similar*), it can be used in two ways:

■ No indefinite article is used and *semejante* precedes the noun:

No sabía que vivían en semejante casa.	I didn't know that they lived in such a house.

■ The indefinite article is used and *semejante* follows the noun:

*No sabía que vivían en **una** casa semejante.*	I didn't know that they lived in such a house.

The Neuter Article *lo*

This article refers to abstract ideas and has only one form, *lo*, which does not indicate gender or number. An equivalent form in English is used with adjectives or adverbs used as nouns. In Spanish, *lo* always precedes the masculine singular form of the adjective or adverb.

***Lo** bueno es eso, claro.*	The good (thing) is that, of course.
***Lo** justo vencerá.*	The just (side) will overcome.
*Me sorprende **lo** bonita que es.*	It surprises me how beautiful she is.
*Se comportó **lo** mejor que pudo.*	He behaved the best he could.
*No me asusta **lo** difícil.*	I am not scared by difficult things.
***Lo** malo de este auto son los frenos.*	The bad thing about this car is the brakes.
*Es interesante **lo** rápido que se supo la noticia.*	It's interesting how fast the news was known.

---

* When a person's name is not known or one does not want to say it, there are four made-up names in Spanish, equivalents to *John Doe* (each of which has corresponding feminine forms as well): *Fulano, Mengano, Zutano,* and *Perengano.* The fictitious name *Fulano de Tal* is used instead of the name of a person on a sample form, application, etc.

Expressions with *lo*

Expressions with *lo* have different meanings in Spanish.

A. Lo que...

This expression is equivalent to *that which, which, what*, or *as far as*:

Lo que importa es llegar a tiempo.	What is important is to arrive on time.
Lo que me preocupa es su ausencia.	What worries me is his absence.
Llegaron tarde, **lo que** molestó a mis padres.	They arrived late, which bothered my parents.
Lo que es yo, pienso viajar.	As far as I am concerned, I intend to travel.
Lo que es eso, no voy a agregarlo en el informe.	As far as that is concerned, I will not add it to the report.

B. Lo... que (how, how much)

When an adjective or an adverb is placed between *lo* and *que*, the expression is equivalent to *how* followed by an adjective or an adverb in English. Observe how the adjectives agree with the nouns in gender and number in the following examples:

Me extraña <u>lo generoso que</u> es tu herma**no**.	It surprises me how generous your brother is.
Es impresionante <u>lo mucho que</u> bebe.	It's amazing how much he drinks.
Es agradable ver <u>lo buenas que</u> son sus hij**as**.	It's nice to see how good her daughters are.
Me comentó <u>lo difícil que</u> era el examen.	She told me how difficult the exam was.

C. Lo de...

Equivalent expressions in English are *the matter of, the subject of, what concerns, what belongs to,* and others.

Lo de Pedro no es nada serio.	What concerns Pedro is not serious at all.
Queremos ver **lo de** Pamela primero.	We want to see Pamela's (what she has or what concerns her) first.
Me ha sorprendido **lo de** su empleo.	The subject of his job has surprised me.

NOTE:

Lo de is also a foreign phrase used to indicate somebody's house:

Fuimos a **lo de** Roberto para repasar las notas.	We went to Roberto's house to review our notes.
Está en **lo de** la tía de ella.	She is at her aunt's.

D. *De lo...*

This expression functions as a superlative when it is followed by *más* (*more*), *menos* (*less*) *mejor* (*better*), or *peor* (*worse*):

Leí un libro *de lo más* interesante.	I read a very interesting (most interesting) book.
Ese color fue *de lo menos* usado en la última temporada.	That color was the least worn during the last season.
Este médico es *de lo mejor* que hay en el hospital.	This doctor is the best there is in the hospital.
Esta película es *de lo más* aburrida.	This film is very boring.
Esta moda es *de lo peor* que apareció.	This fashion is the worst that appeared.

E. *A lo...* (*in the style of . . .*)

In English, a similar construction is rendered by *as a* or *in the style of*:

Se viste *a lo* pobre.	He dresses as a poor person.
Me peiné *a lo* Marilyn.	I wore a Marilyn-style hairdo.
Adornó la casa *a lo* italiano.	She decorated the house Italian style.

F. *Lo* in idiomatic expressions

Some of the most common uses of *lo* in idiomatic expressions include:

A lo lejos se veía una casa blanca.	Far away one could see a white house.
A lo más debes incluir capítulo 4.	At the most, you should include Chapter 4.
A lo mejor ellos vienen esta noche.	Most likely they will come tonight.
A lo menos quiero comprar este libro.	At least I want to buy this book.
A lo sumo Pedro debe tener copia.	At the most, Pedro must have a copy.
Lo menos quiero visitarlo.	At least, I want to visit him.
Por lo común él pasa el verano allá.	Usually, he spends the summer over there.
Por lo general está en su oficina.	Normally, she is in her office.
Por lo menos Pepe vendrá a la fiesta.	At least, Pepe will come to the party.
Por lo pronto los llamaremos.	For the moment, we will call them.
Por lo tanto te veremos mañana.	Therefore, we will see you tomorrow.
Por lo visto ya han llegado.	Evidently, they have already arrived.

Nouns

A noun (*sustantivo* in Spanish) is a word that represents people, animals, things, actions, feelings, or qualities. There are two types of nouns: concrete and abstract.

Concrete nouns are those that represent beings we perceive as existing on their own, even if that happens in our imagination. In Spanish, concrete nouns are divided into proper nouns (*propios*) and common nouns (*comunes*). A proper noun refers to an individual that is distinguished from others belonging to the same category (e.g., **Carmen, Italia, Rocinante, Amazonas, Platero**). A common noun defines all members of the same group or species (e.g., **maestro, oveja, lago, casa**).

Abstract nouns, on the other hand, refer to qualities, feelings, and actions that do not exist by themselves but are, rather, embodied in persons and things. Abstract nouns include *youth* (**la juventud**), *generosity* (**la generosidad**), *wealth* (**la riqueza**), and *happiness* (**la felicidad**).

Gender of Nouns

In Spanish, nouns are masculine, feminine, or neuter. Nouns that apply to males are usually masculine, while those that refer to females are usually feminine. However, gender classification is done only for grammatical purposes, since there are few nouns that are inherently masculine or feminine.

Although gender is usually determined by the ending of the noun (*la casa, el toro*), there are many exceptions to the rules, in which cases the article in front of the noun indicates the proper gender.

In general, Spanish dictionaries indicate the gender of a noun by showing *(m.)* for masculine or *(f.)* for feminine, immediately after the entry. Note these examples:

compás (m.)	compass	*señal (f.)*	signal
luz (f.)	light	*temporal (m.)*	storm

Masculine Nouns

Usually, the following rules will help you to determine which nouns are masculine.

A. Nouns with the following endings are masculine:

-o		*-or*		*-al*	
estío	summer	*picaflor*	humming bird	*general*	general
teatro	theater	*rumor*	rumor	*tribunal*	tribunal
templo	temple	*candor*	candor	*tendal*	tent

-ente		*-ante*		*-ma*	
escribiente	clerk	*estante*	shelf	*programa*	program
poniente	west	*almirante*	admiral	*drama*	drama
coeficiente	coefficient	*pescante*	jib of a crane	*dilema*	dilemma

-aje		*-e*	
maquillaje	makeup	*bronce*	bronze
paje	page	*roce*	friction
ultraje	outrage	*goce*	enjoyment

> **NOTE:**
>
> There are exceptions to this rule, especially in nouns that end in *-e*. Some common feminine words that constitute exceptions to the above rule include: *la mano* (*hand*), *la flor* (*flower*), *la señal* (*signal*), *la creciente* (*swell*), *la lente* (*lens*), *la variante* (*variant*), and *la pose* (*posture*).

B. Nouns that designate someone of obvious male gender are masculine:

el hijo	son	*el hombre*	man
el padre	father	*el monje*	monk
el rector	rector	*el tío*	uncle
el muchacho	young man	*el joven*	young man

> **NOTE:**
>
> Some masculine nouns in this category that end in *-o* or in a consonant have corresponding feminine forms ending in *-a* (instead of the *-o* or after the consonant):
>
> *la muchacha*　　　　　*la tía*　　　　　*la rectora*

C. Names of days, months, boats, and geographical terms for such features as rivers, lakes, oceans, deserts, volcanoes, and gulfs are masculine:

el viernes	*un febrero caluroso*	*el Reina Isabel*	*el Amazonas*
el Titicaca	*el Atlántico*	*el Sahara*	*el Santa Elena*

D. Cardinal numbers are masculine:

el cinco (5)	*el setenta y dos* (72)	*el cuatro* (4)	*el veinte* (20)

E. Names of languages are masculine:

el español	Spanish	*el griego*	Greek
el alemán	German	*el italiano*	Italian

F. Names of colors are masculine:

el verde	green	*el rosado*	pink
el amarillo	yellow	*el blanco*	white

> **NOTE:**
> Some masculine color names have feminine endings. (See Chapter 4, Adjectives, for more information on colors.)
>
> | | | | |
> |---|---|---|---|
> | *el rosa* | pink | *el violeta* | violet |
> | *el lila* | lilac | *el grana* | scarlet |

G. Infinitives that function as nouns are masculine:

*el **Cantar** de Mío Cid*	the *Poem of the Cid*
el poder del tirano	the power of the tyrant

H. Nouns that end in a consonant and represent professions or occupations are masculine.

Note that the corresponding feminine noun is usually formed by adding *-a*:

el pintor	➤	*la pintora*	the painter, the artist
el patrón	➤	*la patrona*	the boss

I. Some masculine nouns that end in **-e, -ante,** or **-ista** have the same form in the feminine:

el (la) estudiante	student	*el (la) recepcionista*	receptionist
el (la) debutante	debutant(e)	*el (la) ascensorista*	elevator operator
el (la) protestante	Protestant	*el (la) ciclista*	cyclist

Feminine Nouns

Usually, the following rules will help you to determine which nouns are feminine.

A. Nouns with the following endings are feminine:

-a		**-d**		**-ión**	
comarca	region	*nerviosidad*	nervousness	*irritación*	irritation
pila	pile	*salud*	health	*confusión*	confusion
rosa	rose	*virtud*	virtue	*religión*	religion

-ie		**-umbre**		**-sis**	
intemperie	unsheltered area	*techumbre*	roof	*crisis*	crisis
		lumbre	fire	*sinopsis*	synopsis
serie	series	*costumbre*	custom	*esclerosis*	sclerosis
especie	species				

-z	
nariz	nose
paz	peace
codorniz	quail

NOTES:

(1) Some masculine nouns that constitute exceptions to the above rule include the following: ***el mapa*** (*map*), ***el alud*** (*avalanche*), ***el envión*** (*push*), ***el alumbre*** (*alum*), ***el oasis*** (*oasis*), ***el lápiz*** (*pencil*).

(2) Special Cases: Feminine nouns that begin with a stressed *a* or *ha* take a masculine article when they are in the singular form. However, they keep the feminine article in the plural:

el águila	➤	*las águilas*	eagles
el ama	➤	*las amas*	housekeepers
el arca	➤	*las arcas*	arks

el arma	➤	las armas	guns
el arte	➤	las artes	arts
el hacha	➤	las hachas	axes

Adjectives that modify these nouns agree with the noun in gender and number:

| el águila negra | ➤ | las águilas negras | the black eagles |
| el haba seca | ➤ | las habas secas | the dried beans |

B. **Nouns that designate someone of obvious female gender are feminine:**

la hija	daughter	la mujer	woman
la muchacha	young woman	la joven	young woman
la madre	mother	la monja	nun
la tía	aunt	la señora	lady

C. **The letters of the alphabet are feminine:**

| la pe (p) | la eme (m) | la hache (h) | la jota (j) |

D. **The names of the sciences, arts, professions, and virtues are feminine:**

| la biología | biology | la escultura | sculpture |
| la ingeniería | engineering | la pureza | purity |

Neuter Nouns

Neuter nouns are preceded by the article *lo* and are usually derived from adjectives. The following nouns, for example, denote the quality of being blue, large, sad, or good.

lo azul

Lo azul de su vestido me atrajo al instante.

The blue (shade) of her dress attracted my attention.

lo grande

Nos maravilló lo grande de la casa.

We marveled at the largeness of the house.

lo triste

Lo triste de su rostro delataba la pena.

The sadness in her face revealed her grief.

lo bueno

Le agradecí <u>lo bueno</u> de su gesto.　　　　I thanked him for the goodness of his gesture.

Nouns of Double Gender

In some cases, the same noun can be both feminine and masculine. The article plays an important role in indicating the gender of such nouns.

A. Nouns that change meaning depending on the article

Several nouns change meaning depending on their gender, indicated by the article that precedes them:

el policía	policeman	*la policía*	police, policewoman
el capital	money, capital	*la capital*	capital city
el parte	communication	*la parte*	part
el cura	priest	*la cura*	healing
el orden	order	*la orden*	command
el mañana	future	*la mañana*	morning

B. Nouns with male and female versions

Some nouns that have the same form for both masculine or feminine use an article (and any adjectives) that agrees with the gender of the person:

el (la) criminal	criminal	*el (la) testigo*	witness
el (la) modelo	model	*el (la) masajista*	masseur, masseuse
el (la) mártir	martyr	*el (la) homicida*	murderer

C. Nouns that stay the same whether they refer to males or females

Some nouns that have the same form for both masculine or feminine use an article (and any adjectives) that agrees with the noun rather than the gender of the person being referred to:

El pobre hombre fue <u>una víctima</u> desgraciada de la sociedad.	The poor man was an unfortunate victim of society.
Ella fue <u>una</u> triste <u>víctima</u> de sus acciones.	She was a sad victim of her actions.
La mujer parecía <u>un monstruo</u> por las cicatrices de las quemaduras.	The woman looked like a monster because of the scars from the burns (she had suffered).

No me gustó *el monstruo* de la película.	I didn't care for the monster in the movie.
Su hija es *un primor*.	His daughter is a darling.
El vecino es *un primor*.	The neighbor is a darling.
Ella es *el mejor personaje*.	She is the best character.
El personaje masculino es viejo.	The male character is old.

Number of Nouns

Regular Plural Forms

In order to make a singular noun plural, the following rules apply.

A. **When a singular noun ends in an unstressed vowel or in a stressed *-e*, add *-s* to make the plural:**

la pera	➤	las peras	pears
el bote	➤	los botes	boats
el yanqui	➤	los yanquis	Yankees
la tribu	➤	las tribus	tribes
el café	➤	los cafés	coffee shops
el hincapié	➤	los hincapiés	emphases

NOTE:

The name of the letter *e*, which becomes *las ees*, is an exception to this rule.

B. **In the following cases, add *-es* to the singular noun to make the plural.**

1. When the singular noun ends in a consonant, add *-es* to make the plural:

el mástil	➤	los mástiles	masts
el examen	➤	los exámenes	exams
la canción	➤	las canciones	songs

2. When the singular noun ends in *-y*, add *-es* to make the plural:

el rey	➤	los reyes	kings
la ley	➤	las leyes	laws
el buey	➤	los bueyes	oxes
la grey	➤	las greyes	congregations

3. When the singular noun ends in a stressed *-a*, *-i*, *-o*, or *-u*, add *-es* to make the plural:

el majá	➤ *los majaes*	snakes
el chajá	➤ *los chajaes*	birds
el rajá	➤ *los rajaes*	rajas
el maní	➤ *los maníes*	peanuts
el ají	➤ *los ajíes*	peppers
el bongó	➤ *los bongoes*	drums
el ñandú	➤ *los ñandúes*	ostriches
el caracú	➤ *los caracúes*	marrows

NOTES:

(1) Some exceptions are:

la mamá	➤ *las mamás*	mothers
el papá	➤ *los papás*	fathers
el sofá	➤ *los sofás*	sofas
el bisturí	➤ *los bisturís*	scalpels

(2) For nouns ending in a stressed *-e*, see previous rule A.

(3) Certain words take a variety of plural forms:

maravedí	➤ *maravedís, maravedíes,* and *maravedises*	coins
tabú	➤ *tabús* and *tabúes*	taboos
esquí	➤ *esquís* and *esquíes*	skis
marroquí	➤ *marroquís* and *marroquíes*	Moroccans

Irregular Plural Forms

Specific rules apply in the formation of irregular plural forms.

A. When the singular noun ends in *-z*, change the *z* to a *c* and then add *-es* to make the plural:

la paz	➤ *las paces*	reconciliation
la raíz	➤ *las raíces*	roots
el pez	➤ *los peces*	fish

B. Singular nouns ending in -*s* or -*x*, with an unstressed last syllable, do not change in the plural:

el análisis	➤ los análisis	analyses
el brindis	➤ los brindis	toasts
la crisis	➤ las crisis	crises
el oasis	➤ los oasis	oases
la hipótesis	➤ las hipótesis	hypotheses
el jueves	➤ los jueves	Thursdays
el paréntesis	➤ los paréntesis	parentheses
el tórax	➤ los tórax	thoraxes
el fénix	➤ los fénix	phoenixes

C. Foreign singular nouns, including those derived from Latin, may add -*s* or -*es* to make the plural:

el álbum	➤ los álbumes	albums
el memorándum	➤ los memorándums	memorandums
el gol	➤ los gols, goles	goals
el club	➤ los clubs, clubes	clubs

NOTE:

In some words, the last letter is dropped and then -*es* is added:

el lord	➤ los **lores**	lords
el chalet	➤ los **chalés**	chalets

D. Singular nouns ending in -*c* change to -*qu*, while names ending in -*g* change to -*gu*, in the plural:

el frac	➤ los fraques	tails (dress coat)
el coñac	➤ los coñaques	cognacs
el zigzag	➤ los zigzagues	zigzags

Nouns with No Plural Form

The following noun categories do not take a plural form, unless the nouns are modified:

A. Proper names:

> el Nilo   Napoleón   el Aconcagua

B. Professions, sciences, and arts:

> la ingeniería   la medicina   la química   la pintura   la arquitectura

C. Metals:

> la plata   el oro   el cobre   el bronce

D. Vices and virtues:

> la codicia   la generosidad   la pulcritud

E. Religions and ideologies:

> el cristianismo   el budismo   el comunismo   el islamismo

Examples of modified nouns from the previous categories, which <u>do</u> take plural forms, are as follows:

El Paraguay y el Uruguay son los <u>Nilos</u> de la Argentina.	The Paraguay and the Uruguay rivers are the Niles of Argentina.
Las diferentes <u>arquitecturas</u> europeas florecieron en aquella época.	The different European architectural expressions bloomed in those times.
Los <u>oros</u> seductores de las Américas despertaron interés.	The seductive gold of the Americas awoke interest.
Las <u>codicias</u> de los países ricos se han puesto en evidencia a través de la historia.	The greed of the rich countries has been demonstrated throughout history.
Los <u>cristianismos</u> alterados de las sociedades mixtas son parte de su cultura.	The altered forms of Christianity in mixed societies are part of their culture.

Nouns Considered as a Whole (Mass Nouns)

A. **Some nouns, called mass nouns, take the singular form when used in a general way:**

Me gusta caminar sobre la arena.	I like to walk on the sand.
El café cuesta mucho.	Coffee costs a lot.

B. **Sometimes these mass nouns are used in the plural form if there is a modifier:**

Las arenas de África son cansadoras para el viajero.	The sand in Africa is tiresome for the traveler.
Los cafés de Brasil son excelentes.	The coffee from Brazil is excellent.

C. **Adding a quantitative expression before the mass noun**

The concept of wholeness may be changed into the idea of parts by the introduction of a quantitative expression before the mass noun:

Se usaron dos toneladas de arena para el proyecto.	Two tons of sand were used for the project.
Se necesitan dos kilos de café para el licor.	Two kilograms of coffee are needed to prepare the liqueur.

> **NOTE:**
>
> Some examples of words that are considered whole nouns in English and may be correctly separated into parts in Spanish are:
>
> | | | |
> |---|---|---|
> | *casa de muebles* (furniture store) | ➤ | *un mueble* (one piece of furniture) |
> | *consejos* (advice) | ➤ | *un consejo* (one piece of advice) |
> | *las noticias* (the news) | ➤ | *una noticia* (a piece of news) |
> | *algodón* (cotton) | ➤ | *tres algodones* (three cotton balls) |
> | *peces de agua salada* (saltwater fish) | ➤ | *cinco peces* (five fish) |
> | *calor* (heat) | ➤ | *los calores del sur* (Southern heat) |
> | *jabón* (soap) | ➤ | *dos jabones* (two bars of soap) |
> | *papel* (paper) | ➤ | *cuatro papeles* (four pieces of paper) |
> | *pan* (bread) | ➤ | *un pan* (one loaf of bread) |
> | *joyas* (jewelry) | ➤ | *una joya* (one piece of jewelry) |
> | *medicinas* (medicine) | ➤ | *dos medicinas* (two types of medicine) |

Nouns with No Singular Form

Nouns that are expressed only in the plural form include:

A. Mountain ranges:

los Alpes   los Andes   los Himalayas

B. Names of countries or cities:

Honduras   Buenos Aires   Caracas

C. Miscellaneous words:

gafas, anteojos (eyeglasses)
Mis gafas (anteojos) se rompieron.   My glasses broke.

nupcias (wedding)
Sus padres piensan venir para las nupcias.   His parents plan to come to the wedding.

exequias (funeral rites)
Las exequias serán el viernes.   The funeral rites will be on Friday.

preces (prayers)
Ahora ella se siente mejor gracias a las preces   Now she feels better thanks to the prayers of
   de su familia.   her family.

víveres (food, provisions)
La Cruz Roja envió víveres a la región.   The Red Cross sent food to the region.

alrededores (sorrounding area)
Los alrededores son bonitos.   The surrounding area is pretty.

comicios (primaries)
Los comicios fueron el martes.   The primaries were on Tuesday.

> **NOTE:**
> The singular forms *boda* and *casamiento* are more commonly used than *nupcias*. In the case of *preces*, the plural *oraciones* is heard in everyday Spanish, while the singular *oración* is also used. *Funeral* and *funerales* may be used instead of *exequias*.

Vinieron para la boda de su sobrina.	They came for their niece's wedding.
Les agradecí sus oraciones.	I thanked them for their prayers.
Necesito que reces una oración por mí.	I need you to say a prayer for me.
El funeral de la princesa fue muy emotivo.	The princess's funeral was very emotional.

Nouns Used in the Plural Form

Ganas is usually used in the plural form, especially with the verbs *tener* and *dar*:

ganas (desire)

Tengo ganas de comer allí.	I feel like eating there.
Le dieron ganas de llamarlo.	She felt like calling him.

However, *ganas* can also be used in the singular form, as in:

Lo hice de mala gana.	I did it reluctantly.
No le da la gana.	She doesn't feel like it.

In this last context, *gana* is <u>not</u> used in the plural:

<u>Incorrect</u>: *No trabaja porque no le dan las ganas.*

Vacaciones is used in the plural when it appears in the phrase *de vacaciones*, meaning *on vacation*:

vacaciones (vacation)

Nos vamos de vacaciones.	We are going on vacation.
<u>Not</u>: *Nos vamos de vacación.*	

Elecciones is used primarily in the plural:

elecciones (elections)

Las elecciones presidenciales serán el año próximo.	The presidential elections will be next year.

NOTE:

There are other nouns that are used in the plural, although their singular forms are also accepted. Included in this category are objects that have two parts, such as *las tijeras* (scissors), *las tenazas* (pliers), and *los pantalones* (pants).

Nouns with Different Meanings in the Plural Form

Some nouns have two plural forms: one that is the plural of the singular noun, and another one that is inherently plural, that is, it is not used in the singular. Observe the following examples:

A. Regular plural of a singular noun:

el grillo	➤	*los grillos*	crickets
la esposa	➤	*las esposas*	wives

B. An inherently plural form:

los grillos	fetters
las esposas	handcuffs

Compound Nouns

Compound nouns are those formed by two words that act together as a single noun:

el altibajo	➤	*los altibajos*	ups and downs
el avemaría	➤	*los avemarías*	Hail Marys
el mapamundi	➤	*los mapamundis*	world maps
el semicírculo	➤	*los semicírculos*	semicircles

The Plural Forms of Compound Nouns

Many compound nouns make their plural form according to the rules already stated. Other nouns, however, follow different rules.

A. Both words in the compound noun take the plural form.

Notice that these words are combinations of two nouns or one noun and one adjective:

la ricadueña	➤	*las ricasdueñas*	ladies; daughters of a noble person
el ricohombre	➤	*los ricoshombres*	grandee; nobility

la casaquinta	➤	las casasquintas	country houses
el gentilhombre	➤	los gentileshombres	gentlemen
la casatienda	➤	las casastiendas	residence and store in the same building

B. Only the first word is pluralized:

| el hijodalgo | ➤ | los hijosdalgo | noblemen |

NOTE:

The word *hijodalgo* originated in the expression *hijo de algo*. The forms *hidalgo* and *hidalgos* are more commonly used.

C. No change in the form of the compound noun

There is no change in the form of the compound noun from singular to plural in the following cases.

1. When the second word of the compound noun is already in the plural:

el paraguas	➤	los paraguas	umbrellas
el sacapuntas	➤	los sacapuntas	pencil sharpeners
el parabrisas	➤	los parabrisas	windshields
el sacacorchos	➤	los sacacorchos	corkscrews
el lavaplatos	➤	los lavaplatos	dishwashers
el rompecabezas	➤	los rompecabezas	puzzles
el escarbadientes	➤	los escarbadientes	toothpicks
el lustrabotas	➤	los lustrabotas	shoeshine boys
el quitamanchas	➤	los quitamanchas	stain removers

NOTE:

The preceding nouns are formed from a verb and a noun, as in *parar aguas*, *sacar puntas*, and *parar brisas*.

2. When the compound noun ends in a verb or in a word that does not change:

| el hazmerreír | ➤ | los hazmerreír | laughingstocks |
| el ir y venir | ➤ | los ir y venir | comings and goings |

NOTE:

There are exceptions to this rule, such as *el vaivén,* which makes the plural *los vaivenes* (see following note E).

D. When two nouns are united by a preposition, only the first word takes the plural:

el ojo de buey	➤ *los ojos de buey*	portholes
la bomba de hidrógeno	➤ *las bombas de hidrógeno*	hydrogen bombs
el alma en pena	➤ *las almas en pena*	distressed souls
un alma de Dios*	➤ *unas almas de Dios*	pious persons
el reloj de arena	➤ *los relojes de arena*	hourglasses
el arma de fuego	➤ *las armas de fuego*	firearms
la cuchara de sopa	➤ *las cucharas de sopa*	soupspoons
el guante de goma	➤ *los guantes de goma*	rubber gloves

NOTE:

The second noun may already be in the plural form, as in

caja de ahorros	➤ *cajas de ahorros*	savings accounts
collar de cuentas	➤ *collares de cuentas*	bead necklaces

E. Most singular compound nouns in certain categories form the plural by adding *-es.*

In most of the compound nouns formed by combinations of two verbs, a verb and a noun, two nouns, an adjective and a noun, a noun and an adjective, or a preposition and a noun, the plural is made by adding *-s* if the word ends in a vowel, and *-es* if it ends in a consonant. (Compare the Note following the preceding Section C. 2.)

el vaivén	➤ *los vaivenes*	swings (i.e. of fortune)
el girasol	➤ *los girasoles*	sunflowers
el puntapié	➤ *los puntapiés*	kicks
el altavoz	➤ *los altavoces*	loudspeakers
la Nochebuena	➤ *las Nochebuenas*	Christmas Eves
la sobrefalda	➤ *las sobrefaldas*	overskirts
un sinvergüenza	➤ *unos sinvergüenzas*	rascals

---

* An indefinite article must be used with this expression; otherwise, it would mean *God's soul.*

Collective Nouns

Collective nouns represent groups of people, animals, or things.

la rosaleda	group of rosebushes
el colmenar	group of beehives (apiary)
el arenal	extension of sand
el paraisal	group of *paraísos* (South American trees)
el ejército	the army
la marina	the navy
la fuerza aérea	the air force
la gente	people
el rebaño	group of sheep
la caballada	group of horses

Many collective nouns derive from other nouns, e.g., *rosaleda* from *rosal* (*rosebush*), *colmenar* from *colmena* (*beehive*), *arenal* from *arena* (*sand*), and *paraisal* from *paraísos*. Others, such as *ejército* (*army*), *gente* (*people*), *grey* (*flock*), *piara* (*herd*), *rebaño* (*herd*), and many others, are counted among the collective nouns that are not derivative.

The Plural Forms of Collective Nouns

Collective nouns follow the general rules already specified for making the plural form, that is, an *-s* is added to words that end in a vowel, and *-es* is added to those that end in a consonant.

Esta rosaleda es preciosa.	This group of rose bushes is beautiful.
Esas rosaledas son lindas.	Those groups of rose bushes are pretty.
El colmenar está en el valle.	The apiary is in the valley.
Sus colmenares son famosos.	Their apiaries are famous.

Uses of Nouns

Nouns perform different functions in the sentence.

A. A noun as the main element of the subject:

*El **perro** negro está ladrando.*	The black dog is barking.
***Jaime** estudia matemáticas.*	Jaime studies mathematics.

B. A noun as an adjective:

*El hombre **rana** descubrió el barco.*   The diver (frogman) discovered the boat.

1. Sometimes the noun being used as an adjective is preceded by a preposition. Note the following examples where a preposition is needed in Spanish but not in English:

   *Llevaré una blusa **de** seda.*   I will wear a silk blouse.
   *La silla **de** ruedas está rota.*   The wheelchair is broken.

2. If there is an adjective in Spanish that corresponds to a prepositional phrase, the adjective is preferred:

   un examen de fin de año   final exam
   *un examen **final***

   la casa de los curas   priests' house
   *la casa **cural***

   una carrera de éxito   successful career
   *una carrera **exitosa***

   el programa del domingo   Sunday program
   *el programa **dominical***

   un reglamento del estado   state rule
   *un reglamento **estatal***

C. A noun as an interjection or exclamation:

¡Madre!   *¡Cielos!*   *¡Niño!*   *¡Jesús!*   *¡Caracoles!*

D. A noun as an adverb (preceded by a preposition):

***A fin** de mayo terminan las clases.*   Classes end at the end of May.
*Haré el pedido **por teléfono**.*   I will place the order by phone.
*La maestra trazó las líneas **con** mucho cuidado*.   The teacher drew the lines very carefully.

*La tormenta se vino **de golpe**.*   The storm came suddenly.

E. A noun as a predicate nominative:

*Ella es una **mujer** inolvidable.*	She is an unforgettable woman.
*Tomás es el **director** de la escuela.*	Tomás is the school principal.

F. A noun as a direct object:

*Compré cinco **libros** ayer.*	I bought five books yesterday.
*Queremos una **casa** grande.*	We want a large house.
*Romeo ama a **Julieta**.*	Romeo loves Juliet.

G. A noun as an indirect object:

*Traje los libros para **María**.*	I brought the books for María.
*Le compró comida al **perro**.*	She bought food for her dog.

H. Nouns in apposition (a noun identifying another noun or pronoun that immediately precedes it):

Buenos Aires, <u>capital de Argentina</u>, es una ciudad cosmopolita.	Buenos Aires, the capital of Argentina, is a cosmopolitan city.
Juan Carlos I, <u>rey de España</u>, desciende de los Borbones.	Juan Carlos I, the king of Spain, is descended from the Bourbons.
Su padre, <u>decano de la universidad</u>, viene todos los meses.	His father, dean of the university, comes every month.

Words That Function as Nouns

A. A pronoun as a noun:

*No quiero ese vaso. **Éste** es el mío.*	I don't want that glass. This one is mine.
*Prefiere mi programa. No le gusta el **suyo**.*	She prefers my program. She does not like hers.

B. An infinitive as a noun, with or without the article:

***Fumar** es dañino para la salud.*	Smoking is harmful to one's health.
***El beber** mucha agua es bueno para las células.*	Drinking plenty of water is good for the cells.

C. An adjective as a noun:

1. Any adjective preceded by the neuter article *lo* becomes an abstract noun:

Lo bueno *es que ganó la beca.*	The good thing is that he got the scholarship.
Lo triste *de esta situación ya ha sido expuesto.*	The sad part about this situation has already been exposed.

2. An adjective functions as a noun by omission of the noun:

*La señora canosa es mi abuela y la **delgada** es mi tía.*	The gray-haired lady is my grandmother and the thin one is my aunt.
*El gato grande es mío y el **pequeño** es de mi hermano.*	The big cat is mine and the small one is my brother's.

D. A clause as a noun:

El hombre que trajo la carta ya se fue.	The man who brought the letter has already left.
*El **que trajo la carta** ya se fue.*	The one who brought the letter has already left.

E. An adverb as a noun:

***El sí** de las niñas es una obra de Moratín.*	El sí de las niñas is a play by Moratín.
*Debes ahorrar para **el mañana**.*	You must save for the future.
***Lo bien** que avanza en los estudios me sorprende.*	It surprises me how well she is progressing in her studies.

Agreement of Nouns

A. Agreement of nouns and articles

1. The article agrees with the noun in gender and number.

la casa	the house
las ruedas	the wheels
el camino	the road
los árboles	the trees

Some exceptions to this rule follow where there is not an agreement in gender between the noun and the article. Notice that the gender of the adjectives—feminine or masculine—agrees with the article:

*la mano **pequeña*** (f.)	*las manos **pequeñas*** (f.)
the small hand	the small hands
*un mapa **moderno*** (m.)	*unos mapas **modernos*** (m.)
a modern map	some modern maps
*una foto **clara*** (f.)	*unas fotos **claras*** (f.)
a clear photo	some clear photos
*el drama **inglés*** (m.)	*los dramas **ingleses*** (m.)
the English drama	the English dramas

NOTE:

See Note 2 in Section A under Feminine Nouns where in expressions such as el alma generosa *(the generous soul) the noun does not agree with the article, but the adjective agrees with the noun.*

2. If several nouns are preceded by one article, the article must agree with the first noun:

La casa, árboles y jardines daban una atmósfera de paz.	The house, the trees, and the gardens formed a peaceful environment.
Los bienes, perseverancia y suerte los ayudaron a progresar en la vida.	Possessions, perseverance, and luck helped them to progress in life.

B. Agreement of nouns and adjectives

1. Adjectives agree in gender and number with the main noun in the sentence.

*un **libro** rojo*	a red book
*los **lápices** cortos*	the short pencils
*una **mujer** buena*	a good woman
*las **toallas** gruesas*	the thick towels
***Rocinante** era un caballo alto y huesudo.*	Rocinante was a tall and bony horse.
***Romeo** y **Julieta** son personajes famosos.*	Romeo and Juliet are famous characters.

2. If one or more adjectives follow two or more nouns, either all masculine or masculine and feminine combined, the adjective or adjectives must be used in the masculine plural form.

*Me compré zapatos, un cinturón y guantes **negros** y **elegantes**.*	I bought elegant black shoes, a belt, and gloves.
*Tiene un cuadro y una estatua **importados** de Italia.*	She has a painting and a statue imported from Italy.

3. When all the nouns are feminine, the feminine plural form of the adjective must be used.

*Las manos, las mejillas y la frente **arrugadas** le daban un aire de sabiduría.*	Her wrinkled hands, cheeks, and forehead gave her an air of wisdom.
*La pulsera y la hebilla **plateadas** son **españolas**.*	The silver-plated bracelet and buckle are from Spain.

4. When the adjective is placed before the nouns, it usually agrees with the first noun and is understood for all the others:

*Tengo **muchas** naranjas y melones en casa.*	I have many oranges and melons at home.
*No quiere recibir **tantos** regalos y flores.*	She doesn't want to receive so many presents and flowers.

5. If the adjective consists of a prepositional phrase with *de*, agreement varies depending on the word order.

*Rocinante no era un caballo **ancho de ancas**.*	Rocinante did not have a wide rump.

The expression *ancho de ancas* refers to *horse* and acts as a unit, therefore *ancho* qualifies *caballo* and is masculine. A literal translation would be *a horse [that is] wide in the rump*.

*Rocinante no era un caballo **de ancas anchas**.*	(Literally) Rocinante was not a horse with a wide rump.

In this case, *anchas* refers solely to *ancas* (*rump*), a feminine noun, and is therefore feminine.

C. Agreement of nouns and pronouns

An introduction to pronouns is presented in this section to demonstrate how pronouns agree in gender and number with the nouns they represent. Consult Chapter 16, Pronouns, for further information.

1. Personal pronouns

Some of the personal pronouns are obviously masculine or feminine:

él	he
ella	she
nosotros	we (masculine)
nosotras	we (feminine)
vosotros	you (masculine plural, used mostly in Spain)
vosotras	you (feminine plural, used mostly in Spain)
ellos	they (masculine)
ellas	they (feminine)

The other personal pronouns can indicate either masculine or feminine gender:

yo	I
tú	you (informal)
usted (Ud.)	you (formal, singular)
ustedes (Uds.)	you (formal and informal plural, mostly used in Latin America)

In the following examples of such pronouns, the gender of the pronoun is made obvious by the gender of the adjective that agrees with it:

Yo (Lucía) soy trabajadora.	I am a hard worker.
Tú (Juan) eres bueno.	You are good.
Ud. (Señora) es una buena directora.	You are a good principal.
Ud. (Señor) está loco.	You are crazy.
Uds. (chicas) están contentas.	You are happy.

NOTES:

Ellos and *Uds.* may need clarification when they occur out of context.

(1) *Ellos* may refer to masculine nouns only or to a combination of masculine and feminine:

Ellos (Juan y María) son buenos estudiantes.	They (Juan and María) are good students.
Ellos (Juan y Pedro) son buenos estudiantes.	They (Juan and Pedro) are good students.

(2) *Uds.* can refer to females only, but can also refer to males only or to a combination of males and females:

Uds. son buenas.	(Luisa and Sara)
Uds. están cansados.	(Miguel and Carlos)

Uds. están cansados.   (Luisa and Alberto)

Uds. son inteligentes. (masculine or feminine, since **inteligente** applies to both genders)

2. Demonstrative pronouns

As opposed to English, Spanish has three different categories for demonstrative pronouns. The pronouns in each of these categories agree in gender and number with the nouns they represent. The third category, which indicates something that is further away in location or time, is expressed in English as *that one over there, those down the hill,* etc.

éste (león)	this (lion)
éstos (leones)	these (lions)
ésta (mentira)	this (lie)
éstas (mentiras)	these (lies)
ése (amigo)	that (friend)
ésos (amigos)	those (friends)
ésa (colmena)	that (beehive)
ésas (colmenas)	those (beehives)
aquél (privilegio)	that (privilege)
aquéllos (privilegios)	those (privileges)
aquélla (planta)	that (plant) over there
aquéllas (plantas)	those (plants) over there
Ése *es el más* **cómico** *de todos. (amigo)*	That one is the funniest of all. (male friend)
Aquéllas están vacías. (casas)	Those over there are empty. (houses)

NOTES:

(1) The use of the accent is now optional for demonstrative pronouns.

(2) The neuter demonstrative pronouns *esto, eso,* and **aquello,** which refer to abstract or undefined nouns, are always expressed in the singular form and take masculine singular adjectives.

Esto es bueno.	This is good.
Eso será ridículo.	That will be ridiculous.
Aquello era obvio.	That was obvious.

3. Possessive pronouns

(a) The possessive pronouns agree in gender and number with the item or thing that is possessed.

la mía (mi casa)	mine (my house)
las mías (mis casas)	(my houses)
el mío (mi auto)	(my car)
los míos (mis autos)	(my cars)
Las mías son más grandes (casas).	Mine are bigger (houses).
la tuya (tu fiesta)	yours, informal (your party)
las tuyas (tus fiestas)	(your parties)
el tuyo (tu soneto)	(your sonnet)
los tuyos (tus sonetos)	(your sonnets)
El tuyo no tiene la rima correcta. (soneto)	Yours doesn't have the correct rhyme. (sonnet)
la suya (su idea)	yours/hers/his/theirs (your/her/his/ their idea)
las suyas (sus ideas)	yours/hers/his/theirs (your/her/his/ their ideas)
el suyo (su perro)	yours/hers/his/theirs (your/her/his/ their dog)
los suyos (sus perros)	yours/hers/his/theirs (your/her/his/ their dogs)

> **NOTE:**
>
> The pronouns *suya, suyas, suyo,* and *suyos* are equivalent to the English *yours* (formal form in Spanish), and also to *his, hers,* and *theirs,* which in English are used to refer to both singular and plural nouns.
>
> | | |
> |---|---|
> | *El suyo tiene pelo negro. (perro)* | Yours (his, hers, theirs) has black hair. (dog) |
> | *Las suyas son excelentes. (ideas)* | Yours (his, hers, theirs) are excellent. (ideas) |

la nuestra (nuestra mesa)	ours (our table)
las nuestras (nuestras mesas)	(our tables)
el nuestro (nuestro cuadro)	(our painting)
los nuestros (nuestros cuadros)	(our paintings)
El nuestro es importado de Japón. (cuadro)	Ours is imported from Japan. (painting)
la vuestra (vuestra lámpara)	yours (your lamp)
las vuestras (vuestras lámparas)	(your lamps)

el vuestro (vuestro país)	(your country)
los vuestros (vuestros países)	(your countries)

NOTE:

Yours, informal plural, used in Spain, indicates one or more things owned by two or more persons.

El vuestro tiene aire acondicionado. (auto)	Yours has air-conditioning. (car)
Las vuestras están en la sala. (maletas)	Yours are in the living room. (suitcases)

(b) The neuter possessive pronouns *lo mío, lo tuyo, lo suyo, lo nuestro,* and *lo vuestro,* which refer to abstract or undefined nouns, are always expressed in the singular form and take masculine singular adjectives.

Lo mío es secreto.	What I have is secret.
Lo tuyo será expuesto.	What you (informal) have will be exposed.
Lo suyo es muy serio.	What you (formal) have is very serious.
	What he (or she) has is very serious.
	What they have is very serious.
Lo nuestro es placentero.	What we have is pleasant.
Lo vuestro es interesante.	What you have is interesting.

4. Relative pronouns

Relative pronouns replace nouns or other words that refer to nouns and that occur in the same sentence. There are four basic relative pronouns: *que* (*that, who, whom, what*), *quien* (*who, whom*), *cual* (*which*), and *cuyo* (*whose*).

(a) *Que* (*that, who, whom, what*) is invariable:

*La <u>cartera</u> **que** me regalaron es de la China.*	The purse they gave me is from China.
*Las <u>personas</u> **que** vinieron van a la conferencia.*	The people who came are going to the conference.

When *que* is preceded by *el, la, los,* or *las,* these words agree in gender and number with the noun that is being referred to by *que.*

La *que está aquí es mi <u>pluma</u>.*	The one here is my pen.
*<u>El artista</u>, **del que** conseguí un autógrafo, es mi favorito.*	The actor, from whom I got an autograph, is my favorite.
*Tus <u>cuadernos</u> son **los que** trajo Oscar.*	Your notebooks are those that Oscar brought.

The neuter article *lo* sometimes precedes *que*. The expression *lo que* has different meanings:

Llegó a tiempo, **lo que** causó una buena impresión.	He arrived on time, <u>which</u> caused a good impression.
Yo sé **lo que** cuesta viajar.	I know <u>how much</u> it costs to travel.
Es tan bueno ver **lo que** le agrada recibir visitas.	It's so good to see <u>how much</u> he enjoys having people over.
Trajeron **lo que** les habíamos pedido.	They brought <u>what</u> we had asked them to bring.

(b) *Quien* has the plural form *quienes*, but does not vary by gender. This pronoun does not use a preceding article, but may follow a preposition. It is used to replace persons only. *Quien* can be replaced by *cual*, preceded by *el, la, los,* or *las*.

<u>Carlos</u>, **quien** (el cual) se ha ido al Perú, es profesor.	Carlos, who has gone to Peru, is a professor.
<u>Mi madre</u>, **quien** (la cual) sabía tocar el piano, era muy paciente.	My mother, who knew how to play the piano, was very patient.
<u>Los niños</u>, con **quienes** (con los cuales) iremos mañana, se portan bien.	The children, with whom we'll go tomorrow, are well-behaved.

(c) *Cual* has the plural form *cuales*, and is always preceded by the article *el, la, los,* or *las*, which indicates the gender. It may replace persons or things.

Las <u>rosas</u> rojas, **las cuales** están en la sala, son de mi jardín.	The red roses, which are in the living room, are from my garden.
El <u>perrito</u> negro, **el cual** está ladrando afuera, tiene trece años.	The little black dog, who is barking outside, is thirteen years old.
Esa <u>niña</u>, **la cual** tiene un vestido verde, es mi sobrina.	That girl, who has a green dress on, is my niece.

If two or more nouns form the antecedent, *cual* agrees in gender and number:

Las <u>rosas</u> y los <u>claveles</u>, **los cuales** están en la sala, son de mi jardín.	The roses and the carnations, which are in the living room, are from my garden.
La <u>blusa</u> verde y <u>la blanca</u>, **las cuales** son de seda, son de mi talla.	The green blouse and the white one, which are made of silk, are my size.

(d) *Cuyo* is used to refer to people or things. As opposed to *que, quien,* and *cual*, it agrees in gender and number with the noun that follows it. It is never preceded by the article *el, la, los,* or *las*.

El estudiante, **cuyos** <u>libros</u> se han perdido, se fue.	The student, whose books got lost, is gone.
La mansión, **cuyo** <u>portal</u> es interesante, perteneció a sus abuelos.	The mansion, whose entrance is interesting, belonged to his grandparents.
Tito, **cuya** <u>hermana</u> trabaja aquí, es muy generoso.	Tito, whose sister works here, is very generous.

D. Agreement of nouns and verbs

The agreement of nouns and verbs in Spanish varies in three different areas.

1. Agreement of the verb with two or more nouns functioning as the subject

(a) When the nouns that form the subject are related to each other as a unit, the verb may be in the singular or in the plural form.

Nuestra <u>atención y dedicación</u> nos **ayudó** a pasar el curso.	Our attention and dedication helped us to pass the course.
Su <u>piedad y generosidad</u> le **dieron** muchas satisfacciones.	His piety and generosity gave him great satisfaction.

However, the plural form of the verb must be used when the nouns are viewed as separate items.

Los lápices, las llaves y el paraguas **estaban** sobre el escritorio.	The pencils, the keys, and the umbrella were on the desk.
Sus abuelos, su tío y su tía **llegaron** por la mañana.	Her grandparents, her uncle, and her aunt arrived in the morning.

(b) When the two nouns that form the subject are joined by *como* (*as*) or *con* (*with*), the verb must be in the plural form:

Tanto el perro como el gato **estaban** comiendo.	Both the dog and the cat were eating.
El presidente con los secretarios **vinieron** a la conferencia.	The president, with the secretaries, came to the conference.

However, notice what happens when the phrase beginning with *con* is placed after the verb:

El presidente **vino** con los secretarios a la conferencia.	The president came with the secretaries to the conference.
El presidente **vino** a la conferencia con los secretarios.	The president came to the conference with the secretaries.

(c) When the two or more nouns that form the subject are joined by *ni* (nor) or *o* (or), the verb may either be in the plural form, if the subject is considered as a whole, or it can agree with the closest noun:

■ *ni*

Ni la madre ni el padre le **permitieron** faltar a la escuela.	Neither his mother nor his father let him miss school.
Ni el rojo ni el verde me **llama** la atención.	Neither red nor green attracts my attention.
Ni los viajes ni el descanso lo **ayudó** a recuperarse.	Neither traveling nor rest helped him to recover.
Ni el descanso ni los viajes lo **ayudaron** a recuperarse.	Neither rest nor traveling helped him to recover.

■ *o*

La madre o el padre le **permitieron** faltar a la escuela.	Either the mother or the father let him miss school.
A mí me **llama** la atención _el rojo o el verde_.	Either red or green attracts my attention.
Los viajes o el descanso lo **ayudó** a recuperarse.	Either traveling or rest helped him to recover.
El descanso o los viajes lo **ayudaron** a recuperarse.	Either rest or traveling helped him to recover.

(d) When the verb precedes two or more nouns that function as the subject, it usually agrees with the first noun.

Siempre le **preocupa** la violencia y la pobreza.	He is always worried about violence and poverty.

NOTES:

(1) The plural form of the verb may also be used:

Siempre le **preocupan** la violencia y la pobreza.	He is always worried about violence and poverty.

(2) If the first noun is plural, the plural form of the verb must be used:

Siempre le **preocupan** los crímenes y la pobreza.	He is always worried about crime and poverty.
Vendrán los hijos, la madre y la abuela.	The children, the mother, and the grandmother will come.

(e) When two or more noun phrases beginning with *que* or *el que* form the subject, the verb must be in the singular form:

*Que lo diga y que lo haga me **sorprende**.*	That she says it and does it, surprises me.
*El que vengan y el que se queden me **tiene** sin cuidado.*	The fact that they will come and stay, doesn't bother me.

(f) When the subject is formed by two or more of the neuter demonstratives *esto*, *eso*, *aquello*, and *lo que,* the verb must be in the singular form:

*Aquello y esto que dijo ahora no **tiene** explicación.*	That, and what he now said, doesn't have an explanation.
*Eso y lo que sugiere María **tiene** sentido.*	That, and what María suggests, makes sense.

(g) When the subject is formed by two or more noun phrases that begin with an interrogative such as *quién*, *cómo*, *cuándo,* or *dónde,* the verb must be in the singular form:

*Quién escriba la carta y cómo lo haga **será** cuestión de decidir.*	Who writes the letter, and how, will have to be decided.
*Dónde encuentre trabajo y cuándo empiece no me **preocupa**.*	Where I'll find a job and when I'll begin don't worry me.

2. Agreement of the verb with collective nouns

(a) A singular collective noun requires a verb to agree with it in the singular form; likewise, any adjectives will agree with the noun in gender and number (singular):

La familia está feliz.	The family is happy.
El ejército italiano se preparó para el ataque.	The Italian army got ready for the attack.

NOTE:

A singular collective noun may require the verb and the adjective to agree with it in the plural form if the following two conditions are met.

(1) The noun represents an undetermined type of people or things, such as *gente* (*people*), *multitud* (*crowd*), or *masa* (*mass*).

(2) The verb and any plural adjective(s) are not next to the noun:

*La multitud se sentó en la iglesia y en cuanto entró el féretro **se pusieron** a llorar.*	The crowd sat in the church, and as soon as the coffin was brought in, they started to cry.
*La gente no aceptaba las condiciones del jefe y por eso **estaban tristes y amargados**.*	The people did not accept the conditions imposed by the boss, and therefore they were sad and bitter.

(b) When a collective expression that indicates quantity such as *la mitad* (*half*), *una parte* (*a part*), and *un millar* (*a thousand*) is followed by a plural noun, the verb is usually in the plural:

*La mitad de los <u>pasteles</u> **fueron** hechos en el horno.*	Half of the pies were made in the oven.
*Parte de los <u>paquetes</u> **llegaron**.*	Part of the packages arrived.

NOTES:

(1) If the collective expression is followed by a singular noun, the verb is in the singular:

*La mitad del <u>colegio</u> se **mudó** a las afueras.*	Half of the school moved to the outskirts.

(2) If the collective expression is preceded by the verb, the verb is in the singular.

***Llegó** parte del pedido.*	Part of the order arrived.
***Entró** una decena de chicos.*	Ten children came in.

(c) If the collective noun is part of an expression with *de*, the adjective and the verb may be used in the plural form. Any adjectives used would also have to be in the plural form:

*La sala estaba decorada con <u>un juego de</u> cuadros que habían sido **colocados** a cada lado de la chimenea.*	The room was decorated with a set of paintings that had been placed on each side of the fireplace.
*Mi padre tiene <u>un par de</u> herramientas **importadas** que **son** muy fáciles de usar.*	My father has a couple of imported tools that are very easy to use.

(d) When the collective noun is in the plural form, representing more than one group, the verb and any adjective(s) must also be in the plural:

*Las <u>comunidades</u> **democráticas** se **adhirieron** a la fiesta.*	The democratic communities joined in the celebration.
*Sus <u>familias</u> **estuvieron presentes**.*	Their families were present.

(e) Some collective nouns take a verb in the singular form in Spanish where in English a plural form would be used:

*La gente de Estados Unidos **es** muy educada.*	People in the United States <u>are</u> well educated.
*La policía latinoamericana **está** informada del problema.*	The Latin American police <u>are</u> informed about the problem.

(f) Other collective nouns in Spanish take a verb in the plural form, whereas in English the verb would be in the singular:

*Dijo que las noticias **fueron** inesperadas.*	He said the news <u>was</u> unexpected.
*Los muebles **son** estilo Mediterráneo.*	The furniture <u>is</u> Mediterranean style.

3. Agreement of the verb *ser* (*to be*) when it is between subject and predicate

When the verb *ser* appears between two nouns, one being the subject of the sentence and the other the predicate, the verb *ser* usually agrees with the subject:

<u>*Hijos y nietos*</u> **son** *la razón para seguir viviendo.*	Children and grandchildren are the reason to continue living.
<u>*Los aztecas*</u> **eran** *una civilización progresista.*	The Aztecs were a progressive civilization.

NOTES:

(1) The verb may agree with the predicate if emphasis is desired.

*Hijos y nietos **es** <u>la razón</u> para seguir viviendo.*	Children and grandchildren <u>is</u> the reason to continue living.
*Los aztecas **era** <u>una civilización</u> progresista.*	(Literally) The Aztecs <u>was</u> a progressive civilization.
*El barco que vi **eran** <u>sólo imágenes</u>.*	(Literally) The boat I saw <u>were</u> only images.

(2) If the adjective *todo(a)* is modified by the verb, *todo(a)* agrees with the subject.

*La <u>religión</u> de los aztecas **era toda** sacrificios y muertes.*	The religion of the Aztecs was all sacrifices and deaths.
*El <u>informe</u> de Norma **es todo** correcciones y marcas.*	Norma's report is all corrections and marks.

The Present Indicative

The infinitive of a verb (expressed in English as *to walk, to read, to write*) can have one of three possible endings in Spanish: *-ar (caminar)*, *-er (leer)*, or *-ir (escribir)*. Based on these endings, verbs are said to belong to the first conjugation (*-ar* verbs), to the second conjugation (*-er* verbs), or to the third conjugation (*-ir* verbs). All other verb forms are derived from the infinitive.

In order to conjugate a verb in the present tense, that is, to assign a form for each subject pronoun such as *I* [*am*], *you* [*are*], *he* [*is*], *she* [*is*], etc., the first step is to eliminate the infinitive ending (*terminación*). The beginning of the verb, or the stem (*raíz*), takes new endings according to the subject pronoun that performs the action denoted by the verb.

Regular Verbs in the Present Tense

Verbs that do not change their stem are called *regular* verbs, while those that undergo changes in the stem are classified as *irregular* verbs. As for the endings, regular verbs and most irregular verbs take the same endings in the present tense, while a few verbs show some spelling differences.

The Present Tense of *-ar* Verbs

The endings for *-ar* verbs are: *-o*, *-as*, *-a*, *-amos*, *-áis*, and *-an*. Notice that *él, ella,* and *Ud.* (*usted*) share the same verb form in the singular, and *ellos, ellas,* and *Uds.* (*ustedes*) share the same verb form in the plural.

hablar (to speak)

*yo habl**o***	I speak	*nosotros/as habl**amos***	we speak
*tú habl**as***	you speak	*vosotros/as habl**áis***	you speak
*él habl**a***	he speaks	*ellos habl**an***	they speak
*ella habl**a***	she speaks	*ellas habl**an***	they speak
*Ud. habl**a***	you speak	*Uds. habl**an***	you speak

NOTES:

(1) *tú* is the informal *you* that is used to address a child, a young adult, a friend, a relative, or a pet.

(2) *Ud.* is the abbreviation of *usted*, and is used to address a person formally, that is, someone who is older, a person whom the speaker does not know, a boss, a teacher, or a professional such as a medical doctor or a dentist. In some regions, the *Ud.* (*usted*) form is also heard between parents and children. The abbreviation *Ud.* is generally used in writing and is always capitalized. When speaking or reading, *Ud.* must be pronounced as the whole word *usted*. The word *usted* is only capitalized when it is the first word in the sentence. The abbreviations **Vd.** and **Vds.** are no longer in use; however, these forms are found in older literary texts and manuscripts.

(3) *Uds.*, or *ustedes* is the plural form of *Ud.*, and is used in Latin America to address two or more people formally or informally. In Spain, however, *ustedes* is used formally, while *vosotros/as* is used to address two or more people informally.

(4) *nosotros* and *vosotros* also have feminine forms: *nosotras* and *vosotras*, respectively.

(5) *ellos*, *nosotros*, and *vosotros* may refer to a group of males or to a group of both males and females, while *ellas*, *nosotras*, and *vosotras* refer only to females.

(6) The *vosotros/as* forms carry an accent in the present tense.

(7) For grammatical purposes, the subject (or personal) pronouns are classified as follows:

yo	first person singular	**nosotros** *or* **nosotras**	first person plural
tú	second person singular	**vosotros** *or* **vosotras**	second person plural
él	third person singular	**ellos**	third person plural
ella	third person singular	**ellas**	third person plural
Ud.	third person singular	**Uds.**	third person plural

(8) Since some subject pronouns share the same endings, *ella, Ud., nosotras, vosotras, ellas,* and *Uds.* will not be included in future conjugations for practical reasons. However, in the examples that illustrate the material being covered, as well as in the exercises in the CD-ROM, these subject pronouns will be varied at random.

The Present Tense of -er Verbs

These verbs take the endings -*o*, -*es*, -*e*, -*emos*, -*éis*, and -*en*.

comer (to eat)

yo com**o**	I eat	nosotros com**emos**	we eat
tú com**es**	you eat	vosotros com**éis**	you eat
él com**e**	he eats	ellos com**en**	they eat

The Present Tense of -ir Verbs

These verbs take the endings -*o*, -*es*, -*e*, -*imos*, -*ís*, and -*en*.

vivir (to live)

yo viv**o**	I live	nosotros viv**imos**	we live
tú viv**es**	you live	vosotros viv**ís**	you live
él viv**e**	he lives	ellos viv**en**	they live

Notice that -*ir* verbs have the same endings as -*er* verbs, with the exception of the *nosotros/as* and *vosotros/as* forms: *comemos* as opposed to *vivimos*, and *coméis* as opposed to *vivís*.

Summary of verb endings in the present tense

amar (to love)	**am**-	o, as, a, amos, áis, an
beber (to drink)	**beb**-	o, es, e, emos, éis, en
escribir (to write)	**escrib**-	o, es, e, imos, ís, en

NOTES:

(1) Since Spanish verb endings indicate who or what the subject of the sentence is, it is not necessary to include the personal (or subject) pronouns. When clarification is needed, as for example *él* or *ella*, *ellos* or *ellas*, *nosotros* or *nosotras*, the subject is used.

(2) The third persons *él*, *ella*, and *Ud.*, which are singular forms, always share the same endings. This rule also applies to the third persons *ellos*, *ellas*, and *Uds.*, which are plural forms.

(3) The verb form must always agree with the subject, even when the subject is left out.

(4) The subject may be

a pronoun	**Tú** *hablas español muy bien.*	You speak Spanish very well.
a noun	**El doctor Juárez** *vive en California.*	Dr. Juarez lives in California.
	Roberto *maneja rápido.*	Roberto drives fast.
a noun and a pronoun	**Juan y yo** *tomamos mucho café. (nosotros)*	Juan and I drink a lot of coffee.
	María y tú *beben agua. (ustedes)*	María and you drink water.
	Carlos y Ud. *comen pollo. (ustedes)*	Carlos and you eat chicken.
excluded	*Recibimos muchas cartas. (nosotros/as)*	We receive many letters.
	Enseña bien la gramática.	He/She teaches grammar well. You (formal) teach grammar well.

(5) When there are two verbs back to back, as in *Jane wants to rest*, the following rules must be taken into consideration:

■ If the second verb in English is an infinitive, as in *to rest*, it is also written in Spanish as an infinitive:

Jane wants <u>to rest</u>.	*Jane quiere **descansar**.*
I need <u>to work</u> on the project.	*(Yo) Necesito **trabajar** en el proyecto.*

■ If the second verb is a gerund in English, as in *waiting*, it is also written in Spanish as a gerund. See more information in Chapter 9, The Present Participle.

I am <u>waiting</u> for the mailman.	*(Yo) Estoy **esperando** al cartero.*
We are <u>listening</u>.	*(Nosotras) Estamos **escuchando**.*

■ If the second part of a compound verb in English is a past participle, such as *walked, done,* or *written*, a past participle is also used in Spanish. This is covered in Chapter 11, The Present Perfect Indicative.

I have <u>finished</u> the homework.	*Yo he **terminado** la tarea.*
You have <u>come</u> early.	*Tú has **venido** temprano.*

Irregular Verbs in the Present Tense

Verbs considered irregular in Spanish fit into one of the following categories:

A. Verbs that change a vowel into another vowel or a diphthong in the present tense

These verbs are also known as stem-changing verbs. There are three main groups. For the first conjugation shown below—the conjugation of *pedir* (*to ask for*) as an example of verbs that change *e* to *i*—we show all the personal pronouns. Notice that *ella* and *Ud.* (*usted*) share the *él* form, and *ellas* and *Uds.* (*ustedes*) share the *ellos* form. Also *nosotras* and *vosotras* have the same form as the masculine *nosotros* and *vosotros*, respectively.

1. Verbs that change *e* to *i* in the present tense:

pedir (to ask)	*pido, pides, pide, pedimos, pedís, piden*
yo pido	*nosotros/nosotras pedimos*
tú pides	*vosotros/vosotras pedís*
él pide	*ellos piden*
ella pide	*ellas piden*
Ud. pide	*Uds. piden*

NOTES:

(1) Some of the other common verbs in this category include *concebir, corregir, elegir, medir, reír, seguir, sonreír, teñir, vestir,* as well as other verbs that contain some of these verbs, such as *conseguir, desmedirse, desteñir, desvestirse, impedir, reelegir,* etc.

(2) The first vowel of the *nosotros/as* and *vosotros/as* forms does not change.

(3) When the stem has two *e*s, the second *e* is the one that undergoes the change:

repetir (to repeat)	*repito, repites, repite, repetimos, repetís, repiten*

There are no changes in the stem for *nosotros/as* and *vosotros/as*.

(4) For practical purposes, only the forms for *yo, tú, él, nosotros, vosotros,* and *ellos* will be given in subsequent examples.

2. Verbs that change *e* to *ie* in the present tense:

pensar (to think)	*pienso, piensas, piensa, pensamos, pensáis, piensan*
preferir (to prefer)	*prefiero, prefieres, prefiere, preferimos, preferís, prefieren*

NOTES:

(1) Some of the other common verbs in this category include *comenzar, despertar, divertirse, empezar, encender, entender, mentir, perder, querer, sentir,* as well as other verbs that contain some of these verbs, such as *desmentir, resentir,* etc.

(2) *adquirir* (to acquire) is an exceptional verb that changes *i* to *ie* in all persons with the exclusion of *nosotros/as* and *vosotros/as*, which maintain the *i* of the infinitive:

adquiero, adquieres, adquiere, adquirimos, adquirís, adquieren

3. Verbs that change *o* to *ue* in the present tense:

    poder (can, to be able)   *puedo, puedes, puede, podemos, podéis, pueden*

NOTES:

(1) Some of the other common verbs in this category include *acordarse, contar, dormir, encontrar, morir, mostrar, recordar, resolver,* as well as others that might contain some of these verbs, such as *demostrar, desencontrar, recontar,* etc.

(2) *Oler* (*to smell*) is a particular verb that changes *o* to *hue* for all persons but *nosotros/as* and *vosotros/as: huelo, hueles, huele, olemos, oléis, huelen*

(3) *jugar* (to play a sport or a game) is an exceptional verb that changes *u* to *ue*:

juego, juegas, juega, jugamos, jugáis, juegan

    The Spanish verb for *to play an instrument*, however, is *tocar*, which also means *to touch*.

B. Verbs that undergo a change in the first person singular of the present tense

These verbs are also known as first-person irregular verbs. While the first person is the only one to undergo the specific change indicated in this section, some verbs also show additional irregularities in the other persons. For example, *venir* (*to come*) picks up a *g* in the *yo* form and the other persons, aside from *nosotros/as* and *vosotros/as*, change *e* to *ie*, as outlined in the preceding section A: *vengo, vienes, viene, venimos, venís, vienen*. Other verbs, such as *poner* (*to put*), pick up a *g* in the first person, but the rest of the verb conjugation behaves like a regular verb, with no changes in the stem: *pongo, pones, pone, ponemos, ponéis, ponen*. In some cases the spelling change is made in order to preserve the pronunciation of the infinitive form.

1. Verbs that add *-g* in the first person singular of the present tense:

tener (to have) *tengo, tienes, tiene, tenemos, tenéis, tienen*

NOTES:

(1) Some of the other common verbs in this category include *asir, decir, hacer, oír, salir, valer,* as well as other verbs that contain some of these forms, such as *abstenerse, convenir, deshacer, desoír, disponer, reponer, suponer,* etc.

(2) For other irregularities of *oír,* consult Section C, Other irregular forms in the present tense, that follows.

(3) *Tener* is a peculiar verb since it has specific functions, which need to be clarified:

■ It indicates possession and is equivalent to the English verb *to have* in that sense, as in:

Tengo un perro. I have a dog.

■ When the infinitive appears as *tener que,* however, this verb is equivalent to the English *to have to* as in:

Tengo que comprar un perro. I have to buy a dog.

In this case, the irregularities are the same: *tengo que, tienes que, tiene que, tenemos que, tenéis que, tienen que*; these forms are then followed by an infinitive: *tengo que comprar, tienes que venir, tiene que hablar,* etc.

■ *Tener* is used in expressions where English uses the verb *to be*:

Tengo frío.	I am cold.
Usted tiene calor.	You are hot.
Tenemos sed.	We are thirsty.
Tenéis miedo.	You are afraid.

■ *Tener* is also used in expressions which are equivalent to the English *to feel like*:

Tengo ganas de escribir una carta. I feel like writing a letter.

Notice that a gerund (*writing*) is used in English, while the infinitive (*escribir*) is used in Spanish. The infinitive of the Spanish verb is *tener,* but the expression *ganas de* must follow the conjugated form of *tener*:

tienes ganas de escribir, tenemos ganas de beber, tenéis ganas de hablar... you (informal) feel like writing, we feel like drinking, you (*vosotros*) feel like speaking . . .

2. Verbs that add *-ig* in the first person singular of the present tense:

traer (to bring)   *traigo, traes, trae, traemos, traéis, traen*

> **NOTE:**
> Some of the other common verbs in this category include *caer* and other verbs that contain *caer* or *traer*, such as *abstraer, atraer, contraer, distraer, recaer, sustraer,* etc.

3. Verbs that change *c* to *g* in the first person singular of the present tense:

hacer (to do)   *hago, haces, hace, hacemos, hacéis, hacen*

> **NOTES:**
> **(1)** Some of the other common verbs in this category include *satisfacer* and *decir*, as well as other verbs that contain some of these verbs, such as *contradecir, desdecir, deshacer, maldecir,* etc.
>
> **(2)** *decir* and its derivatives, such as *desdecir*, have the additional change of *e* to *i* for all persons except *nosotros/as* and *vosotros/as*:
>
> contradecir   *contradigo, contradices, contradice, contradecimos, contradecís, contradicen*

4. Verbs that change *g* to *j* in the first person singular of the present tense:

recoger (to collect)   *recojo, recoges, recoge, recogemos, recogéis, recogen*

> **NOTES:**
> **(1)** Some of the other common verbs in this category include *coger, dirigir, elegir, exigir, proteger,* as well as other verbs that contain these verbs, such as *acoger, escoger, recoger, reelegir,* etc.
>
> **(2)** This change in the first person preserves the pronunciation of the infinitive: *yo recojo* instead of *yo recogo*.
>
> **(3)** *elegir* and other similar verbs also have a change from *e* to *i* in all persons except *nosotros/as and vosotros/as*:
>
> *elijo, eliges, elige, elegimos, elegís, eligen*

5. Verbs that change *gu* to *g* in the first person singular of the present tense:

seguir (to follow)   *sigo, sigues, sigue, seguimos, seguís, siguen*

(1) Some of the other common verbs in this category include *distinguir* and *extinguir,* as well as other verbs that contain these verbs, such as *conseguir, perseguir, proseguir,* etc.

(2) *seguir* and other similar verbs also have a change from *e* to *i* in all persons except *nosotros/as* and *vosotros/as*:

consi**g**o, consigues, consigue, conseguimos, conseguís, consiguen

(3) The change preserves the pronunciation of the infinitive: *yo sigo* instead of *yo siguo*.

6. Verbs that change *c* to *z* in the first person singular of the present tense:

vencer (to win, to defeat)   ven**z**o, vences, vence, vencemos, vencéis, vencen

NOTES:

(1) Some of the other common verbs in this category include *ejercer, mecer, torcer,* as well as other verbs that contain these verbs, such as *convencer* and *retorcer.*

(2) *torcer* also changes from *o* to *ue* in all persons, except the *nosotros/as* and the *vosotros/as* forms:

t**ue**rzo, t**ue**rces, t**ue**rce, torcemos, torcéis, t**ue**rcen

(3) The change from *c* to *z* is not meant to preserve the sound, and this applies to both Peninsular and Latin American Spanish. In Spain, the *z* is pronounced like the English *th* in *think*. The combinations *c* + *e* and *c* + *i* are also pronounced the same way. Therefore, all the forms in the present tense of *vencer* are pronounced with the English *th* sound in Spain, regardless of the orthographical change. In Latin America, the *z*, as well as the combinations *c* + *e* and *c* + *i*, are pronounced like the English *s* in *same*. Therefore, all the forms of the present tense of *vencer* are pronounced with the *s* sound, regardless of the orthographical change.

7. Verbs that change *c* to *zc* in the first person singular of the present tense:

conocer (to know)   cono**zc**o, conoces, conoce, conocemos, conocéis, conocen

NOTE:

Some of the other common verbs in this category include *agradecer, aparecer, complacer, crecer, deducir, establecer, introducir, merecer, obedecer, producir, reducir, rejuvenecer, traducir,* as well as other verbs that contain these verbs, such as *desagradecer, desconocer, reaparecer, reconocer, restablecer,* etc.

C. Other irregular forms in the present tense:

There are verbs that show other irregularities that do not fit into any of the previous categories. A list with examples follows.

1. Changes in the stem of the first person singular in the present tense:

caber (to fit)	**cab ➤ quep**	*quepo, cabes, cabe, cabemos, cabéis, caben*
delinquir (to commit a crime)	**qu ➤ c**	*delinco, delinques, delinque, delinquimos, delinquís, delinquen*

2. Changes in the endings of the first person singular in the present tense:

dar (to give)	*do**y**, das, da, damos, dais, dan*
estar (to be)	*esto**y**, estás, está, estamos, estáis, están*
saber (to know)	*s**é**, sabes, sabe, sabemos, sabéis, saben*
ver (to see)	*v**e**o, ves, ve, vemos, veis, ven*

3. Irregular forms in all persons in the present tense:

ir (to go)	*voy, vas, va, vamos, vais, van*
ser (to be)	*soy, eres, es, somos, sois, son*
haber (to have)	*he, has, ha, hemos, habéis, han*

4. Some verbs add *-y* in the present tense:

oír (to hear)	*oigo, oyes, oye, oímos, oís, oyen*
huir (to flee)	*huyo, huyes, huye, huimos, huís, huyen*

> **NOTE:**
> Some of the other common verbs in this category include *concluir, construir, incluir, restituir*, as well as other verbs that contain these verbs, such as *reconstruir*.

5. Some verbs add an accent on the *i* or *u* in the present tense:

esquiar (to ski)	*esquío, esquías, esquía, esquiamos, esquiáis, esquían*
continuar (to continue)	*continúo, continúas, continúa, continuamos, continuáis, continúan*

Reflexive Verbs

Reflexive verbs have the suffix *se* attached to the infinitive. These verbs are conjugated like all other verbs, aside from the suffix, which changes according to the subject (*yo, tú*, etc.) and is placed before the conjugated verb. If a verb is made reflexive with the addition of *se*, all the usual irregularities will also appear in the present tense. The verb *dormirse*, for example, shows all the irregularities of *dormir*, which is a verb that changes *o* to *ue* in the stem. Reflexive verbs are covered in the section on Reflexive Pronouns in Chapter 16, Pronouns.

dormirse (to fall asleep)	*yo **me** duermo*	*nosotros/as **nos** dormimos*
	*tú **te** duermes*	*vosotros/as **os** dormís*
	*él **se** duerme*	*ellos **se** duermen*
	*ella **se** duerme*	*ellas **se** duermen*
	*Ud. **se** duerme*	*Uds. **se** duermen*
caerse (to fall down)	*yo **me** caigo*	*nosotros/as **nos** caemos*
	*tú **te** caes*	*vosotros/as **os** caéis*
	*él **se** cae*	*ellos **se** caen*
	*ella **se** cae*	*ellas **se** caen*
	*Ud. **se** cae*	*Uds. **se** caen*

Verbs like *gustar*

Besides reflexive verbs, there are certain other verbs in Spanish that are also used with a pronoun. *Gustar* (*to like*) is one of them. The uses of such verbs are covered in the section on Constructions with *se* in Chapter 16, Pronouns. As a preview, notice the following sentences in which *gustar* has only two forms in the present: *gusta*, which is used when the verb is followed by a singular noun or by one or more verbs in the infinitive, and the plural form *gustan*, followed by plural nouns.

*A mí **me gusta** el flan.*	I like flan.
*A los chicos **les gustan** los programas.*	The children like the programs.
***Nos gusta** escuchar música clásica.*	We like to listen to classical music.
*¿A ti **te gusta** leer y escribir poemas?*	Do you like to read and write poems?

The subject pronouns *yo, tú, él, ella*, etc. are not used with *gustar*; they are replaced by indirect object pronouns:

***Me** gusta la música. (yo)*	***Nos** gusta la primavera. (nosotros/as)*
***Te** gusta hablar español. (tú)*	***Os** gustan las empanadas. (vosotros/as)*

Le gusta el café. (él)   *Les gustan las vacaciones. (ellos)*
Le gusta venir a clase. (ella) *Les gusta viajar y comprar cosas. (ellos)*
Le gustan las frutas. (Ud.)   *Les gusta mi auto nuevo. (Uds.)*

Uses of the Present Indicative

The present indicative is used in the following situations.

A. Actions that take place at the time of speaking:

*Enrique **dice** que va a venir mañana.*   Enrique says he is going to come tomorrow.

B. Actions in progress:

***Hablo** por teléfono ahora.*   I am talking on the phone now.

(Note, however, that in this case it is better to use the present progressive in Spanish: ***Estoy hablando** ahora.*)

C. Habitual actions:

*María **escribe** poemas.*   María writes poems.

D. Actions that have no limits in time or that represent well-known facts:

*El sol **da** vida al universo.*   The sun gives life to the universe.
*Para cocinar langosta no **se quita** la   In order to cook lobster, it is not necessary to
caparazón.*   remove the shell.

E. Future events in a statement or question:

***Sale** esta noche.*   He is leaving tonight.
***Va a salir** esta noche.*   He is going to leave tonight. / He will leave
                              tonight.

*¿Cuándo **vamos** al cine?*   When are we going to the movies?

F. Events that are very likely to take place in the future, when *si* has the meaning of *if*:

Si **nieva** no voy.   If it snows, I will not go.

> **NOTE:**
>
> The future is used when *if* means *whether*:
>
> No me dijo si vendrá mañana. (future tense)   He didn't tell me if/whether he would come
>   tomorrow.

G. A request or a command:

Y Ud. la **llama** por teléfono después de la   And you, call her on the phone after the
reunión, por favor.   meeting, please.

Tú se lo **das** cuando venga mañana.   You give it to him when he comes tomorrow.

H. Actions that began in the past and are still going on in the present:

Los países **sufren** la consecuencia de tener   The countries suffer the consequences of
gobiernos débiles.   having weak governments.

Estudia en la universidad.   She studies at the university.

I. The present indicative is used with *desde* (or *desde hace*) + a time expression:

Estudio música desde el verano.   I have studied music since the summer.

Practico natación desde hace dos años.   I have practiced swimming for two years.

J. The present indicative is used with the expression *hace* + a time expression + *que*:

Hace dos años que **estudio** música.   I have been studying music for two years.

K. The present indicative is used with *cuando* to indicate a routine situation:

Nunca **salgo** cuando llueve.   I never go out when it rains.

L. The present indicative is used for a narration of past, literary, or historical events to make them more vivid:

Estaba estudiando y de repente lo **veo** entrar.   I was studying and all of a sudden I see him
                                                    come in.

La mujer **se levanta** y **cierra** la puerta.   The woman gets up and closes the door.

Colón **llega** en 1492.   Columbus arrives in 1492.

M. The present indicative is used to express an action in progress with the present progressive tense:

1. With the verb *estar*:

Está <u>tomando</u> la sopa.	He is having soup.

2. With other verbs, the continuity of the action is emphasized:

Ella **continúa/sigue** <u>estudiando</u>.	She continues studying.
Ella **anda** <u>trabajando</u> mucho estos días.	She has been working a lot these days.
Voy <u>aprendiendo</u> despacio.	I have been gradually learning.

N. The present indicative is used to express a temporary or permanent state or condition using *ser* or *estar*:

Jim **está** preocupado.	Jim is worried.
Marte **está** cerca de la luna.	Mars is near the Moon.
María **es** muy inteligente.	María is very intelligent.
Todos **somos** humanos.	Everybody is human.

O. The present indicative is used to express an action that has just been completed, using *acabar de* + infinitive:

Acabo de comer.	I have just finished eating.
Acaban de recibirlo.	They have just received it.

P. The present indicative is used to express an action that was almost completed in the past:

Casi lo **echan** del trabajo.	They almost fired him.
Por poco **me caigo**.	I almost fell.

The Verbs *ser* and *estar*

The verbs *ser* and *estar* in Spanish are two versions of the English verb *to be*. The conjugation of these verbs is presented here only in the present tense.

ser	estar	to be
yo soy	yo estoy	I am
tú eres	tú estás	you are (singular, informal)

él es	*él está*	he is
ella es	*ella está*	she is
Ud. es	*Ud. está*	you are (singular, formal)
nosotros/as somos	*nosotros/as estamos*	we are
vosotros/as sois	*vosotros/as estáis*	you are (plural, informal in Spain)
ellos son	*ellos están*	they are
ellas son	*ellas están*	they are
Uds. son	*Uds. están*	you are (plural, formal/informal)

Differences Between and Uses of *ser* and *estar*

Some of the most common uses of *ser* and *estar* follow.

A. The verb *ser* is used in the following circumstances.

1. The verb *ser* is used to indicate a permanent or inherent characteristic of the noun:

El terciopelo es suave.	Velvet is smooth.
Soy feliz. Tengo una linda familia.	I'm a happy person. I have a nice family.
Mi abuelo es muy generoso.	My grandfather is very generous.
El flan es muy rico.	Flan is very good.

   NOTE:

"Ser o no ser."	"To be or not to be."

2. The verb *ser* is used to give information about the location of an event:

La carrera es en el autódromo de Daytona.	The race is at the Daytona Speedway.

3. The verb *ser* is used to identify a noun:

Esos son los jugadores del equipo.	Those are the team's players.
Esta es la habitación de los huéspedes.	This is the guests' room.

4. The verb *ser* is used to give information about a profession:

Sara es dentista.	Sara is a dentist.
Esos hombres son electricistas.	Those men are electricians.

Also:

Yo soy estudiante de primer año.	I am a freshman.

5. The verb *ser* is used to provide the date:

Hoy es el 14 de abril.	Today is April 14th.
La independencia es el 4 de julio.	Independence Day is on July 4th.
La inauguración del edificio es mañana.	The inauguration of the building is tomorrow.

6. The verb *ser* is used to mention day and time and to ask about the time:

Hoy es sábado.	Today is Saturday.
¿Qué hora es ahora?	What time is it now?
Es la una de la tarde.	It is one P.M.
Son las 5 y media de la mañana.	It is 5:30 in the morning.

7. The verb *ser* is used to express the passive voice:

Los exámenes fueron corregidos por el maestro, no por el ayudante.	The exams were corrected by the teacher, not by his assistant.
El francés es hablado en Haití.	French is spoken in Haiti.

8. The verb *ser* is used with an adverb of time:

Es temprano para comer ahora.	It's early for eating now.
"Nunca es tarde cuando la dicha es buena."	It's never late when things are going well. (popular proverb)
Es hora de recibir un aumento.	It's time to get a raise.

9. The verb *ser* is used to explain what something is made of:

Los escalones son de madera dura.	The steps are made of hard wood.
La cacerola es de acero inoxidable.	The pot is made of stainless steel.

10. The verb *ser* is used followed by *de* to express nationality or the origin of a noun:

Mi padre es de España.	My father is from Spain.
El florero es de Tánger.	The flower vase is from Tangier.
La rosa amarilla que me dio el florista es de Holanda.	The yellow rose that the florist gave me is from Holland.

11. The verb *ser* is used to indicate possession:

La valija negra es de mi hermano.	The black bag is my brother's.
Estos lápices son míos.	These pencils are mine.
Estas plantas son las de Maggie.	These are Maggie's plants.

12. The verb *ser* is used to name the seasons:

Ahora es verano en Inglaterra.	Now it's summer in England.
Cuando en Estados Unidos es otoño es primavera en Sudamérica.	When it's fall in the United States, it's spring in South America.

13. The verb *ser* is used with impersonal expressions:

Es increíble que duermas tanto.	It's incredible that you sleep so much.
Fue bueno que ella alquilara la casa.	It was good that she rented the house.

But:

Está mal que ella no responda.	It's bad that she is not answering.
Está bien que vosotros hayáis venido.	It's good that you have come.

14. The verb *ser* is used to ask for the total amount of a purchase:

¿Cuánto es? or ¿Cuánto es todo?	How much is it?

15. The verb *ser* is used to indicate religious preference and political affiliation:

La reina Isabel de España era católica.	Queen Elizabeth of Spain was Catholic.
Note: *Esta tortilla no **está** muy católica.*	This omelet is not very good.
Su familia es presbiteriana.	Her family is Presbyterian.
El asistente de María es republicano.	María's assistant is a Republican.
No sé si Jorge es republicano o liberal.	I don't know if Jorge is a Republican or a liberal.

B. **The verb *estar* is used in the following circumstances.**

1. The verb *estar* is used to indicate a temporary or transitional characteristic of a noun:

Las noches están más frescas ahora.	The evenings are cooler now.
La tenista está cansada.	The tennis player is tired.
Estoy feliz. Vamos a viajar pronto.	I am happy. We are going to travel soon.

Mi abuelo está generoso hoy: acaba de darme dinero para mis libros.	My grandfather is generous today: he just gave me money for my books.
El postre está rico. No tiene mucho azúcar.	The dessert is good. It doesn't have too much sugar.

2. The verb *estar* is used to give the location of a noun:

Nuestra escuela está cerca del centro.	Our school is near the downtown area.
Nashville está en Tennessee.	Nashville is in Tennessee.
Marta está en casa.	Marta is at home.
El perro está en la casucha.	The dog is in the doghouse.

3. The verb *estar* is used in the present progressive tense to express an action in progress:

¿Vosotros estáis esperando a los niños?	Are you waiting for the children?

4. The verb *estar* is used to indicate the result of an action:

Los exámenes ya están corregidos.	The exams are already corrected.

5. The verb *estar* is used to denote specific, temporary situations:

Mis vecinos están de fiesta.	My neighbors have a party going on.
Martín está de vacaciones.	Martin is on vacation.
La novia estaba de blanco.	The bride had a white gown on.
Estoy a dieta. Quiero adelgazar.	I'm on a diet. I want to lose weight.
La familia está de luto.	The family is in mourning.
Los panaderos están de huelga.	The bakers are on strike.
Ya estoy de vuelta.	I just came back.
"Cuando ella va, yo ya estoy de vuelta."	I am smarter than she is. (popular proverb)
Estamos de parabienes; nuestra hija acaba de tener un bebé.	We feel lucky; our daughter just had a baby.

6. The verb *estar* is used to describe an ailment:

Raúl está con jaqueca.	Raúl has a migraine.
Hilda está con un resfrío bárbaro.	Hilda has a bad cold.
Estoy con dolor de estómago.	I have a stomachache.
Estaba congestionada.	I was congested.
Mi hermano está engripado.	My brother has the flu.

7. The verb *estar* is used to indicate a condition related to time:

Estoy adelantado con el pago.	I am early with the payment.
Estamos atrasados. Perdón.	We are late. Excuse us.

8. The verb *estar* is used to show the immediacy of an action:

Estaba por llamarte cuando viniste.	I was about to call you when you came.
La aerolínea estaba por cerrar.	The airline was about to close down.
La secretaria estaba a punto de venir.	The secretary was about to come.

9. The verb *estar* is used to express a condition contrary to what is expected:

La sopa está fría.	The soup is cold.
Los fideos están duros.	The noodles are hard.
Su hijo está más maduro. ¡Qué bien!	Their son is (has become) more mature. That's good!
¡Qué verde está el pasto!	How green the grass is!

10. The verb *estar* is used to describe a position of the body:

Estamos sentados.	We are seated.
El gobernador está de pie.	The governor is standing.
Nadie está parado.	Nobody is standing.
La enferma está recostada.	The patient is lying down.
Juancito está acostado.	Juancito is in bed.
Papá ya está levantado.	Dad is already up.
La monja está de rodillas.	The nun is kneeling.

11. The verb *estar* is used to indicate a job or position occupied at a particular time:

Mi prima está de cajera en esa tienda.	My cousin works as a cashier in that store.
Laura está de maestra suplente del primer grado.	Laura is working as a substitute first grade teacher.

12. The verb *estar* is used to talk about the weather:

Hoy está nublado.	Today it's cloudy.
Hoy está ventoso.	Today it's windy.
Hoy está precioso.	It's beautiful today.
Hoy está caluroso. / Hace calor.	It's hot.
Está un poco frío. / Hace un poco de frío.	It's a little bit cold.

NOTE:

Estar is used in the present progressive tense, as described in item 3 previously, to show an action in progress. This tense can also be used to describe the weather:

Está lloviendo, nevando, garuando. (raining, snowing, drizzling)

13. The verb *estar* is used to ask about a price:

¿A cuánto están las rosas?	How much are the roses?

14. The verb *estar* is used to say whether someone is alive or dead:

¿Sus abuelos están vivos?	Are your grandparents alive?
El padre de Martín está muerto.	Martin's father is dead.

Cases in Which Either *ser* or *estar* Is Used

A. In indicating marital status, either *ser* or *estar* can be used, depending on the context:

Jorge es casado.	Jorge is married.
Jorge está casado ahora.	Jorge is married now.
Está casado con Luisa.	He is married to Luisa.
Su hijo es soltero.	Their son is single.
Su hijo está soltero todavía.	Their son is still single.

■ To refer to a married couple:

Carlos y Sara están divorciados.	Carlos and Sara are divorced.
Pepa y Juan están separados.	Pepa and Juan are separated.

NOTE:

The reflexive verbs *divorciarse* and *separarse* are also very common:

Carlos y Sara se divorciaron.	Carlos and Sara got divorced.
Pepa y Juan se separaron.	Pepa and Juan separated.

■ To refer to individuals not related to each other:

Tony y Marta son divorciados.	Tony and Marta are divorced.
Manuel, Catalina y Pedro son separados.	Manuel, Catalina, and Pedro are separated.
¿Tu mamá es viuda?	Is your mom a widow?
¿Cuánto tiempo hace que ella está viuda?	How long has she been a widow?
Él es divorciado.	He is divorced.

Ella es separada.	She is separated.
Eugenia es solterona.	Eugenia is an old maid.
Reinaldo es solterón.	Reinaldo is a confirmed bachelor.

NOTE:

quedarse soltero/a	to stay single
Juan se quedó soltero.	Juan stayed single.
Ruth se quedó soltera. Su novio murió.	Ruth stayed single. Her fiancé died.

B. To describe status related to work, both *ser* and *estar* can be used:

Mi hermano es jubilado.	My brother is retired.

But:

Mi hermano no trabaja ahora porque está jubilado.	My brother doesn't work now because he is retired.
El Dr. Pérez es médico pero está retirado; va a dedicarse a escribir.	Dr. Pérez is a medical doctor, but he is retired; he will spend his time writing.

Different Meanings of Adjectives Depending on the Use of *ser* or *estar*

El dueño de la tienda es rico.	The store owner is wealthy.
Esta salsa está rica.	This sauce is delicious.
Raimundo es listo.	Raimundo is smart.
Raimundo está listo.	Raimundo is ready.
Es una chica muy viva.	She is a vivacious child.
Su abuela está viva.	Their grandmother is alive.
Su esposo es ciego.	Her husband is blind.
Su esposo está ciego.	Her husband doesn't realize what's going on.
Mi primo es sordo.	My cousin is deaf.
Mi primo está sordo.	My cousin doesn't want to hear.
Esteban es maduro.	Esteban is mature.
Las peras están maduras.	The pears are ripe.
La espinaca es verde.	Spinach is green.
Las peras están verdes.	The pears are not ripe.
Es tarde.	It's late.
Estoy atrasado.	I'm late.

Es temprano.	It's early.
Llegué temprano.	I'm early.
Juana es muy interesada. Siempre quiere favorecerse con todo.	Juana is very self-interested. She always tries to benefit from everything.
Juana está interesada en las noticias que le di.	Juana is interested in the news I gave her.
Mabel es/está consciente de sus deberes como madre.	Mabel is aware of her duties as a mother.
El paciente está consciente después de la operación.	The patient is conscious after the surgery.
Esa presentación fue muy aburrida.	That presentation was very boring.
Todos los chicos estaban aburridos.	All the children were bored.
Carlos es muy orgulloso. No acepta ninguna crítica constructiva.	Carlos is very proud. He doesn't accept any constructive criticism.
Javier está orgulloso. Fue ascendido a gerente.	Javier is very proud. He was promoted to work as a manager.

4

Adjectives

Adjectives are used to modify a noun, either by giving a description of that particular noun in order to distinguish it from others of its class, or by indicating its location, ownership, or the exact or vague quantity of the noun. Adjectives are also used to ask questions and to express feelings. Besides single words, phrases or sentences may also function as adjectives, as in these examples:

el jarrón <u>chino</u>	the Chinese vase
muchos jarrones <u>con figuras chinas</u>	many vases with Chinese figures
ese jarrón <u>que tiene figuras chinas</u>	that vase that has Chinese figures

Classification of Adjectives

Adjectives in Spanish are classified into two main groups:

A. Descriptive adjectives (*adjetivos calificativos*) show a quality of the noun, as in *río extenso* (*long river*), *casa chica* (*small house*), or *niño inteligente* (*intelligent child*).

B. Determinative adjectives (*adjetivos determinativos*) give specific information regarding the noun. These adjectives are classified according to what they specify:

- *Demonstrative* adjectives (*demostrativos*): location

- *Possessive* adjectives (*posesivos*): ownership

- *Numeral* adjectives (*numerales*): exact quantity

- *Indefinite* adjectives (*indefinidos*): vague quantity

- *Interrogative* adjectives (*interrogativos*): questions

- *Exclamatory* adjectives (*admirativos*): exclamations

Descriptive Adjectives

Descriptive adjectives have ending variations that correspond to the gender and number of the nouns to which they refer.

Endings

A. Adjectives ending in *o*

Adjectives that end in *o* have four different endings to agree with masculine and feminine nouns, both singular and plural:

o	*os*	*a*	*as*

The feminine is formed by changing the final *o* into *a*. For the plural, an *s* is added to both masculine and feminine forms:

el bosque oscuro	the dark forest
los bosques oscuros	the dark forests
la calle oscura	the dark street
las calles oscuras	the dark streets

B. Adjectives ending in *a* (or *ista*)

Adjectives ending in *a* (or *ista*) have the same form for masculine and feminine. For the plural, an *s* is added to the singular form:

a (or *ista*) and s

el comentario realista	realistic comments
la muchacha realista	realistic girl
los asuntos realistas	realistic subjects
las resoluciones realistas	realistic resolutions
el hombre alerta	the alert man
los hombres alertas	the alert men
la mujer alerta	the alert woman
las mujeres alertas	the alert women

C. Adjectives ending in e

Adjectives ending in *e* have the same form for masculine and feminine. For the plural, an *s* is added to the singular form:

e and s

el banco fuer**te**	the strong bench
los bancos fuer**tes**	the strong benches
la mesa fuer**te**	the strong table
las mesas fuer**tes**	the strong tables

D. Adjectives ending in i

There are not many adjectives ending in *i*, and they take the following forms:

1. If the stress is on the next to last syllable (*penúltima sílaba*), they have the same form for masculine and feminine. For the plural, an *s* is added to the singular form:

i and s

el hombre pars**i**	the Parsic man
los hombres pars**is**	the Parsic men
la dama pars**i**	the Parsic lady
las damas pars**is**	the Parsic ladies
la palabra curs**i**	the affected word
las palabras curs**is**	the affected words
la mujer yanqu**i**	the Yankee woman
las mujeres yanqu**is**	the Yankee women

2. If the stress is on the last syllable, the plural is formed by adding *es* and placing an accent mark on the *i*:

i and es

bengalí, bengal**íes**	Bengali
guaraní, guaran**íes**	Guarani
iraní, iran**íes**	Iranian
iraquí, iraqu**íes**	Iraqi
sefardí, sefard**íes**	Sephardi
carmesí, carmes**íes**	red (color)

E. Adjectives ending in *u*

Adjectives ending in *u* have one form for both genders, and usually form the plural by adding *es*. Since the stress is on the last syllable, the *u* carries an accent mark:

u and es

la chica zulú	Zulu girl
los cantos zulúes	Zulu songs
la túnica hindú	Hindu tunic
las túnicas hindúes	Hindu tunics

F. Adjectives that end in a consonant change according to the following rules.

1. When masculine and feminine have the same form, *es* is added to form the plural:

consonant and es

el ejercicio útil	the useful exercise
los ejercicios útiles	the useful exercises
la regla útil	the useful rule
las reglas útiles	the useful rules

> **NOTE:**
> Other adjectives that fall under this rule are those that end in *s*, *un*, and *z*, as in *cortés/corteses* (*courteous*), *común/comunes* (*common*), and *audaz/audaces* (*audacious*). Note that in adjectives that end in -*z*, the *z* is changed to a *c*, and then *es* is added to the word.

2. When the feminine is formed by adding an *a* to the masculine, as in *cantor/cantora* (*singer*), *s* is added for the feminine plural and *es* for the masculine plural.

masculine	**feminine**
singular: ends in consonant	singular: ends in consonant + *a*
el profesor	*la profesora*
plural: ends in consonant + *es*	plural: ends in consonant + *as*
los profesores	*las profesoras*

Adjectives that follow this rule are:

(a) Some adjectives of nationality or origin:

el diario español	the Spanish newspaper
*los diarios español**es***	the Spanish newspapers
*la revista español**a***	the Spanish magazine
*las revistas español**as***	the Spanish magazines

Some other examples are: ***alemán, irlandés, portugués,*** and ***vienés.***

(b) Adjectives ending in *on*, *an*, or *or*:

el niño llorón	the crying boy
*los niños llor**ones***	the crying children / boys
*la niña llor**ona***	the crying girl
*las niñas llor**onas***	the crying girls

Some other examples are: ***haragán*** (*lazy*); ***mandón*** (*bossy*); ***narrador*** (*narrator*).

However, there are other adjectives that end in *or* and have only two possible forms: singular and plural. These adjectives form the plural by adding *es*:

el patio exterior	outside patio
*los patios exterio**res***	outside patios
la pared exterior	outside wall
*las paredes exterio**res***	outside walls

Other examples include ***anterior, inferior, interior, posterior,*** and ***superior.***

> **NOTE:**
> The noun *superior* has the feminine form *superiora,* which defines a nun in charge of a religious community. This noun usually follows *madre,* as in *madre superiora.*
>
> | | |
> |---|---|
> | *El superior presidió la reunión.* | The superior presided over the meeting. |
> | *La (madre) superiora habló con las monjas.* | The mother superior talked to the nuns. |

(c) Adjectives ending in *in*:

Juan es un bailarín profesional.	Juan is a professional dancer.
*Ellos son bailar**ines**.*	They are dancers.
*María es bailar**ina**.*	María is a dancer.
*Ellas son bailar**inas**.*	They are dancers.

A few other examples include *chiquitín, pequeñín* (*small*); *saltarín* (*a person who jumps*, not necessarily a *parachutist*, which is called *paracaidista*); *pillín* (*rascal*); *chiquilín* (*small child*).

NOTE:

An exception to this rule is *ruin* (*mean*), which has the same form for the feminine. Both masculine and feminine plural forms take *es*:

*el hombre ru**in***	mean man
*los hombres ru**ines***	mean men
*la mujer ru**in***	mean woman
*las mujeres ru**ines***	mean women

G. Invariable ending

Some adjectives have a unique form that does not change for gender or number. Some examples are:

animals

*una hiena **macho***	a male hyena
*un avestruz **hembra***	a female ostrich
*una niña **prodigio***	a wonder girl

colors

*pantalones color **vino***	wine-colored pants
*labios **coral***	coral-shaded lips
*sandalias **limón***	lemon-colored sandals

Agreement Between Descriptive Adjectives and Nouns

Although descriptive adjectives usually agree with nouns in gender and number, agreement varies depending on the following conditions.

- The position of the adjectives (after or before the noun or nouns)

- The gender and number of the nouns involved

- Whether the adjectives qualify equally all the nouns involved

- Whether different adjectives qualify different nouns in the sentence

Agreement When Descriptive Adjectives Follow the Noun

A. Agreement between one adjective and one noun

If only one adjective qualifies a noun (singular or plural), the adjective takes the ending that corresponds to that noun:

la calle larga	the long street
los niños torpes	the clumsy children

B. Agreement between one adjective and two nouns

If only one adjective qualifies two nouns (singular or plural), the adjective takes the following endings:

1. Feminine nouns ➤ feminine plural ending for the adjective:

una puerta y una ventana estrechas	a narrow door and a narrow window
la puerta y las ventanas estrechas	the narrow door and the narrow windows
las ventanas y la puerta estrechas	the narrow windows and the narrow door

2. Masculine nouns ➤ masculine plural ending for the adjective:

el lápiz y el cuaderno rojos	the red pencil and the red notebook
los lápices y los cuadernos rojos	the red pencils and the red notebooks

3. Mixed-gender nouns ➤ masculine plural ending for the adjective:

la calle y el barrio sencillos	the plain street and the plain neighborhood
las calles y los barrios sencillos	the plain streets and the plain neighborhoods
la niña y los niños extranjeros	the foreign girl and the foreign boys
hombres y mujeres extranjeros	foreign men and foreign women

NOTES:

(1) Sometimes the speaker considers the nouns as a whole idea rather than isolated entities. In these cases, the adjective that modifies the nouns may agree in gender and number with the closest noun:

pavor y angustia repentina	sudden fear and anguish
ojos y pelo negro	black eyes and black hair

(2) When the nouns are joined by either *o* (*or*) or *ni* (*nor*), the adjective that qualifies both nouns takes the plural form according to the rule of agreement:

Quiero un pastel o una tortilla frescos.   I want a fresh pie or a fresh omelet.
No pediré ni un pastel ni una ensalada   I will order neither a Mexican pie nor a
  mexicanos.   Mexican salad.

C. Agreement between one adjective and more than two nouns

If only one adjective qualifies more than two different nouns (singular or plural), the adjective takes the following endings:

1. Feminine nouns ➤ feminine plural endings for the adjective:

las ventanas, la puerta y la galería estrechas   the narrow windows, the narrow door, and the narrow gallery

2. Masculine nouns ➤ masculine plural endings for the adjective:

el león, los tigres y los caballos domesticados   the tamed lion, the tamed tigers, and the tamed horses

3. mixed-gender nouns ➤ masculine plural endings

el vestido, los zapatos y la blusa blancos   the white dress, the white shoes, and the white blouse

NOTE:
The *y* is not preceded by a comma as *and* would be in English in a series of nouns.

D. Agreement between two adjectives and one singular noun

If two adjectives qualify a singular noun, the adjectives are connected by *y* and each one takes the ending that corresponds to that noun:

La casa estaba cerrada y silenciosa.   The house was closed and silent.

E. Agreement between two adjectives and one plural noun

There are two cases.

1. If two adjectives qualify a plural noun and the noun is considered as a whole concept, each adjective takes the ending that corresponds to that noun:

los ojos profundos y tristes	the deep, sad eyes
las manos blancas y suaves	the smooth, white hands
las casas pequeñas y pobres	the small, poor houses

Here, both eyes, both hands, and all the houses are equally modified by the adjectives.

2. If two adjectives qualify a plural noun, and the noun cannot be considered as a whole concept but as being formed by two different entities (two nouns different from each other), one adjective must agree with one of the items, and the other adjective should function as a noun.

Reference made to <u>two novels</u>:

Incorrect: *Prefiero las novelas corta y larga.*	(Literally) I prefer the novels short and long.
Correct: *Prefiero la novela corta y la larga.*	I prefer the short novel and the long one.

Reference made to <u>two dogs</u>:

Incorrect: *Prefiero los perros blanco y negro.*	(Literally) I prefer the dogs white and black.
Correct: *Prefiero el perro blanco y el negro.*	I prefer the white dog and the black one.

Reference to <u>two wines</u>:

Incorrect: *Trajo los vinos tinto y blanco.*	(Literally) He brought the wines red and white.
Correct: *Trajo el vino tinto y el blanco.*	He brought the red wine and the white one.

F. Agreement between two adjectives and two nouns

If two adjectives qualify equally two nouns (singular or plural), they are connected by *y* and take the following endings:

1. Feminine nouns ➤ feminine plural endings for the adjectives:

la <u>blusa</u> y la <u>falda</u> rojas y cortas (both singular nouns)	the short, red blouse and skirt
las <u>blusas</u> y las <u>faldas</u> rojas y cortas (both plural nouns)	the short, red blouses and skirts

la *blusa* y las *sandalias* blancas y modernas (singular/plural nouns)	the modern, white blouse and sandals

2. Masculine nouns ➤ masculine plural endings for the adjectives:

el *pantalón* y el *cinturón* negros y elegantes (both singular nouns)	the elegant, black pair of pants and belt
los *pantalones* y los *zapatos* negros y elegantes (both plural nouns)	the elegant, black pants and shoes
los *pantalones* y el *cinturón* negros y elegantes (plural/singular nouns)	the elegant, black pants and belt

3. Mixed-gender nouns ➤ masculine plural endings for the adjectives:

la *corbata* y el *pantalón* negros y elegantes (both singular nouns)	the elegant, black tie and pants
el *suéter* y las *medias* viejos y sucios (singular/plural nouns)	the old, dirty sweater and socks

G. **Agreement between two adjectives and more than two nouns**

If two adjectives qualify more than two nouns, the adjectives are connected by *y* and take the following endings.

1. Feminine nouns ➤ feminine plural endings for the adjectives:

la *blusa*, la *falda* y la *cartera* blancas y modernas	the modern, white blouse, skirt, and purse
las *medias*, la *falda* y la *cartera* blancas y modernas	the modern, white socks, skirt, and purse

2. Masculine nouns ➤ masculine plural endings for the adjectives:

el *baño*, el *comedor* y el *patio* amplios y limpios	the spacious, clean bathroom, dining room, and patio
el *niño*, el *padre*, el *tío* y el *abuelo* cansados y aburridos	the tired and bored boy, father, uncle, and grandfather

3. Mixed-gender nouns ➤ masculine plural endings for the adjectives:

la *madre*, el *padre* y los *niños* entusiasmados y divertidos	the enthusiastic and fun mother, father, and children
la *mesa*, las *sillas* y el *sillón* importados y caros	the expensive, imported table, chairs, and sofa

NOTE:

The *y* before the last noun is not preceded by a comma as *and* would be in English in a series of nouns.

H. Agreement between more than two adjectives and one noun

If more than two adjectives qualify one noun (singular or plural), the adjectives take the endings that correspond to that noun. No commas are placed before the *y*:

receta corta, fácil y buena	short, easy, and good recipe
recetas cortas, fáciles y buenas	short, easy, and good recipes
día lluvioso, oscuro y triste	rainy, dark, and sad-looking day
días lluviosos, oscuros y tristes	rainy, dark, and sad-looking days

NOTE:

It is also possible to place one of the adjectives in front of the noun to indicate emphasis:

algunos tristes días lluviosos y oscuros	some sad-looking days, rainy and dark
una buena receta corta y fácil	a good recipe, short and easy

I. Agreement between more than two adjectives and two nouns

If more than two adjectives qualify equally two nouns (singular or plural), the adjectives take the following endings.

1. Feminine nouns ➤ feminine plural endings for the adjectives:

las palabras y las frases cortas, buenas y exactas	the short, good, and exact words and phrases
la funda y las sábanas blancas, limpias y suaves	the clean, smooth, and white pillowcase and sheets

2. Masculine nouns ➤ masculine plural endings for the adjectives:

un perro y un gato hambrientos, somnolientos y cansados	a hungry, sleepy, and tired dog and cat
unos perros y un gato negros, viejos y hambrientos	some black, old, and hungry dogs and a cat

3. mixed gender nouns ➤ masculine plural endings

el tío y la tía generosos, buenos y amables	the good, generous, and amiable uncle and aunt
las tías y los abuelos buenos, generosos y simpáticos	the good, generous, and nice aunts and grandparents

NOTE:
The *y* that connects the last two adjectives is not preceded by a comma.

J. Agreement between more than two adjectives and more than two nouns

In the case of multiple adjectives that qualify equally more than two nouns (singular or plural), the adjectives take the following endings.

1. Feminine nouns ➤ feminine plural endings for the adjectives:

la pluma, la tiza y la carpeta blancas, pequeñas y nuevas	the small, new, and white pen, chalk, and folder

2. Masculine nouns ➤ masculine plural endings for the adjectives:

el lápiz, el marcador y el borrador negros, viejos y gastados	the old, worn out, and black pencil, marker, and eraser

3. Mixed-gender nouns ➤ masculine plural endings for the adjectives:

el lápiz, las lapiceras y el borrador nuevos, baratos y buenos	the new, cheap, and good pencil, pens, and eraser

NOTE:
The *y* is not preceded by a comma as *and* would be in English in a series of nouns.

Agreement When Descriptive Adjectives Precede the Noun

Sometimes adjectives are placed before nouns to produce a form that is more poetic, or simply to intensify the quality of the noun. The following rules apply.

A. Agreement between one adjective and one noun (singular or plural)

If only one adjective qualifies a noun, the adjective agrees in gender and number with the noun:

un caluroso día	a hot day
los atractivos platos	the attractive dishes

B. Agreement between one adjective and two singular nouns

If the nouns are singular, the adjective agrees in gender and number with the closest noun. In the following examples, the (f.) stands for feminine and the (m.) for masculine.

Pude notar su <u>profundo candor</u> y fe (f.)   or *... profundo candor y fervor* (m.)
I noticed her deep candor and her faith.
<u>But</u>: *Pude notar su candor y fe profundos.*

Tenía <u>excesiva angustia</u> y dolor (m.).   or *... excesiva angustia y pena* (f.)
She felt excessive anguish and grief.
<u>But</u>: *Tenía angustia y dolor excesivos.*

C. Agreement between one or two adjectives and a combination of singular and plural nouns

If one adjective (or more than one) qualifies a combination of singular and plural nouns, the idea is better expressed when the adjectives <u>follow</u> the nouns instead of preceding them:

los campos y la colina <u>fértiles</u>	the fertile fields and hill
los campos y la colina <u>frescos y fértiles</u>	the cool, fertile fields and hill

Another possibility is for one adjective to precede one of the nouns and for related adjectives to be placed before the other nouns:

los <u>fértiles</u> campos y la <u>fecunda</u> colina	the fertile fields and the fruitful hill
(or) *los <u>fértiles</u> campos y la <u>fecunda</u> y <u>verde</u> colina*	the fertile fields and the fruitful, green hill

D. Agreement between one or more adjectives and two or more plural nouns

If the nouns are plural, the adjectives agree in gender and number with the closest noun. Agreement with the other noun or nouns is implied.

las anchas avenidas y parques	the wide avenues and parks
los verdes y frescos valles y colinas	the cool, green valleys and hills
los verdes y frescos valles, colinas y campos	the cool, green valleys, hills, and fields
las blancas, suaves y pequeñas ovejas y corderos	the small, smooth, white sheep and lambs

Notice that the order of the adjectives in Spanish does not correspond to the order of the adjectives in English.

> **NOTES:**
>
> **(1)** The *y* that connects the last two nouns is not preceded by a comma.
>
> **(2)** Two adjectives must be joined by a *y*.
>
> **(3)** When there are more than two adjectives, the *y* that joins the last two adjectives is not preceded by a comma.

When Different Adjectives Qualify Different Nouns

A distinction must be made in the sentence when the adjective or adjectives agree with certain nouns only, regardless of whether the adjectives precede or follow the nouns.

las anchas avenidas y los pequeños parques	the wide avenues and the small parks
los fértiles y frescos valles y las aldeas antiguas	the cool, fertile valleys and the ancient villages
los valles fértiles y frescos y las antiguas aldeas	

Notice that the order of the adjectives in Spanish does not correspond to the order of the adjectives in English.

When Descriptive Adjectives Precede and Follow the Noun

Sometimes adjectives are placed before and after the noun, either to give emphasis to a quality or qualities of the noun or to agree with specific positional rules. Agreement with the noun will follow the general rules of agreement. (See the section on Position of Descriptive Adjectives that follows). Observe the following examples of multiple adjectives that qualify a noun:

| hermosas rosas otoñales | beautiful fall roses |
| elegantes pantalones veraniegos | elegant summer pants |

una ancha playa solitaria y tranquila	a wide, quiet, and solitary beach
espesas y frescas arboledas provincianas	thick and cool provincial groves

Agreement Between Nouns and Adjectives of Color

When colors are used as nouns they take the masculine form:

El gris es un color triste.	Gray is a sad color.
El verde es mi color preferido.	Green is my favorite color.
Los rojos de este cuadro son vivos.	The reds (red tones) in this painting are vivid.
El violeta está de moda este invierno.	Violet is in fashion this winter.

As adjectives, colors follow specific rules for gender and number agreement according to their endings, as shown below. The word *color* or the expression *de color* may also precede a specific color, in which case all colors appear in the masculine singular form *(color rojo, de color rojo)*. Some of the most common colors are used in the following examples.

A. Colors ending in *o* have four different forms: *o, a, os, as*:

amarillo	➤	*zapatos amarillos*	yellow shoes
anaranjado	➤	*blusa anaranjada*	orange blouse
blanco	➤	*nubes blancas*	white clouds
morado	➤	*uva morada*	dark violet grape
negro	➤	*sombrero negro*	black hat
rojo	➤	*labios rojos*	red lips

B. Colors that end in *a* follow specific rules:

crema	**one form**
zapatos crema	cream-colored shoes
paredes color crema	cream-colored walls
uñas de color crema	cream-colored nails
lila	**one form; sometimes used in the plural**
vestido lila	lilac dress
flores lilas	lilac flowers
tarjeta de color lila	lilac card
guantes color lila	lilac gloves

naranja	**one form**
blusa color naranja	orange blouse
pantalones naranja	orange pants
auto de color naranja	orange car

rosa	**one form**
blusa de color rosa	pink blouse
sombrero color rosa	pink hat
guantes color de rosa	pink gloves
la vida color de rosa	life through rose-colored glasses
labios rosa	pink lips

violeta	**one form for both genders; sometimes used in the plural**
blusa violeta	violet blouse
ojos violeta	violet eyes
paredes violetas	violet walls
papel color violeta	violet paper
sábana de color violeta	violet sheet

púrpura	**one form**
mangas púrpura	purple sleeves
capa color púrpura	purple cape
collares de color púrpura	purple necklaces

malva	**one form**
abrigo malva	mauve coat
uñas malva	mauve nails

C. Colors ending in *e* follow specific rules:

beige*	**one form**
autos beige	beige cars
bolsas de color beige	beige bags
crema color beige	beige cream

café	**one form**
platos café	brown dishes
medias de color café	brown socks
zapatos color café	brown shoes

---

* A widely used French word. The *g* is pronounced like the *g* in *generous or large*.

NOTE:

In many countries *marrón* is used for *brown*.

celeste	**one form for both genders; used also in the plural form**
cintas celestes	light-blue ribbons
lápiz celeste	light-blue pencil
ojos de color celeste	light-blue eyes
bandera color celeste	light-blue flag
verde	**one form for both genders; used also in the plural form**
ojos verdes	green eyes
casa verde	green house
anteojos de color verde	green glasses
caja color verde	green box

D. Colors ending in *i* have forms which are affected by the stress of the word:

caqui* or *kaki	**one form (stress on penultimate syllable)**
uniformes caqui	khaki uniforms
gorra color caqui	khaki cap
camisa de color caqui	khaki shirt
carmesí	**two forms: one singular and one plural**
pañuelo carmesí	red handkerchief
labios carmesíes	red lips

NOTE:

The singular form is also sometimes used for the plural:

labios carmesí or *labios color carmesí*

E. Colors ending in a consonant vary only by number

Colors ending in a consonant have one form for both genders (*caja azul, auto azul*) and add *es* for the plural (*casas azules, autos azules*). The forms *color azul* and *de color azul* are also used.

azul	➤	*cajas azules*	blue boxes
cajas de color azul			
cajas color azul			

Other examples such as the following will also show the three possibilities:

gris   ➤   cabellos grises   gray hair
cabellos de color gris
cabellos color gris

marrón   ➤   pantalones marrones   brown pants
pantalones de color marrón
pantalones color marrón

Other Variations of Adjectives of Color

Sometimes certain words or expressions are used as modifiers. When colors are modified, they do not change for gender and number. A modified color may apply to singular or plural nouns.

A. Adjectives to specify intensity of color

Some of the adjectives that may be added to any color to specify its intensity are:

claro (light) ➤	ojos azul <u>claro</u>	light blue eyes
oscuro (dark) ➤	suéter verde <u>oscuro</u>	dark green sweater
pálido (pale) ➤	blusa rosa <u>pálido</u>	pale pink blouse
vivo (vivid) ➤	rosas rojo <u>vivo</u>	vivid red roses

The expressions *color (verde)* and *de color (verde)* may also be used when the color is modified, as follows:

(de) color verde claro
silla color verde claro   light green chair
sillas de color verde claro   light green chairs

(de) color marrón oscuro
zapatos color marrón oscuro   dark brown shoes
zapatos de color marrón oscuro   dark brown shoes

(de) color rojo vivo
cinta rojo vivo   vivid red ribbon
sombrero de color rojo vivo   vivid red hat

B. Nouns or adjectives to suggest a specific color shade

Nouns or adjectives may be added to suggest a specific color shade:

pared verde agua	light green wall
vestido azul cielo	sky-blue dress
suéter color cereza	cherry-colored sweater
blusa limón	light yellow blouse
verde militar	army green
azul marino	navy blue
azul eléctrico	electric blue
adorno color cobre	copper-colored ornament
rojo furioso (colloquial)	bright red
rosa viejo	dusty rose

> **NOTE:**
>
> Whenever a noun is used to describe a color, such as *cielo* (*sky*), *vino* (*wine*), *limón* (*lemon*), etc., the modifying noun is invariable:
>
> | | |
> |---|---|
> | *ojos cielo* | sky-colored eyes |
> | *una camisa vino* | a wine-colored shirt |
> | *pantalones limón* | lemon-colored pants |

C. Adjectives derived from colors

Adjectives derived from colors have four endings: *o, a, os, as.* Some examples are:

amarillo	➤	*amarillento (a ,os, as)*	yellowish
azul	➤	*azulado, azulino*	bluish
blanco	➤	*blancuzco, blanquecino*	whitish
gris	➤	*grisáceo*	grayish
lila	➤	*liláceo*	lilac-ish
púrpura	➤	*purpúreo, purpurino*	purplish
rojo	➤	*rojizo*	reddish
rosa	➤	*rosado, rosáceo*	pinkish
verde	➤	*verdoso*	greenish
violeta	➤	*violáceo*	violet-ish

THE BIG RED BOOK OF SPANISH GRAMMAR

D. Colors used with certain nouns

Some color words are used specifically with certain nouns:

cabello castaño (not *marrón*)	brown hair
ojos pardos (not *marrones*)	brown eyes
cabello canoso (also *gris*)	gray hair
cabello rubio	blonde hair
mujer pelirroja (not *pelo rojo*)	red-haired woman
mujer morena	dark-skinned woman
mujer negra	black woman
hombre blanco	Caucasian man

Agreement of Compound Adjectives

Compound adjectives formed by two words agree with the noun in gender and number. Notice that the first adjective appears in the masculine singular form:

los problemas socioeconómicos	socioeconomic problems
las obras grecolatinas	Greco-Latin works
la asociación hispanohablante	Hispanic-American association
los temas religiosoculturales	religious and cultural subjects
las obras teóricoprácticas	theoretical and practical works
los tratados francoespañoles	Franco-Spanish treaties

Agreement Between Adjectives and Collective Nouns

The adjective agrees with the preceding noun:

un grupo de hombres enfurecidos	a group of infuriated men
un grupo enfurecido de hombres	an infuriated group of men
una comunidad de familias religiosas	a community of religious families
una comunidad religiosa de familias	a religious community of families

Agreement of Adjectival Expressions That Are Preceded by *de*

When a noun is modified by another noun preceded by *de*, as in *lapicera de plástico* (pen made of plastic), and there is an adjective in the sentence, the adjective must agree with the noun it is modifying.

la lapicera de plástico rojo	the pen made of red plastic
la lapicera roja de plástico	the red pen made of plastic
una caja de plástico barato	a box made of cheap plastic
una caja barata de plástico	a cheap box made of plastic
una casa de ladrillos vieja y fea	an old, ugly brick house
una casa vieja de ladrillos	an old brick house
una casa de ladrillos viejos	a house made of old bricks

Position of Descriptive Adjectives

Descriptive adjectives are placed before or after the noun according to their specific role in the sentence. Check the section immediately preceding this one, Agreement Between Descriptive Adjectives and Nouns, for information on gender and number variations for single and multiple adjectives that follow or precede the noun or nouns.

Descriptive Adjectives Placed After the Noun

In general, descriptive adjectives that add more information about the noun, with the idea—intentional or not—of distinguishing the noun from others of its kind, are placed after the noun:

El pueblo está al final de un camino largo.	The town is at the end of a long road. (There are also short roads).
El sol se veía por debajo de las nubes bajas.	The sun could be seen below the low clouds. (There were also clouds at other altitudes).
Dos ratas enormes se escaparon al vernos.	Two huge rats ran away when they saw us. (There were also rats of other sizes.)

NOTE:

If more than one descriptive adjective is used, the speaker will give subjective priority to the adjectives based on their position:

El pueblo está al final de un camino largo y polvoriento.	(The length is more significant than the condition [*dusty*] of the road).
El sol se veía por debajo de las nubes finas y bajas.	(The thinness of the clouds is more significant than the position of the clouds in the sky).

Other Categories of Descriptive Adjectives Placed After the Noun

A. Colors placed after the noun

Apareció una sonrisa entre sus labios rojos.	A smile appeared upon her red lips.
But: *Sus rojos labios insinuaron una leve sonrisa.* (poetic)	Her red lips suggested a quick smile.

If other descriptive adjectives are added to the color to modify the noun, the adjective of color must be close to the noun.

1. One adjective + the color:

Se compró una cartera verde hermosa. (information)	
Se compró una hermosa cartera verde. (emphasis)	She bought a beautiful green bag.

2. Two or more adjectives + the color:

Tenía un pantalón negro, viejo y arrugado.	She had on a black, old, and wrinkled pair of pants.

Negro gives information about the color of the pants. The fact of being old is more important to the speaker than the condition of the pants. Changing the order of the adjectives to *arrugado y viejo* would emphasize the appearance as being more important in the mind of the speaker:

Tenía un pantalón negro, arrugado y viejo.

B. Nationalities placed after the noun

Adjectives of nationality represent essential information that is not subjective or emphatic and must be placed after the noun.

las costumbres españolas	Spanish customs
los barcos ingleses	English boats
la secretaria alemana	German secretary

> **NOTE:**
>
> Adjectives of nationality are not capitalized in Spanish.

If other descriptive adjectives are used to modify the noun, the adjective of nationality must be close to the noun. Notice that the adjective that is most closely associated with the noun is the first one in the series:

las costumbres españolas antiquísimas	ancient Spanish customs
los barcos ingleses usados y reparados	used and repaired English boats
la secretaria alemana joven, inteligente y simpática	nice, young, intelligent German secretary

Notice that the order of the adjectives in English does not correspond to the order of the adjectives in Spanish.

> **NOTE:**
>
> In the previous example, *secretaria alemana* forms a single unit of thought; therefore, there is no comma placed after *alemana*. The adjectives *joven, inteligente,* and *simpática* qualify the unit of thought. If, instead, *alemana* were considered by the speaker as just another characteristic or qualification of the secretary, a comma should be placed:
>
> | | |
> |---|---|
> | *secretaria alemana, joven, inteligente y simpática* | a secretary who is German, young, intelligent, and nice |

C. Conditions placed after the noun

Most adjectives and other adjectival expressions that indicate a condition resulting from an action follow the noun:

las manos sucias	dirty hands
las latas recicladas	recycled cans
el sombrero mojado	wet hat
huevos revueltos	scrambled eggs

D. Scientific or technical adjectives placed after the noun

Adjectives that supply essential information of a scientific or technical nature are placed after the noun:

el ejercicio gramatical	grammatical exercise
el misterio arqueológico	archeological mystery
la agencia meteorológica	meteorological agency
la presión sanguínea	blood pressure
la zona geográfica	geographical zone

E. Forms or shapes placed after the noun

Adjectives that give information as to the form or shape of a noun are placed after the noun:

la figura octogonal	octogonal figure
el organismo unicelular	unicellular organism
la caja cuadrada	square box
la oficina oval	oval office
los caballeros de la mesa redonda	knights of the round table

F. Adjectives formed by *de* + noun

Modifiers can be created by adding the preposition *de* before a noun.

1. *de* + noun to indicate the materials nouns are made of:

la reja de hierro	iron grill
el piso de baldosas	tile floor
la silla de madera	wooden chair
las medias de seda	silk stockings
la pulsera de oro	gold bracelet

2. *de* + noun to indicate a specific category of the noun:

el reloj de arena	hourglass
la lluvia de verano	summer rain
la lata de sardinas	sardine can
la tarjeta de cumpleaños	birthday card
la ensalada de camarones	shrimp salad

Adjectives Placed Before the Noun

Descriptive adjectives are normally placed before the noun in the following cases:

A. Adjective before noun to enhance a specific quality of the noun

Descriptive adjectives are placed before the noun to enhance a specific quality of the noun without comparing it to others of its kind:

El _generoso profesor_ le dio el dinero para el libro.	The generous professor gave him the money for the book.
But: El _profesor generoso_ fue el único que lo ayudó.	The generous professor was the only one who helped him. (a distinction is implied: no other professors helped him)

Sus ojos estaban fijos en las _tranquilas aguas_ del lago.	His eyes were fixed on the quiet waters of the lake.
But: Después de la tormenta, el bote se movía suavemente en las _aguas tranquilas_.	After the storm, the boat moved smoothly on the quiet waters. (a distinction between stormy and smooth waters is implied)

B. Adjective before noun to produce a poetic effect

Descriptive adjectives are placed before the noun to produce a poetic effect, mainly in literary pieces:

El pueblo está al final de un _largo camino_.	The town is at the end of a long road.
El sol sonreía por debajo de las _grises nubes_.	The sun smiled under the gray clouds.
Los _hambrientos ratones_ se convirtieron en _elegantes caballos_ antes de la medianoche.	The hungry mice became elegant horses before midnight.

C. Adjective before noun to emphasize a subjective appraisal

Descriptive adjectives are placed before the noun to emphasize a quality or characteristic of the noun as an indication of a subjective appraisal done by the speaker, not necessarily meaning an intrinsic quality of the noun:

Ayer la visité en su _hermosa casa de campo_.	I visited her yesterday in her beautiful country house.
Su esposo le regaló una _elegante cartera_ negra de cuero.	Her husband gave her an elegant black leather bag.

However, note the following examples where the adjectives represent widely known facts, not only the opinion of the speaker:

Cervantes es un renombrado escritor español.	Cervantes is a renowned Spanish writer.
No pudieron soportar las heladas noches del polo.	They could not bear the frozen nights at the Pole.

D. Adjective before noun to express an inherent characteristic of the noun

Descriptive adjectives that express an inherent characteristic of the noun are called *epítetos* (*epithets*) and can be removed without altering the meaning of the sentence:

El furioso tornado aplastó las casas.	The furious tornado flattened the houses.
Su cabeza golpeó contra la dura roca.	His head hit against the hard rock.
Escondió la carta bajo el suave terciopelo del vestido.	She hid the letter under the soft velvet of her dress.

Adjectives Placed Before and After the Noun

A. Position of adjectives when a noun is modified by more than one descriptive adjective

When a noun is modified by more than one descriptive adjective, the position of the adjectives before and after the noun must follow the specific rules outlined previously for each category:

extraordinarios hechos históricos (emphasis; essential)	extraordinary historical facts
conocido poeta cubano (inherent; nationality)	well-known Cuban poet
preciosos zapatos rojos (subjective; color)	beautiful red shoes

B. Position of adjectives to indicate relative priority

The position of descriptive adjectives before or after the noun may also indicate the priority of the adjectives in the mind of the speaker. This modality also renders the language more poetic. Notice the following sentence, where the length of the road is more important to the speaker than its condition:

El pueblo está al final de un largo camino polvoriento.	The town is at the end of a long, dusty road.

In the following sentence, both the length and the condition are important:

El pueblo está al final de un <u>largo</u> y <u>polvoriento</u> camino.

However, notice the next two sentences as well. In the first one, the condition is emphasized; in the second one, both the condition and the length are important to the speaker:

El pueblo está al final de un <u>polvoriento</u> camino <u>largo</u>.   The town is at the end of a long, dusty road.

El pueblo está al final de un <u>polvoriento</u> y <u>largo</u> camino.

Notice that the order of the adjectives in English does not correspond to the order of the adjectives in Spanish.

Shortened Forms

Some adjectives adopt a shortened form when they are placed before masculine singular nouns. This form is called *apócope* in Spanish (English *apocope*).

malo	➤	*un <u>mal</u> momento*	a bad moment
bueno	➤	*un <u>buen</u> rato*	a good time
alguno	➤	*<u>algún</u> chico*	a child
ninguno	➤	*<u>ningún</u> libro*	no book
primero	➤	*<u>primer</u> amor*	first love
tercero	➤	*<u>tercer</u> examen*	third exam
postrero	➤	*<u>postrer</u> pedido*	last request
uno	➤	*<u>un</u> maletín*	one briefcase
cualquiera	➤	*<u>cualquier</u> partido*	any game

NOTES:

(1) The short forms *algún* and *ningún* carry a written accent.

(2) The adjective *santo,* capitalized, takes the short form *San* before saints' names: *San Antonio, San Juan, San Carlos,* etc., with exceptions such as *Santo Tomás* and *Santo Domingo.* In other cases, the whole word *santo* is used before and after the noun:

un santo hombre or *un hombre santo*   a holy man

el santo rosario   the holy rosary

el Santo Padre   the Holy Father / the Pope

(3) *grande* takes the shortened form *gran* in front of a masculine or feminine singular noun. However, there is a change in meaning from *large* to *grand* or *great* if used in this position:

La boda tuvo lugar en un <u>gran</u> patio cubierto.	The wedding took place in a grand, covered patio.
La boda tuvo lugar en una <u>gran</u> mansión.	The wedding took place in a grand mansion.

(4) When another adjective follows the apocope, the short form is usually maintained:

Fue el <u>primer</u> <u>increíble</u> relato que le escuché contar.	It was the first incredible story that I heard him tell.

However, when the adjectives are linked by the conjunction *y* or *e*—both meaning *and*—the long form is used:

Fue el <u>primero</u> y <u>último</u> relato que le escuché contar.	It was the first and last story that I heard him tell.

Other examples:

Es el <u>tercer</u> <u>excelente</u> concierto que presentaron.	It is the third excellent concert they have presented.
Es el <u>tercero</u> y <u>último</u> concierto al que pienso asistir.	It is the third and last concert I plan to attend.

(5) The short form *cien* is used before plural nouns, and also before *mil* (*one thousand*) and *millones* (*millions*). *Ciento* is used to count from *ciento uno* (101) to *ciento noventa y nueve* (199).

cien libros	one hundred books
cien mil pesos	one hundred thousand pesos
cien millones de habitantes	one hundred million inhabitants

Please note that 100% is widely read *cien por ciento* instead of *ciento por ciento*.

(6) The masculine plural form stays the same in most cases:

malo	➤	malos momentos	bad moments
bueno	➤	buenos ratos	good times
alguno	➤	algunos chicos	some children
primero	➤	primeros calores	first hot days

Please note that:

- *Ninguno* is not used in the plural form:

No hay **ningún** libro.   There are no books.

- *Tercero* is used in the plural form as a noun. The noun can be left out:

Los primeros exámenes del semestre fueron   The first exams of the semester were good;
  buenos, los segundos, mejores, y los   the second ones were better; and the
  terceros, excelentes.   third ones were excellent.

(7) The feminine singular form does not change in front of a noun:

mala	➤	una mala acción	a bad deed
buena	➤	una buena cosa	a good thing
alguna	➤	alguna mujer	a woman
ninguna	➤	ninguna casa	no house
primera	➤	primera carta	first letter
tercera	➤	tercera apuesta	third bet

(8) The feminine plural form stays the same in most cases when placed in front of a noun:

malas acciones	bad deeds
buenas cosas	good things
algunas mujeres	some women
primeras cartas	first letters

Please note that *ninguna* is not used in the plural form:

No hay **ninguna** mujer.   There are no women.

Adjectives That Change Meaning Depending on Placement

Some adjectives change their meaning depending on whether they are placed before or after the noun. Notice that some adjectives are invariable and are used with masculine or feminine nouns:

algún(o, a)

¿Tienes algún libro?	Do you have any books?
No tengo libro alguno.	I don't have any.
¿Quieres alguna galleta	Do you want any cookies?
No, no quiero galleta alguna.	No, I don't want any.

alto(a)

Es un alto ejecutivo.	He is a top official.
Ella es una alta dama.	She is a high-class lady.
Es un hombre alto.	He is a tall man.
Ella es una mujer alta.	She is a tall woman.

antiguo(a)

Fue la antigua capital.	It was the former capital.
Es su antiguo jefe.	He is her former boss.
Es una capital antigua.	It's an ancient capital.
Es un documento antiguo.	It is an ancient document.

bueno(a)

Es un buen hombre.	He is a simple man.
Es un hombre bueno.	He is a good man.
Es una buena maestra.	She is a good teacher.
Es una maestra buena.	She is a gentle/generous teacher.
Tuvo una buena sorpresa.	He had a big surprise.
Fue una sorpresa buena.	It was a good surprise.
Recibió una buena cantidad.	He received a large amount.
Es una cantidad buena.	It is a sufficient amount.

cierto(a)

Oyó ciertas historias.	She heard certain stories.
Son historias ciertas.	They are true stories.
Vino un cierto día.	He came on a certain day.
Vino el día cierto.	He came on the right day.

cualquier(a)

Quiero cualquier perro.	I want any dog (of the ones you have).
Quiero un perro cualquiera.	I want just any dog (the breed is not important).
Me gustaría cualquier marca.	I would like any brand (of the ones you have).
Me gustaría una marca cualquiera.	I would like just any brand.

dulce

¡Dulces sueños!	Sweet dreams!
galletas dulces	sweet cookies

grande

Es un gran coche.	It's a great car.
Es un coche grande.	It's a large car.

mismo(a)

Vi al mismo chico.	I saw the same child.
Vi al chico mismo.	I saw the child himself.
Saludé a la misma chica.	I greeted the same girl.
Saludé a la chica misma.	I greeted the girl herself.

nuevo(a)

Recibió un nuevo libro.	She received another book.
Recibió un libro nuevo.	She received a new book.
Me dio una nueva receta.	She gave me another recipe.
Me dio una receta nueva.	She gave me a new recipe.

pobre

La pobre señora se murió.	The unfortunate lady died.
La señora pobre se murió.	The poor (not rich) lady died.

propio(a)

Vino con su propio auto.	He came with his own car.
Es un regalo propio para él.	It's a gift especially for him.
Hizo su propia casa.	He built his own house.
Hizo una casa propia para él.	He built a house according to his taste.
Italia es un nombre propio.	Italy is a proper name.

puro(a)

Eran puros cuentos.	They were sheer stories.
Eran cuentos puros.	They were pure (decent) stories.
Son puras historias.	They are sheer stories.
Son historias puras.	They are pure (decent) stories.

raro(a)

Es un raro evento.	It is a rare event.
Tienen costumbres raras.	They have strange customs.
Es una rara ocasión.	It is a rare occasion.
Es una ocasión rara.	It is a strange occasion.

NOTE:

In the expression *raras veces* (*seldom*), the adjective is always placed before the noun:

Raras veces asistía a los conciertos.	She very seldom attended the concerts.

simple

Fue un simple pedido.	It was a mere request.
Fue un pedido simple.	It was a simple request.

triste

Me dio una triste tarjeta.	She only gave me a card.
Me dio una tarjeta triste.	She gave me a sad card.

único(a)

Es la única caja.	It's the only box.
Es una caja única.	It's a unique box.
Él es el único hijo que tienen.	He is the only son they have.
Él es un hijo único.	He is a unique son.

varios(as)

Usó varios colores.	He used several colors.
Usó colores varios.	He used different colors.
Había varias tortas.	There were several cakes.
Había tortas varias.	There were different cakes (types).

viejo(a)

Esa es su vieja casa.	That's his former house.
Esa es su casa vieja.	That is his old house.
Él es un viejo amigo.	He is an old friend (of long standing).
Él es un amigo viejo.	He is an aged friend.

Comparative and Superlative Forms

Any adjective is in a comparative degree when it possesses its inherent quality to a degree that is higher than, lower than, or equal to that of the adjectives to which it is compared. In English, the ending -er is usually added in the comparative form to adjectives that have one or two syllables. With adjectives that have more than two syllables, the word *more* or the formula *more + adjective + than* is generally used. A lower degree, however, is indicated by the word *less* or a combination of *less + adjective + than*. To compare adjectives that possess the same degree of a specific quality, the word *as* is placed before and after the adjective.

> My room is large. Your room is larger.
> This report is explicit. The other report is more explicit.
> That report is more explicit than Bill's.
> This lesson is less difficult.
> This movie is less interesting than the previous one.
> His explanation is as clear as hers.

When an adjective has the highest degree of a particular characteristic, the ending -est is added to the adjective. Notice also the addition of the article *the* before the superlative adjective.

> My room is large, your room is larger, but Mary's is the largest.
> Mary's room is the largest of all.

If the adjective represents the lowest degree of a specific quality, the word *least* is used in English. The article is also added before the adjective.

> *My car is expensive, your car is less expensive, and Peter's is the least expensive.*
> *Peter's car is the least expensive of the three.*

There are a few adjectives in English that have irregular forms when used to make comparisons. Some of those are:

Adjective	Comparative Form	Superlative Form
good	better	the best
bad	worse	the worst
little	less	the least
far	farther/further	the farthest/furthest

In Spanish, as in English, there are also three levels of comparison: comparison of inequality (*more/less than*), comparison of equality (*as . . . as*), and the superlative degree (*the most/least*).

Comparison of Inequality—Adjectives

To compare two nouns, singular or plural, the expressions *más ... que* (*more . . . than*) and *menos ... que* (*less . . . than*) are used around the adjective. The comparatives involved in these sentences are called in Spanish *comparativos de superioridad* and *comparativos de inferioridad*, respectively:

El clavel es **más** perfumado **que** la rosa.	The carnation is more scented than the rose.
Tus libros son **más** caros **que** mi diccionario.	Your books are more expensive than my dictionary.
Mi auto gris es **menos** rápido **que** tu auto nuevo.	My gray car is less fast than your new car.
Noviembre y diciembre son **menos** calurosos **que** enero y febrero en el Cono Sur.	November and December are less hot than January and February in the Southern Cone.

When the second element of a comparison is a pronoun, the same expressions are used:

Mi clavel es **más** perfumado **que** el tuyo.	My carnation is more scented than yours.
Soy **menos** inteligente **que** tú.	I am less intelligent than you.
Estos relojes son **más** baratos **que** aquellos.	These watches are cheaper than those.

NOTE:

The meanings of the preceding sentences can be maintained with other formulations as well.

(1) By inverting the word order and changing the comparative expression:

Tu clavel es **menos** perfumado **que** el mío.	Your carnation is less scented than mine.
Tú eres **más** inteligente **que** yo.	You are more intelligent than I.
Aquellos relojes son **menos** baratos **que** éstos.	Those watches are less cheap than these.

(2) By changing the sentences to the negative, using the formula *no* + verb + *tan* + adjective + *como:*

Tu clavel **no** es **tan** perfumado **como** el mío.	Your carnation is not as scented as mine.
Yo **no** soy **tan** inteligente **como** tú.	I am not as intelligent as you.
Aquellos relojes **no** son **tan** baratos **como** éstos.	Those watches are not as cheap as these.

Adjectives with Irregular Forms

Just as in English, there are a few adjectives in Spanish that have irregular forms when used in a comparative degree:

bueno (good)	*mejor* (better)	*el mejor* (the best)
malo (bad)	*peor* (worse)	*el peor* (the worst)
grande (large)	*mayor* (larger)	*el mayor* (the largest)
pequeño (small)	*menor* (smaller)	*el menor* (the smallest)

*Esta lapicera roja es **mejor que** la azul.*	This red pen is better than the blue one.
*Esa solución es **peor que** la que sugieres.*	That solution is worse than the one you suggest.
*Esta caja es **mayor que** aquéllas.*	This box is larger than those.
*Estos guantes son **menores que** los de cuero.*	These gloves are smaller than the leather ones.

NOTES:

(1) The adjectives *bueno*, *malo*, and *pequeño* agree with the noun in gender and number.

(2) The adjective *grande* agrees with the noun only in number.

(3) The comparatives *mayor* and *menor* agree with the noun in number and are also used in the following situations:

■ With reference to age, as in:

*Mi hermano es **mayor que** yo.*	My brother is older than I.
*Miguel es mi hermano **mayor**.*	Miguel is my older brother.
*Mi hermana es **menor que** yo.*	My sister is younger than I.
*Maggie es mi hermana **menor**.*	Maggie is my younger sister.
*Greta es una persona **mayor**.*	Greta is almost a senior citizen.
*Respetan a los **mayores**.*	They respect their elders.
*No apta para **menores**.*	Not suitable for underage persons.
*Hay que ser **mayor** de edad.*	You must be of age.
*Vengan con un **mayor**.*	Come with an adult.

■ *Mayor* and *menor* are usually replaced by *más grande* and *más chico(a)* when referring to things, both in their singular and plural forms:

*Nuestra casa es **más grande que** la casa del vecino.*	Our house is larger than the neighbor's house.
*Estos vasos son **más chicos que** los otros.*	These glasses are smaller than the others.

With reference to people, the expressions *más grande* and *más chico(a)* are used to indicate the size of the person:

*Julio es **más grande que** tú.*   Julio is bigger than you.

*Carlitos es **más chico que** su hermano.*   Carlitos is smaller than his brother.

■ *Mayor* is the equivalent of *greatest* in:

*El premio que recibió fue el **mayor** homenaje a su patriotismo.*   The award he received was the greatest homage paid to his patriotism.

■ *Menor* is the equivalent of *least* in:

*Quiero que lo haga con el **menor** esfuerzo posible.*   I want you to do it with the least effort possible.

Comparison of Inequality—Nouns

To make a comparison of inequality involving nouns, the formula *más* or *menos* + noun + *que* is used.

*Roy recibió **más** regalos **que** su hermano.*   Roy received more gifts than his brother.

*Hoy tengo **menos** trabajo **que** Lola.*   Today I have less work than Lola.

NOTE:

The meanings of the preceding sentences can also be preserved with other formulations:

(1) By inverting the order of each sentence and changing the comparative expression:

*Su hermano recibió **menos** regalos **que** Roy.*   His brother received fewer gifts than Roy.

*Hoy Lola tiene **más** trabajo **que** yo.*   Today Lola has more work than I.

(2) By changing the sentences to the negative using this formula: *no* + verb + *tanto/a/os/as* + noun + *como:*

*Su hermano **no** recibió **tantos** regalos **como** Roy.*   His brother didn't receive as many gifts as Roy.

*Hoy **no** tengo **tanto** trabajo **como** Lola.*   Today I don't have as much work as Lola.

For comparisons of inequality using verbs and other adverbs, see Chapter 18, Adverbs.

Comparison of Equality—Adjectives

To compare two adjectives, singular or plural, which share equally a specific characteristic, the expression *tan* + adjective + *como* is used. In Spanish these forms are called *comparativos de igualdad*.

Tu camisa es **tan** *elegante* **como** *la de Martín.*	Your shirt is as elegant as Martín's.
Molly es **tan** *aplicada* **como** *su hermano Johnny.*	Molly is as diligent as her brother Johnny.
Los leones son **tan** *salvajes* **como** *los tigres.*	Lions are as wild as tigers.

NOTES:

(1) The meaning of the preceding sentences can be preserved while inverting the word order:

La camisa de Martín es **tan** *elegante* **como** *la tuya.*	Martín's shirt is as elegant as yours.
Su hermano Johnny es **tan** *aplicado* **como** *Molly.*	Her brother Johnny is as diligent as Molly.

(2) To negate these sentences, the word *no* is placed in front of the verb, in which case the sentence becomes a comparison of inequality:

Tu camisa **no** es **tan** *elegante* **como** *la de Martín.*	Your shirt is not as elegant as Martín's.

Comparison of Equality—Nouns

Comparisons of equality using nouns are made with the following formula: *tanto/a/os/as* + noun + *como*. Notice that *tanto* agrees in gender and number with the noun:

Tiene **tanto** *miedo* **como** *yo.*	He is as afraid as I am.
Demuestra **tanta** *paciencia* **como** *su padre.*	She shows as much patience as her father.
Recibió **tantas** *felicitaciones* **como** *se merecía.*	He received as many congratulations as he deserved.
La compañía tiene **tantos** *problemas* **como** *su competidora.*	The company has as many problems as its competitor.

NOTES:

(1) The meaning of these sentences can be preserved while inverting the word order:

*Tengo **tanto** miedo **como** él.*	I am as afraid as he is.
*Su padre demuestra **tanta** paciencia*	Her father shows as much patience as she
*****como** ella.*	does.

(2) To negate these sentences, the word *no* is placed in front of the verb, in which case the sentence becomes a comparison of inequality:

*No tengo **tanto** miedo **como** él.*	I am not as afraid as he is.
*Su padre **no** demuestra **tanta** paciencia*	Her father doesn't show as much patience as
*****como** ella.*	she does.

For comparisons of equality using verbs and other adverbs, see Chapter 18, Adverbs.

Superlatives

An adjective is classified as superlative when it shows the highest or lowest degree of its inherent characteristic.

There are several ways of forming the superlative in Spanish:

A. Using the expression *el/la/los/las más* or *menos* + adjective + *de* or *entre* to form the superlative:

*El Parque Central es **el más** <u>extenso</u> **de** la ciudad de Nueva York.*	Central Park is the largest in New York City.
*****Entre** todas las empleadas, Estela es **la** persona **más** <u>responsable</u>.*	Among all the employees, Estela is the most responsible person.
*Esos cuadros son **los menos** <u>coloridos</u> **de** la exposición.*	Those paintings are the least colorful in the art show.

B. Adding the ending *-ísimo* or *-ísima*, or their plural forms, to the adjective to form the superlative:

*Este libro es buen**ísimo**.*	This book is very, very good.
*Estaba encantad**ísima**.*	She was extremely delighted.

NOTES:

(1) The difference between A. and B. is that the sentences in A. identify the subjects within a specific group: the city of New York, an undefined office, and a particular art show. Outside of these limits, there might be other parks, employees, or paintings that enjoy a higher (or lower) degree of the characteristics addressed here.

In the sentences in B., there is no comparison with other subjects. The qualities mentioned (goodness and extreme happiness) are absolute, not being compared with the same type of qualities that might be possessed by other subjects.

(2) In order to add *-ísimo* or *-ísima* to an adjective, some basic spelling changes occur, although there are exceptions.

■ The last vowel is dropped before adding *-ísimo* or *-ísima*:

chico cansad**o**	➤	cansad*ísimo*	very tired
vajilla rot**a**	➤	rot*ísima*	badly broken
bandera verd**e**	➤	verd*ísima*	deep green

■ The ending *-c* plus a vowel changes to *-qu* to preserve pronunciation:

pato blan**co**	➤	blanqu*ísimo*	very white
mañana fres**ca**	➤	fresqu*ísima*	very cool

■ The ending *-g* plus a vowel changes to *-gu* to preserve pronunciation:

avenida lar**ga**	➤	largu*ísima*	very long
trago amar**go**	➤	amargu*ísimo*	very bitter

■ The ending *-gu* plus a vowel changes to *-qu:*

documento anti**guo**	➤	antiqu*ísimo*	very old

■ The ending *-ble* changes to *-bil*:

momento agrada**ble**	➤	agrada*bil*ísimo	extremely nice
persona afa**ble**	➤	afa*bil*ísima	very nice

■ The ending -z changes to *-c:*

hombre andalu**z**	➤	andalu*c*ísimo	very Andalusian
matrimonio feli**z**	➤	feli*c*ísimo	very happy

■ An existing accent is dropped:

| campo *fértil* | ➤ | fertil*ísimo* | very fertile |
| caja *útil* | ➤ | util*ísima* | very useful |

■ The ending *-iente* changes to *-ente:*

| café cal*iente* | ➤ | cal*entísimo* | very hot |
| soldado val*iente* | ➤ | val*entísimo* | very valiant |

(3) Not all adjectives can take the superlative *-ísimo*, *-ísima*, or their plural forms. Examples of some of the categories are given here:

■ Augmentatives (*casona*), diminutives (*mujercita*), adjectives with many syllables (*incomprensible*), adjectives that do not accept degrees because of their intrinsic qualities (*eterno*), and numerals (*octavo*), among others, do not take the superlative form *-ísimo*. Comparatives are another category of adjectives that do not take the *-ísimo* form or its variations since they have their own specific superlative structures, as shown here:

bueno	➤	mejor	➤	óptimo
malo	➤	peor	➤	pésimo
pequeño	➤	menor	➤	mínimo
grande	➤	mayor	➤	máximo
alto	➤	superior	➤	supremo
bajo	➤	inferior	➤	ínfimo

■ Adjectives that end in *-í* (*carmesí*) do not take the superlative form *-ísimo* or its variations.

■ Adjectives that carry a written accent in the antepenultimate syllable and end in *-eo* (*momentáneo*); *-imo* (*legítimo*); *-ico* (*estático*); or *-fero* (*mortífero*), do not take the superlative form *-ísimo* or its variations.

■ A few adjectives take the ending *-érrimo* instead of *ísimo*, including:

pobre ➤ paup*érrimo*   célebre ➤ celeb*érrimo*   mísero ➤ mis*érrimo*   salubre ➤ salub*érrimo*

C. Adding words or expressions such as:

Muy (*very*), **sumamente** (*exceedingly*), **extremadamente** (*extremely*), **inmensamente** (*immensely*), **bien** (with the meaning of *very, very*), and others. All of these forms are invariable.

sumamente triste	very, very sad
muy fatigadas	very tired
extremadamente pálido	extremely pale
inmensamente feliz	very, very happy
bien alegre	very, very happy, content

D. Plurals of superlative adjectives

The plurals of superlative adjectives that end in *-ísimo* and *-ísima* are formed according to the rules used for basic adjectives:

Los novios estaban felicísimos.	The bride and the groom were very, very happy.
Las madres estaban ocupadísimas.	The mothers were extremely busy.

Other forms, such as those mentioned previously, are invariable.

For the use of superlatives with verbs and other adverbs, see Chapter 18, Adverbs.

Demonstrative Adjectives

Demonstrative adjectives (*adjetivos demostrativos*) refer to the noun and give an idea of its distance from the speaker, either in space or in time. There are three categories of demonstrative adjectives in Spanish, which correspond to the English forms *this, these, that*, and *those*. As with other adjectives, demonstrative adjectives agree in gender and number with the noun they modify.

Categories of Demonstrative Adjectives

A. Near the speaker (*this, these*):

este *pueblo*	(this town)	**estos** *libros*	(these books)
esta *señora*	(this lady)	**estas** *flores*	(these flowers)

B. Near the person spoken to or both the speaker and the listener (*that, those*):

ese *pueblo*	(that town)	**esos** *libros*	(those books)
esa *señora*	(that lady)	**esas** *flores*	(those flowers)

C. Far from both speaker and listener (*that, those over there*):

aquel pueblo	(that town over there)
aquella señora	(that lady in the corner)
aquellos libros	(those books in the basement)
aquellas flores	(those flowers in the back yard)

NOTES:

(1) The preceding forms become pronouns when they are used without a noun. As pronouns, they may or may not carry a written accent since this practice is now optional. In some cases the written accent helps to clarify the situation:

Estas flores son lindas.	These flowers are pretty.
Éstas son lindas.	These ones are pretty.
Estas flores son rojas y ésas amarillas.	These flowers are red and those are yellow.

(2) The forms *esto, eso*, and *aquello* are pronouns and never carry a written accent. They do not have feminine or plural forms, and are used to refer to non-specific things or ideas:

Eso es muy serio.	That (situation) is very serious.
No me gustó aquello.	I didn't like that.

(3) The pronouns *estotro (este otro)* and *esotro (ese otro)* and their feminine and plural forms are no longer used. They appear in older manuscripts and literary works, such as *La Celestina* and *Don Quijote de la Mancha*.

Position of Demonstrative Adjectives

Demonstrative adjectives are usually placed before the noun:

Estos libros son buenos.	These books are good.

Sometimes they are placed after the noun, mainly to express contempt or to refer to a noun previously mentioned:

No me gustan los libros estos.	I don't like these books.
Es muy chica la casa esa.	That house is very small.

Uses of Demonstrative Adjectives

A. If more than one noun is modified by demonstrative adjectives, the adjectives must be repeated:

Esta cartera y estos guantes son importados.   This bag and these gloves are imported.

Esta blusa y esta falda me gustan.   I like this blouse and this skirt.

B. When the nouns represent the same person or object, however, only one demonstrative is used:

Esa buena madre y enfermera pasó la noche cuidándolo.   That good mother and nurse spent all night taking care of him.

Ese local y biblioteca está muy bien diseñado.   That site and library is very well designed.

C. When a demonstrative adjective precedes the noun, no article is used before that noun:

Ese hombre salió rápido.   That man left quickly.

(<u>Not</u>: *Ese el hombre salió rápido.*)

D. When a demonstrative adjective follows the noun, the article must be used:

Salió rápido el hombre ese.   That man left quickly.

E. Demonstratives used to cover a pause

In spoken Spanish, and sometimes even in informal writing, the demonstratives *este* and *esto* can be used to express hesitation in the sentence:

Me lo dio... este... pero no dijo nada.   She gave it to me . . . **uh** . . . but didn't say anything.

Bueno... esto... dije que no quiero que vengas.   Well . . . **uh** . . . I said I don't want you to come.

F. *Tal* and *tales* to replace *ese* and *aquel*

The words *tal* and *tales* sometimes replace *ese* and *aquel,* their plural forms *esos* and *aquellos,* and the feminine forms *esa(s)* and *aquella(s)*:

¡No me gustó tal (esa) sorpresa!   I didn't like a surprise like that.

Tales (Esos) problemas eran cosa de todos los días.   Problems like those were an everyday thing.

G. *Ese* and *aquel* to indicate past time

Ese and *aquel* and their feminine and plural forms are used to indicate a period of time in the past. *Aquel* gives the idea of further back in time, or of something that no longer exists:

En **ese** tiempo vivíamos en Quilmes.	At that time we lived in Quilmes.
En **esa** época todo estaba bien.	At that time, everything was fine.
Aquellas veces yo me quedaba en su casa.	I would stay at her house back then.
Vivían en **aquella** casa que estaba en la esquina.	They lived in that house that used to be on the corner.
En **aquellos** años yo era muy chica.	In those years, I was very small.

H. Forms of *aquel* in idiomatic expressions

Aquel, or one of its variations, is used exclusively in some idiomatic expressions:

¡Qué bailes **aquellos**! Ya no existen fiestas así.	What dances those were! There are no parties like those any more.
¡Qué muchacho **aquel**! Nunca llegaba a tiempo.	What a guy he was! He never arrived on time.

Possessive Adjectives

Possessive adjectives (*adjetivos posesivos*) indicate which person is the possessor of the item expressed by the noun. In <u>My chair is brown</u>, it is obvious that the chair belongs to me. These adjectives are usually placed before the noun in Spanish, although they may be placed after the noun for emphasis, in which case they have a different form.

Prenominal Position (Before the Noun) of Possessive Adjectives

A. Singular possessor

	Single Item		Plural Items	
my	*mi* jardín	garden	*mis* jardines	gardens
	mi lapicera	pen	*mis* lapiceras	pens
your (informal)	*tu* gato	cat	*tus* gatos	cats
	tu casa	house	*tus* casas	houses
his, her,	*su* pie	foot	*sus* pies	feet
its, your (formal)	*su* cama	bed	*sus* camas	beds

B. Plural possessor

	Single Item		**Plural Items**	
our	**nuestro** perro	dog	**nuestros** perros	dogs
	nuestra casa	house	**nuestras** casas	houses
your (informal, Spain)	**vuestro** coche	car	**vuestros** coches	cars
	vuestra loma	hill	**vuestras** lomas	hills
your (formal)	**su** maleta	suitcase	**sus** maletas	suitcases
	su papel	paper	**sus** papeles	papers
their	**su** regalo	gift	**sus** regalos	gifts
	su tía	aunt	**sus** tías	aunts
	su gato	cat	**sus** gatos	cats
	su cama	bed	**sus** camas	beds

NOTES:

(1) *Nuestro/a/os/as* (*our*) and *vuestro/a/os/as* (*your*, plural) agree with the noun in gender and number; all other forms agree only in number (*mi/mis, tu/tus, su/sus*).

(2) *Vuestro* and its variations are used in Spain. Latin American speakers use *su* and *sus* in prenominal position (before the noun). Notice the following two versions of a question to a couple about their car:

¿**Vuestro** coche es nuevo?	Is your car new?
¿**Su** coche es rojo?	Is your car red?

(3) The article *(el, la, los, las)* is omitted before the noun when the possessive adjective is in prenominal position (before the noun):

Tu resumen es bueno.	Your summary is good.
(Not: *Tu* **el** *resumen es bueno.*)	
Llegaron nuestros amigos.	Our friends arrived.
(Not: *Llegaron nuestros* **los** *amigos.*)	

Postnominal Position (After the Noun) of Possessive Adjectives

A. Singular possessor

	Single Item		**Plural Items**	
my	*jardín mío*	garden	*jardines míos*	gardens
	gorra mía	cap	*gorras mías*	caps

your (informal)	gato tuyo	cat	gatos tuyos	cats
	casa tuya	house	casas tuyas	houses
his, her, its,				
your (formal)	cama suya	bed	camas suyas	beds
	pie suyo	foot	pies suyos	feet

B. Plural possessor

	Single Item		Plural Items	
our	perro nuestro	dog	perros nuestros	dogs
	casa nuestra	house	casas nuestras	houses
your (informal, Spain)	coche vuestro	car	coches vuestros	cars
	loma vuestra	hill	lomas vuestras	hills
your (formal)	regalo suyo	gift	regalos suyos	gifts
	lámpara suya	lamp	lámparas suyas	lamps
their	gato suyo	cat	gatos suyos	cats
	cama suya	bed	camas suyas	beds

NOTES:

(1) All postnominal possessives (i.e., those positioned after the noun) agree with the noun in gender and number.

(2) *Vuestro* and its variations (*vuestra/os/as*) are used in Spain. Latin American speakers use *suyo/a/os/as*:

*¿Este es el libro **vuestro**?*	Is this your book?
*¿El auto **suyo** es nuevo?*	Is your car new?

The form *de ustedes* is also widely used in Latin America:

*¿Los autos **de ustedes** son importados?*	Are your cars imported?

(3) The article must precede the noun when the possessive adjective comes after the noun:

<u>El</u> resumen tuyo es bueno.	Your summary is good.
Llegaron <u>los</u> amigos nuestros.	Our friends arrived.
Traigan <u>los</u> discos de ustedes.	Bring your CDs.

Uses of Possessive Adjectives

A. Possessive adjectives used with more than one noun

When the nouns are considered independently, a possessive adjective is used with every noun:

Su abrigo y su bastón estaban en la sala.　　　His coat and his cane were in the living room.

However, only one adjective may be used in the following cases.

1. When the nouns are considered together as a whole concept:

Nuestra paz y prosperidad dependen del pueblo.　　　Our peace and prosperity depend on our people.

2. When the nouns refer to the same person or object:

Ella es mi hermana y confidente.　　　She is my sister and confidante.

B. Possessive adjectives used (or not) with parts of the body

Possessives are not used with parts of the body unless the sentence is ambiguous:

*Puse **los** pies en agua tibia.*　　　I put my feet in warm water.
(Not: *Puse mis pies en agua tibia.*)
*Tiene **los** pies cansados.*　　　Her feet are tired.
(Not: *Tiene sus pies cansados.*)

> **NOTES:**
>
> (1) If the body part is the subject of the verb, the possessive is used instead of the article to avoid ambiguity:
>
> ***Sus** dientes eran blancos.*　　　Her teeth were white.
> But: *Los dientes eran blancos.*　　　The teeth were white. (It is not clear whose teeth the speaker is referring to.)
>
> ***Mi** cabeza daba vueltas.*　　　My head was turning around.
> But: *La cabeza daba vueltas.*　　　The head was turning around. (It is not clear whose head the speaker is referring to.)
>
> (2) Possessives are not used when the verb is reflexive:
>
> *Me duele **la** cabeza.*　　　My head hurts.
> (Not: *Me duele mi cabeza.*)

　　　THE BIG RED BOOK OF SPANISH GRAMMAR

*Se lavó **las** manos.*	She washed her hands.
(<u>Not</u>: *Se lavó sus manos.*)	
*Me seco **la** cara.*	I dry my face.
(<u>Not</u>: *Me seco mi cara.*)	

C. Possessive adjectives used with family members

A possessive adjective must be used if the member of the family *(hermana, padres, hija)* belongs to a subject of the verb indicated by the personal pronoun *yo, tú, Ud. (usted), nosotros/as, vosotros/as* or *Uds. (ustedes):*

*(yo) Fui al cine con **mi** hermana a ver "Cautivos de amor".*	my sister
*(tú) ¿Hablaste con **tus** padres anoche?*	your parents
*¿Ud. almorzó con **su** cuñado?*	your brother-in-law
*(nosotros) Iremos con **nuestras** hijas.*	our daughters
*(vosotros) Iréis con **vuestra** madre.*	your mother
*Uds. verán a **sus** hijos.*	your sons

However, with the third persons, both singular and plural, indicated by *él, ella, ellos,* or *ellas,* either the possessive adjective or the article may be used:

*El salió con **su** (**el**) hermano.*	his brother
*María vio a **sus** (**las**) primas ayer.*	her cousins

D. Possessive adjectives used with persons other than relatives

To indicate relationships with persons other than members of the family, the use of the possessive adjective is optional with all the pronouns:

*Lo vi a **mi** (**al**) jefe.*	my/the boss
*Hablaste con **tu** (**el**) empleado.*	your/the employee
*Uds. verán a **su** (**al**) médico.*	your/the doctor
*Carlos vino con **su** (**el**) amigo.*	his friend

E. Possessive adjectives used with personal items, particularly items of clothing

The use of the possessive adjective is optional when there is no question about the owner:

*Llevé **mi** (**el**) bolso azul.*	I took my blue bag.
<u>But</u>: *Llevé **mi** bolso azul porque no encontré **el tuyo**.*	I took my blue bag because I couldn't find yours.

NOTES:

(1) When the verb is reflexive, the possessive is not necessary, unless the meaning is ambiguous:

*Se puso **el (su)** abrigo negro.*	She put on her black coat.
*Me senté en **la (mi)** silla.*	I sat on my chair.

However:

*Se puso **su** abrigo viejo porque **el de María** no le quedaba bien.*	She put on her old coat because María's coat did not fit her very well.

(2) When the owner of the item is indicated by an indirect object, the possessive adjective is not used:

***Nos** dejó **las** camas sin hacer.*	She left our beds unmade.
<u>Not</u>: *Nos dejó <u>nuestras</u> camas sin hacer.*	
*Siempre **me** devuelve **los** libros cuando me los pide prestados.*	He always returns my books when he borrows them.
<u>Not</u>: *Siempre me devuelve <u>mis</u> libros.*	

(3) If the item possessed is the subject of the verb, the possessive is used instead of the article to avoid ambiguity:

***Mi** cama estaba sin hacer.*	My bed was unmade.
But: *<u>La</u> cama estaba sin hacer.*	The bed was unmade. (It could be anybody's bed.)

F. Possessive adjectives used after the verb *ser*

When the possessive adjective is in *prenominal* position (before the noun) following the verb *ser*, there is a mere indication of possession, and the article is not used:

*Esa es **nuestra** carta.*	That one is our letter.
*¿Estos son **tus** zapatos?*	Are these your shoes?

When the possessive adjective is in *postnominal* position (after the verb) following the noun, there is a distinction implied, and the article must be used:

*Esa es <u>la</u> casa **nuestra**; la de al lado es la de Ester.*	That one is our house; the one next door is Ester's.
*¿Estos son <u>los</u> zapatos **tuyos** o los de Juan?*	Are these your shoes or Juan's?

G. Possessive adjectives used with definite or indefinite articles

The meaning of the sentence using a possessive adjective changes in Spanish depending on whether the article is present or absent and on the type of article that is used.

1. Possessive adjective used with no article:

*Elena es amiga **mía**.*	Elena is my friend.

Here the possessive article merely gives information on the relationship.

2. Possessive adjective used with an indefinite article:

*Elena es **una** amiga **mía**.*	Elena is a friend of mine.

Here the possessive article identifies Helen as one of the speaker's friends and suggests the possibility that the speaker has other friends besides Helen.

3. Possessive adjectives used with a definite article:

*Elena es **la** amiga que yo tengo.*	Elena is the friend I have.
*Elena es **la** amiga **mía** que siempre está lista para ayudarme.*	Elena is the friend of mine who is always ready to help me out.
*Elena es **la** amiga **mía**; Juana es la amiga de Clara.*	Elena is my friend; Juana is Clara's friend.

In the first sentence above, there is an indication that the speaker has only one friend. In the second sentence there is a clear distinction made among the speaker's friends. In the third sentence, there is a possibility that the speaker has other friends but is specifically referring to one person.

H. Ambiguous third person forms (singular and plural) of possessive adjectives

The Spanish forms *su* and *sus*, as well as *suyo* and its variations *suya*, *suyos*, and *suyas*, may lead to confusions regarding the possessor when used out of context. A practical way of clarifying the utterance is to use the preposition *de* and a *personal pronoun* (third person singular or plural, as in *de él*, *de ellos*, covered in the section Practical Uses of Possessive Adjectives that follows). The following examples show the multiple possible meanings of these:

1. Prenominal *su, sus* (*his, her, its, your, their*)

*Me gusta **su** paciencia.*	I like his/her/its/your/their patience.
*Hay algo en **sus** ojos tristes.*	There is something in his/her/its/your/their sad eyes.

2. Postnominal *suyo/a/os/as* (*his, her, its, your, their*)

Me gusta la paciencia **suya**.	I like his/her/its/your/their patience.
Hay algo en los tristes ojos **suyos**.	There is something in his/her/its/your/their sad eyes.

Practical Uses of Possessive Adjectives

In order to clarify the identity of the possessor or to avoid redundancy of the possessive adjective or pronoun, a form of *de* plus a *personal pronoun* is used instead of the prenominal or postnominal possessive in the following cases:

A. *De* plus a pronoun with persons

la familia **de él**	his family
los hijos **de ella**	her children
el artículo **de Ud.**	your article
el perro **de ellos**	their dog
las latas **de ellas**	their cans
el examen **de Uds.**	your exam

Compare the following sets of sentences using *de* plus a *personal pronoun*, the possessive adjective or pronoun, or a possessive expression with the article plus *de*, as in *el de*, *la de*, etc., that functions as a possessive adjective or pronoun.

Prefiero el lápiz **suyo**.	I prefer his/her/your/their pencil.
Prefiero **su** *lápiz*.	I prefer his/her/your/their pencil.
Prefiero el lápiz **de él**.	I prefer his pencil.
Prefiero **el** *(lápiz)* **de él**.	I prefer his (pencil).
Prefiero **el** *(lápiz)* **de María**.	I prefer María's (pencil).
Prefiero **su** *(adj.) lápiz porque el* **suyo** *(pron.) no escribe bien.*	I prefer his/her/your/their pencil because his/hers/yours/theirs does not write well.
Prefiero el lápiz **suyo** *(adj.) porque el* **suyo** *(pron.) no escribe bien.*	I prefer his/her/your/their pencil because his/hers/yours/theirs does not write well.
Prefiero el lápiz **de ella** *(adj.) porque el* **suyo** *(pron.) no escribe bien.*	I prefer her pencil because his/hers/yours/theirs does not write well.

Prefiero **su** (adj.) *lápiz porque* **el de** (pron.) *Juan no escribe bien.*	I prefer his/her/your/their pencil because John's does not write well.
Prefiero el lápiz **de ella** (adj.) *porque* **el de** Ud. (pron.) *no escribe bien.*	I prefer her pencil because yours does not write well.

B. *De* with inanimate nouns

In order to avoid ambiguity, the possessive adjective may be left out with inanimate nouns. Neither the expression *de* + *personal pronoun* (*él, ella, ellos, ellas*) nor the post-nominal possessives are used:

El precio **del coche** es bueno.	The price of the car is good.
Not clear:	
Su precio es bueno.	Its/his/her/your/their price is good.
El precio **de él** es bueno.	Its/his price is good.
El precio **suyo** es bueno.	Its/his/her/your/their price is good.
Las ventanas **de los cuartos** son grandes.	The windows of the rooms are large.
Not clear:	
Sus ventanas son grandes.	Their/its/her/his/your windows are large.
Las ventanas **de ellos** son grandes.	Their (could refer to the rooms or to people) windows are large.
Las ventanas **suyas** son grandes.	Its/her/his/your/their windows are large.

C. Possessive adjectives used with nonhuman animate nouns

In order to avoid ambiguity, the possessive adjective may be left out. Neither the expression *de* + *personal pronoun* (*él, ella, ellos, ellas*) nor the postnominal possessives are used:

Los dientes **de los leones** son afilados.	Lions' teeth are sharp.
Not clear:	
Sus dientes son afilados.	Their/its/her/his/your teeth are sharp.
Los dientes **de ellos** son afilados.	Their (could refer to the lions or to people) teeth are sharp.
Los dientes **suyos** son afilados.	Their/its/his/her/your teeth are sharp.

More Uses of Possessive Adjectives

Possessive adjectives are also used in the following situations:

A. **Possessive adjectives used to address a person in written or spoken language**

1. The *postnominal* form is used. The article is left out:

Estimados señores **nuestros**:	Dear Sirs:
Muy señores **míos**:	Gentlemen:
Hija **mía:**	My daughter,

2. If other words are added to modify the nouns, either the *prenominal* or the *postnominal* form may be used. The article is left out:

Mi estimada señora:	(My) dear Madam:
Estimada señora **mía**:	
Nuestros recordados colegas:	(Our) well-remembered colleagues:
Recordados colegas **nuestros**:	

B. **The use of *nuestro* instead of *mi***

Nuestro is used in place of *mi*, particularly in formal writing, in order to avoid the use of the first person *yo* (implied) as the subject of the sentence, indicated by the possessive *mi*. This is normally done in English to make the writing less subjective: *Our intention is*, rather than *My intention is*.

Nuestra intención es presentar el documento mañana. Not: **Mi** intención es...	Our intention is to present the document tomorrow.
Nuestros datos indican que hay una diferencia. Not: **Mis** datos indican...	Our data indicate that there is a difference.

C. **Idiomatic expressions with possessive adjectives**

The following are some examples of idiomatic expressions that use possessive adjectives:

1. Expressions with prepositions (postnominal possessive adjective):

a instancia nuestra	at our request
a costa suya	at his expense
a pesar nuestro	in spite of us
de parte mía	on my behalf
por causa suya	because of her
por culpa mía	because of me

2. Expressions without prepositions (postnominal possessive adjective):

*No tenemos carta **tuya**.*	We haven't received a letter from you.
*No hubo comunicación **suya**.*	There was no communication from him.
*Han recibido autorización **nuestra**.*	They have received our authorization.
*Pediré referencias **suyas**.*	I will request references about him.

D. Possession expressed by a prepositional phrase with *de*

Possession may be expressed in three different ways: by a possessive in prenominal position, a possessive in postnominal position, or by *de* + a personal pronoun:

*Esta es **nuestra** <u>casa</u>.*	This is our house.
*Esta es la <u>casa</u> **nuestra**.*	
*Esta es la <u>casa</u> **de nosotros**.*	

*Me gusta **su** <u>traje</u>.*	I like his suit.
*Me gusta el <u>traje</u> **suyo**.*	
*Me gusta el <u>traje</u> **de él**.*	

The third form listed above (*de* + personal pronoun) may be used with all the personal pronouns, with the exception of the first and second persons singular *yo* and *tú*.

*Esta es **mi** <u>casa</u>.*	This is my house.
*Esta es la <u>casa</u> **mía**.*	
<u>Not</u>:	
*Esta es la <u>casa</u> de **yo** (or **de mí**).*	

*Me gusta **tu** <u>cartera</u>.*	I like your purse.
*Me gusta la <u>cartera</u> **tuya**.*	
<u>Not</u>:	
*Me gusta la <u>cartera</u> de **tú** (or **de ti**).*	

E. Possession expressed by the verb *pertenecer* (*to belong*)

Possession may be indicated using the verb ***pertenecer*** and an indirect object pronoun (***me, te, le, nos, os, les***). This verb is conjugated like ***gustar***. The indirect object may also be used, for emphasis:

*Estos libros **me** pertenecen (a mí).*	These books belong to me.
*El sombrero **le** pertenece (a él).*	The hat belongs to him.

> **NOTE:**
>
> Without an indirect object pronoun, ***pertenecer*** means *to be part* of something. It is conjugated in all the forms.
>
> | | |
> |---|---|
> | *(Yo) pertenezco al grupo de competidores.* | I am part of the group of competitors. |
> | *Nosotros pertenecemos a esta sociedad.* | We are members of this society. |

Numerals

Numerals are adjectives that refer to a noun and indicate the amount or the order in which the units appear. There are six categories of numerals:

A. Cardinal numerals (*cardinales*):

dos *plantas*	two plants

B. Ordinal numerals (*ordinales*):

*la **tercera** carta*	the third letter

C. Partitive numerals (*partitivos*):

*la **octava** parte*	the eighth part

D. Multiple or proportional numerals (*múltiples o proporcionales*):

*el **doble***	double

E. Distributive numerals (*distributivos*):

sendos/as	to one another, each other

F. collective numerals (*colectivos*):

un **centenar** de caballos   one hundred horses

Cardinal Numerals

These numeral adjectives point to the noun and specify its number. They answer the question *How many?*

¿Cuántos amigos? Tres.   How many friends? Three.
¿Cuántas tiendas? Cinco.   How many stores? Five.

Gender of Cardinal Numerals

Numbers in Spanish are masculine because *número* is a masculine noun (*el número dos, el número cuarenta*):

El tres es número de suerte.   Three is a lucky number.
Llegaremos **el ocho** de marzo.   We'll arrive on March 8th.
Hay un ejercicio en la página (**número**)   There is an exercise on page 205.
  doscientos cinco.

> **NOTE:**
>
> Numbers do not change gender before a feminine noun:
>
> cinco lápices (masculine noun)   five pencils
> cinco camas (feminine noun)   five beds
> veinte platos   twenty plates
> veinte almohadas   twenty pillows
>
> However, exceptions to this rule are the number one (*uno* ➤ *una*), as well as all the combinations with *cientos*, from *doscientos* to *novecientos* (including five hundred, *quinientos*), each of which has a feminine form: *doscientas, quinientas*. See the following section titled Uses and Changes in Form for each set of numbers.

Numbers from 0 to 30

0 *cero*

Zero is an arithmetical sign. It has no numerical value by itself, but when placed to the right of a number it multiplies the value of that number by ten: 0, 20, 200.

1 *uno*	11 *once*	21 *veintiuno*
2 *dos*	12 *doce*	22 *veintidós*
3 *tres*	13 *trece*	23 *veintitrés*
4 *cuatro*	14 *catorce*	24 *veinticuatro*
5 *cinco*	15 *quince*	25 *veinticinco*
6 *seis*	16 *dieciséis*	26 *veintiséis*
7 *siete*	17 *diecisiete*	27 *veintisiete*
8 *ocho*	18 *dieciocho*	28 *veintiocho*
9 *nueve*	19 *diecinueve*	29 *veintinueve*
10 *diez*	20 *veinte*	30 *treinta*

Uses and Changes in Form of Numbers from 0 to 30

A. *Uno* becomes *un* before masculine singular nouns

Uno takes the short form *un* before masculine singular nouns, even when the noun is preceded by another adjective:

Tengo **uno**.	I have one.
But:	
Tengo **un** amigo.	I have one friend.
Tengo solamente **un** fiel amigo.	I have only one faithful friend.

B. All numerals that end in *uno* take the shortened form *un* before masculine nouns:

Hay veinti**ún** chicos.	There are twenty-one boys.
ciento **un** hombres	one hundred men

> **NOTE:**
>
> This rule also applies when the cardinal precedes *mil* (*thousand*), *millón* (*million*), *billón* (*billion*), *trillón* (*trillion*), etc.:
>
> | | |
> |---|---|
> | veinti**ún** mil dólares | 21,000 dollars |
> | treinta y **un** millones | 31 million |
> | cincuenta y **un** billones | 51 billion |

C. *Uno* becomes *una* before a feminine singular noun

Uno changes to *una* before a feminine singular noun even when the noun is preceded by another adjective:

*Tengo **una**.*	I have one.
*Tengo **una** amiga.*	I have one friend.
*Tengo solamente **una** fiel amiga.*	I have only one faithful friend.
*Me quedé con **una** copia.*	I was left with one copy.

NOTES:

(1) Expressions such as *un amigo* and *una copia* (*one friend, one copy*) can also just mean *a friend* or *a copy*, depending on context, since the numeral has the same form as the indefinite article:

*Compré **un** lápiz azul y dos rojos.*	I bought one (a) blue pencil and two red ones.
*Tengo **un** buen lápiz para corregir los ejercicios.*	I have one (a) good pencil for correcting the exercises.

(2) The number *one* (*uno, una*) never has a plural form. If it appears in the plural, it is an indefinite article:

*Vi **un** árbol allí.* (adj./art.)	I saw one (a) tree there.
*Vi **unos** árboles allí.* (art.)	I saw some trees there.
*Vi solamente **una** planta, no tres, como dices.* (adj.)	I saw only one plant, not three as you say.
*Hay **unas** plantas.* (art.)	There are some plants.

D. *Una* becomes *un* before a stressed *a*

When a feminine singular noun begins with a stressed *a*, *una* becomes *un* for phonetic purposes. The form *una* is also accepted, although it is used less frequently.

*Noé construyó **un** arca.*	Noah built an (one) ark.
*Noé construyó **un** arca enorme.*	Noah built a huge ark.

However, if another adjective is placed before the noun to show emphasis, the complete form *una* is used:

*Noé construyó **una** enorme arca, no dos.*	Noah built one huge ark, not two.

E. *Una* and *un* before feminine plural nouns

All numerals that end in *uno* take the ending *una* before a feminine plural noun, and *un* before a feminine plural noun that begins with stressed *a*:

Hay veinti**una** <u>chicas</u> aquí.	There are twenty-one girls here.
Encontraron veinti**ún** <u>arcas</u> en la excavación.	They found twenty-one arks in the excavation.

> **NOTE:**
>
> If the feminine cardinal precedes *mil* (*thousand*), *millón* (*million*), *billón* (*billion*), etc., the shortened form *un* is always used:
>
> | | |
> |---|---|
> | veinti**ún** mil especies | 21,000 species |
> | treinta y **un** millones de estrellas | 31 million stars |
> | cuarenta y **un** mil maestras | 41,000 teachers |

F. Numbers from *dieciséis* to *diecinueve* (16-19) and from *veintiuno* to *veintinueve* (21-29)

Numbers from *dieciséis* to *diecinueve* (16-19) and from *veintiuno* to *veintinueve* (21-29) are usually written as one word. They may also be written as three words (*diez y ocho*, *veinte y tres*), although these forms are becoming obsolete. Even when written in the long form, numbers between twenty-one and twenty-nine are pronounced as one word.

G. Plural form of numerals

Although numerals greater than one are necessarily plural and do not change form (*cinco lápices*, *five pencils*), they have a plural form when used as a noun:

Quiero los **ocho** pedazos.	I want the eight pieces. (There are eight in all.)
But:	
No me gusta este **ocho**. Es muy grande.	I don't like this number eight. It's too large.
No me gustan estos **ochos**; píntalos de rojo.	I don't like these eights; paint them red.

H. Numerals that designate the hours are feminine

Numerals from one to twelve that are used to designate the hours are feminine because the noun *hora* (*hour*) is feminine:

la una	one o'clock
las dos	two o'clock
las doce	twelve o'clock

The verb *ser* (*to be*) agrees in number with the hour specified:

Es la una.	It is one o'clock.
Es la una en punto.	It is one o'clock sharp.
Son las tres.	It is three o'clock.
Son las once.	It is eleven o'clock.

To indicate what time it is, *a la* (*at*) is used with *one o'clock*, and *a las* with the hours between two and twelve:

a la una	at one o'clock
a las ocho	at eight o'clock

The time is usually spelled out:

LLegaron a las cuatro y media.	They arrived at four thirty.

NOTE:

In schedules, such as departures and arrivals, military time is used:

18:30, 22:00, etc.

18:30 may be read as *dieciocho y treinta* (formal) or *seis y media* (informal).

I. Writing out numbers

When numbers appear in letters, notes, etc., it is better to write them out, beginning with one, although figures are accepted up to nine:

Trajeron una botella.	They brought one bottle.
Me dio ocho botellas.	She gave me eight bottles.

However, if exact figures are given, as in specific amounts of items, figures are used:

Esperan vender 475 cajas de herramientas.	They expect to sell 475 tool boxes.

If the amount is approximate, words are used:

Creen que venderán unas cuatrocientas cajas.	They think that they will sell about four hundred boxes.

Numbers from 30 to 199

30 *treinta*	31 *treinta y uno*
40 *cuarenta*	44 *cuarenta y cuatro*

50 cincuenta	55 cincuenta y cinco
60 sesenta	66 sesenta y seis
70 setenta	77 setenta y siete
80 ochenta	88 ochenta y ocho
90 noventa	99 noventa y nueve
100 cien (ciento)	101 ciento uno
150 ciento cincuenta	151 ciento cincuenta y uno
190 ciento noventa	199 ciento noventa y nueve

Uses and Changes in Form of Numbers from 30 to 199

A. Compound numbers between thirty-one and ninety-nine

Compound numbers between thirty-one and ninety-nine are written and pronounced using three words each (*cincuenta y dos*, *treinta y cuatro*), although the pronunciation *cincuentidós*, *treinticuatro* is widely heard. Notice the use of *y* (*and*) in the Spanish numerals:

cuarenta y tres	forty-three
setenta y nueve	seventy-nine

B. *Un*, the shortened form of *uno* (*one*), is not used before the numbers *cien* and *ciento*:

cien gallinas	one hundred hens
ciento un pollos	one hundred and one chickens

C. Beyond 100, there is no *y* (*and*) right after the hundreds, as there would be in English:

ciento uno	one hundred and one
doscientos tres	two hundred and three
cuatrocientos cincuenta	four hundred and fifty
trescientos cuarenta y dos	three hundred and forty-two

NOTE:
It is *ciento uno* (101) (<u>not</u>: *un ciento uno*).

D. Spelling changes

There are slight changes in the spelling of the original single digit when it becomes part of a larger number:

6 seis	➤	60 sesenta
7 siete	➤	70 setenta
9 nueve	➤	90 noventa

E. Cien

Cien is a shortened form for *ciento* (*a hundred*), and is invariable. It is used in the following contexts.

1. *Cien* is used before a noun, preceded or not by a modifying word:

cien maestros	one hundred teachers
cien lámparas	one hundred lamps
cien hermosas chicas	one hundred pretty girls

2. *Cien* is used before nominalized adjectives:

   | Salieron cien valientes. | One hundred valiant (men) came out. |
   | Eligieron a las cien más bonitas. | They chose the prettiest one hundred (girls). |

3. *Cien* is used when the number stands by itself:

   | Quiero cien. No me des más. | I want one hundred (of them). Don't give me more. |
   | Sólo tengo cien. | I only have one hundred. |

   NOTE:

   The use of *ciento* is becoming obsolete in this case, although it was previously considered the correct form.

4. *Cien* is used before *mil* (*thousand*), *millón* (*million*), *billón* (*billion*), etc.:

   | cien mil años | one hundred thousand years |
   | cien millones de dólares | one hundred million dollars |

   NOTES:

   (1) *Mil* has a plural form only when it functions as a collective noun:

   | Hay miles de estrellas. | There are thousands of stars. |

   (2) *Un billón* is *a thousand millions*, as in English.

(3) If a number from one to ninety-nine is added to one hundred, *cien* becomes *ciento*, even before *mil, millones, billones,* etc.:

ciento dos mil pesos	102,000 pesos
ciento cincuenta millones	150,000,000
But:	
cien mil pesos	100,000 pesos

F. **Ciento is used in the following contexts:**

1. *Ciento* is used when a number from one to ninety-nine is added to one hundred:

ciento un maestros	101 teachers
ciento una lámparas	101 lamps
ciento cincuenta libros	150 books
ciento noventa y nueve días	199 days
ciento treinta y cuatro mil habitantes	134,000 inhabitants

2. *Ciento* is used to indicate a percentage:

Tuvieron un cien (ciento)* por ciento de ganancias.	They made a hundred-percent profit.
Los resultados fueron buenos en el cuatro por ciento de los estudiantes.	The results were good for four percent of the students.

Numbers from 200 to 999

200 *doscientos*	201 *doscientos uno*
300 *trescientos*	322 *trescientos veintidós*
400 *cuatrocientos*	433 *cuatrocientos treinta y tres*
500 *quinientos*	555 *quinientos cincuenta y cinco*
600 *seiscientos*	666 *seiscientos sesenta y seis*
700 *setecientos*	777 *setecientos setenta y siete*
800 *ochocientos*	888 *ochocientos ochenta y ocho*
900 *novecientos*	999 *novecientos noventa y nueve*

---

* Although *ciento por ciento* (100%) has been considered the correct form, the expression *cien por ciento* is widely used.

Uses and Changes in Form of Numbers from 200 to 999

A. *Doscientos* and *trescientos* are also spelled *docientos* and *trecientos*.

B. *Cientos* (*hundreds*)

Cientos (*hundreds*) is part of every number from *two hundred* (*doscientos*) to *nine hundred* (*novecientos*). It has a feminine ending, which is used before feminine nouns:

trescientos soldados	three hundred soldiers
setecientos años	seven hundred years
seiscientas páginas	six hundred pages
doscientas ovejas	two hundred sheep
cuatrocientas vacas	four hundred cows

C. *Cientos* by itself is a collective noun that means *hundreds* and is always masculine:

Tiraron cientos de botellas.	They threw out hundreds of bottles.
Había cientos de soldados muertos.	There were hundreds of dead soldiers.
Hay cientos de páginas para leer.	There are hundreds of pages to read.

D. *Quinientos*

Quinientos has a different form from all other numbers in the sequence from *doscientos* to *novecientos*. It also has a feminine ending, which is used before feminine nouns:

Había quinientas armas en el granero.	There were five hundred guns in the silo.
La biblioteca recibió quinientos libros.	The library received five hundred books.

> **NOTE:**
> *Las mil y quinientas* takes the meaning of *very late* in a popular saying:
>
> *Se fueron a las mil y quinientas esa noche.* — They left very late that night.

E. *Y* (*and*) in cardinal numbers

Notice that *y* (*and*) is not used right after the hundreds, as would be done in English, but it is used after the tens:

doscientos cuarenta	two hundred <u>and</u> forty
quinientos treinta y seis	five hundred <u>and</u> thirty-six

Numbers 1000 and Beyond

There are several uses and changes in form for these numbers.

A. *Mil* (one thousand)

1. *Un*, the shortened form of *uno* (*one*) is not used before *mil*:

mil viajes	one thousand trips
mil leguas	one thousand leagues
mil gracias	many, many thanks

   However, *un* is used when the multiple of *mil* (i.e., the number of thousands) ends in *uno*:

500.000	(English: 500,000)	quinientos mil
But:		
501.000	(English: 501,000)	quinientos **un** mil

2. *Mil* has the plural form *miles,* followed by *de*, only when used as a collective noun meaning *thousands*.

mil hojas	one thousand leaves
miles de hojas	thousands of leaves

   Miles does not have a feminine form:

unos miles de hormigas	a few thousand ants
(Not: unas miles de hormigas)	

   > **NOTE:**
   > *Millar* is a group of one thousand units. The plural form, *millares*, is used to indicate a large number of items. It does not have a feminine form, either:
   >
   > | | |
   > |---|---|
   > | Había un millar de estrellas. | There were a thousand stars. |
   > | Había millares de estrellas. | There were thousands of stars. |

3. In order to write a multiple of *mil*, numbers from 2 to 999 are placed in front of *mil*:

mil	one thousand
dos mil	two thousand

cincuenta mil	fifty thousand
trescientos mil	three hundred thousand
novecientos noventa y nueve mil	nine hundred ninety-nine thousand

NOTES:

(1) In Spanish, a period is used to indicate the thousands instead of a comma:

3.500	7.221	10.422

(2) A comma is used to indicate decimals:

0,25	3,14	1.300,75

(3) The thousands cannot be expressed as hundreds, as is sometimes done in English:

English	Spanish
twelve hundred	*mil doscientos* (one thousand two hundred)
fourteen ninety-two	*mil cuatrocientos noventa y dos* (one thousand four hundred and ninety-two)
nineteen ninety-nine	*mil novecientos noventa y nueve* (one thousand nine hundred and ninety-nine)

4. Numbers from 1 to 999 are added to the thousands to make all possible combinations up to one million:

23.877	*veintitrés mil ochocientos setenta y siete*
999.999	*novecientos noventa y nueve mil novecientos noventa y nueve*
1.005	*mil cinco* (one thousand and five)

NOTES:

(1) In Spanish, *y* (*and*) is not used after the thousands or hundreds, but it is used after the tens, as in 2.348:

5.007	*cinco mil siete*
3.220	*tres mil doscientos veinte*
2.348	*dos mil trescientos cuarenta y ocho*

(2) The expression ***las mil y una***, as in the popular saying ***Me hizo las mil y una*** (*She treated me very badly*), does not mean literally *one thousand and one*, but *many, many times plus one more time*.

B. *Millón, billón, trillón,* etc.

These words have the following characteristics:

1. They are collective nouns and have a plural form (*millones,* *billones*):

un millón de pesos	one million pesos
dos millones de dólares	two million dollars

2. They do not have a feminine form:

un millón de tarjetas	one million cards
un millón de gracias	one million thanks
dos millones de monedas	two million coins

3. They represent, respectively, the following numbers:

1.000.000	*un millón*	one million
1.000.000.000	*un billón*	one billion
1.000.000.000.000	*un trillón*	one trillion

4. As nouns, they may be preceded by articles (art.), adjectives (adj.), or numerals (num.), as clarified below. They can also be implied after a pronoun (pro.):

<u>un</u> *millón de cepillos* (num.)	one million brushes
el millón de libros pedidos (art.)	the million books ordered
<u>El</u> *millón de dólares lo estaba esperando.* (art.)	The million dollars were waiting for him.
<u>tres</u> *millones de latas* (num.)	three million cans
<u>Ese</u> *(millón) desapareció.* (pro.)	That one disappeared.
El suculento millón desapareció. (adj.)	The succulent million disappeared.

5. They are followed by the preposition *de* if no other numerals are added: (See point 6 that follows.)

*tres millones **de** entradas*	three million tickets
*dos billones **de** pesos*	two billion pesos

However, in context, *de* and the noun may be left out:

*Pidieron un billón **de** dólares.*	They asked for a billion dollars.
Recibieron un millón.	They received one million.
<u>But:</u>	
*Recibieron **el billón** que habían pedido.*	They received the billion that they had asked for.

6. If numerals are added to the basic units *un millón*, *un billón*, etc., the indefinite article is kept, and the whole expression is written without the preposition *de*.

un millón quinientas mil estrellas	1,500,000 stars
un billón doscientos mil pesos	1,000,200,000 pesos

7. The multiples of *un millón, un billón*, etc., are expressed in the plural form:

tres millones de monedas	3 million coins
tres millones cincuenta mil monedas	3,050,000 coins
dos billones de euros	2 billion euros
dos billones trescientos dos puntos	2,000,000,302 dots

8. Some more numbers that follow *billón* (*billion*) are: *trillón*, *cuatrillón*, and *quintillón*.

Position of Cardinal Numerals

Cardinal numerals are placed before the noun in most cases:

tres ratones	three mice
mil años	a thousand years

NOTES:

(1) Sometimes a cardinal numeral functions as an ordinal numeral, and, therefore, it does not answer the question *How many?* but rather *Which one?* In these cases, the adjective follows the noun:

*Juan XXIII (Juan **veintitrés**)*	John XXIII
*capítulo **cuarenta y dos***	Chapter 42
*siglo XIX (siglo **diecinueve**)*	19th century
*el día **trece** de junio*	June 13th

(2) With days of the month, as in *el trece de junio*, cardinal numerals are used for all the days with the exception of the first day of the month, which takes the ordinal *primero* (*first*), as in English. It is placed before the month: *el primero de agosto* (*August 1st*). The numeral is followed by *de*, and then the month:

el 1° (primero) de agosto	August 1st
el 2 (dos) de julio	July 2nd
el 15 (quince) de febrero	February 15th

When writing out dates, the following rules apply:

- The month is not capitalized unless it is the first word in a sentence, mainly when dating a letter:

Agosto 4, 2005	*4 de agosto, 2005*	*4 de agosto de 2005*
Vamos a ir en septiembre.	We are going in September.	
Septiembre ha sido un mes caluroso.	September has been a hot month.	

- In a four-digit year, the thousands are not separated by a period: *1999* and not *1.999.*

- The definite article, rather than the preposition *en* (*on*), is used to express a date:

Iremos el 28 de enero.	We will go on January 28th.

- When writing dates with figures, the day comes first:

7/6/94 (siete de junio de 1994) = June 7, 1994 (6/7/94)

(3) Cardinal numerals are generally used to refer to pages and chapters. They are placed after the noun:

página uno (page 1)	*capítulo once* (chapter 11)
página trece (page 13)	*capítulo veinticinco* (chapter 25)

Ordinal numerals may also be used to refer to pages and chapters, mainly for the numbers from 1 to 10. They are usually placed before *página (primera página, segunda página),* and before or after *capítulo*:

tercer* capítulo or *capítulo tercero*	Chapter 3
cuarto capítulo or *capítulo cuarto*	Chapter 4
octavo capítulo or *capítulo octavo*	Chapter 8

(4) To designate centuries, cardinal numerals are placed after the word *siglo.* Notice that Roman numerals are used in Spanish:

el siglo XII (doce)	12th century
el siglo XX (veinte)	20th century
el siglo XXI (veintiuno)	21st century

(5) When cardinal and ordinal numerals appear together, the cardinals may be placed before or after the ordinals:

---

* *Primero* and *tercero* become *primer* and *tercer* before a masculine singular noun.

| los <u>seis primeros</u> resultados | the first six results |
| los <u>primeros seis</u> recibos | the first six receipts |

Ordinal Numerals

Ordinal numerals point to nouns and indicate the order in which those nouns appear. They answer the question *Which one?*

| Esta es la **primera** vez. | This is the first time. |
| Ha sido el **segundo** atentado. | This has been the second attack. |

Gender and Number of Ordinal Numbers

Spanish ordinal numerals agree in gender and number with the noun they modify:

la cuarta vez	the fourth time
los primeros libros	the first books
la vigesimoprimera edición	the twenty-first edition

Ordinal Numerals from *First* to *Nineteenth* (1st to 19th)

primero	first
segundo	second
tercero	third
cuarto	fourth
quinto	fifth
sexto	sixth
séptimo or sétimo	seventh
octavo	eighth
noveno	ninth
décimo	tenth
undécimo	eleventh
duodécimo	twelfth
decimotercero or decimotercio	thirteenth
decimocuarto	fourteenth
decimoquinto	fifteenth
decimosexto	sixteenth

decimoséptimo or *decimosétimo*	seventeenth
decimoctavo	eighteenth
decimonoveno or *decimonono*	nineteenth

NOTES:

(1) *Primero*, *tercero*, and *noveno* each have an alternate form: *primo*, *tercio*, and *nono,* respectively:

materias primas (primeras)	raw materials
una tercia parte	one third
Pío Nono (IX)	Pius IX

(2) *Primero* and *tercero* become *primer* and *tercer* before a masculine singular noun:

el primer hombre	the first man
el tercer salario	the third salary
But: *los primeros hombres*	the first men
la primera mujer	the first woman

(3) The form *primer* before a feminine noun is used occasionally in cases such as *la primer página* and *la primer entrevista*.

(4) All combinations of ordinals that end in the word *primero* or *tercero* also drop the *o* before a masculine singular noun: *vigesimoprimer corredor* (see following).

(5) All combinations of ordinals that include the word *décimo*, such as *undecimoprimero* or *decimoquinto*, form the feminine form by changing only the final *o* to *a*, as in *undecimoprimera*, *decimoquinta*. The feminine forms *undecimaprimera* and *decimaquinta* are accepted, but the above forms are preferred.

Ordinal Numerals from Twentieth to Ninety-Ninth (20th to 99th)

vigésimo	twentieth
vigesimoprimero	twenty-first
trigésimo	thirtieth
trigesimosegundo	thirty-second
cuadragésimo	fortieth
cuadragesimotercero	forty-third
quincuagésimo	fiftieth
quincuagesimocuarto	fifty-fourth

sexagésimo	sixtieth
sexagesimoquinto	sixty-fifth
septuagésimo	seventieth
septuagesimosexto	seventy-sixth
octagésimo	eightieth
octagesimoséptimo	eighty-seventh
nonagésimo	ninetieth
nonagesimonoveno	ninety-ninth

NOTE:

All ordinal numbers that end in *primero, tercero*, and *noveno* can also have the endings *primo, tercio*, and *nono*, respectively.

Ordinal Numerals from *One Hundredth* to *One Thousand and First* (100th to 1001st)

centésimo	100th
centesimoprimero	101st
ducentésimo	200th
ducentesimosegundo	202nd
tricentésimo	300th
tricentesimotercero	303rd
cuadringentésimo	400th
cuadringentesimocuarto	404th
quingentésimo	500th
quingentesimoquinto	505th
sexcentésimo	600th
sexcentesimosexto	606th
septingentésimo	700th
septingentesimoséptimo	707th
octingentésimo	800th
octingentesimoctavo	808th
noningentésimo	900th
noningentesimonoveno	909th
milésimo	1000th
milesimoprimero	1001st

NOTES:

(1) All ordinal numbers that end in *primero, tercero*, and *noveno* can also have the endings *primo, tercio*, and *nono*, respectively.

(2) The word *enésimo* is a mathematical term that represents *an undetermined number of times*:

la enésima potencia   the nth power

(3) *Millonésimo* is the equivalent of *millionth*.

(4) For practical purposes, large ordinal numerals, as in *the 300th anniversary*, are usually read as *el trescientos aniversario* rather than *el tricentésimo aniversario*.

Position and Uses of Ordinal Numerals

Ordinal numerals are placed before or after the noun, depending on specific conditions.

A. Ordinal numerals for chapters

With chapters, ordinal numerals may be used before or after the noun, *up to ten*.

tercer capítulo	third chapter (Chapter 3)
capítulo tercero	
octavo capítulo	eighth chapter (Chapter 8)
capítulo octavo	

NOTE:

Cardinal numerals may also be used for chapter numbers from *one to ten*. Cardinals *always* follow the noun (*capítulo uno, capítulo cinco*); ordinals may precede or follow the noun (*primer capítulo* or *capítulo primero; quinto capítulo* or *capítulo quinto*). After ten, cardinal numerals are generally used:

capítulo trece	Chapter 13
capítulo veinte	Chapter 20

B. Ordinal numerals for pages

With pages, ordinal numerals may be used *up to nine*. They are always placed before the word *página*, and not after.

primera página	(Not: página primera)
tercera página	(Not: página tercera)

NOTE:

Cardinals may also be used for page numbers up to ten; they are *always* placed after the word *página*: *página uno*, *página seis*. Beginning with ten, cardinals are generally used:

página diez	(<u>Not</u>: *décima página*)
página dieciocho	(<u>Not</u>: *decimoctava página*)

C. Ordinal and cardinal numerals with days of the month

Primero is the only ordinal numeral used with the days of the month: *el primero de febrero* (*February 1st*). For the other days, cardinal numerals are used:

1º (primero) de febrero de 1898	February 1st, 1898
2 (dos) de febrero de 1942	February 2nd, 1942
31 (treinta y uno) de julio	July 31st

D. *Primero* as an adverb

Primero also functions as an adverb, just like *primeramente* or *en primer lugar*:

Primero le escribiré.	First, I will write to her.
Primeramente irá a verla.	First, he will go see her.
En primer lugar lo llamaré.	First of all, I will call him.

It is also used with the meaning of *rather*, or *it is better to*:

Primero preguntar que cometer un error.	Rather ask than make a mistake. (It is better to ask than to make a mistake.)
Primero averiguar que sospechar.	Rather make sure than suspect. (It is better to make sure than to suspect.)

E. *Primero* preceded by *lo*

Primero, preceded by the neuter article *lo*, is equivalent to *the first thing* or *whatever comes first*:

*Mi hija es **lo primero**.*	My daughter comes first.
*La salud es **lo primero**.*	Health comes first.
***Lo primero** que vimos fue la estatua.*	The first thing we saw was the statue.

F. Ordinal and cardinal numerals with names of kings and popes

With names of kings and popes, ordinals are generally used for numbers up to ten. They are placed after the proper noun and are expressed with Roman numerals:

Carlos V (quinto)   *Alfonso X (décimo)*   *Juan Carlos I (primero)*

However, cardinal numerals are used beyond ten and merely indicate a number in a sequence. They are also written with Roman numerals: *Pío XII (doce), Juan XXIII (veintitrés), Benedito XVI (dieciséis)*. Note how the following titles are read:

Pío XII: Pío doce   (<u>Not</u>: *Pío el doce*)
Alfonso X: Alfonso décimo   (<u>Not</u>: *Alfonso el décimo*)

G. *Segundo* as an adverb

Segundo also functions as an adverb, just like *en segundo lugar*:

Segundo, no me interesa.   Secondly, I am not interested.
En segundo lugar, estudiaremos el otro plan.   Secondly, we'll study the other plan.

H. Ordinal and cardinal numerals with centuries

With centuries, ordinals are generally used with numbers up to ten, while cardinals are used beyond ten. Both ordinals and cardinals follow the word *siglo*:

en el siglo primero   in the first century
en el siglo sexto   in the sixth century
en el siglo trece   in the thirteenth century
el siglo XX (veinte)   the twentieth century

I. Placement of ordinal numerals

If the ordinal is used to emphasize an item in a sequence, it is placed before the noun:

*Carlos es el **segundo** chico que saca una A.*   Carlos is the second boy who has gotten an A.
*Es la **tercera** vez que lo veo.*   It's the third time I've seen him.

J. With the words *centenario* (*one hundred years*), and *aniversario* (*anniversary*), ordinal numerals are also used:

*el **cuarto** centenario de la conquista*   the 400th anniversary (literally, the fourth
  de América   centenary) of the conquest of America

el **quincuagésimo** aniversario de la inauguración	the fiftieth anniversary of the inauguration

NOTE:

It is common to use cardinals instead of ordinals in informal situations:

Celebran el *cuatrocientos* aniversario de la fundación de la ciudad.	They're celebrating the 400th anniversary of the founding of the city.

K. Expressing birthdays

Birthdays are not expressed with ordinals as in English. The sentence *We are going to celebrate Molly's 70th birthday* may be expressed in one of the following ways:

Vamos a celebrar los setenta años de Molly.	We are going to celebrate Molly's seventy years (of age).
Vamos a celebrar sus setenta años.	We are going to celebrate her seventy years (of age).
Vamos a celebrar el cumpleaños de Molly, que cumple setenta (años).	We are going to celebrate Molly's birthday, who will be seventy (years of age).

Partitive Numerals

These numerals represent the number of parts into which the noun is divided:

media página	half a page
tres cuartos de una manzana	three quarters of an apple
la segunda parte de la novela	the second part of the novel
dos décimos de la lotería	two tenths of a lottery number

Partitives from *One Half* to *One Tenth* (½ to ⅒th)

With the exception of **medio** (*one half*) and **un tercio** (*one third*), all the other partitives are the same as the ordinals:

½ medio	one half
⅓ un tercio	one third
¼ un cuarto	one fourth
⅕ un quinto	one fifth
⅙ un sexto	one sixth

⅐ un séptimo	one seventh
⅛ un octavo	one eighth
⅑ un noveno	one ninth
⅒ un décimo	one tenth

Partitives Beyond *One Tenth* (⅒**th**)

Fractions beyond one tenth add the ending *-avo* to the cardinals, with some spelling modifications. The exceptions are ***centésimo*** and ***milésimo*** (*one hundredth* and *one thousandth*). These numerals are used to express mathematical operations:

¹⁄₁₁	un onceavo	one eleventh
¹⁄₁₂	un doceavo	one twelfth
¹⁄₁₃	un treceavo	one thirteenth
¹⁄₁₄	un catorceavo	one fourteenth
¹⁄₁₅	un quinceavo	one fifteenth
¹⁄₁₆	un dieciseisavo	one sixteenth
¹⁄₁₇	un diecisieteavo	one seventeenth
¹⁄₁₈	un dieciochoavo	one eighteenth
¹⁄₁₉	un diecinueveavo	one nineteenth
¹⁄₂₀	un veinteavo	one twentieth
¹⁄₂₄	un veinticuatravo	one twenty-fourth
¹⁄₃₀	un treintavo	one thirtieth
¹⁄₄₀	un cuarentavo	one fortieth
¹⁄₅₀	un cincuentavo	one fiftieth
¹⁄₆₀	un sesentavo	one sixtieth
¹⁄₇₀	un setentavo	one seventieth
¹⁄₈₀	un ochentavo	one eightieth
¹⁄₉₀	un noventavo	one ninetieth
¹⁄₁₀₀	un **centésimo**	one hundredth
¹⁄₁₂₀	un cientoveinteavo	one hundred and twentieth
¹⁄₂₀₀	un doscientavo	one two hundredth
¹⁄₁₀₀₀	un **milésimo**	one thousandth

NOTES:

(1) The word *centésimo*, which designates ¹⁄₁₀₀ (*one hundredth*) has another form, *centavo*, but that is used exclusively to refer to *one cent* in the monetary system.

(2) When the first numeral changes to ***dos, tres, cuatro***, etc., the second numeral stays the same but in the plural form. Compare these numbers:

⅓	un *tercio*	one third
⅔	dos *tercios*	two thirds
³⁄₂₀	tres veinteavos	three twentieths
⁸⁄₁₀₀	ocho centésimos	eight hundredths
²⁄₁₀₀₀	dos milésimos	two thousandths

Uses of Partitives

There are specific uses for partitives:

A. **Medio(a)** means *half*, with reference to weights, measurements, and time:

2 *metros y medio*	2.5 meters
4 *kilos y medio*	4.5 kilograms
2 *libras y media*	2.5 pounds
medio kilo	½ kilogram
media manzana	half an apple
media hora	half an hour

B. **Medio** (masculine form only), followed by an adjective, means *a little* or *somewhat*:

medio ocupado	a little busy
medio enferma	a little sick
medio enterados	somewhat aware
medio confundidas	somewhat confused

C. **Centavo** (*one hundredth*) is used to designate *a cent*:

un centavo	one cent
cinco centavos	five cents

D. When partitives precede the word *parte(s)* (*part/s*), they take the feminine gender:

una cuarta parte de la clase	one quarter of the class
tres quintas partes de la casa	three fifths of the house

Multiple or Proportional Numerals

These numerals indicate the number of times that the noun is repeated: onefold, threefold, etc. Some examples of multiple numerals are:

doble or *duplo(a)*	twofold, double
triple or *triplo(a)*	threefold, triple
cuádruple, cuádruplo(a)	fourfold, quadruple
quíntuplo(a)	fivefold
séxtuplo(a)	sixfold
séptuplo(a)	sevenfold
óctuplo(a)	eightfold
nónuplo(a)	ninefold
décuplo(a)	tenfold
undécuplo(a)	elevenfold
duodécuplo(a)	twelvefold
terciodécuplo(a)	thirteenfold
céntuplo(a)	one hundredfold

NOTES:

(1) *Simple* (*single*) is the name given to what is not double, triple, etc.:

una hoja simple	a single sheet

In Spanish, there are equivalents of *single* that do not use the word *simple*, as in the following examples:

single room	*habitación individual* (or *para una persona*)
single-handed	*sin ayuda, solo*
single man	*hombre soltero*
single life	*vida de soltero, celibato*
single state	*estado civil soltero*
not a single (book, house)	*ningún libro, ninguna casa* (or *ni un libro, ni una casa*)

(2) *Duplicado* (*triplicado, cuadruplicado*, etc.) is the name given to a copy of a document:

Hay que firmar el duplicado.	The copy must be signed.
El documento debe ser por duplicado (triplicado, cuadruplicado, etc.).	The document must be in duplicate (triplicate, quadruplicate, etc.).

(3) The word *double* is used in English in many contexts where Spanish uses different expressions. Some of the most common ones are:

double bed	*cama para dos personas (camera, de matrimonio, de dos plazas)*
double boiler	*baño de María*
double-breasted jacket	*saco cruzado*
double chin	*papada*
double cross	*traición*
double date	*cita de dos parejas*
double-edged	*de dos filos*
double entry	*partida doble* (in accounting)
double-faced	*falso, hipócrita*
double feature	*programa de dos películas*
double meaning	*doble sentido*
double-minded	*vacilante*
double room	*habitación con dos camas* (or *para dos personas*)
double talk	*lenguaje ambiguo*
double door	*puerta de dos hojas*

Distributive Numerals

These numerals indicate a distribution of a plural noun to each one of the recipients. In the examples that follow, *regalos* (*gifts*), *sonrisas* (*smiles*), and *huesos* (*bones*) are the nouns:

*María y Elena se dieron **sendos** regalos.*	María and Elena gave each other a gift.
*Los niños hicieron **sendas** sonrisas a la maestra.*	Each one of the children smiled at the teacher.
*El hombre compró **sendos** huesos para los cuatro perros.*	The man bought the four dogs one bone each.

NOTES:

(1) It is incorrect to use *ambos* or *ambas* (*the two of them*) with the meaning of *sendos, sendas* (*one each*). Observe the following sentences:

*Los niños le dieron **sendos** regalos.* (one gift each)

*Los niños le dieron **ambos** regalos.* (the two children together gave her two gifts)

(2) It is incorrect to use *sendo(a)*, *sendos(as),* to give the idea of *large, impressive,* or *two of them*:

Incorrect: *Se vino con sendo coche.*   He came with a huge car.

Correct: un coche grande

Incorrect: *Llegó con sendas cajas llenas*   She came with two boxes full of clothes.
  de ropa.

Correct: dos cajas

Collective Numerals

These numerals are nouns that represent a group (*couple, dozen, thousand,* etc.).

*Me dio **un par** de guantes.*	She gave me a pair of gloves.
*Hay **una decena** de patos.*	There are ten ducks.
*Compré **una docena** de huevos.*	I bought a dozen eggs.
*Vino **una veintena** de hombres.*	Twenty men came.
*Había **centenas** de personas.*	There were hundreds of people.
*Hubo **un centenar** de chicos.*	There were a hundred kids.
***Miles** de pájaros volaron.*	Thousands of birds flew away.
*Hay **un millar** de aficionados.*	There are a thousand fans.
*Sacó **un millón** en la lotería.*	She won a million in the lottery.

NOTES:

(1) While nouns like *veintena* and *treintena* represent *twenty* and *thirty*, *quincena* (*fifteen*) and *cuarentena* (*forty*) are also used without the preposition *de* to indicate *a two-week period* and *a quarantine*, respectively:

*La compañía empleó a una **quincena de***   The company hired about fifteen men.
  hombres.

*Le pagan por **quincena**.*   The pay him every fifteen days.

*Estuvieron en **cuarentena**.*   They were in quarantine.

(2) If the collective numeral is followed by *de* and a plural noun, the verb appears in the plural:

***Miles de** pájaros volaron.*   Thousands of birds flew away.

However, if the numeral is designating a specific number, the singular form of the verb is used:

***Una docena** cabía en la caja.*   One dozen fit in the box.

*Una **docena de huevos** cabía en la caja.*   One dozen eggs fit in the box.

Indefinite Adjectives

Indefinite adjectives point to the noun and indicate its number in an indefinite or imprecise manner. Many of these adjectives have four different endings to agree with the gender and number of the nouns. Some indefinite adjectives vary in either number or gender, while others are used exclusively in the plural form. There are also a few invariable adjectives.

Indefinite Adjectives with Variations of Gender and Number

A. The indefinite adjective *alguno* (*some, any, a*)

1. This adjective agrees in gender and number with the noun it qualifies (*alguno/a, algunos/as*), and takes the shortened form *algún* before masculine singular nouns. It can refer to animate and inanimate nouns and is usually placed before the noun:

Prefiero **algún** artículo más moderno.	I'd prefer a more modern article.
Quiero **alguna** novela corta.	I want a novel that is short.
Esperaba a **algunos** amigos.	He was waiting for some friends.
Llegarán de sorpresa **alguna** tarde.	Some afternoon they will arrive unexpectedly.

2. When placed after the noun, *alguno/a* takes the meaning of *ninguno/a* (*not any*). Notice that the sentences are in the negative:

No fue a fiesta **alguna**.	She didn't go to any party whatsoever.
No tuve informe **alguno**.	I didn't receive any reports at all.

3. *Alguno* is not the equivalent of the partitive *some* used in English. To convey the same idea, Spanish uses either the expression *un poco de* or the mass noun by itself.

Aceptaré **un poco de** dinero.	I'll accept some money.
¿Prefieres café?	Would you prefer some coffee?

   (Not: *Aceptaré* algún dinero. This is the short form of **alguno**, which is used before a masculine noun.)

There are some nouns, such as *bread*, which are mass nouns in English but not in Spanish. It is correct to say ***algún pan***, with the meaning of *a* or *any* loaf of bread.

Quiero algún pan de trigo que no tenga sal.	I want any loaf of wheat bread that doesn't have salt.

4. In some cases, *algunos* does not have exactly the same meaning as *unos*, even when both can be translated as *some* in English.

*Vi a **unos** chicos en la calle.*	I saw some children in the street. (indefinite amount; the street was not empty)
*Había **algunos** chicos en la calle.*	There were some children in the street. (a few; not all the ones I usually see)
*Cómpreme **unas** manzanas cuando vaya al mercado.*	Buy me some apples when you go to the market. (indefinite amount; the quantity is not important)
*Tráigame **algunas** manzanas para hacer dulce.*	Bring me some apples to make jam. (just a few)

The preposition *a* is used before an indefinite adjective or pronoun when it refers to a person (except after the verbs ***tener*** and ***haber***):

*Vi **a** algunos chicos.*	I saw some children.
Tengo algunos estudiantes.	I have some students.
Hay algunos estudiantes.	There are some students.

5. In order to negate a question where any forms of *alguno* appear, these adjectives are replaced by *ningún* or *ninguna*. *Ningún* is the short form of *ninguno* used before a masculine singular noun.

*¿Tienes **algún** sobre como éste que pueda usar?*	Do you have any envelopes like this one that I can use?
*No, no tengo **ningún** sobre de ese tamaño.*	No, I don't have any envelopes of that size.
*¿Recibió **alguna** carta hoy?*	Did you receive any letters today?
*No, **ninguna** carta ha llegado.*	No, no letters have arrived.

To avoid the repetition of the nouns ***sobre*** and ***carta*** in the preceding examples, the pronoun *ninguno* or *ninguna* may be used in the answers:

No, no tengo **ninguno*** de ese tamaño.	No, I don't have any of that size.
No, no recibí **ninguna**.	No, I didn't receive any.
¿Viste las películas de OO7?	Did you watch the OO7 movies?
No, no vi ninguna.	No, I didn't watch any.

6. The expression *alguno que otro* and its variations are used with the meaning of *a few*. Similar expressions in Spanish are *unos cuantos*, *unas cuantas*, *unos pocos*, *unas pocas*, *algunos*, and *algunas*:

Había **alguno que otro** árbol en medio del parque.	There were a few trees in the middle of the park.
Me dieron **alguna que otra** foto de recuerdo.	They gave me a few pictures as souvenirs.
En esa tienda encontré **unos cuantos** bolsos importados.	I found quite a few imported bags in that store.
Tenía **unas pocas** cosas amontonadas en el cuarto.	He had a few things piled up in his room.

B. The indefinite adjective *cierto* (certain)

This adjective agrees in gender and number with the noun it qualifies (*cierto/a*, *ciertos/as*).

Me contó **ciertas** cosas que no pude creer.	He told me certain things that I couldn't believe.
Hablamos de **cierta** persona responsable.	We discussed a certain person who was responsible.

NOTES:

(1) *Cierto* has the following meanings:

■ *fixed, determined, specific*

Quedaron en verse a **cierta** hora.	They agreed to see each other at a specific time.

■ *some*

Ciertos médicos hablan de una cura.	Some doctors talk of a cure.

The *singular* indefinite article (*un, una*) may precede *cierto* or *cierta*, in which case the vagueness of the meaning is emphasized:

Siento **un cierto** temor cuando hay tormenta.	I feel a certain fear when there is a storm. (I can't quite explain it.)

---

* The short form is not used because the adjective is not followed by the noun. As pronouns, *ninguno* and *ninguna* always appear in the singular form.

Tiene *una cierta* gracia al hablar.	She has a certain grace when she speaks. (I don't know how to define it.)

Also, *un cierto* and *una cierta* are synonyms of *un tal* and *una tal* (a certain), with reference to an unidentified person:

Recibí una carta de *un cierto (un tal)* Torres que trabaja en esa oficina.	I received a letter from a certain man named Torres, who works in that office.
Hablé con *una cierta (una tal)* María Pérez, que lo conocía.	I spoke with a certain woman named María Perez, who knew him.

(2) When placed after the noun, *cierto* takes the meaning of *sure* or *accurate*. In this position, the four variations of gender and number are used:

Se lleva la dirección **cierta**.	She is taking the right address with her.
Tenemos una lista con los nombres **ciertos**.	We have a list of the right names.

(3) Other uses of *cierto* include:

A ciencia cierta (with certainty, for sure)

No lo sé <u>a ciencia cierta</u> pero creo que Juan lo compró.	I don't know for sure, but I think that Juan bought it.

Por cierto, de cierto, ciertamente (certainly, truly)

Es muy bueno <u>por cierto</u>.	Certainly it is very good.
<u>De cierto</u> les digo que no tendremos vacaciones.	Truly, I tell you that we will not have a vacation.
<u>Ciertamente</u> lo ha probado.	She certainly has proved it.

Por cierto que (indeed, in fact)

<u>Por cierto que</u> es muy bonita.	She is very pretty indeed.

Lo cierto es que (the fact is that)

<u>Lo cierto es que</u> llamó.	The fact is that he called.

Exception: The English expression *certain other*, as in *certain other laws*, is rendered into Spanish as *algunas otras leyes* (Not: *ciertas otras leyes*).

C. The indefinite adjective *cuanto* (all the, every)

1. This adjective is always placed before the noun and agrees with it in gender and number (*cuanto/a, cuantos/as*). Without an accent mark, *cuanto* refers to the whole amount, and is equivalent to *all (of) the* or *everybody*:

Cuanto cuidado puso en esa tarea fue inútil.	All the care he put into that task was useless.
Cuanta gente vino, recibió una entrada gratis.	Everybody who came received a free ticket.
Agruparon a **cuantos** hombres se voluntarizaron.	They grouped all the men who volunteered.
Puedes darme **cuantas** excusas quieras.	You can give me all the excuses you want.

NOTES:

(1) *Cuanto,* and its variations, can be replaced by the equivalent forms of *todo el* (*all the*), plus *que*:

Todo el cuidado **que** puso en esa tarea fue inútil.	All the care he put into that task was useless.
Puedes darme **todas las** excusas **que** quieras.	You can give me all the excuses you want.

(2) *Cuantos/as*, preceded by *unos/as,* means *a few (of)* or *some*. Although these expressions are considered equivalent to *algunos/as* and *unos pocos, unas pocas,* they really give the idea of a larger amount:

Tiene **unas pocas** plantas en el jardín.	She has a few (some) plants in the garden.
Tiene **algunas** plantas.	She has a few plants.
Tiene **unas cuantas** plantas.	She has (quite) a few plants.

The phrase **unas cuantas** in this example indicates more plants than **unas pocas** or simply **algunas**.

2. With an accent mark, *cuánto* is used as an exclamatory adjective to show the magnitude of a certain thing (how much or how many):

¡Cuánto cuidado puso en eso!	How much care she put into that!
¡Cuánta gente vino!	(Look) How many people came!
¡Cuántos hombres lo dijeron!	How many men said it!
¡Cuántas excusas me dio!	How many excuses she gave me!

D. The indefinite adjective *demasiado* (*too much, too many*)

This adjective is always placed before the noun and agrees with it in gender and number (*demasiado/a, demasiados/as*). It always indicates excess in some way:

Puso **demasiado** queso en el pastel.	She put too much cheese in the pie.
Tenía **demasiada** salsa y no lo comí.	It had too much sauce and I did not eat it.
Ha cometido **demasiados** errores.	He has made too many mistakes.
Me ha hecho **demasiadas** promesas.	She has made me too many promises.

NOTES:

(1) All the variations of *demasiado* function as pronouns when the noun is not present:

Tenemos demasiados. *(vasos)*   We have too many. (glasses)

(2) *Demasiado* also functions as an adverb:

Trabajó demasiado hoy.	You worked too much today.
Pepa se arregló demasiado.	Pepa fixed herself up too much.
¡No comas demasiado!	Don't eat too much!
La necesito demasiado para dejarla ir.	I need her too much to let her go.

(3) When *demasiado* precedes a form of *poco*, it is used in the singular and means *not enough*. It can also be replaced by *muy* (*very*):

Muestra demasiado poca fe.	She does not show enough faith.
Tiene demasiado pocos apuntes.	He does not have enough notes.
Compró demasiado pocas manzanas.	He did not buy enough apples.
Muestra muy poca fe.	She shows very little faith.
Tiene muy pocos apuntes.	He has very few notes.
Compró muy pocas manzanas.	He bought very few apples.

(4) The English expression *too many other*, as in *They have too many other subjects to choose from*, could be rendered into Spanish as *Aparte de esas, ellos tienen demasiadas materias para elegir*.

E. The indefinite adjective *mismo* (same, similar, own)

This adjective agrees with the noun in gender and number (*mismo/a*, *mismos/as*).

1. When placed before the noun, it may be preceded by the definite article, in which case it has the meaning of *same*:

Tenía <u>el</u> **mismo** vestido.	She had the same dress on.
Viven en <u>la</u> **misma** casa.	They live in the same house.
Me gustan <u>los</u> **mismos** deportes.	I like the same sports.
Siempre veo <u>las</u> **mismas** caras.	I always see the same faces.
Esto es <u>del</u> **mismo** tamaño.	This is (of) the same size.

2. If preceded by a possessive adjective, *mismo* shows identity and is translated as *own*. The adjective *propio* is also used in similar cases, in all its variations of gender and number:

*Vivía en su **misma** casa.*	He lived in his own house.
*Lo pintó con sus **propias** manos.*	She painted it with her own hands.

3. When placed after the noun, *mismo* takes the meaning of *self* or *very*:

*Llamó el doctor **mismo**.*	The doctor himself called.
*Estaba parado en la puerta **misma**.*	He was standing at the very door.
*Se lo pidieron los estudiantes **mismos**.*	The students themselves asked him.
*Las secretarias **mismas** invitaron a sus jefes.*	The secretaries themselves invited their bosses.

4. After a personal pronoun or the name of a person, *mismo* means *self*. It varies by gender and number:

*Me lo entregó él **mismo**.*	He himself gave it to me.
*Vendrán ellas **mismas**.*	They themselves will come.
*Se lo trajo Miguel **mismo**.*	Miguel himself brought it to her.

5. After adverbs, *mismo* means *exactness*:

*Te llamaré mañana **mismo**.*	I will call you tomorrow (without delay, for sure).
*Lo recibimos ahora **mismo**.*	We received it just now.
*Estaba allí **mismo**.*	It was right there.

NOTES:

(1) If expressions like *mañana*, *tarde*, *noche*, and *medianoche* are preceded by a demonstrative adjective, *mismo* usually agrees with the noun:

*Aquella tarde **misma(o)**.*	That very afternoon.
*Esta noche **misma(o)**.*	Tonight. (this very night)

(2) If the definite article precedes the noun, *mismo* must agree in gender and number with the article:

*en las tardes **mismas** en que venía á vernos*	in those afternoons when she came to see us
*Ella tenía un cordón en el paraguas **mismo**.*	She had a string in the umbrella itself.

Notice the change introduced by the definite article in the following sentence:

Hasta China **mismo(a)** está involucrada.   Even China itself is involved.
Hasta la China **misma** está involucrada.   Even China itself is involved.

The same idea could also be expressed as follows:

Hasta **mismo** (la) China está involucrada.   Even China itself is involved.
Hasta la **misma** China está involucrada.   Even China itself is involved.

If the article is part of the noun, either form is used:

El Palacio Municipal está en La Habana   The Municipal Palace is right in La Habana.
   mismo(a).

6. *Lo mismo* is a nominalized form that represents the following expressions:

(a) *the same thing* (*la misma cosa, igual*):

Para mí es lo mismo.   It is the same to me.
A mí me da lo mismo.   It makes no difference to me.

(b) *just the same, in spite of, anyway*:

Lo quiero lo mismo.   I love him just the same (in spite of it).
Lo haremos lo mismo.   We'll do it anyway.

(c) *the same old thing*:

Es lo mismo de siempre.   It is the same old thing.

(d) *the same as*:

Será lo mismo que una visita al museo.   It will be the same as a visit to the museum.

NOTES:

The expression *el mismo* translates as:

(1) *he himself* (with an accent mark on *él*, since it is a pronoun in this case):

Está muy bien hecho. **Él mismo** lo hizo.   It is very well done. He did it himself.

Being a pronoun, *él* changes to *ella*, *ellos*, or *ellas*, depending on the subject:

¡Qué lindo! Ella misma lo hizo.   How pretty! She did it herself.

(2) *his usual self*, referring to a human being:

Juan es **el mismo** muchacho de siempre.   Juan is the same old guy. He'll never change.
   No cambiará.

(3) *the same* (masculine singular):

Quiero **el mismo** producto.	I want the same product.

The preceding examples merely compare the meaning of **el mismo** to **lo mismo**. However, it is necessary to remember that in Notes (2) and (3), the other three definite articles (*la, los,* and *las*) may also be used as needed, in which case *mismo* agrees in gender and number:

María es **la misma** de siempre.	María is the same old girl.
Quiero **los mismos** productos.	I want the same products.
Me interesan **las mismas** materias.	I am interested in the same subjects.

7. Common idiomatic expressions with *mismo*:

al mismo tiempo *(at the same time)*

Salieron de vacaciones al mismo tiempo.	They went on vacation at the same time.

así mismo *(regardless, anyway, all the same)*

Lo invitaremos así mismo.	We'll invite him all the same.

eso mismo *(phrase that indicates approval)*

Sí, eso mismo.	Yes, that's right.
Eso mismo.	That's right.

por eso mismo *(for that reason, precisely)*

Por eso mismo lo decimos los dos.	For that reason (That's why) the two of us say it.

el mismo de siempre *(same as always; no change)*

Juan es el mismo de siempre. Insiste en quedarse en casa.	Juan hasn't changed. He insists on staying home.

NOTE:

Mismo agrees in gender and number with any of the definite articles *(el, la, los, las).*

F. The indefinite adjective *mucho* (much, a lot of, many)

This adjective agrees with the noun in gender and number (*mucho/a, muchos/as*). As an adjective, it is always placed before the noun:

Tiene **mucho** orgullo de su familia.	He is very proud of his family.
El cerdo tiene **mucha** grasa.	Pork has a lot of fat.

La leche tiene **muchas** calorías.	Milk has a lot of calories.
Hay **muchos** chicos aquí.	There are many boys here.

NOTES:

(1) *Mucho* (and all its variations) is also a pronoun:

Esta comida tiene **mucha** (grasa), pero es deliciosa.	This meal has a lot (of fat) but is delicious.

(2) *Mucho* functions as an adverb. In this case it has only one form:

Siempre estudia **mucho**.	She always studies hard.

(3) *Mucho* (and its variations) also indicates *too much, too many, plenty*, and is a synonym of *demasiado*:

No me des más. Eso es **mucho**.	Don't give me more. That's too much.
Te daré algunas. Son **muchas** para mí.	I'll give you some. There are too many for me.

(4) *Lo mucho* is a nominalized form of the adjective:

Es muy sencilla por **lo mucho** que tiene.	She is very modest considering how much (money) she has.

(5) When *mucho*, followed by *más* or *menos*, precedes a noun, it must agree with the noun in gender and number:

Quiero **muchos más** <u>tomates</u> que los que me das.	I want many more tomatoes than the ones you give me.
Los trabajadores tienen **muchas menos** <u>esperanzas</u> con ese sindicato.	The workers have a lot less hope with that union.
Necesito **mucho más** <u>dinero</u>.	I need a lot more money.
Prefiero **mucha más** <u>tranquilidad</u>.	I prefer much more tranquility.

(6) When *mucho*, followed by *más* or *menos*, precedes an adjective, it is invariable:

La lección es **mucho más** <u>difícil</u>.	The lesson is a lot more difficult.
Era **mucho menos** <u>probable</u>.	It was a lot less probable.

(7) With the comparatives of inequality *mejor, peor, mayor*, and *menor, mucho* is invariable:

Juan es **mucho mayor** que yo.	Juan is a lot older than I am.
La fiebre está **mucho peor** hoy que ayer.	The fever is much worse today than yesterday.

G. The indefinite adjective *ninguno* (*none, no one, not any*)

This adjective agrees with the noun in gender and number (*ninguno/a*, *ningunos/as*). Before a masculine singular noun, *ninguno* becomes *ningún*:

*No tengo **ningún** amigo.*	I have no friends.
*No queremos **ninguna** planta.*	We don't want any plants.

NOTES:

(1) The singular form *ningún* or *ninguna* is used even when the context indicates a plural noun:

*No había **ninguna** chica linda.*	There were no pretty girls.
*No tenían **ningún** libro bueno.*	They didn't have any good books.

However, the plural forms are generally used when the nouns are plural in nature, as in words like ***tenazas*** (*tongs*), ***tijeras*** (*scissors*) or ***pantalones*** (*pants*), although the singular forms are also used:

*No tenían **ningunas** tenazas que fueran baratas.*	They didn't have any tongs that were cheap.
*No encontré **ningunos** pantalones de algodón.*	I didn't find any cotton pants.
*No hay **ninguna** tijera en el cajón.*	There are no scissors in the drawer.
*No quiero **ningún** pantalón de lana.*	I don't want any woolen pants.

(2) When *ninguno* functions as a pronoun, the singular forms *ninguno* and *ninguna* are usually used, even for plural meanings (the shortened form *ningún* is not used as a pronoun):

*¿Tienes **algún** lápiz que pueda usar?*	Do you have a pencil that I can use?
*No, no tengo **ninguno**.*	No, I don't have any.
*¿Hay **algunas** peras en la cesta?*	Are there any pears in the basket?
*No, no hay **ninguna**.*	No, there are none.
*¿Hay **algunos** pesos en el cajón?*	Are there any pesos in the drawer?
*No, no hay **ninguno**.*	No, there aren't any.

(3) If the noun is inherently plural, the singular form is usually preferred:

¿Viste las tijeras sobre la mesa?	Did you see the scissors on the table?
*No, no vi **ninguna**.*	No, I didn't see any.
¿Quiere llevarse los pantalones rojos?	Do you want to take the red pants?
*No, no quiero llevar **ninguno**.*	No, I don't want to take any.

(4) If *ninguno* precedes the verb, the negative *no* is not used:

***Ninguna** vi.*	I have not seen any.
***Ninguno** quiero llevar.*	I do not want to take any.
But: ***No** vi **ninguna**.*	
***No** quiero llevar **ninguno**.*	

H. The indefinite adjective *otro* (*another, other*)

This adjective agrees with the noun in gender and number (*otro/a*, *otros/as*). It is always placed before the noun:

*Ahora tienen **otro** niño.*	Now they have another child.
*Escucharé **otra** canción.*	I will listen to another song.
*Vinieron **otros** estudiantes.*	Other students came.
*Esas son **otras** razones.*	Those are other reasons.

NOTES:

(1) As a pronoun, *otro* varies in gender and number:

*Quiero **otro**.*	I want another one.
***Otra** llegó.*	Another one came.
*Había **otros** en la caja.*	There were others in the box.
*Teníamos **otras** blancas.*	We had other white ones.

The pronouns *otros* and *otras*, preceded by *algunos(as)*, have the meaning of *a few*:

*Quisiera **algunos otros**. Estos no son suficientes.*	I would like a few others. These are not enough.

(2) A definite article may precede any of the forms of *otro*:

***El otro** niño lo quería.*	The other child wanted it.
***La otra** mañana lo vi.*	I saw him the other morning.
*Compré **los otros** tomates.*	I bought the other tomatoes.
*Trajo **las otras** cosas.*	He brought the other things.

El otro and *la otra* are used with the meaning of *the other man* or *the other woman*, in the context of a love triangle:

*Estaba con **la otra** chica.*	He was with the other girl.

This connotation is more emphatic when *otro* or *otra* is used as a pronoun:

*La vieron con **el otro**.*	They saw her with the other one. (the other man)

(3) *Otro* preceded by indefinite articles: as opposed to the English use of *another* and *one other* before the noun, the indefinite articles **un** and **una** are <u>not</u> used before *otro* in Spanish:

*Déme **otra** oportunidad.*	Give me another opportunity.
*Había **otro** recurso.*	There was one other resource.

(4) *Otro* may be preceded by possessive adjectives:

*Aquí están **tus otras** medias.*	Here are your other socks.
***Su otro** amigo le mandará el boleto.*	His other friend will send him the ticket.

(5) *Otro* may be preceded by demonstrative adjectives or pronouns:

*Me gustan **estos otros** duraznos.*	I like these other peaches.
*No me dé **esas otras**.*	Don't give me those other ones.

(6) *Otro* follows other indefinite adjectives. It can function as an adjective or a pronoun:

Otro as an adjective:

*No me lo pidas. Tengo **muchas otras** cosas que hacer.*	Don't ask me. I have many other things to do.
*Visitó **muchos otros** museos interesantes.*	She visited many other interesting museums.

<u>Not</u>: *muchos otros interesantes museos* (The expression *muchos otros* must immediately precede the noun.)

Otro as a pronoun:

*Encontraron **algunas otras**.*	They found other ones.
*Lo dijo **alguna otra**.*	Someone else said it. (a woman)

(7) The indefinite adjective *tantos/as* (*so many*) may be placed before or after *otros/as*, although there is a change in meaning. Notice that *otros/as* may function as an adjective or a pronoun:

*Hice **tantos otros** (planes) que ni recuerdo ahora.*	I made so many others (other plans) that I don't even remember now.
*Tenía diez postales y yo le di **otras tantas** (postales) para su colección.*	She had ten postcards and I gave her an equal amount (of them) for her collection.

(8) The English expression *every other*, as in *every other day*, is rendered into Spanish as *por medio*:

*Van al médico día **por medio**.*	They go to the doctor every other day.

(9) Cardinal numerals follow *otros/as* in Spanish:

*Compré **otros dos** cuadernos.*	I bought two other notebooks.

(10) The English expression *other than* is not rendered in Spanish as a form of *otro* plus *que*; instead, Spanish uses *diferente(s) de* or a subjunctive phrase with *que* and the negative form of *to be* (*ser*) in the required tense: *que no sea(n), que no fuera(n)*, etc:

*Prefiero un anillo **diferente de** éste.*	I prefer a ring other than this.
*Puedes encontrar este tema en algunos poemas **diferentes de** los que están incluidos aquí.*	You can find this theme in poems other than the ones included here.
*Quieren comprar una casa **que no sea** la que les ofreció él.*	They want to buy a house other than the one he offered them.

I. The indefinite adjective *poco* (*little, a little, few, a few, some*)

This adjective agrees with the noun in gender and number (*poco/a, pocos/as*):

*Tengo **poco** tiempo.*	I don't have much time.
*Me queda **poco** dinero. Tendré que ir al banco.*	I have little money left. I'll have to go to the bank.
*Tendrá **poca** paciencia con él.*	She will have little patience with him.
*Hay **pocos** autos en la calle hoy. Será por el feriado.*	There are few cars in the street today. It must be because of the holiday.
*Tiene **pocas** ambiciones.*	He has few ambitions.

NOTES:

(1) Synonyms of *pocos* and *pocas* are *alguno que otro, alguna que otra; uno que otro, una que otra:*

*Trajo **alguna que otra** cosa.*	He brought a few (some) things.
*Agrégale **una que otra** pasa.*	Add just a few raisins.

Although the expressions *unos cuantos* and *unas cuantas* translate into English as *a few* or *some*, they suggest a larger amount than what is indicated by the preceding expressions:

*Trajo **unas cuantas** cosas.*	He brought quite a few things.

(2) The combination *a few other* plus a noun is translated into Spanish as ***algún otro, alguna otra, algunos otros, algunas otras***:

Me devolvió el párrafo con **algunas otras** sugerencias.	He gave me back the paragraph with a few other suggestions.

<u>Not</u>: *con otras pocas (or pocas otras) sugerencias*

The negative form *not many other*, used instead of *a few* as in *with not many other suggestions*, is rendered into Spanish as ***sin*** (*without*) ***muchas otras sugerencias***, rather than the phrase ***con no muchas otras sugerencias***.

(3) *Poco* also functions as an adverb and is usually placed after the verb in everyday use:

Siempre <u>como</u> **poco** de noche.	I always eat little at night.
Poco <u>se sabe</u> del accidente.	Little is known about the accident.

(4) *Un poco de* plus the noun means *a little (bit) of* or *some*. Only the masculine singular form *poco* is used:

Requiere **un poco de** atención.	It requires a little bit of attention.
Agregue **un poco de** arroz.	Add a little bit of rice.

■ Although this expression (*un poco de*) is mostly used with mass nouns, it is also common with plural nouns that are seen as a whole:

Quisiera **un poco de** arvejas.	I would like some peas.

■ *Un poco de* may be replaced by *algo de* to express *some, a little (bit) of*:

Agregue **algo de** arroz.	Add a little bit of rice.
Debemos **algo de** dinero.	We owe some money.

■ The expressions *algo de comer* and *algo de beber* are very common and are used to indicate *something to eat or drink*:

¿Quieres **algo de comer**?	Do you want anything to eat?

(5) *Un poco* modifies adjectives and verbs, and functions as an adverb:

Debe estudiar **un poco**.	He must study a little.
Manejo **un poco**, pero siempre de día.	I drive a little, but always during the day.
Es **un poco** complicado.	It is a little complicated.
Su madre está **un poco** cansada.	Her mother is a little tired.

Un poco may be replaced by *algo* when the meaning is *somewhat*:

*Está **un poco (algo)** triste estos días.*	She is somewhat sad lately.

The plurals *unos pocos* and *unas pocas* function as adjectives or pronouns, and translate as *a few*:

*Llegaron **unos pocos** cajones.*	A few crates arrived.
*Quedan **unas pocas** (hojas) en el cerezo.*	A few (leaves) remain on the cherry tree.

(6) When *demasiado* (*too*) precedes a form of *poco*, it is used in the masculine singular:

*Tiene **demasiado poco** interés.*	He shows too little interest.
*Dice **demasiado pocas** verdades.*	She makes too few truthful statements. / She doesn't make too many truthful statements.

J. The indefinite adjective *raro* (*few, not frequent, not many*)

This adjective agrees with the noun in gender and number (*raro/a, raros/as*). However, as an indefinite adjective, it is more commonly used in the feminine form:

***Rara** vez vino a vernos.*	He didn't come to see us much.
*Lo veíamos en **raras** ocasiones.*	We saw him on just a few occasions.
***Raro** sermón evidenciaba lo que él realmente insinuaba.*	An occasional sermon would show what he was really suggesting.
*Mamá leía en **raros** momentos.*	Mom would read on very few occasions.

NOTES:

(1) The adjective *raro* in the expression *¡Qué raro!* means *strange*:

*¡**Qué raro** que ella lo haya dicho!*	How strange it is for her to have said it!
*¡**Qué raro** es Juan! No lo entiendo a veces.*	How strange Juan is! I do not understand him sometimes.

(2) The adverb *raramente* means *rarely, seldom*:

*Venía **raramente** a la clase.*	He would rarely come to class.

It also means *oddly* or *strangely*, but it is not used very often in that form:

*Los muebles estaban **raramente** distribuidos en el cuarto.*	The furniture was oddly arranged in the room.

Better:

*Los muebles estaban distribuidos en el cuarto de una manera muy **rara**.*	The furniture was arranged in the room in a very odd fashion.

K. The indefinite adjective *tanto* (*so much, so many*)

1. This adjective agrees with the noun in gender and number (*tanto/a*, *tantos/as*) and is always placed before the noun:

No quiere **tanto** té.	He doesn't want so much tea.
Tanta alegría me conmueve.	So much happiness moves me.
¡No sabía que tenías **tantos** alumnos!	I didn't know that you had so many students!
Había **tantas** cosas bonitas que gastamos todo el dinero.	There were so many nice things that we spent all the money.

2. As a <u>pronoun</u>, *tanto* is usually placed after the verb. The position before the verb adds emphasis to the pronoun. In this case, the pronoun is also pronounced more emphatically than the rest of the sentence (the expression is underlined in English for illustration only):

No quiere **tanto**. *(café)*	He doesn't want so much (coffee).
¡**Tanto** no quiere! *(café)*	He doesn't want <u>so much</u>! (coffee)
¡**Tanta** me conmueve! *(generosidad)*	<u>So much</u> (generosity) moves me!
No sabía que tenías **tantos**.	I didn't know you had so many.
¡No sabía que **tantos** tenías!	I didn't know you had <u>so many</u>!
Había **tantas** que gastamos todo el dinero. *(gangas)*	There were so many that we spent all the money. (bargains)
¡**Tantas** había que gastamos todo el dinero!	There were <u>so many</u>, that we spent all the money!

3. As an <u>adverb</u>, only the masculine singular form *tanto* is used. It may be placed before or after the verb:

Viaja **tanto** que no tiene tiempo para descansar.	She travels so much that she does not have any time to rest.
Tanto estudia que sacará una A.	He studies so much that he will get an A.

Before an adjective or another adverb, *tanto* becomes *tan:*

Era **tan** <u>buena</u> que la extrañé cuando se fue.	She was so good that I missed her when she left.
No me gusta algo **tan** <u>triste</u>.	I don't like something so sad.
Lo hizo **tan** <u>bien</u> que lo felicité.	He did it so well that I congratulated him.

4. Other uses of *tanto* include:

(a) *por tanto, por lo tanto* (*therefore*)

Por lo tanto, lo haremos ahora.   Therefore, we'll do it now.

(b) a numeral plus *y tantos* (*more than*)

Tenía cincuenta y tantos años.   He was fifty-something.

(c) *algún tanto* (*a little*)

Me habló algún tanto.   He spoke to me a little.

(d) *un tanto* (*a little*)

Estaba un tanto nerviosa.   She was a little nervous.

(e) *un tanto* (*a certain, fixed amount*)

Recibe un tanto por hora.   He makes (earns) a certain amount per hour.

(f) *tanto* (as a noun, it means *point* or *goal* in a game)

Ganaron por dos tantos a uno.   They won two to one.

(g) *un tanto por ciento* (*a percentage*)

Le dan un tanto por ciento de las ganancias.   They give him a percentage of the profits.

(h) *entre tanto, en tanto* (*in the meantime*)

Entre tanto lo haremos.   We'll do it in the meantime.

(i) *tanto mejor; tanto peor* (*so much the better; too bad*)

Si lo acepta, tanto mejor.   If he accepts it, so much the better.
Si no viene, tanto peor.   If he does not come, too bad.

(j) *con tanto que, con tal que* (*provided*)

Te lo diré con tanto que te lo guardes.   I'll tell you, provided you keep it to yourself.

(k) *estar al tanto* (*to know; to be familiar with*)

Estoy al tanto del programa.   I know about the program.

(l) *tanto más* (*especially*)

Vamos a practicar, tanto más (más aún)   We'll practice, especially now that he has
cuando él lo ha sugerido.   suggested it.

(m) *no es para tanto* (*it is not so bad*)

Se queja pero no es para tanto.   She complains, but it is not so bad.

L. The indefinite adjective *todo* (*each, every, all of it, all of them, whole*)

This adjective agrees with the noun in gender and number (*todo/a, todos/as*). Depending on its meaning, it may be placed before or after the noun. Observe the following cases:

1. *every, each*: before the noun (used in the singular form):

***Todo** problema tiene una solución.*   Every (each) problem has a solution.
***Toda** regla será obedecida.*   Every rule will be obeyed.

2. *whole; all over*: before the noun (used in the singular form):

***Todo** el pastel se comió.*   He ate the whole pie.
*Hay moscas en **toda** la casa.*   There are flies all over the house.
*Recibió noticias de él durante **todo** un año.*   She received news from him for a whole year.
*Llovió **toda** una semana.*   It rained for a whole week.

NOTES:

(1) The expression *all of it* cannot be translated into Spanish as *todo de él* or *todo de ella*. To express this, include the noun, as in *todo el pastel*, or a direct object pronoun such as *lo*:

*Se comió **todo** el pastel.*   He ate all the pie.
*Se lo comió **todo**.*   He ate all of it.

(2) When *todo/a/os/as* precedes another adjective, it means *entirely, completely, extremely, all*:

*El teatro está **todo** lleno.*   The theater is completely full.
*Estaba **toda** contenta.*   She was all happy.
*El está **todo** triste.*   He is all sad.
*La blusa está **toda** arrugada.*   The blouse is entirely wrinkled.
*El patio está **todo** cubierto de nieve.*   The patio is all covered with snow.
*Estaban **todos** tristes.*   They were extremely sad.
*But: **Todos** estaban tristes.*   All of them were sad.

(3) With personal pronouns, *todos/as* is placed before or after the pronoun:

Todas *ellas estaban allí.*	All of them were there.
Deben hacerlo ustedes **todos**.	All of you must do it.

(4) Meaning *all the, all of the, todos/as* is placed before the noun:

Todos *los chicos lo saben.*	All the children know it.
Todas *las azucenas son blancas.*	All of the lilies are white.

■ When the noun is preceded by the neuter article *lo*, the masculine singular form *todo* is placed before the article:

Todo *lo trágico sucedió.*	Everything tragic happened.
Trajeron **todo** *lo demás.*	They brought the rest.

■ The definite article is generally left out in several fixed expressions, such as the following:

a toda prisa	fast
a toda velocidad	fast
a todo vapor	fast
con toda tranquilidad	very calmly
de todo tipo	of all types
en todo momento	always, at all times
a todas partes	everywhere
de todas maneras	anyway
de todas formas	anyway
de todos colores	(of) all colors
de todos calibres	of all sizes
por todos lados	everywhere, all over
por todas partes	everywhere, all over

M. The indefinite adjective *uno que otro* (*just a few, some*)

This adjective agrees with the noun in gender and number. It is usually used in the singular form:

Había **uno que otro** *niño en el patio de la escuela.*	There were just a few children in the school yard.
Una que otra *calle del pueblo estaba arbolada.*	A few of the streets in the town had trees.

As a pronoun, both the singular and the plural forms are used, although *algunos(as)* is a better choice for the plural:

Había **uno que otro** en el patio de la escuela.	There were just a few in the school yard.
Una que otra estaba arbolada.	A few had trees.
Todas las casas del barrio tienen fondo y **unas que otras** (**algunas**) también tienen jardín al frente.	Every house in the neighborhood has a back yard, and a few also have a garden in the front.
Unos que otros (**Algunos**) se adhirieron a la huelga. (trabajadores)	A few (workers) joined the strike.

Indefinite Adjectives That Vary Only in Number or Gender

A. The indefinite adjective *bastante* (*enough, plenty, quite a few, considerable*)

This indefinite adjective varies only in number (*bastante-s*). It also functions as a pronoun:

Ya tengo **bastante** café. No me des más.	I already have enough coffee. Don't give me any more.
Hubo **bastante** lluvia en Florida.	There was plenty of rain in Florida.
Tuvimos **bastantes** clases juntos.	We had quite a few classes together.
Habrá **bastantes** alumnos allí.	There will be plenty of students there.
Tiene **bastante** (dinero) para vivir bien.	He has enough (money) to live well. [pronoun]
No quiere ver más cuadros. Ya vio **bastantes**.	She doesn't want to see any more paintings. She has already seen enough. [pronoun]

B. The indefinite adjective *cual* (*which*)

This indefinite adjective varies only in number (*cual-es*). It is also called an interrogative adjective, depending on how it is used, and indicates a selection of one or more items among others. Without the noun, it becomes an indefinite (or interrogative) pronoun. As an interrogative, it must carry an accent mark called an occasional accent because it distinguishes different functions.

¿**Cuál** (libro) leíste?	Which one (book) did you read?
¿**Cuáles** (monedas) se usaron durante la dictadura?	Which ones (coins) were used during the dictatorship?
No me dijo **cuál** quería. (cuadro)	He didn't tell me which one he wanted. (painting)

Notice the cases where *cual* does not carry an accent mark in the following note.

NOTE:

The indefinite adjective or pronoun *cual* must not be confused with the relative pronoun, which has an antecedent (underlined noun in the example below) and is preceded by a definite article. As a relative pronoun, it does not carry an accent mark:

Indefinite adjective: ¿**Cuál** vestido te gusta?	Which dress do you like?
Indefinite pronoun: ¿**Cuál** te gusta?	Which one do you like?
Relative pronoun: Ese <u>vestido</u>, **el cual** cuesta mucho, es de seda.	That <u>dress</u>, which costs a lot, is made of silk.

Some expressions with *cual* include forms with and without accent marks:

- **a cuál más** (*each one*)

Tenía muchas flores, a cuál más bonita.	She had many flowers and each one was prettier than the last.

- **cuál más cuál menos** (*all*)

Cuál más cuál menos, todos trajeron algo.	Some more, some less, everybody brought something.

- **cual si** (*as if*)

Reaccionó cual si fuera el dueño.	He reacted as if he were the owner.

- **tal cual** (*just as it is; as*)

Él me lo dio tal cual estaba.	He gave it to me just as it was.

- **tal para cual** (*similar*

María y Pedro son tal para cual.	María and Pedro resemble each other.

- **cada cual** (*everyone*)

Cada cual hace lo que quiere.	Each one does what (s)he wants.

C. The indefinite adjective *cualquier* (*any, anyone, anybody*)

Although this indefinite adjective has only one form for both genders before the noun, it takes the form *cualquiera*, also for both genders, when placed after the noun:

cualquier libro, un libro cualquiera	any book
cualquier maleta, una maleta cualquiera	any suitcase

As a pronoun, ***cualquiera*** means *anyone, anybody*:

Se lo dieron a cualquiera.   They gave it to anybody.

D. The indefinite adjective *múltiple* (*multiple, complex*)

This indefinite adjective varies only in number (*múltiple-s*). It may be placed before or after the noun:

*Falleció por causa de sus **múltiples** heridas.*   He died of multiple wounds.

*Es un proceso **múltiple** que requiere mucha*   It is a complex process that requires a lot of
atención.   attention.

E. The indefinite adjective *semejante* (*such, of that type*)

This indefinite adjective varies only in number (*semejante-s*):

No entiendo cómo ha podido darme   I can't understand how she could have given
***semejante** excusa.*   me such an excuse.

*Es increíble que tenga **semejantes** problemas.*   It's incredible that he has such problems.

If *semejante-s* is placed after the noun, the indefinite article precedes the noun:

*¡Cómo ha podido decirte una cosa **semejante**!*   How could he tell you such a thing!

NOTES:

(1) After a noun, ***semejante a*** means *similar to*:

*No creo que tenga problemas **semejantes a***   I don't think she has problems similar to mine
los míos.   (like mine).

(2) Before the noun, ***semejante(s)*** and ***tal(es)*** have the same meaning:

No acepté semejante (tal) proposición.   I didn't accept such a proposal.

F. The indefinite adjective *suficiente* (*enough*)

This indefinite adjective varies only in number (*suficiente-s*). It may be used before or after the noun:

*Me gustaría tener **suficiente** dinero para eso.*   I would like to have enough money for that.

*Creo que ella tiene razones **suficientes**.*   I think she has enough reasons.

Tiene suficientes (demasiadas) razones para no hacerlo. | She has enough (other) reasons not to do it.

Not: Tiene suficientes otras razones para no hacerlo.

G. The indefinite adjective *tal* (such, such a, that)

This indefinite adjective varies only in number (*tal-es*):

No sé qué haría yo en **tales** circunstancias.	I don't know what I would do in such circumstances.
Lo dijo con **tal** seriedad que todos lo creímos.	He said it so seriously that all of us believed it.
Es la primera vez que admite **tal** cosa.	It's the first time that she has admitted such a thing.
Creo que fue a **tal** hotel en Madrid.	I think he went to that hotel (that you mentioned) in Madrid.

NOTE:

When *tal* is used before a proper noun and is preceded by an article, the expression has a contemptuous connotation:

Me presentó a **una tal** Pepa que vivía allí.	She introduced me to a certain Pepa who lived there.
La tal Pepa se consideraba su amiga.	That Pepa considered herself her friend.

The Indefinite Adjective *Varios* (*Several*), Used Only in the Plural Form

This indefinite adjective varies only in gender. The feminine form is *varias*:

Hay **varios** documentos para firmar.	There are several documents to be signed.
Tiene **varias** clases los lunes.	She has several classes on Mondays.
Las clases que tiene que tomar son **varias**.	There are several classes he has to take.

When *varios* is placed after the noun, it means *different:*

Pintó el cielo con colores varios.	He painted the sky with different colors.

But:

Pintó el cielo con varios colores.	He painted the sky with several colors.

Indefinite Adjectives That Are Invariable in Form

A. The indefinite adjective *cada* (*each*)

Although it is an indefinite adjective, *cada* has a distributive value and is used only in the singular form:

Cada *documento tiene un sello.*	Each document has a stamp.
*Le dieron un recibo a **cada** persona.*	They gave each person a receipt.

As a pronoun, *cada* is followed by *uno* or *una* (*each one*), according to the noun:

Cada uno *tiene un sello.*	Each one has a stamp.
*Le dieron un recibo a **cada una**.*	They gave each one a receipt.

B. The indefinite adjective *harto* (*rather, very*)

This indefinite adjective is not used in some regions. It is the equivalent of *muy* (*very*):

*Dijo cosas **harto** interesantes.*	She spoke about things that were very interesting.

It is also the irregular past participle of the verb *hartar* (*to satisfy, to fill to excess*). When this participle functions as an adjective, it agrees with the noun in gender and number (*harto/a, hartos/as*) and has the meaning of *tired to the limit, full, completely satisfied with food*:

*Estoy **harta** de todo.*	I'm fed up with everything.
*Los chicos están **hartos** de los días de lluvia.*	The children are tired of the rainy days.
*Están **hartas**; no quieren el postre.*	They are full; they don't want the dessert.

Interrogative and Exclamatory Adjectives

The words *qué*, *cuál(-es),* and *cuánto/-a/-os/-as* are indefinite adjectives that become interrogative and exclamatory adjectives when they are placed before the noun in questions or exclamations. All of them carry accent marks.

Qué

Qué is invariable in form and is equivalent to *what* in English. Notice that the indefinite article (*un* or *una*) is not used in Spanish before the singular noun when *qué* is an exclamatory adjective:

¡**Qué** tragedia la de Alberto!	What a tragedy happened to Alberto!
¡**Qué** libro interesante!	What an interesting book!
¡**Qué** pueblitos lindos hay en España!	What pretty little towns there are in Spain!
¡**Qué** chicas inteligentes son sus hijas!	How intelligent his daughters are!
¿**Qué** receta quieres?	What recipe do you want?
¿**Qué** estudiantes faltaron a clase?	What students missed class?

Other Uses of *Qué* Depending on the Following Word

A. The expression *Qué* + an adjective is the equivalent of English *how:*

¡**Qué** triste!	How sad!

B. *Qué* plus a verb is translated in English as *what*:

¡**Qué** te parece!	What do you think! *or* Look at that!
¿**Qué** te parece esto?	What do you think about this?

C. *Qué* followed by an adverb is equivalent to *how* in English:

¡**Qué** bien lo hizo!	How well he did it!

Cuál

Cuál has a plural form, *cuáles,* but does not change for gender. It is used more as an interrogative pronoun, however, without the noun:

*¿**Cuál** quieres, la receta de sopa o la de guiso?*	Which recipe do you want, the one for soup or the one for stew?
*¿**Cuáles** vas a comprar, las uvas de Chile o las de California?*	Which grapes are you going to buy? The ones from Chile or those from California?
*¿**Cuáles** se perdieron?*	Which ones got lost?

NOTES:

(1) When the noun is present in sentences like the preceding one, *qué* is used more often than *cuál* or *cuáles*. The use of *cuál* or *cuáles* seems to signal more the fact that there is a selection:

*¿**Qué** receta quieres?*	Which recipe do you want?
*¿**Cuál** de estas recetas quieres?*	Which one of these recipes do you want?

(2) When *cuál(es)* keeps its function as an interrogative word within a sentence, it carries the accent mark:

*No tengo idea **cuál(es)** quiere.*	I have no idea which one(s) he wants.

Cuánto

Cuánto varies for gender and number and becomes *cuánta, cuántas,* and *cuántos*. It is translated into English as *how much* or *how many*:

*¡**Cuánto** arroz fue importado!*	How much rice was imported!
*¡**Cuánta** grasa tiene la comida!*	How much fat this meal has!
*¿**Cuántas** chicas llegaron?*	How many girls came?
*¿**Cuántos** escritores vinieron?*	How many writers came?

5

The Future Tense

The Spanish future tense is equivalent to the English tense formed with the auxiliary words *shall* and *will*. There are three ways of representing future actions in Spanish: the informal future, the simple future, and the future perfect.

The Informal Future

This tense is most frequently used to express future actions in spoken Spanish. It is formed with the present tense of *ir* (to go), the preposition *a*, and the infinitive of the main verb. (In English, the present continuous or progressive form of *to be* is used with the infinitive of the main verb.)

Present tense of *ir*	*a* + infinitive	Present Progressive in English
yo voy	a cantar	I am going to sing
tú vas	a comer	you are going to eat
él va	a vivir	he is going to live
ella va	a cenar	she is going to have dinner
Ud. va	a preguntar	you are going to ask
nosotros/as vamos	a dormir	we are going to sleep
vosotros/as vais	a reír	you are going to laugh
ellos van	a llorar	they are going to cry
ellas van	a decidir	they are going to decide
Uds. van	a caminar	you are going to walk

NOTE:

The informal future may be replaced by the present tense of the verb that appears in the infinitive, without changing the meaning of the sentence.

Yo voy a cantar mañana.　　I'm going to sing tomorrow.
Yo canto mañana.　　I sing tomorrow.

The Simple Future

The simple future is built on a single base word, which happens to be the infinitive of the verb. To form the simple future of *-ar*, *-er*, and *-ir* verbs, the endings *-é, -ás, -á, -emos, -éis,* and *-án* are added to the infinitive of the verb. The six basic personal pronouns are used in the following examples:

	mirar	**conocer**	**sentir**
yo	mirar**é**	conocer**é**	sentir**é**
tú	mirar**ás**	conocer**ás**	sentir**ás**
él	mirar**á**	conocer**á**	sentir**á**
nosotros	mirar**emos**	conocer**emos**	sentir**emos**
vosotros	mirar**éis**	conocer**éis**	sentir**éis**
ellos	mirar**án**	conocer**án**	sentir**án**

Practicarás mucho castellano.	You will practice a lot of Spanish.
Comeremos en este lugar.	We will eat in this place.
Vivirá aquí hasta julio.	He will live here until July.
Me levantaré a las seis.	I will get up at six.
No **tendremos** lluvia.	We will not have rain.

NOTES:

(1) All the forms have an accent mark on the last syllable, with the exception of the *nosotros/as* forms, which are stressed on the next-to-last syllable but do not carry a written accent.

(2) To conjugate reflexive verbs such as ***levantarse*** (*to get up*), write the corresponding reflexive pronoun (*me, te, se, os,* or *nos*) in front of the verb and add the infinitive with the corresponding endings:

yo	me	levantar**é**
tú	te	levantar**ás**
él	se	levantar**á**
ella	se	levantar**á**
Ud.	se	levantar**á**
nosotros/as	nos	levantar**emos**
vosotros/as	os	levantar**éis**
ellos	se	levantar**án**
ellas	se	levantar**án**
Uds.	se	levantar**án**

Me vestiré temprano.	I will get dressed early.

(3) To negate a sentence with a verb in the future tense, the word *no* is placed after the personal pronoun, if given, and before the conjugated verb. If the verb is reflexive, the word *no* has to be placed before the reflexive pronoun:

Tú no cantarás en el coro.	You will not sing in the choir.
No me vestiré tarde.	I will not get dressed late.

Irregular Forms of the Simple Future

There are many verbs that show irregularities in the stem. The following are examples of the irregular forms. The personal pronoun *yo* is used in these examples.

A. The last vowel of the infinitive changes to a *d* in the simple future:

poner (to put)	*pon(e)r*	➤	*pondré*
salir (to go out)	*sal(i)r*	➤	*saldré*
tener (to have)	*ten(e)r*	➤	*tendré*
valer (to be worth)	*val(e)r*	➤	*valdré*
venir (to come)	*ven(i)r*	➤	*vendré*

B. The *ec* or *ce* of the infinitive is dropped in the simple future:

decir (to say)	*d(ec)ir*	➤	*diré*
hacer (to do/make)	*ha(ce)r*	➤	*haré*

C. The final vowel of the infinitive is dropped in the simple future:

caber (to fit)	*cab(e)r*	➤	*cabré*
haber (to have)	*hab(e)r*	➤	*habré*
poder (can)	*pod(e)r*	➤	*podré*
querer (to want)	*quer(e)r*	➤	*querré*
saber (to know)	*sab(e)r*	➤	*sabré*

NOTES:

(1) Endings remain the same for all verbs, whether the stems are regular or irregular:

-é, -ás, -á, -emos, -éis, -án

(2) To determine which verbs have a regular or irregular conjugation, consult a book of verb conjugations or a dictionary.

(3) Verbs that contain one of the aforementioned verbs, such as *convenir* (*to agree*), *contener* (*to contain*), *rehacer* (*to do again*), and many others, also show the irregular stem in the future form:

(yo) contener ➤ *con**tendré***   *convenir* ➤ *con**vendré***   *rehacer* ➤ *re**haré***

Uses of the Simple Future

A. The simple future is used to indicate events that will or will not happen in the future:

*Carlos **leerá** unos informes.*	Carlos will read some reports.
*Nos **mudaremos** a una casa.*	We will move to a house.
*Mañana no **hará** frío.*	It won't be cold tomorrow.

B. The simple future may be replaced by the *present tense* in the following cases.

1. To indicate future events:

*Mañana **llega** Matilde.*	Matilde arrives tomorrow.
*Te **veo** a la tarde.*	I'll see you in the afternoon.

2. To indicate a lack of possibility in negative sentences, Spanish uses the present tense of *querer* (*to want*) and not the future tense, as English does:

*El niño **no quiere** responder.*	The child won't answer.
*La imagen **no quiere** venir.*	The image won't come in.

3. To indicate a polite request, *querer* (*to want*) and *poder* (*can*) are used in the present tense in Spanish instead of the future tense:

*¿**Quieres** llevar esta carta?*	Will you take this letter?
*¿**Pueden** ponerse de pie?*	Will you stand?

C. The simple future is used to express doubt, wonder, or probability, mainly when asking questions:

¿Cuántos días de vacaciones **tendrán**?	How many days of vacation do you think they'll have?
¿**Serán** las cinco?	Do you think it is five o'clock?
Creo que **serán** las seis.	I think it is about six o'clock.
¿Qué **estará** pensando Miguel ahora?	What do you think Miguel is thinking about right now?

D. The simple future is used to express a command:

¡Ud. lo **tendrá** listo para mañana sin falta!	You will have it ready for tomorrow, for sure!
¡**Estarás** de vuelta a las diez!	You will be back at ten!

E. The simple future is used to express a possibility, where English uses *might* or *may*:

Será fácil como tú dices, sin embargo no lo haré.	It might be easy as you say; however I will not do it.
Ganará mucho dinero, pero no lo demuestra.	He might make a lot of money, but he doesn't show it.
Será inteligente, pero no sale bien en los exámenes.	She may be intelligent, but she does not do well in the exams.

Uses of the Simple Future in Combination with Other Tenses

Simple Future and Subjunctive

When the fulfillment of a future event depends upon a hypothetical action, this second action (or the dependent clause) will be in the subjunctive. Expressions such as *tan pronto como* (*as soon as*), *mientras que* (*as long as*), *después de que* (*after*), *cuando* (*when*), *enseguida que* (*as soon as*), and others, precede the subjunctive form:

Nos acostaremos tan pronto como <u>lleguen</u> los niños.	We'll go to bed as soon as the children arrive.
Tomaré un café con él cuando <u>venga</u>.	I'll have coffee with him when he comes.
Irán a casa enseguida que <u>terminen</u>.	They will go home as soon as they finish.
La chica **esperará** aquí mientras que el profesor <u>prepare</u> el ejercicio.	The girl will wait here while the professor prepares the exercise.

However, if the second action is a habitual action, the present tense is used instead of the future in both the main clause and the dependent clause:

Nos acostamos *tan pronto como* <u>*llegan*</u> *los niños.*	We go to bed as soon as the children arrive.
Tomo *un café con él cuando* <u>*viene*</u>.	I have coffee with him when he comes.
Van *a casa enseguida que* <u>*terminan*</u>.	They go home as soon as they finish.

NOTES:

(1) The expressions *antes que* and *antes de que* are always followed by the subjunctive, whether the main sentence is in the future or in the present, because the dependent clause is describing a situation that still has to happen:

Limpiaré *el coche antes que él* <u>*llegue*</u>.	I'll clean the car before he arrives.
Siempre **limpio** *el coche antes de que él* <u>*llegue*</u>.	I always clean the car before he arrives.

(2) The expressions *después que* and *después de que* are followed by the subjunctive when the main sentence is in the future because the dependent clause which they introduce refers to events that have not happened yet:

Preparará *la comida* **después que** *los chicos* <u>*vengan*</u>.	She will prepare the meal after the children come.

Please note that if a habitual action is intended, the present tense is used in both the main clause and the dependent clause, even when *después que* is used:

Mamá **calienta** *la comida después que Papá* **llega**.	Mom warms up the food after Dad arrives.

(3) If there are no dependent clauses, and the two actions take place in the future, the future tense is used for both:

Limpiaré *el auto y él lo* **secará**.	I will clean the car and he will dry it.

Simple Future and Present

If the future action does not depend upon a hypothetical, unreal action but will take place because of an action that is happening in the present, the second verb is in the present:

hypothetical:

Compraré *la fruta que tú* <u>*quieras*</u>.	I'll buy the fruit that you want (whenever you tell me what fruit you want).

present:

Compraré la fruta que tú quieres.   I'll buy the fruit that you want (and you have indicated which one).

The Future Perfect Tense

The future perfect tense is formed with the future of the auxiliary verb *haber* and the past participle of the main verb. *Haber* is one of the irregular verbs that drop the final vowel of the infinitive in order to form the future stem.

As for the past participle, there are regular and irregular forms. The verbs that have regular past participles take the following endings: *-ado* for *-ar* verbs, and *-ido* for *-er* and *-ir* verbs. There is not a specific rule for the formation of the irregular past participles. In English, verbs have forms that end in *-ed* (*walked, jumped, visited*), and irregular forms (*gone, left, eaten*). For a review of the most common ones, consult Chapter 10, The Past Participle.

Future tense of *haber*	Past Participle	
yo habr**é**	terminado	I will have finished
tú habr**ás**	cantado	you will have sung
él habr**á**	puesto	he will have put
ella habr**á**	dormido	she will have slept
Ud. habr**á**	hablado	you will have spoken
nosotros/as habr**emos**	dicho	we will have said
vosotros/as habr**éis**	venido	you will have come
ellos habr**án**	salido	they will have gone out
ellas habr**án**	recordado	they will have remembered
Uds. habr**án**	esperado	you will have waited

Uses of the Future Perfect Tense

A. The future perfect is used to express an action that will be completed at a certain point in the future:

Para mayo ya **habré terminado** mis cursos.   By May I will have finished my courses.

Cuando salgas del trabajo mañana **habremos llegado** a Ponce.   By the time you leave work tomorrow we will have arrived in Ponce.

B. The future perfect is used to indicate probability:

Ella **habrá tenido** *miedo.*	She may have been afraid.
Los niños **habrán salido**, *seguramente.*	The children have probably gone out.

C. The future perfect is used to admit a possibility about a situation in the past with the introduction of a condition or clarification:

Tú **habrás sido** *generosa, pero eso no te impide que des dinero otra vez.*	You may have been generous, but that does not keep you from giving money again.
Yo **habré estado** *descansando, sin embargo terminé el trabajo.*	I may have been resting, but regardless, I finished the job.

6

The Preterit Tense

The preterit tense describes an action that was completed at one point in the past or that lasted during a specified period of time and is viewed as a whole. The action could have taken place as a series of repeated events that ended at a specific time and that are not considered as a habitual or continuous action in the past with no specified beginning or ending, as in *I used to sing*.

Preterit Endings for Regular Verbs

There are two sets of regular endings for the preterit:

-ar verbs: *-é, -aste, -ó, -amos, -asteis, -aron*
-er and *-ir* verbs: *-í, -iste, -ió, -imos, -isteis, -ieron*

hablar	**comer**	**vivir**
yo hablé	*yo comí*	*yo viví*
tú hablaste	*tú comiste*	*tú viviste*
él habló	*él comió*	*él vivió*
ella habló	*ella comió*	*ella vivió*
Ud. habló	*Ud. comió*	*Ud. vivió*
nosotros/as hablamos	*nosotros/as comimos*	*nosotros/as vivimos*
vosotros/as hablasteis	*vosotros/as comisteis*	*vosotros/as vivisteis*
ellos hablaron	*ellos comieron*	*ellos vivieron*
ellas hablaron	*ellas comieron*	*ellas vivieron*
Uds. hablaron	*Uds. comieron*	*Uds. vivieron*

NOTES:

(1) The final syllable of the *yo, él, ella,* and *Ud.* forms is stressed and carries an accent mark.

(2) The forms *nosotras* and *vosotras* share the same forms as their corresponding masculine pronouns *nosotros* and *vosotros*.

(3) The final syllable of the *tú* form does not end in *-s*.

(4) The forms for the first person plural *nosotros* of *-ar* and *-ir* verbs are identical to their corresponding forms for the present. The correct tense has to be deduced from context:

*Siempre **hablamos** castellano en clase.* [present]	We always speak Spanish in class.
*Ayer **hablamos** mucho en la clase de conversación.* [preterit]	Yesterday we spoke a lot in our conversation class.
***Vivimos** en la calle San Martín.* [present]	We live on San Martín Street.
***Vivimos** en San Juan el año pasado.* [preterit]	We lived in San Juan last year.

Irregular Preterit Forms

There are several irregular forms in the preterit.

A. *Ser (to be)*, *ir (to go)*, and *dar (to give)* are entirely irregular in the preterit.

The six basic personal pronouns are used below to show the conjugation of these verbs in the preterit:

ser / ir	*dar*
*yo **fui***	*yo **di***
*tú **fuiste***	*tú **diste***
*él **fue***	*él **dio***
*nosotros **fuimos***	*nosotros **dimos***
*vosotros **fuisteis***	*vosotros **disteis***
*ellos **fueron***	*ellos **dieron***

NOTE:

Ser and *ir* share the same forms in the preterit. *Dar* takes the endings of *-er* and *-ir* verbs, but without any accents.

B. Some -*ar*, -*er*, and -*ir* verbs have irregular stems.

However, note that there are groups of these verbs that share common letters in their stems, and that all of these verbs share the following set of endings. Also notice that none of these endings carry accent marks:

-e	-iste	-o	-imos	-isteis	-ieron

uv

andar	anduve, anduviste, anduvo, anduvimos, anduvisteis, anduvieron
estar	estuve, estuviste, estuvo, estuvimos, estuvisteis, estuvieron
tener	tuve, tuviste, tuvo, tuvimos, tuvisteis, tuvieron

u

caber	cupe, cupiste, cupo, cupimos, cupisteis, cupieron
haber	hube, hubiste, hubo, hubimos, hubisteis, hubieron
poder	pude, pudiste, pudo, pudimos, pudisteis, pudieron
poner	puse, pusiste, puso, pusimos, pusisteis, pusieron
saber	supe, supiste, supo, supimos, supisteis, supieron

i

hacer	hice, hiciste, hizo, hicimos, hicisteis, hicieron
querer	quise, quisiste, quiso, quisimos, quisisteis, quisieron
venir	vine, viniste, vino, vinimos, vinisteis, vinieron

j

conducir	conduje, condujiste, condujo, condujimos, condujisteis, condujeron
decir	dije, dijiste, dijo, dijimos, dijisteis, dijeron
traducir	traduje, tradujiste, tradujo, tradujimos, tradujisteis, tradujeron
traer	traje, trajiste, trajo, trajimos, trajisteis, trajeron

NOTE:

While the ending of the third person plural is -*ieron,* the *j* group drops the *i*:

conduj**eron**	dij**eron**	traduj**eron**	traj**eron**

Changes in the Verb Stem in the Preterit

Several verbs undergo changes in the stem of the infinitive when they are conjugated in the preterit. For practical purposes, only the six basic personal pronouns are shown in the following conjugation.

A. *Hacer* changes *c* to *z* in the third person singular of the preterit:

yo hice	nosotros hicimos
tú hiciste	vosotros hicisteis
él hi**z**o	ellos hicieron

B. Spelling changes to preserve pronunciation

In order to preserve the consonant sound of the infinitive, verbs that end in *-car* and *-gar* undergo a change in the spelling of the first person, *yo.*

1. Endings in *-car: (buscar)*

   In Spanish, *c* before *e* or *i* is pronounced as *s*, while *c* before *a*, *o*, or *u* is pronounced as *k*. Since the first person, *yo,* ends in *é* in the preterit, the *k* sound is preserved by changing the *c* to *qu*:

   buscar: bus**qu**é, buscaste, buscó, buscamos, buscasteis, buscaron

   > NOTE:
   > A list of additional common verbs that show the same change in the first person includes, but is not limited to:
   >
   > educar, explicar, marcar, recalcar, sacar, secar, tocar

2. Endings in *-gar: (pagar)*

   In Spanish, *g* before *e* or *i* has a sound similar to the strong sound of *h* in *ham,* while *g* before *a*, *o*, or *u* is pronounced like the English *g* in *gone*. Since the first person, *yo,* ends in *é* in the preterit, the *g* sound is preserved by changing the *g* to *gu*:

   pagar: pa**gu**é, pagaste, pagó, pagamos, pagasteis, pagaron

   > NOTE:
   > A list of additional common verbs that show the same change in the first person includes, but is not limited to:
   >
   > apagar, colgar, entregar, jugar, llegar, negar, rogar

C. Changes in verbs that end in *-zar*

Verbs that end in *-zar* change the *z* to *c* in the *yo* form. This change is not made to preserve pronunciation in either Continental or Latin American Spanish. In Spain, the *z* as well as the *c* before *e* or *i* are pronounced like the English *th* in *think*. In Latin America, both the *z* and the *c* before *e* or *i* are pronounced as *s*. Observe the following verbs:

realizar

<u>In Spain</u> (all persons pronounced with the sound of *th* in *think*):

realicé, realizaste, realizó, realizamos, realizasteis, realizaron

almorzar

<u>In Latin America</u> (all persons pronounced with the sound of *s* in *same*):

almorcé, almorzaste, almorzó, almorzamos, almorzasteis, almorzaron

NOTES:

(1) A list of additional common verbs that show the same change in the first person includes, but is not limited to:

comenzar, empezar, gozar, rezar, utilizar

(2) All *-ar* and *-er* verbs that undergo stem changes in the present tense (called stem-changing verbs) do not have any changes in the preterit:

	Present	**Preterit**
contar	*(yo)* **cuen**to	*(yo)* conté
perder	*pie*rdo	*perdí*

(3) All *-ir* verbs that have a stem change in the present keep the *e* or the *o* of the infinitive when they are conjugated in the preterit, except in the third person singular and plural, where they change *e* to *i* and *o* to *u*:

Present	**Preterit**	
pedir		
yo pido	*yo pedí*	
tú pides	*tú pediste*	
él pide	*él pidió*	*e* to *i*
nosotros pedimos	*nosotros pedimos*	
vosotros pedís	*vosotros pedisteis*	
ellos piden	*ellos pidieron*	*e* to *i*

repetir	
yo repito	*yo repetí*
tú repites	*tú repetiste*
él <u>repite</u>	*él <u>repi</u>tió* e to i
nosotros repetimos	*nosotros repetimos*
vosotros repetís	*vosotros repetisteis*
ellos <u>repiten</u>	*ellos <u>repi</u>tieron* e to i
do<u>r</u>mir	
yo duermo	*yo dormí*
tú duermes	*tú dormiste*
él <u>due</u>rme	*él <u>du</u>rmió* o to u
nosotros dormimos	*nosotros dormimos*
vosotros dormís	*vosotros dormisteis*
ellos <u>due</u>rmen	*ellos <u>du</u>rmieron* o to u

Changes in the Endings in the Preterit

The following rules apply.

A. **The preterit ending changes when the stem of an *-er* or *-ir* verb ends in a vowel.**

If the stem of an *-er* or *-ir* verb ends in a vowel, a *y* replaces the *i* of the third person singular and plural:

    <u>*leer:*</u> *(le er)*   *leí, leíste, leyó, leímos leísteis, leyeron*
    <u>*oír:*</u> *(**o** ír)*   *oí, oíste oyó, oímos, oísteis, oyeron*

B. **The preterit ending changes for verbs that end in *-uir*.**

Verbs that end in *-uir* also substitute a *y* for the *i* in the third person singular and plural of the preterit tense:

    construir: *construí, construiste, construyó, construimos, construisteis, construyeron*
    atribuir: *atribuí, atribuiste, atribuyó, atribuimos, atribuisteis, atribuyeron*

Uses of the Preterit Tense

The preterit tense is used in Spanish to describe the following situations.

A. **The preterit is used to describe a completed action in the past.**

This usage is equivalent to the English preterit tense:

Me **compré** un coche nuevo.	I bought a new car.
Ella **invitó** a sus amigas para conversar.	She invited her friends to chat.
Juan **trabajó** para mi padre de mayo a septiembre.	John worked for my father from May to September.
Mis amigos **llegaron** a las cinco.	My friends arrived at five.

B. **The preterit is used to describe an action that lasted for some time in the past and is viewed as a whole.**

~~In English, the expression *used to* plus a verb in the infinitive might be used in such a context:~~

Mi hermano **estudió** en esa universidad.	My brother ~~used to study~~ *studied* at that university.
María **fue** secretaria en su oficina.	María ~~used to be~~ *was* a secretary in his office.
Ellos **vivieron** en Santa Fe.	They ~~used to~~ live in Santa Fe.

 The preterit is used to indicate a completed action in the past that extends its effect into the present.

In English, the present perfect tense is used here:

Acabé de limpiar la casa.	I have just finished cleaning the house.
Mis vecinos **terminaron** de mudarse.	My neighbors have finished moving.
Ya **salió** para el aeropuerto.	He has already left for the airport.

> **NOTE:**
>
> The preceding sentences may also be expressed using the present perfect in Spanish (used mostly in Spain) and the preterit in English:
>
> Ya <u>ha salido</u> para el aeropuerto.   He already <u>left</u> for the airport.

D. The preterit is used to describe an event that took place before another event in the past.

English uses the past perfect here:

Juan dijo que María **fue** su mejor amiga en la escuela.	Juan said that María had been his best friend at school.
Me contaron que **viniste** a verlos.	They told me that you had come to see them.

E. The preterit is used to describe a series of events delimited within a specific period of time:

El semestre pasado **fui** a clases todos los jueves.	Last semester I attended classes every Thursday.
Cuando **estuvo** en la Marina siempre nos escribió.	When he was in the Navy, he always wrote to us.
Durante el verano **tomé** clases de natación.	During the summer I took swimming lessons.
Escuché música por dos horas.	I listened to music for two hours.

NOTE:

If there is no adverbial phrase such as *el semestre pasado*, the imperfect tense has to replace the preterit:

Iba a clases todos los jueves.	I used to go to classes every Thursday.

However, if it is understood in context that the length of time had a beginning and an end, the preterit is used:

¿Qué hiciste el semestre pasado?	What did you do last semester?
Fui a clase todos los jueves.	I went to class every Thursday.

F. The preterit is used to describe an event of certain duration that has a specific beginning or end or that began and ended in the past:

Almorzamos a las dos.	We had lunch at two. (beginning)
Leí el diario hasta tarde.	I read the newspaper until late. (end)
Asistí a clase de mayo a julio.	I attended class from May to July.

G. The preterit is used to describe a situation governed by a verb of action or movement:

Jaime **trabajó** toda la tarde.	Jaime worked all afternoon.
Carlos **manejó** sin parar.	Carlos drove without stopping.

The preterit of *deber* plus an infinitive is used to describe an obligation or a duty:

Ellos ***debieron*** *llegar más temprano.*	They should have arrived earlier.
Debí *preparar el informe antes de su llegada.*	I should have prepared the report before his arrival.

NOTE:

The sentence ***Ellos debieron llegar más temprano*** could also be interpreted as an assumption, as in *They might have arrived earlier.*

I. **The preterit is used to describe a sudden change in time or condition:**

Se hizo *la una y tuve que volver.*	Suddenly, it was one o'clock and I had to return.
Hubo *una cantidad enorme de gente en la plaza.*	There was a big crowd in the public square.
Mi sobrino ***cumplió*** *tres años en octubre.*	My nephew turned three in October.

The preterit is used to describe a change that is expressed by a reflexive or reciprocal verb:

Se volvió *loca con tanto sufrimiento.*	She went crazy with so much suffering.
Se casaron *el sábado pasado.*	They got married last Saturday.
Su hija ***se puso*** *pálida con la noticia.*	Her daughter turned pale when she heard the news.
La familia de Juan ***se quedó*** *sin un centavo.*	Juan's family was left without even a cent.

K. **The preterit of *irse* plus the present participle of the main verb is used to describe the progression of an event:**

A medida que hablaba ***se fue*** *tranquilizando.*	As she talked, she calmed down little by little.
Después de vivir allí tres meses ***nos fuimos*** *ajustando.*	After living there for three months we gradually got used to it.

L. **The preterit is used to describe a completed event in the past, of specific duration:**

Charlamos *por teléfono por dos horas.*	We chatted on the phone for two hours.
Se quedaron *en ese motel por una semana.*	They stayed in that motel for one week.

Verbs That Change Their Meaning in the Preterit

Some Spanish verbs have a different meaning when they are used in the preterit tense than when they are used in the present:

acabar de
(to have just done)

Acabo de hacer los ejercicios.
I have just finished doing the exercises.

(to finish)

Acabé de leer y me dormí.
I finished reading and I fell asleep.

conocer
(to know)

Ellos conocen al profesor.
They know the professor.

(to meet)

Ellos conocieron al profesor ayer.
They met the professor yesterday.

saber
(to know)

Yo sé donde vive Juana.
I know where Juana lives.

(to find out)

Yo supe anoche que vive allí.
I found out last night that she lives there.

poder
(to be able)

Tú puedes hablar bien el castellano.
You can speak Spanish well.

(to manage)

¡Tú pudiste decirlo todo sin parar!
You managed to say it all without stopping!

querer
(to want)

Queremos ir a España en las vacaciones.
We want to go to Spain on our vacation.

(to try to)

Quisimos ir pero no había asientos.
We tried to go but there were no seats.

no querer
(not to want)

María no quiere hablar con Carlos.
María doesn't want to talk to Carlos.

(to refuse)

María no quiso hablar con Carlos.
María refused to talk to Carlos.

Contrasts Between the Preterit Tense and the Imperfect Tense

The preterit, as well as the imperfect, represents actions that happened in the past. There are specific situations where one or the other tense must be used. Included in the following list are some of the most common of those situations:

Uses of the Preterit

a. A one-time, completed action in the past:
Vendí mis libros.
I sold my books.

b. An action that lasted for a while and is viewed as a whole:
Tomé clases el año pasado.
I took classes last year.

c. A completed action in the past that extends its effect into the present:
Acabé de leer la novela.
I just finished reading the novel.

d. An action that happened before another action in the past:
Me dijeron que te recibiste.
They told me you had graduated.

e. A completed action in the past with a beginning and an ending:
Trabajó allí por un año.
He worked there for a year.

f. A series of events within a specific period of time:
Pedro nos visitó todo el tiempo que estuvo en la casa de sus abuelos.
Pedro came to visit us all the time he lived with his grandparents.

Uses of the Imperfect

a. Habitual actions in the past:
Siempre almorzaba allá.
I always had lunch over there.

b. Actions that lasted in the past without specific duration:
Llevaba zapatos de taco alto.
She had high-heeled shoes on.

c. Actions in progress that took place simultaneously:
Mamá barría el patio mientras yo lustraba los muebles.
Mom swept the patio while I polished the furniture.

d. An action in progress that is interrupted by an action in the preterit:
Cuando estudiaba en la biblioteca, oí un ruido sordo.
When I was studying in the library, I heard a muffled noise.

e. Description of a scene in the past:
Estaba nevando y el viento soplaba los copos.
It was snowing and the wind was blowing the snowflakes.

f. Description of physical characteristics in the past:
Era alto y tenía el pelo oscuro.
He was tall and had dark hair.

g. The beginning of an event of certain duration:

Fuimos al teatro a las seis.

We went to the theater at 6 P.M.

h. A situation controlled by a verb of action:

Bailó toda la noche.

She danced all night.

i. To indicate obligation with the verb ***deber***:

Tú debiste avisarme antes.

You should have told me in advance.

j. A sudden change of condition:

Obtuvo el aumento de sueldo.

She got a raise.

k. A change expressed with a reflexive or reciprocal verb:

Me volví caritativa después de la experiencia que tuve.

I became very charitable after the experience I had.

Se comprometieron en el Caribe.

They got engaged in the Caribbean.

l. The progression of an event, with ***irse*** plus a present participle:

Me fui acostumbrando a la nueva casa.

I slowly got used to the new house.

g. To tell the time in the past:

Me dijo que eran las dos.

He told me that it was two o'clock.

Cuando viniste era la una.

When you came it was one o'clock.

h. Age in the past:

Juana tenía un año cuando vino aquí.

Juana was one year old when she came here.

Pedro no alcanzaba a los veinte.

Pedro was not even 20 years old.

i. The expression *Once upon a time . . .* in children's stories:

Había una vez...

NOTES:

(1) The preterit tense and the imperfect tense can both occur in the same sentence. There is usually a situation that has been going on and is interrupted by another action:

Cuando estudiaba en la biblioteca, oí un ruido sordo.

When I was studying in the library, I heard a muffled noise.

Empezó a nevar cuando estaba subiendo la montaña.

It began to snow when I was going up the mountain.

(2) There are cases when the choice between the preterit or the imperfect depends on the emphasis desired by the speaker:

Esos dos meses en Buenos Aires siempre íbamos a tomar el té en el Café Tortoni.	We always went to have tea at the Café Tortoni those two months (that I was) in Buenos Aires.

Although there is a specific length of time given in the preceding sentence, it is the frequency of the action that is emphasized. In the following sentence, however, the speaker is viewing the actions in a mental time frame:

Siempre fuimos a tomar el té al Café Tortoni cuando estuve en Buenos Aires.

7

The Imperfect Tense

The imperfect tense is used in Spanish to describe an action that took place during some time in the past. This action may have occurred habitually or repeatedly during that time. The main difference between the imperfect and the preterit, both tenses representing actions in the past, is that in the imperfect the beginning and end of the action are not exactly known or determined. To indicate a similar idea, English uses the expressions *used to*, *would*, or the preterit tense.

Regular Verbs in the Imperfect

All except three Spanish verbs are considered regular in the imperfect. The three irregular verbs (*ser*, *ir*, and *ver*) will be discussed in the following section. Below you will find endings and sample conjugations for the regular verbs.

Endings for Regular Verbs

-ar verbs: **-aba, -abas, -aba, -ábamos, -abais, -aban**
-er and *-ir* verbs: **-ía, -ías, -ía, -íamos, -íais, -ían**

Sample Conjugations of Regular Verbs

cantar	beber	escribir
yo cant**aba**	yo beb**ía**	yo escrib**ía**
tú cant**abas**	tú beb**ías**	tú escrib**ías**
él cant**aba**	él beb**ía**	él escrib**ía**
ella cant**aba**	ella beb**ía**	ella escrib**ía**
Ud. cant**aba**	Ud. beb**ía**	Ud. escrib**ía**

nosotros cant**ábamos**	nosotros beb**íamos**	nosotros escrib**íamos**
nosotras cant**ábamos**	nosostras beb**íamos**	nosotras escrib**íamos**
vosotros cant**abais**	vosotros beb**íais**	vosotros escrib**íais**
vosotras cant**abais**	vosotras beb**íais**	vosotras escrib**íais**
ellos cant**aban**	ellos beb**ían**	ellos escrib**ían**
ellas cant**aban**	ellas beb**ían**	ellas escrib**ían**
Uds. cant**aban**	Uds. beb**ían**	Uds. escrib**ían**

NOTES:

(1) The pronouns *yo*, *él*, *ella*, and *Ud.* share the same verb form. The pronouns *ellos*, *ellas*, and *Uds.* also share the same verb form. *Nosotras* and *vosotras* share the same forms of their corresponding masculine pronouns *nosotros* and *vosotros*.

(2) In the conjugation of *-ar* verbs, *nosotros* and *nosotras* are the only forms that carry an accent. However, all forms of *-er* and *-ir* verbs have accents on the *i*.

(3) A habitual or repeated action in the past may also be expressed with the imperfect form of *estar* plus the present participle, that is, a verb that has the ending *-ando* or *-iendo*, represented by the *-ing* ending in English:

Yo **estaba cocinando** cuando oí la noticia. (or Yo cocinaba...)	I was cooking when I heard the news.
Estábamos almorzando. (or Nosotros almorzábamos.)	We were having lunch.

Irregular Verbs in the Imperfect

As already mentioned, there are only three irregular verbs in the imperfect in Spanish: *ser (to be)*, *ir (to go)*, and *ver (to see)*. For practical purposes, only the six basic personal pronouns are shown in the conjugations below.

ser	*ir*	*ver*
yo *era*	yo *iba*	yo *veía*
tú *eras*	tú *ibas*	tú *veías*
él *era*	él *iba*	él *veía*
nosotros *éramos*	nosotros *íbamos*	nosotros *veíamos*
vosotros *erais*	vosotros *ibais*	vosotros *veíais*
ellos *eran*	ellos *iban*	ellos *veían*

(1) *Ser* changes its stem entirely in the preterit; the endings it uses are the *-er* endings of the imperfect, as in *bebía, bebías,* etc., but without the *i*. (These are also the endings for *-ar* verbs in the past subjunctive, which is also called the imperfect subjunctive: *cantara, cantaras,* and so on).

(2) The imperfect of *ir* consists of the *-ir* endings of the imperfect, as in *escribía, escribías,* etc., with the addition of a *b* inserted between the *i* and the *a*.

(3) *Ver* picks up an *e* in the stem and uses the *-er* endings of the imperfect, as in *bebía, bebías,* etc.

Uses of the Imperfect Tense

The Spanish imperfect tense is used to indicate several types of actions in the past.

A. The imperfect tense to express habitual actions in the past:

Siempre **viajábamos** a la playa.	We always traveled to the beach.
Yo **cantaba** en el coro cuando era niña.	I used to sing in the choir when I was a child.
Ella **venía** a casa los viernes.	She would come home on Fridays.

B. The imperfect tense to express actions that happened in the past without a specific duration:

Carmen nos **visitaba**.	Carmen used to visit us.
Llevaba puestos unos anteojos.	He had glasses on.
En ese entonces, **íbamos** a fiestas.	At that time, we would go to parties.

C. The imperfect tense to express actions in progress that took place simultaneously:

Yo **cantaba** mientras el **leía**.	I would sing while he read.
Cuando Juan **entraba**, Carlos **salía** del cuarto.	When Juan was coming in, Carlos was leaving the room.

D. The imperfect tense to express an action in progress that was interrupted by an action in the preterit tense:

Cuando **caminaba** por el parque <u>tuve</u> una idea magnífica.

While I was walking in the park I had a great idea.

El <u>llamó</u> cuando yo **dormía**.

He called while I was asleep.

E. The imperfect tense to describe a scene in the past:

El cielo **estaba** azul y **hacía** un poco de calor.

The sky was blue and it was a little hot.

Había árboles a cada lado del camino.

There were trees on each side of the road.

F. The imperfect tense to describe physical characteristics in the past:

Sus manos **eran** pequeñas.

Her hands were small.

La expresión de su rostro **reflejaba** sus sentimientos.

The expression on her face reflected her feelings.

G. The imperfect tense to describe time in the past:

Eran las cuatro cuando vino.

It was four o'clock when he came.

Era la medianoche.

It was midnight.

Era la una de la tarde.

It was one o'clock in the afternoon.

H. The imperfect tense to describe age in the past:

Tenía 20 años cuando me casé.

I was twenty when I got married.

No **llegaba** a cincuenta y se creía un hombre viejo.

He was not even fifty and he considered himself an old man.

I. The imperfect tense to describe a general physical condition in the past:

<u>Estaba</u> cansada y <u>sentía</u> un malestar en la pierna.

I was tired and had discomfort in my leg.

La cabeza me <u>daba</u> vueltas.

My head was spinning.

J. The imperfect tense to express *Once upon a time . . .* in children's stories:

Había una vez una princesita...

Once upon a time there was a little princess . . .

Typical Expressions That Trigger the Imperfect Tense

When expressions such as the following appear in a sentence, the verb is usually in the imperfect. (See Chapter 6, The Preterit Tense, for contrasts between the use of the preterit and the imperfect.)

a veces	sometimes
cada día (mañana, tarde, noche)	each day (morning, afternoon, night)
cada dos días	every two days
con frecuencia / frecuentemente	frequently, often
cuando era niño (joven, viejo)	when he was a child (young, old)
de vez en cuando	every once in a while
día por medio	every other day
durante el verano (invierno, otoño)	during the summer (winter, fall)
generalmente	usually
los fines de semana	on weekends
los lunes (martes, miércoles)	on Mondays (Tuesdays, Wednesdays)
nunca	never
raras veces	seldom
siempre	always
todos los días (meses, años)	every day (month, year)
todas las mañanas (tardes, noches)	every morning (afternoon, night)
cuando yo quería	whenever I wanted to

The Conditional Tense

The conditional tense, called *condicional* or *potencial* in Spanish, corresponds to the English form *would* plus the infinitive of the main verb. A sentence that has a verb in the conditional indicates the possibility that an action could take place. These types of actions can be represented in Spanish with either the conditional tense (*I would go*), which is a one-verb form, or the compound form called the conditional perfect tense (*I would have gone*).

Regular Forms of the Conditional Tense

To form the conditional tense, the following endings are added to the infinitive of -*ar*, -*er*, and -*ir* verbs, regardless of whether the verbs have regular or irregular stems.

Conditional Endings

-*ía*, -*ías*, -*ía*, -*íamos*, -*íais*, -*ían*

Sample Conditional Conjugations

pensar	*entender*	*recibir*
yo pensar*ía*	yo entender*ía*	yo recibir*ía*
tú pensar*ías*	tú entender*ías*	tú recibir*ías*
él pensar*ía*	él entender*ía*	él recibir*ía*
ella pensar*ía*	ella entender*ía*	ella recibir*ía*
Ud. pensar*ía*	Ud. entender*ía*	Ud. recibir*ía*
nosotros pensar*íamos*	nosotros entender*íamos*	nosotros recibir*íamos*
nosotras pensar*íamos*	nosotras entender*íamos*	nosotras recibir*íamos*
vosotros pensar*íais*	vosotros entender*íais*	vosotros recibir*íais*
vosotras pensar*íais*	vosotras entender*íais*	vosotras recibir*íais*

ellos pensarían	ellos entenderían	ellos recibirían
ellas pensarían	ellas entenderían	ellas recibirían
Uds. pensarían	Uds. entenderían	Uds. recibirían

Iría a Madrid el año que viene.	I would go to Madrid next year.
¿**Comerías** una manzana?	Would you eat an apple?
Escribiríamos la carta.	We would write the letter.
Se acostaría temprano.	He would go to bed early.
¿**Vendríais** con vuestros padres?	Would you come with your parents?

NOTES:

(1) If the verb is reflexive, as in **acostarse** *(to go to bed)*, the corresponding reflexive pronoun *me, te, se, os,* or *nos* is placed in front of the verb, which is conjugated as indicated above:

acostarse ➤ yo **me** acostaría

me acostaría, te acostarías, se acostaría, nos acostaríamos, os acostaríais, se acostarían

(2) The endings of the conditional tense are the same as the endings for the *-er* and *-ir* forms of the imperfect tense. To recognize the tenses out of context, remember that the endings of the conditional are added to the infinitive of the verb, while the endings of the imperfect are added to the stem of the verb after deleting the infinitive endings *-er* or *-ir*:

beber	imperfect: *beb ía*	conditional: *beber ía*
asistir	imperfect: *asist ía*	conditional: *asistir ía*

(3) All the endings in the conditional tense carry an accent mark.

Irregular Stem Forms

Some verbs show the following irregularities in the stem, which are the same irregularities as appear in the irregular forms of the future tense. The **yo** form is shown in these examples:

A. Changing of the last vowel into *d* in the conditional:

poner (to put)	*pon(**e**)r*	➤	*pon**dr** ía*
salir (to go out)	*sal(**i**)r*	➤	*sal**dr** ía*
tener (to have)	*ten(**e**)r*	➤	*ten**dr** ía*

| *valer* (to be worth) | *val(e)r* | ➤ | *valdr ía* |
| *venir* (to come) | *ven(i)r* | ➤ | *vendr ía* |

B. Dropping of *ec* or *ce* in the conditional:

| *decir* (to say) | *d(ec)ir* | ➤ | *dir ía* |
| *hacer* (to do / make) | *ha(ce)r* | ➤ | *har ía* |

C. Dropping of the final vowel of the infinitive in the conditional:

caber (to fit)	*cab(e)r*	➤	*cabr ía*
haber (to have)	*hab(e)r*	➤	*habr ía*
poder (to be able)	*pod(e)r*	➤	*podr ía*
querer (to want)	*quer(e)r*	➤	*querr ía*
saber (to know)	*sab(e)r*	➤	*sabr ía*

NOTES:

(1) Endings remain the same for the three conjugations, whether the stems are regular or irregular.

(2) Verbs that contain one of the above-mentioned verbs, such as *convenir* (*to agree*), *contener* (*to contain*), *rehacer* (*to do again*), and several others, keep the irregular stems in the conditional forms:

contener ➤ *con**tendría***   *convenir* ➤ *con**vendría***   *rehacer* ➤ *re**haría***

Uses of the Conditional Tense

The conditional tense is used in the following circumstances.

A. The conditional to indicate possibility

The conditional is used to indicate the possibility of an action in the case of a hypothetical situation. In English, such a hypothetical situation is known as an *if clause* or a *contrary-to-fact statement*:

| ***Compraríamos** la casa de la esquina si tuviéramos dinero.* | We would buy the house on the corner if we had money (contrary to fact). |
| *¿**Vendrías** mañana si pudieras?* | Would you come tomorrow if you could? (situation less likely to happen). |

NOTES:

(1) The phrases *si tuviéramos* and *si pudieras* are in the imperfect subjunctive form. (See Chapter 14, The Subjunctive for details about *if clauses*.)

(2) The condition may be implicit, as follows:

Compraríamos la casa de la esquina.	We would buy the house on the corner.
¿Vendrías mañana?	Would you come tomorrow?

B. The conditional to express doubt, wonder, or probability

The conditional is used to express doubt or wonder about an action that already happened or the probability that an action could have happened in the past, where English uses *must*, *could*, or *might*:

*¿Cuantos días **tendrían** de vacaciones?*	How many days of vacation could they have had?
*¿**Serían** las seis?*	Could it have been six o'clock?
*Creo que **serían** las cinco.*	I think it might have been five o'clock.
*¿Qué **estaría** pensando Juan cuando dijo eso?*	I wonder what Juan could have been thinking when he said that.

C. The conditional to ask a question or to request something in a very polite manner:

*¿Me **podrías** alcanzar el lápiz?*	Could you give me the pencil, please?
*¿Me **daría** Ud. tiempo para resolver este asunto?*	Would you give me some time to solve this problem?

D. The conditional to indicate an expected action in the future from a specific point in the past:

*Oí decir que **llegaría** hoy.*	I heard that she would come today. (I don't know if she will.)
*Me dijo que me **compraría** el boleto esta semana.*	He said that he would buy my ticket this week. (I don't know yet whether he has done it).

E. The conditional to change a sentence with a verb in the future tense into indirect discourse:

Vendré mañana a la tarde.	I'll come tomorrow afternoon.
*Me dijo que **vendría** mañana a la tarde.*	She told me that she would come tomorrow afternoon.

| Te *llamaré* más tarde. | I'll call you later. |
| *Dijo que me **llamaría** más tarde.* | He said he would call me later. |

NOTE:

If the verb in the future tense is a command, the indirect discourse will be in the subjunctive instead of the conditional:

¡Llegarás más temprano!	Arrive earlier!
Me mandó que llegara más temprano.	He ordered me to arrive earlier.
¡No te quedarás aquí!	Don't stay here!
Me dijo que no me quedara allí.	He told me not to stay there.

F. Imperfect instead of conditional

When English uses *would* to show a habitual action in the past, Spanish uses the imperfect tense, not the conditional:

| *Todas las tardes el coro practicaba las canciones.* | Every afternoon the choir would practice the songs. |
| *Siempre salían juntos.* | They would always go out together. |

NOTE:

The verbs *soler* and *acostumbrar* are also used, with the infinitive of the main verb, to indicate a customary action when English uses *would*:

| *Ella acostumbraba llamar todas las tardes.* | She would call every afternoon. |
| *Mamá solía escuchar música correntina en la cocina.* | Mom would listen to music from Corrientes in the kitchen. |

G. Use of present subjunctive or imperfect subjunctive

When English uses *would* (or *will*) after an expression of wish, Spanish uses the present subjunctive or the imperfect subjunctive, according to the situation:

Ojalá que vengas.	I wish you would come.
Espero que me escribas.	I hope you will write to me.
(present subjunctive)	

Ojalá sacara la lotería.	I wish I would win the lottery.
Ojalá vinieras.	I wish you would come.
(imperfect subjunctive)	

The imperfect subjunctive (*sacara*, *vinieras*) makes the possibility far more remote than the present subjunctive (*escribas*, *vengas*).

H. Use of the negative form of *querer*

When English uses *would* and a negative expression to indicate a refusal to do something, Spanish uses a negative form of the verb *querer* (*to want*) in the imperfect or the preterit, depending on the situation:

Ella nunca <u>quería</u> decir la verdad. (imperfect)	She would never tell the truth. (ongoing situation)
Él no <u>quiso</u> venir a verla cuando estuvo en el pueblo. (preterit)	He wouldn't come to see her when he was in town. (one time)

I. Use of the conditional form of *deber* or *ser*

When English uses *should* to indicate the desirability of an action to be taken, Spanish uses the conditional form of *deber* or *ser:*

Deberías escucharlo.	You should listen to him.
No **sería** conveniente que Ud. cortara esas flores.	You shouldn't cut those flowers.

NOTE:

If *should* is used in English to denote a question or a cause for wonder, Spanish uses the conditional of the auxiliary verb *haber*, followed by the preposition *de* and the infinitive of the main verb:

¿Por qué **habrías de** pagar esa cuenta?	Why should you pay that bill?
No sé por qué él **habría de** decírselo a su hermano.	I don't know why he should tell his brother about that.

J. Expressing possibility depending on likelihood

When English uses *should* to indicate a condition with *if clauses*, Spanish uses the present tense if there is a strong possibility of the event happening or the imperfect subjunctive if the possibility is remote:

Si <u>alquilas</u> la casa, quiero verla primero.	If you should rent the house, I want to see it first.
Si <u>alquilaras</u> la casa, querría verla primero.	Should you rent the house, I would want to see it first.

The Conditional Perfect Tense

The conditional perfect is formed with the conditional of the auxiliary verb *haber* and the past participle of the main verb. *Haber* is one of the verbs that drop the *e* of the infinitive in order to form the conditional stem, which is covered in the section Irregular Stem Forms, previously in this chapter.

As for the past participle, there are regular and irregular forms. The verbs that have regular past participles take the following endings: *-ado* for *-ar* verbs, and *-ido* for *-er* and *-ir* verbs. There is no specific rule for the formation of the irregular past participles. In English, verbs have forms that end in *-ed* (*walked, jumped, visited*), and irregular forms (*gone, left, eaten*). For a review of the most common irregular past participles in Spanish, consult Chapter 10, The Past Participle:

yo habría **venido**	I would have come
tú habrías **dicho**	you would have said
él habría **hablado**	he would have spoken
ella habría **pensado**	she would have thought
Ud. habría **contemplado**	you would have contemplated
nosotros habríamos **recibido**	we would have received
nosotras habríamos **ido**	we would have gone
vosotros habríais **roto**	you would have broken
vosotras habríais **estado**	you would have been
ellos habrían **escrito**	they would have written
ellas habrían **dado**	they would have given
Uds. habrían **esperado**	you would have waited

Uses of the Conditional Perfect Tense

The conditional perfect tense is used in the following situations.

A. The conditional perfect is used to express an action that would have been completed at a certain point in the past:

Marta **habría venido** ayer.	Martha would have come yesterday.
¿Tú me **habrías llamado**?	Would you have called me?

B. The conditional perfect is used to indicate probability within a specific context in the past:

Ella **habría sufrido** mucho.	She would have suffered a lot.
Yo **habría tenido** cuidado.	I would have been careful.

C. The conditional perfect is used to show the probability of an action being completed before another action in the past.

Notice the use of the imperfect subjunctive after *antes (de) que*:

Dijo la maestra que nosotros **habríamos tenido** las notas antes de que terminara el curso.	The teacher said that we would have had the grades before the course was finished.
Miguel explicó que ellos **habrían salido** antes que llegaran los chicos.	Michael explained that they would have gone out before the children arrived.

9

The Present Participle

The present participle, also known as the gerund (*gerundio*), is used to form sentences which are equivalent to the present progressive sentences. While in English all verbs take the *-ing* ending, there are regular and irregular endings for the present participle in Spanish.

Endings of the Present Participle

Regular Endings

To form the present participle of verbs that take regular endings, drop the infinitive ending *-ar, -er,* or *-ir*, and add *-ando* to the stem of *-ar* verbs, and *-iendo* to the stem of *-er* and *-ir* verbs:

-ar verbs: -ando	-er verbs: -iendo	-ir verbs: -iendo
hablar (to speak)	*correr* (to run)	*vivir* (to live)
hablando (speaking)	*corriendo* (running)	*viviendo* (living)

Irregular Endings

A. When the stem of *-er* and *-ir* verbs ends in a vowel, the *i* of the *-iendo* ending changes to a *y:*

traer	*leer*	*huir*	*oír*	*excluir*
trayendo	*leyendo*	*huyendo*	*oyendo*	*excluyendo*

> **NOTE:**
>
> The present participle of the verb *ir* (*to go*) is *yendo* (*going*):
>
> *Estás **yendo** muy rápido con este proyecto.*   You are going very fast with this project.

B. *-er* and *-ir* verbs that have stems ending in *ll* or *ñ* drop the *i* of the *-iendo* ending:

bullir	*bullendo*	*mullir*	*mullendo*
entullir	*entullendo*	*reñir*	*riñendo*
escabullirse	*escabulléndose*	*tañer*	*tañendo*
gruñir	*gruñendo*	*teñir*	*tiñendo*

Stems of the Present Participle

Regular Stems

Stem-changing verbs that end in *-ar* and *-er* do not change the stem for the present participle:

Verb	Present Tense	Present Participle
almorzar	*yo almuerzo*	*almorzando*
empezar	*yo empiezo*	*empezando*
entender	*yo entiendo*	*entendiendo*
pensar	*yo pienso*	*pensando*
perder	*yo pierdo*	*perdiendo*
volver	*yo vuelvo*	*volviendo*

Exception

poder	*yo puedo*	*pudiendo*
jugar	*yo juego*	*jugando*

Irregular Stems

Stem-changing verbs that end in *-ir* show the following changes:

A. Verbs whose stem changes from *e* ➤ *i* in the present tense keep an *i* in the stem:

Verb	Present Tense	Present Participle
pedir	*yo pido*	*pidiendo*
seguir	*yo sigo*	*siguiendo*

(1) The letter *u* is inserted after the *g* in *siguiendo* to preserve the pronunciation of the infinitive.

(2) A few verbs that have stems ending in a vowel drop the *i* of the *-iendo* ending to avoid having two *i*'s together:

freír	*yo frío*	*fri**endo***
reír	*yo río*	*ri**endo***
engreír(se)	*yo me engrío*	*engri**endo***

(3) Verbs like *decir* and *venir* have exceptional forms:

decir	*yo digo*	*diciendo*
venir	*yo vengo*	*viniendo*

B. Verbs whose stem changes from *e* ➤ *ie* in the present tense keep an *i* in the stem of the present participle:

Verb	Present Tense	Present Participle
sentir	*yo siento*	*sintiendo*
preferir	*yo prefiero*	*prefiriendo*

NOTE:

If there are two *e*'s in the stem, the second one is the one that changes.

C. Verbs whose stem changes from *o* ➤ *ue* in the present tense keep a *u* in the stem:

Verb	Present Tense	Present Participle
dormir	*yo duermo*	*durmiendo*
morir	*yo muero*	*muriendo*

Uses of the Present Participle

The present participle is used in the following situations.

A. The present participle in the progressive tense

In combination with the verb *estar* (*to be*), the present participle forms the progressive tenses, which denote an action in progress:

hablar:	*yo estoy hablando*	I am speaking
	tú estás hablando	you are speaking
	él está hablando	he is speaking
	ella está hablando	she is speaking
	Ud. está hablando	you are speaking
	nosotros estamos hablando	we are speaking
	nosotras estamos hablando	we are speaking
	vosotros estáis hablando	you are speaking
	vosotras estáis hablando	you are speaking
	ellos están hablando	they are speaking
	ellas están hablando	they are speaking
	Uds. están hablando	you are speaking
correr:	*yo estoy corriendo*	I am running
vivir:	*yo estoy viviendo*	I am living

NOTES:

(1) The form of the present participle is invariable for all persons.

(2) Besides the present progressive, *estar* is also conjugated in the following tenses:

yo **estuve** *hablando*	I was speaking
tú **estabas** *escribiendo*	you were writing
él **estará** *durmiendo*	he will be sleeping
ella **estaría** *viajando*	she would be traveling
Ud. **ha estado** *trabajando*	you have been working
nosotros **habíamos estado** *viendo*	we had been seeing
nosotras **habremos estado** *oyendo*	*we* will have been hearing
vosotros **habríais estado** *cocinando*	you would have been cooking
vosotras **estén** *estudiando*	you are studying
ellos **estuvieran** *planeando*	they were planning
ellas **hayan estado** *practicando*	they have been practicing
Uds. **hubieran estado** *jugando*	you had been playing

The boldfaced forms of *estar* in the preceding examples include the preterit, imperfect, future, conditional, present perfect, past perfect, future perfect, conditional perfect, and the four subjunctive forms (the last four examples): present, imperfect, present perfect, and past perfect or pluperfect.

(3) With verbs of motion, the gerund is used after *estar* in idiomatic expressions to indicate location:

Mi casa está yendo derecho por esta calle.	My house is straight down on this street.
La farmacia estaba doblando la esquina.	The drugstore was around the corner.
La escuela está siguiendo, a la izquierda.	The school is straight ahead on the left.
El banco está subiendo un poco.	The bank is [going] up there a little.

Verbs such as *encontrarse*, *estar localizado*, *estar ubicado*, and *quedar* are also used to express the same idea, but not with the present participle:

Mi casa se encuentra más adelante en esta calle.	My house is straight down on this street.
La farmacia estaba localizada a la vuelta de la esquina.	The drugstore was around the corner.
La escuela queda allá derecho, a la izquierda.	The school is straight ahead, on the left.
El banco está ubicado cerca de la plaza.	The bank is near the public square.

B. The present participle as an adverb

When it is not used with an auxiliary verb, the present participle functions as an adverb that modifies the action of the verb:

Pasó el día mirando televisión.	She spent the day watching TV.
Salió hablando con Marta.	He left talking to Martha.
Viviendo en el centro, era fácil visitar los museos.	While I lived downtown, it was easy to visit the museums.
Me vino a ver, teniendo ella tiempo entre conferencias.	She came to see me, since she had time between conferences.

C. The present participle and the idea of a continuous action

In combination with verbs of motion such as *andar*, *ir*, *seguir*, and *venir*, the present participle emphasizes the idea of a continuous action:

Andan revisando todo en la oficina.	They have been checking everything in the office.
Va saliendo de la depresión.	He is [gradually] coming out of his depression.
Seguimos estudiando mucho.	We keep on studying a lot.
Vengo sintiendo un malestar.	I've been feeling discomfort.

D. The present participle to imply a conditional statement:

Nosotros lo haríamos, **siendo** necesario.	We would do it if it were necessary.
Estando en la ciudad, yo visitaría el museo.	If I were in the city, I would visit the museum.
Considerando todo, podríamos aprovechar el tiempo.	If we consider everything, we would be able to take advantage of the time.

E. The present participle to denote an extended action

After verbs of perception such as *oír*, *ver*, *observar*, and *escuchar*, the present participle is used instead of the infinitive to denote an extended action:

La *oí* **llorando** a la madrugada.	I heard her crying at dawn.
Te *vimos* **regando** el jardín.	We saw you watering the garden.
Los *observé* **mezclando** las acuarelas.	I watched them while they were mixing the watercolors.
Me *escuchó* **hablando** con Luis.	He heard me talking to Luis.

When the verbs of perception are used with verbs of motion, the infinitive may also be used:

La *vi* **entrar**. (entrando)	I saw her coming in.
Los *escuchamos* **salir**. (saliendo)	We heard them going out.

F. Replacements for the present participle

In some cases, the gerund or present participle is replaced in Spanish by a relative clause, an adjective, or an adjectival phrase.

1. A relative clause replacing the present participle:

First, notice where the gerund in Spanish functions as a secondary verb:

Leyó los poemas **mencionando** el origen de su inspiración.	She read the poems and mentioned the source of her inspiration.
Le dieron los documentos **identificando** los problemas.	They gave him the documents and identified the problems.

Now observe the use of the relative clause:

Leyó los poemas **que mencionaban** el origen de su inspiración.	She read the poems that mentioned the source of her inspiration.
Le dieron los documentos **que identificaban** los problemas.	They gave him the documents that identified the problems.

2. An adjective (not formed with a present participle) or an adjectival phrase replacing the present participle:

an adjective

una película **espeluznante**	a horrifying movie
un signo **interesante**	an interesting sign
la selva **viviente**	the living forest
compañía **embotelladora**	bottling plant

an adjectival phrase

papel **de envolver**	wrapping paper
aceite **de cocinar**	cooking oil
goma **de mascar**	chewing gum
hilo **de bordar**	embroidery thread
aguja **de tejer**	knitting needle
punto **de fusión**	melting point

G. Use of the infinitive as a noun

Although in English the gerund is used as a noun, Spanish uses the infinitive, with or without the definite article:

Comer bien es saludable.	Eating well is healthy.
El leer instruye.	Reading educates.

H. The gerund to indicate manner

Although English uses *by* + the gerund to indicate the manner in which something may be accomplished, Spanish uses only the gerund:

Puedes hablar con ella **llamándola** a la oficina.	You may talk to her by calling her in her office.
Aprenderán a manejar **practicando** todos los días.	You will learn how to drive by practicing every day.

NOTES:

(1) With some prepositions, Spanish uses the *infinitive* while in English the *gerund* is used as the object of the preposition:

<u>Sin</u> **estudiar** no pasarás.	Without studying you will not pass.
<u>Con</u> **venir** no ganarás nada.	By coming you will not gain anything.
No veo nada malo <u>en</u> **comprar** lo necesario.	I don't see anything wrong in buying what is necessary.

(2) To indicate the justification of an action, Spanish uses the *gerund* or other equivalent expressions:

La llamé **diciéndole** la verdad.	I called her, telling (to tell) her the truth.
La llamé para decirle la verdad.	I called her to tell her the truth.
... porque quería decirle...	. . . because I wanted to tell her . . .
... al querer decirle...	. . . since I wanted to tell her . . .
... como quería decirle...	. . . since I wanted to tell her . . .
... puesto que quería decirle...	. . . because I wanted to tell her . . .
... ya que quería decirle...	. . . because I wanted to tell her . . .

I. Use of the infinitive as the object of a verb

Although English uses the *gerund* as the object of a verb, Spanish uses the *infinitive*:

Me gusta **escuchar** música.	I like listening to music.
Odiamos **venir** tarde a clase.	We hate coming late to class.
Ella dejó de **pensar** en el problema.	She stopped thinking about the problem.

J. Use of the past participle to describe states or conditions

Although English uses the *gerund* to describe posture or other states or conditions, Spanish uses the *past participle*:

La niña está **parada**.	The girl is standing.
La silla está **recostada** en la puerta.	The chair is leaning on the door.
La señora está **recostada**.	The lady is lying down.
El diploma está **colgado** en la pared.	The diploma is hanging on the wall.

K. Direct and indirect objects attached to the gerund (present participle)

If direct and/or objects are used, these are attached to the *gerund* in Spanish:

Viéndola enojada, me fui.	Seeing that she was upset, I left.
Su madre se acercó, **dándoselo**.	Her mother came closer, giving it to her.

NOTES:

(1) If the progressive tense is used, the object pronouns may be placed before the verb *estar* or attached to the gerund:

Su madre <u>se</u> <u>lo</u> está dando. / Su madre está dánd<u>oselo</u>.

(2) With reflexive or reciprocal verbs, the pronouns are placed before the verb or attached to the gerund:

<u>Me</u> estoy **peinando**.	I am combing my hair.
Estamos **escribiénd<u>onos</u>**.	We are writing to each other.

10

The Past Participle

The past participle is a verb derivative that functions as a verbal form, an adjective, and a noun. Some examples from the three Spanish conjugations are:

hablar ➤ hablado (spoken)   romper ➤ roto (broken)   vivir ➤ vivido (lived)

Forms of the Past Participle

Regular Forms

Regular past participles end in *-ado* or *-ido*. These endings replace the ending of the corresponding infinitive:

-ar verbs: *-ado*	cantar	➤	cantado	sung
	eliminar	➤	eliminado	eliminated
-er verbs: *-ido*	entender	➤	entendido	understood
-ir verbs: *-ido*	sufrir	➤	sufrido	suffered

Irregular Forms

Irregular past participles do not end in *-ado* or *-ido*. The following list shows some of the most common past participles:

abrir	abierto	opened; open
cubrir	cubierto	covered
decir	dicho	said
escribir	escrito	written
exponer	expuesto	exposed
hacer	hecho	done
morir	muerto	died; dead
poner	puesto	put

resolver	*resuelto*	resolved
romper	*roto*	broken
satisfacer	*satisfecho*	satisfied
ver	*visto*	seen
volver	*vuelto*	returned

NOTE:

Past participles of verbs that derive from verbs with irregular forms maintain the same irregularity as manifested in the original verbs:

describir	*descrito*	described
descubrir	*descubierto*	discovered
deshacer	*deshecho*	undone
devolver	*devuelto*	returned
imponer	*impuesto*	imposed
reabrir	*reabierto*	reopened

Verbs with Both Regular and Irregular Forms

Some verbs have two different past participles: a regular form that is used in the compound tenses (*ellos han prendido; they have caught*) and an irregular form used as an adjective or a noun (*preso; caught*). The irregular form cannot be used in compound tenses. These are some examples:

	Regular	Irregular
bendecir (to bless)	*bendecido*	*bendito*
elegir (to elect)	*elegido*	*electo*
extender (to extend)	*extendido*	*extenso*
fijar (to fix)	*fijado*	*fijo*
freír (to fry)	*freído*	*frito*
maldecir (to curse)	*maldecido*	*maldito*

NOTE:

All regular and irregular past participles used to form compound tenses end in *o* regardless of the gender and number of the subject that performs the action of the verb:

<u>Inés</u> *ha comprad**o** un coche.*	Ines has bought a car.
<u>Juan</u> *ha vendid**o** su casa.*	Juan has sold his house.
<u>Ellos</u> *han vist**o** la foto.*	They have seen the photo.

Uses of the Past Participle

A. The past participle as a verbal form

The past participle is used in Spanish in combination with the verb *haber* (the auxiliary *to have*) to form the compound tenses called *perfect tenses*, as in the English forms *I have done*, *we have written*, or *they have walked*.

The forms of *haber* are presented here to facilitate the comprehension of the past participle. They are covered in detail in the sections of each chapter that refer to the perfect (or compound) tenses:

Forms of *haber*

yo he	I have	*nosotros/as hemos*	we have
tú has	you have	*vosotros/as habéis*	you have
él ha	he has	*ellos han*	they have
ella ha	she has	*ellas han*	they have
Ud. ha	you have	*Uds. han*	you have

NOTE:

Haber may be conjugated in the present (*yo he*), past (*yo había*), preterit perfect (*yo hube*), future (*yo habré*), conditional (*yo habría*), present subjunctive (*yo haya*), and past or pluperfect subjunctive (*yo hubiera*) to form the following tenses or moods:

present perfect	*yo he andado*	I have walked
past perfect	*tú habías comido*	you had eaten
preterit perfect*	*ella hubo dicho*	she had said
future perfect	*Juan habrá visto*	Juan will have seen
conditional perfect	*nosotros habríamos ido*	we would have gone
present perfect subjunctive	*vosotros hayáis permitido*	you have allowed
pluperfect subjunctive	*ellos hubieran seguido*	they had followed

B. The past participle as an adjective

Past participles used as adjectives must agree in gender and number with the nouns they modify. Notice that the verb *haber* is not used in these examples:

*Me gusta la blusa raya**da**.*	I like the striped blouse.
*Sus manos están arruga**das**.*	His hands are wrinkled.
*Lo miró con ojos hundi**dos**.*	She looked at him with sunken eyes.
*El espacio es reduci**do**.*	The space is limited.

---

* This tense is no longer used in spoken Spanish. It is seldom seen in the written form, but is found in literary works.

Combined with some verbs, past participles used as adjectives indicate specific states or conditions. Note the following examples:

1. With **tener** (*to have*), past participles used as adjectives indicate the result of an action. The verb may be conjugated in any tense:

*Tiene escrit**os** dos libros.*	He has two books written.
*Tendrán la casa pintad**a**.*	They will have the house painted.
*Nos tuvo recopilad**os** los datos.*	He had the data gathered for us.
*Yo ya le tengo dich**o**.*	I have already told him.

2. With the verb **estar** (*to be*), past participles used as adjectives indicate the result of an action and are used to describe people, places, and things:

*La luz está encendid**a**.*	The light is (turned) on.
*El chico estaba acalorad**o**.*	The child was hot.
*El banco estará cerrad**o**.*	The bank will be closed.
*Las puertas estuvieron abiert**as**.*	The doors were open.

3. With **ser** (*to be*), past participles used as adjectives show an action or event in passive sentences, when the element acted upon becomes the subject of the sentence. This construction is called the *passive voice*. The verbs may be conjugated in any tense, while the agent of the action is stated or implicit:

*La puerta fue abiert**a**.*	The door was opened.
*Los votos fueron contad**os** por la secretaria.*	The votes were counted by the secretary.
*El informe es dad**o** por el jefe.*	The report is given by the boss.
*Los perros fueron soltad**os**.*	The dogs were set loose.
*La obra es representad**a**.*	The play is staged.

NOTES:

(1) When the subject is not specified, the impersonal *se* construction is widely used:

Se soltaron los perros.	The dogs were set loose.
Se representará la obra.	The play will be staged.
Se leyó el poema.	The poem was read.
Se firman los documentos al final de la reunión.	The documents are signed at the end of the meeting.

(2) When past participles are used as adjectives with verbs of motion such as *andar, ir, llegar, salir, seguir, venir,* and *volver,* the idea of continuous state or condition is emphasized:

Anda cansado.	He has been feeling tired.
Salió entristecida.	She went out sad.
Siguen desesperados.	They are still desperate.
Fui esperanzada.	I went with big hopes.

C. The past participle as a noun

Past participles used as nouns vary in gender and number and are used with definite and indefinite articles. Some examples follow:

los bordados	*el pescado*	*el vuelto*
un conocido	*el bañado*	*el rapto*
un expreso	*el sujeto*	*unas disputas*
la extinta	*las presas*	*el recién casado*
el herido	*una empleada*	*los puestos*
los muertos	*el estado*	*una corrida*
el resto	*el puesto*	*la venida*
la salida	*un revuelto*	*la bebida*

Past participles also become nouns in combination with the article *lo.* In this case, they always take the masculine singular form, and are modified by adverbs instead of adjectives:

Lo bien expresado es digno de aplauso.	What is well said is worthy of praise.
Lo hablado claramente puede ahorrar malentendidos.	What is said clearly can avoid misunderstandings.
Lo mal higienizado es peligroso.	What is not sanitized is dangerous.

D. The past participle as an adverb

Sometimes, past participles modify the subject and the verb, in which case they agree in gender and number with the subject:

Comió apurada.	She ate in a hurry.
Se quedó rendido.	He ended up exhausted.
Salieron sorprendidos.	They left surprised.
Llegaron decepcionadas.	They were disappointed when they arrived.

E. The past participle as an independent statement

Past participles indicate termination and agree in gender and number with the noun they modify:

*Una vez <u>hech**a**</u> <u>la comida</u>, ella se fue al trabajo.*	Once the food was cooked, she went to work.
*<u>Vendid**os**</u> <u>los productos</u>, se hicieron ricos.*	Having sold the products, they became rich.
<u>Terminado</u> <u>el examen</u>, recibirá la nota.	When the exam is finished, he will receive the grade.
<u>Cansada</u> de escucharlo, <u>ella</u> se quejaba a su madre.	Being tired of listening to him, she complained to her mother.

F. The past participle to denote *position* or *posture*

As mentioned in Chapter 9 under uses of the present participle, Spanish uses the past participle to denote position or posture, while English uses the gerund:

Elena está <u>sentada.</u>	Helen is seated.
El niño se quedó <u>acurrucado</u> en el rincón de miedo que tenía.	The child stayed huddled up in the corner because of fear.
La mujer está <u>arrodillada</u>.	The woman is kneeling.
El hombre está <u>doblado</u> por el dolor de espalda.	The man is bending down because of his back pain.

11

The Present Perfect Indicative

The present perfect in Spanish is equivalent to the present perfect in English. It usually describes an action that happened in the past and continues into the present or that may be repeated in the present. It can also indicate an action that has taken place in the recent past.

Forms of the Present Perfect Tense

The present perfect is formed with the present tense of the auxiliary verb *haber* (the auxiliary *to have* in English) plus the past participle of the main verb. Past participles end in *-ado*, *-ido*, or have irregular endings. Consult Chapter 10, The Past Participle, to review the forms:

yo	**he** visto	I have seen
tú	**has** comprado	you have bought
él	**ha** escrito	he has written
ella	**ha** dormido	she has slept
Ud.	**ha** puesto	you have put
nosotros/as	**hemos** venido	we have come
vosotros/as	**habéis** hecho	you have done
ellos	**han** oído	they have heard
ellas	**han** vuelto	they have returned
Uds.	**han** dicho	you have said

NOTES:

(1) The form *ha habido* (*there has been*) is the present perfect of *hay* (there is, there are).

Ha habido unos problemas en la mina. — There have been some problems in the mine.

*Dicen que no **ha habido** nadie en la conferencia.* — They said nobody was at the conference.

(2) No words can be placed between *haber* and the past participle.

*Yo no se lo **he dicho**.*	I have <u>not</u> told him that.
*Tú ya lo **has repetido**.*	You have <u>already</u> repeated it.

(3) The verb *haber* is rarely used as a transitive verb with the meaning of *tener* (*to have* as a possession):

(Rare: *yo he habido*)   ➤   More common: *yo he tenido*   ➤   I have had

Uses of the Present Perfect Tense

There are several uses for the present perfect tense.

A. The present perfect is used for an action that began in the past and continues into the present:

Él ha estado escribiendo.	He has been writing.
Hemos estado esperando.	We have been waiting.

B. The present perfect is used for an action that may be repeated in the present:

Él ha venido llegando tarde a clase estos días.	He has been arriving late to class these days.
Ella ha estado llamando por teléfono.	She has been calling on the phone.

C. The present perfect is used for an action that was terminated in the recent past:

Mi padre ha llegado hoy.	My father arrived today.
Ha terminado de comer.	He has finished eating.

D. The present perfect is used for an action that happened once in the past:

Mi secretaria ha recibido un aumento de sueldo.	My secretary has received a raise.
El preso ha confesado.	The inmate has confessed.

NOTE:

This form is widely used in Spain, while in Latin America the preterit is more common:

Mi secretaria recibió un aumento de sueldo.	My secretary received a raise.
El preso confesó.	The inmate confessed.

E. The present perfect is used for an action that culminated in the present as a result of events in the past:

He aprendido mucho este año.	I have learned a lot this year.
Mi hermana ha adelgazado mucho con ese régimen.	My sister has lost a lot of weight with that diet.
Finalmente he aceptado la verdad de los hechos.	I have finally accepted the truth about those facts.

12

The Past Perfect Indicative

In Spanish, the past perfect indicative (*pluscuamperfecto de indicativo*) is equivalent to the past perfect in English. Its function is basically to describe an action that happened before another action in the past: *I had sent the letter before you came back.*

Forms of the Past Perfect Tense

The past perfect is formed with the imperfect of the auxiliary verb *haber* (the auxiliary *to have* in English) plus the past participle of the main verb. Past participles end in *-ado*, *-ido*, or have irregular endings. Consult Chapter 10, The Past Participle, to review the forms:

yo	**había** visto	I had seen
tú	**habías** comprado	you had bought
él	**había** escrito	he had written
ella	**había** leído	she had read
Ud.	**había** puesto	you had put
nosotros/as	**habíamos** venido	we had come
vosotros/as	**habíais** hecho	you had done
ellos	**habían** vuelto	they had returned
ellas	**habían** hablado	they had spoken
Uds.	**habían** dicho	you had said

NOTES:

(1) The form *había habido* (*there had been*) is the past perfect of *hay* (*there is* or *there are*):

Había habido mucho viento antes de la tormenta.	There had been a lot of wind before the storm.
Creo que había* habido muchos artículos sobre la inflación.	I think there had been many articles about inflation.

---

* This form is used only in the singular.

(2) No words can be placed between *haber* and the past participle:

*Él ya lo **había traído** a casa antes de que tú llegaras.*	He had <u>already</u> brought it home before you arrived.
*Carlos no me las **había dado** cuando me viste.*	Carlos had <u>not</u> given them to me when you saw me.

(3) Adverbs like *ya* (*already*) or *todavía* and *aún* (*yet*) may be placed before *haber* or after the past participle:

*Ellos **ya** habían venido.*	They had already come.
*Ellos habían venido **ya**.*	They had already come.
*No habían venido **todavía**.*	They had not come yet.
***Todavía** no habían venido.*	They had not come yet.
***Aún** no habían llegado.*	They had not arrived yet.
*No habían llegado **aún**.*	They had not arrived yet.

In a preverbal position, *todavía* and *aún* must precede the negative *no*:

***Todavía no** lo había terminado.*	He had not finished it yet.
***Aún no** nos habían dado la fecha.*	They had not given us the date yet.

The same sentences may also be written as follows:

***No** lo había terminado **todavía**.*	He had not finished it yet.
***No** nos habían dado la fecha **aún**.*	They had not given us the date yet.

There are several ways to answer in the negative in Spanish using *todavía* or *aún*, which are equivalent to the expression *not yet* in English:

¿Terminaste el libro?	Did you finish the book?
No todavía.	Not yet.
Todavía no.	Not yet.
No, todavía no.	No, not yet.
Aún no.	Not yet.

Uses of the Past Perfect Tense

This tense is used to indicate an action that took place before another action in the past. There are several possibilities to express this type of situation.

A. The two actions may appear in the sentence:

Nosotros **habíamos comido** antes de salir.   We had eaten before we went out.

El niño ya **había terminado** cuando la   The boy had already finished when the teacher
  maestra lo llamó.   called him.

B. The most recent action may be left out:

Había llovido.   It had rained.

Mis padres **habían escrito.**   My parents had written.

C. Multiple actions may occur in the same sentence:

Laura ya **había visto** y **leído** la carta   Laura had already seen and read the letter
  cuando vino y me dijo la verdad.   when she came and told me the truth.

D. Replacements for the past perfect in spoken language

In spoken language, the preterit, preceded by expressions such as *en cuanto*, *luego que*, *después que,* or *tan pronto como,* replaces the past perfect:

Él se **había sacado** el sombrero antes de   He had taken off his hat before coming into
  entrar a la oficina.   the office.

Después que se sacó el sombrero, él entró   After he took off his hat, he came into his
  en la oficina.   office.

Yo recién **había hablado** con él cuando   I had just spoken to him when Cecilia
  Cecilia me llamó.   called me.

Luego que hablé con él, Cecilia me llamó.   Right after I talked to him, Cecilia called me.

Tito **había comido** antes de irse.   Tito had eaten before going out.

En cuanto comió, Tito se fue.   As soon as he ate, Tito went out.

E. The preterit perfect

To indicate an action that happened immediately before another action in the past, the *preterit perfect*, or **pretérito anterior**, is sometimes used in writing. This tense also follows expressions such as the ones mentioned in D., above.

The forms of the preterit of **haber**, which are used to make the preterit perfect (along with the past participle of the main verb), are as follows:

hube, hubiste, hubo, hubimos, hubisteis, hubieron

*Después que **hubo comido**, se fue a la escuela.*	As soon as he ate, he went to school.
*Así que **hubo entrado**, se quitó los zapatos mojados.*	As soon as he came in, he took off his wet shoes.

NOTE:

The form *hubieron* is only used as the auxiliary form of *haber* in compound tenses. It is incorrect to use *hubieron* with the meaning of *there were* as in the following examples:

Incorrect: *Hubieron tres ensayos para preparar la obra.*

Correct: ***Hubo** tres ensayos para preparar la obra.*

Incorrect: *Me enteré que hubieron dos chicos que faltaron.*

Correct: *Me enteré que **hubo** dos chicos que faltaron.*

F. The perfect infinitive

After expressions such as ***después de***, ***sin***, ***a pesar de***, and ***al***, the *perfect infinitive* is used to indicate two actions that took place in the past. This tense is formed with the infinitive of *haber* plus the past participle of the main verb. In this case, English would use the gerund of the verb *to have* and the past participle of the main verb:

*Entró después de **haber golpeado** la puerta.*	Having knocked on the door, he entered.
*A pesar de **haber bajado** el precio no pudieron vender el terreno.*	In spite of having lowered the price, they were not able to sell the lot.
*Salió sin **haber saludado**.*	He left without having said good-bye.
*Al **haber venido** tan tarde, pidió disculpas.*	Having arrived so late, he apologized.

13

The Infinitive

The infinitive is used to describe the action denoted by the verb in an abstract manner. It does not give any information about a subject nor the time in which the action may take place. Examples in English are *to talk*, *to go*, *to write*, etc. The infinitive has three possible endings in Spanish: *-ar*, *-er*, and *-ir*. Classified according to these endings, verbs are said to belong to the first, second, or third conjugation:

1st conjugation	2nd conjugation	3rd conjugation
hablar (to speak)	*comer* (to eat)	*vivir* (to live)
sentarse (to sit down)	*ser* (to be)	*dormir* (to sleep)

The infinitive is an impersonal mood because there are no variations in the form to indicate the person doing the action of the verb. In the following sentences, the equivalent English and Spanish infinitive forms function in just the same way:

*Quiero **hablar** castellano.*	I want to speak Spanish.
*Quieres **hablar** portugués.*	You want to speak Portuguese.

Uses of the Infinitive

A. Sometimes, English may use the gerund (*-ing* form) when Spanish uses the infinitive:

*Me gusta **cantar** en la lluvia.*	I like singing in the rain.
*Odia **levantarse** temprano.*	She hates getting up early.

B. When the two verbs used in the sentence share the same subject, the second verb must be in the infinitive form:

*Quiero **comprar** un coche nuevo.*	I want to buy a new car.
*Vamos a **mandar** la carta por vía aérea.*	We are going to send the letter via air mail.

NOTES:

(1) If the two verbs share the same subject but indicate a continuous action, the first verb may be one like *estar*, *seguir*, or *continuar* while the second verb takes the gerund ending *-ando* or *-iendo*, corresponding to the English *-ing*. This tense is called the *present progressive* if the first verb is in the present tense, the *past progressive* if the first verb is in the preterit or the imperfect, and so on. Consult Chapter 9, The Present Participle, for more information on the progressive tenses:

Juan *está esperando* noticias.	Juan is waiting for news.
Los estudiantes *continúan escribiendo* los ejercicios.	The students continue writing the exercises.
Los operarios *seguirán protestando*.	The workers will continue protesting.
Yo *estaba escuchando* música.	I was listening to music.

(2) With verbs of assertion, denial, doubt, or fear, such as *creer*, *decir*, *dudar*, *parecer*, *saber*, *sospechar*, *temer*, and others, the infinitive or a clause introduced by *que* (*that*) may be used even when there is only one subject:

Dijo que tiene bastante dinero.	
Dijo **tener** bastante dinero.	He said (that) he has enough money.
Le parece que está enfermo.	
Le parece **estar** enfermo.	He thinks (that) he is sick.
Temo que no pueda verlos.	
Temo no **poder** verlos.	I'm afraid I won't be able to see them.

(3) When the second verb points to an action that took place before the action of the first verb, the infinitive *haber* is used, followed by a past participle. The combination of *haber* plus a past participle is called *infinitivo compuesto* (*compound infinitive*) as opposed to *infinitivo simple* (*simple infinitive*) (as in *haber recibido* versus *recibir*):

Me alegra **haber** *recibido* la carta.	I am happy to have received the letter.
Lamento **haber** *llegado* tarde.	I am sorry to have arrived late.

C. **When the two verbs used in the sentence have different subjects, a clause in the indicative or in the subjunctive must be used for the second verb in Spanish.**

English uses the infinitive, a tense of the indicative (present, preterit, etc.), or the *-ing* construction in this case:

Estoy segura *que ella lo conoce.* (indicative)	I am sure she knows him.

No le gusta _que dejes_ el coche allá en la entrada del garaje. (present subjunctive)	He doesn't like you to leave the car there in the driveway.
Quería _que ella te dijera_ la verdad. (past or imperfect subjunctive)	I wanted her to tell you the truth.
Me parece _que ella se preocupa_ por los resultados.	It seems to me that she is wondering about the results.

> **NOTE:**
>
> With verbs of persuasion such as **_pedir, aconsejar_**, and **_recomendar_**, or verbs that refer to the senses, such as **_escuchar, mirar, oír, sentir_**, or **_ver_**, Spanish may or may not take the infinitive in the second verb when there are different subjects:
>
> | Le pedí **venir** esta tarde. | |
> | Le pedí _que viniera_ esta tarde. | I asked him to come this afternoon. |
> | Oigo **golpear** la lluvia en la ventana. | |
> | Oigo _que la lluvia golpea_ en la ventana. | I hear the rain hitting the window. |
> | Miraba **acercarse** el auto por la avenida. | |
> | Miraba _que se acercaba_ el auto por la avenida. | I watched the car approaching down the avenue. |

D. **The infinitive is used in Spanish after the following prepositions.**

1. _a_

The infinitive is used after the preposition _a_ in the following cases.

(a) _a_ plus infinitive after a verb that requires the preposition _a_. Some of these verbs are:

acostumbrarse, aprender, atreverse, comenzar, decidirse, dedicarse, empezar, enseñar, ir, lanzarse, llegar, and resignarse, among others

| El grupo _va **a cantar**_ en la iglesia. | The group is going to sing in church. |
| Los jefes _llegaron **a arreglar**_ el conflicto. | The managers managed to solve the conflict. |

(b) _a_ plus infinitive to imply a command (in this case the _a_ may also be omitted):

| ¡**A estudiar**! | Study! |
| ¡**Terminar** pronto! | Finish up soon! |

(c) _a_ plus infinitive after verbs such as **_comenzar, empezar, echar(se)_**, or **_ponerse_**, to indicate the beginning of an action, or after **_volver_**, in the sense of _repeating an action_:

*El coro <u>comenzó</u> **a cantar**.*	The choir began singing.
*Nos <u>echamos</u> **a correr**.*	We started to run.
*El niño <u>se puso</u> **a llorar**.*	The boy started crying.
*El <u>volvió</u> **a estudiar** el capítulo.*	He studied the chapter again.

The infinitive is also used after the preposition *a* with verbs such as ***llegar,*** in the sense of *coming to the point of*:

*Yo <u>llegué</u> **a imaginar**me la situación.*	I got to the point of imagining the situation. (I was able to imagine the situation.)
*Hasta ella <u>vino</u> **a suponer** lo que estaba pasando.*	Even she came to realize what was going on.

2. *con*

The infinitive is used after verbs that require this preposition:

*No <u>se gana</u> nada **con quejarse**.*	You cannot gain anything by complaining.
*Pablo <u>amenazó</u> **con decir** lo que sabía.*	Pablo threatened to say what he knew.

3. *de*

The infinitive is used after the prepositon *de* in the following cases.

(a) *de* plus infinitive to express a possibility:

***De ir** ustedes, ella les dará las notas.*	
(Si ustedes van, ella les dará las notas.)	If you go, she will give you the grades.
***De ofrecer** historia medieval, tomaré la clase.*	
(Si ofrecen historia medieval, tomaré la clase.)	If they offer medieval history, I'll take the class.

NOTE:

If the second verb is in the conditional tense instead of the future, the possibility is more remote:

***De ir** ustedes, ella les <u>daría</u> las notas.*	
(Si ustedes fueran, ella les daría las notas.)	If you went, she would give you the grades.

Notice the use of the imperfect subjunctive in the first verb of the second example sentence above, to agree with the second verb, which is in the conditional. This is a contrary-to-fact statement.

To indicate the same idea in the past, use *de* + *haber* + the past participle:

De haber ido ustedes, ella les habría dado las notas.

(*Si hubieran ido* ustedes, ella les habría dado las notas.)

If you had gone, she would have given you the grades.

NOTE:

The clauses above that begin with *si* belong to the category of *if clauses in the past,* or contrary-to-fact statements.

(b) The infinitive follows *de* when it is used in expressions such as ***a pesar de*** (*in spite of*), ***antes de*** (*before*), ***después de*** (*after*), ***en lugar de*** (*instead of*), and ***en vez de*** (*instead of*):

Vino <u>a pesar</u> ***de sentirse*** mal.

He came although he did not feel too well.

Me lo mandó <u>antes</u> ***de venir***.

She sent it to me before she came.

Lo llamaré a Emilio <u>después</u> ***de regresar***.

I'll call Emilio after I come back.

Maggie fue a la tienda <u>en lugar</u> ***de venir*** por acá.

Maggie went to the store instead of coming here.

Se compraron un auto <u>en vez</u> ***de ahorrarse*** el dinero.

They bought a car instead of saving the money.

(c) The infinitive follows *de* when it is used after an adjective:

Es <u>difícil</u> ***de entender*** que no haya llamado.

It is hard to understand that he has not called.

Era <u>interesante</u> ***de ver*** todas las casitas en fila a lo largo del río.

It was interesting to see all the little houses lined up along the river.

(d) The infinitive follows *de* when it is used after a noun (in which case *de* plus the infinitive functions as an adjective):

Mamá tenía una vieja <u>máquina</u> ***de coser*** marca Singer.

Mom had an old Singer sewing machine.

El niño necesita una <u>goma</u> ***de borrar***.

The child needs an eraser.

Me dieron una <u>máquina</u> ***de afeitar*** eléctrica.

They gave me an electric razor.

(e) The infinitive follows *de* when it is used in the expression ***tener ganas de,*** with the meaning of *to feel like*:

<u>Tiene ganas</u> ***de salir*** pronto de vacaciones.

She feels like going on vacation soon.

<u>Tuvimos ganas</u> ***de bailar***.

We felt like dancing.

(f) The infinitive is used after *de* when it appears in the expressions ***dejar de*** (*to stop doing something*), ***acabar de*** (*to have just* + a past participle, as in *to have just eaten*), and ***tratar de*** (*to try*):

*El hombre dejó **de llamar**la por teléfono.*	The man stopped calling her on the phone.
*Acabo **de leer** su última novela.*	I have just finished reading his latest novel.
*Traté **de convencer**la, pero no lo conseguí.*	I tried to convince her, but I couldn't.

(g) The infinitive is used after *de* following verbs such as *acordarse, alegrarse, cansarse, darse cuenta*, and *olvidarse*, which require the preposition:

*Se alegró **de salir** de compras con ella.*	She was happy to go out shopping with her.
*Nos olvidamos **de mandar** la carta.*	We forgot to send out the letter.
*Me cansé **de solicitar** empleo en esas compañías.*	I got tired of applying for jobs in those companies.

4. *en*

The infinitive is used after the preposition *en* in the following cases.

(a) The infinitive after verbs that require the preposition *en*:

*Gasta su herencia **en viajar** a lugares exóticos.*	He spends his inheritance traveling to exotic places.
*Están interesados **en comprar** la hacienda.*	They are interested in buying the ranch.
*Piensa sólo **en trabajar**.*	She only thinks about working.

A list of additional common verbs that require *en* includes, but is not limited to:

complacerse (to be pleased), *consistir* (to consist), *convenir* (to agree), *insistir* (to insist), *tardar* (to be delayed)

(b) The infinitive after *en* following an adjective or a pronoun such as *primero, segundo, último*, or *único*:

*Molly fue la primera chica **en aprender** la lección.*	Molly was the first girl to learn the lesson.
*Roberto será el último **en salir**.*	Roberto will be the last one to leave.

5. *hasta*

When the two verbs joined by *hasta* share the same subject, the infinitive is used for the second one:

*Va a insistir **hasta conseguir** lo que quiere.*	She will insist until she gets what she wants.
*Voy a quedarme **hasta terminar** la tarea.*	I'm going to stay until I finish the task.

However, if there is a change of subject, the subjunctive is used for the second verb:

*Voy a quedarme **hasta** que <u>ella</u> **termine** la tarea.*	I'm going to stay until she finishes the task.

6. *para*

The infinitive after *para*, meaning *in order to*:

*Compramos entradas **para ver** esa obra musical.*	We bought tickets (in order) to see that musical.
***Para apreciar** la naturaleza tienes que visitar Iguazú.*	(In order) To appreciate nature, you must visit Iguazu.

7. *por*

The infinitive after *por*, to indicate exchange or reason:

*Daría cualquier cosa **por ir** a Japón.*	I would give anything to go to Japan.
*Me retaron **por llegar** tarde.*	They scolded me for coming late.
*Me ofreció un café **por ayudar**lo con su trabajo.*	He offered me a cup of coffee for helping him with his work.

8. *sin*

When a verb follows *sin* (*without*) it must be in the infinitive. English uses the present participle or other expressions:

*Lo hizo **sin chistar**.*	He did it without saying a word.
*Se casaron **sin pensar**lo dos veces.*	They got married without thinking twice.
*Nos encontramos **sin querer**.*	We met by coincidence.
*Aceptó **sin titubear**.*	She accepted without hesitation.

E. After *que*, when English uses an infinitive or the gerund, Spanish uses the infinitive:

*Tengo mucho **que hacer**.*	I have a lot to do.
*No tienen **que comer** ahora.*	They do not have to eat now.
*No hace más **que leer**.*	All he does is read.
*Caminar me gusta más **que correr**.*	I like walking more than running.

If an accent mark is placed on *que* in the second sentence above, the meaning changes, as follows:

*No tienen **qué** comer ahora.*	They don't have anything to eat now.

F. After *ser* (to be), as predicate of the sentence, when English uses either the infinitive or the gerund, Spanish uses the infinitive:

*Lo que quiero **es hablar** contigo.*	What I want is to talk to you.
*Lo que me gusta **es caminar** en la lluvia.*	What I like is walking in the rain.

G. The infinitive is used after *tener que, haber de*, and *haber que,* to indicate a moral or personal obligation:

*Tengo que **estudiar** para el examen.*	I have to study for the exam.
*Hemos de **pedir**le que se quede.*	We must ask him to stay.
*Hay que **escribir** todo el párrafo.*	You have to write the whole paragraph.

H. The infinitive after *al*

The infinitive is used after the contraction *al* to indicate an action that took place at the same time as another action or as an immediate consequence of the other action. In this case, English uses *upon* plus the gerund:

*Se sacó el sombrero **al entrar**.*	He took off his hat upon entering.
***Al oír** la verdad se puso a llorar.*	Upon hearing the truth, she started crying (to cry).

The same construction in Spanish can also be used to show the results of an action (when the sentence in English would use *because* or *since*, instead of *upon* + the gerund):

***Al** no **recibir** noticias, la llamó por teléfono.*	Since (Because) she had not received any news, she gave her a call.
*Se rompió la pierna **al caerse** de la escalera.*	She broke her leg because she fell from the stepladder.

I. The infinitive is used as a noun, as follows.

1. The infinitive used as a noun may or may not take the definite article. If it does, the masculine singular form of the article is used. Notice that in English, either the infinitive or the gerund may be used:

Caminar es bueno para la salud.	To walk is good for our health.
El saber estudiar requiere habilidad.	Knowing how to study requires skills.

The predicate may be another infinitive, but never a gerund, as may be the case in English:

Amar es ir más allá de la obligación.	To love is to go the extra mile. / Loving is going the extra mile.
Decir la verdad es mostrar integridad.	To tell the truth is to show integrity.

2. If an adverb follows the infinitive used as a noun, the use of the article is optional:

(El) Fumar demasiado puede causar cáncer.	Smoking excessively may cause cancer.
(El) Participar en actividades es bueno para la comunidad.	Participating in activities is good for the community.

3. If a subject pronoun (*yo, tú*, etc.) follows the infinitive used as a noun, the article must be used:

El venir tú con ese plan me sorprende.	The fact that you are coming with that plan surprises me.
El ir y venir ellos es insinuante.	The fact that they are coming and going is suggestive.

4. If an adjective modifies the infinitive that is acting as a noun, the infinitive must be preceded by an article, a demonstrative adjective, or a possessive adjective:

El comer descontrolado es perjudicial.	Eating without self-control is harmful.
Ese penetrante mirar me atemorizaba.	That penetrating way of looking frightened me.
Su andar pausado me recordaba a mi padre.	His slow walking reminded me of my father.

5. Some infinitives have become true nouns, such that they take a plural form like other nouns. When the infinitive used as a noun is plural, the masculine plural form of the article and any adjective(s) should be used. If the infinitive as a noun is the subject of a verb, the verb must be conjugated in the third person plural:

Me fascina el amanecer a la orilla del mar.

*Me <u>fascinan</u> <u>los</u> **amaneceres** a la orilla del mar.*   Every dawn at the seashore fascinates me.
(Dawns at the seashore fascinate me.)

El poder absoluto del jefe es incuestionable.

<u>Los</u> **poderes** <u>absolutos</u> del jefe <u>son</u>   The absolute power(s) of the boss is (are)
incuestionables.   unquestionable.

    In English, some infinitives become nouns by using the form of the gerund, which does not happen in Spanish. Some of those nouns in English are *rating(s)*, *painting(s)*, *feeling(s)*, *greeting(s)*, and *closing(s)*.

Los cuadros de Goya son impresionantes.   Goya's paintings are impressive.
Paula te manda saludos.   Paula sends you greetings.

J. The infinitive is used to indicate a command or a request, with emphasis on the action:

*La profesora <u>me mandó</u> **cerrar** la puerta.*   The teacher ordered me <u>to close</u> the door.

However, if the emphasis is on the subject of the action, the subjunctive is used:

*La profesora **me** mandó que **cerrara** la puerta.*   The teacher ordered <u>me</u> to close the door.

In English, the stress on the word *me* would help to indicate this emphasis.

K. With impersonal expressions, the infinitive is used if no subject is specified:

*Es aconsejable **hacer** ejercicios físicos.*   It is advisable to exercise.
*Era importante **combatir** los momentos*   It was important to fight the sad moments.
tristes.

    If a subject is specified, the infinitive is used when the emphasis is on the action. Notice that the subject appears as an indirect object pronoun or after the preposition *para*:

*No <u>me</u> es posible **escribir** esa carta ahora*   It is impossible for me to write that letter
mismo.   right now.

*Es importante <u>para</u> él **asistir** a esa*   It is important for him to attend that
conferencia.   conference.

However, when the emphasis is on the subject of the action, the subjunctive is used. These are typical subjunctive sentences, with impersonal expressions and a second subject:

*Es imposible que **yo escriba** esa carta.*	It is impossible for me to write that letter.
*Es importante que **él asista** a esa conferencia.*	It is important for him to attend that conference.

L. The infinitive is used to show a negative reaction:

*¡**Marcharse** sin despedirse de nadie!*	Can you imagine that he left without saying good-bye!
*¿**Viajar** en avión yo? ¡Olvídalo!*	You want me to travel by plane? Forget it!

M. The infinitive is used in the passive voice, where English uses the gerund:

*Se lo vio **bajar** la escalera.*	He was seen coming down the stairs.
*¡Qué cantora! Se la oyó **cantar** en los mejores teatros.*	What a singer! She was heard singing in the best theaters.

N. In the active voice, Spanish uses the infinitive when English uses either the infinitive or the gerund:

*Ellos lo vieron **hablar** con el jefe.*	They saw him talk (talking) with the boss.
*El público la oyó **cantar** en los mejores teatros.*	The audience heard her sing (singing) in the best theaters.

O. Object pronouns may be attached to the infinitive or placed in front of the conjugated verb:

*Quiero **comprárselo**.*	I want to buy it for him.
***Se lo** quiero **comprar**.*	I want to buy it for him.

The same rule applies to reflexive verbs in the infinitive:

*Tengo que **lavarme** las manos.*	I have to wash my hands.
***Me** tengo que **lavar** las manos.*	I have to wash my hands.

P. The infinitive may function as an adverb:

***A juzgar** por las noticias, no creo que vaya.*	Judging by the news, I don't think she will attend.
***A decir verdad**, esta lección es muy difícil.*	To tell the truth, this lesson is very difficult.

14

The Subjunctive

The subjunctive is a verbal mood used mostly in a dependent clause, which is a group of words that cannot stand alone as a sentence. The subjunctive mood shows the point of view or the feelings of the subject about the action indicated in the sentence. These feelings may indicate, among others, a command, a wish, a piece of advice, a necessity, a negation, or an emotion. The action may also reflect a hypothetical, contrary-to-fact, or doubtful occurrence. For the correct use of the subjunctive, several elements must be present. The absence of one of these elements in the sentence will preclude the use of the subjunctive mood.

Elements of a Subjunctive Sentence

There are three main elements of a subjunctive sentence:

1. Two different subjects

2. The relative pronoun *que*

3. Two verbs with the following characteristics:

   (a) The verb that accompanies the first subject (in the main clause) must denote will (*querer, recomendar, aconsejar*); emotions (*sentir, alegrarse*); denial (*negar, no querer*); nonexistence (*no haber, faltar*); indefiniteness (*buscar, necesitar*) or impersonal expressions, which are formed by a combination of *ser* and an adjective such as *interesante*, *conveniente*, or *bueno*, as in:

Es bueno que vengas mañana.	It is good that you are coming tomorrow.
Es interesante que Uds. quieran viajar.	It is interesting that you want to travel.

   (b) The verb that follows the second subject (in the dependent clause) must be conjugated in the subjunctive form, as indicated in the subsections on endings and stems within the sections about the forms of each subjunctive tense, below. This verb may be in the present subjunctive or in the imperfect subjunctive (also called past subjunctive), depending on the tense indicated by the verb in the main clause.

Structure of a Subjunctive Sentence

Note the various parts of each sentence in the two examples of subjunctive sentences that follow:

El médico recomienda que Ud. camine todos los días.	The doctor recommends that you walk every day.
two different subjects	*el médico, Ud.*
relative pronoun	*que*
a verb of advice in the indicative	*recomienda*
a verb in the subjunctive form	*camine*

Mis padres quieren que nosotros vengamos mañana a las ocho.	My parents want us to come tomorrow at eight.
two different subjects	*mis padres, nosotros*
relative pronoun	*que*
a verb of will	*quieren*
a verb in the subjunctive form	*vengamos*

NOTES:

(1) When there is no change in the subject, an infinitive is used. Observe the following sentences:

■ two subjects: subjunctive

*(Tú) Te alegras de que <u>ellos</u> **tengan** paciencia.*	You are glad that they are patient.

■ one subject: infinitive

Te alegras de <u>tener</u> paciencia.	You are glad that you are patient.

■ two subjects: subjunctive

*(<u>Yo</u>) Dudo que <u>María</u> **pueda** venir.*	I doubt that María can come.

■ one subject: infinitive

*Dudo <u>poder</u> venir.**	I doubt that I can come.
*Dudo que (yo) **pueda** conseguir el dinero.*	I doubt I can get the money.
(Dudo poder conseguir el dinero.)	(I doubt I can get the money.)
*Dudo que (ella) **pueda** conseguirlo.*	I doubt she can get it.

---

* Although the examples given here show the grammatically correct usage, it is widely accepted that when the first verb is a verb of doubt, the second verb is in the subjunctive form, even when both verbs have the same subject. When the subject of the second verb might be ambiguous, the context can make it clear.

THE BIG RED BOOK OF SPANISH GRAMMAR

No creo que (yo) tenga interesados cuando (yo) quiera vender la casa.	I don't think I'll have people interested whenever I want to sell the house.
(No creo tener interesados cuando quiera vender la casa.)	(I don't think I'll have people interested whenever I want to sell the house.)
No creo que (Pedro) tenga interesados cuando (él) quiera vender la casa.	I don't think (Pedro) will have people interested whenever he wants to sell the house.

(2) The personal pronouns may be left out in subjunctive sentences, just as with all other sentences in Spanish:

Nosotros necesitamos que Uds. **manden** la carta.	We need you to send the letter.
Necesitamos que **manden** la carta.	We need you to send the letter.

Since the subject of *manden* could be *Uds. ellos*, or *ellas*, the right subject is determined by context. Clarification may be needed.

Verbs That Trigger the Subjunctive in the Dependent Clause

The following is a partial list of verbs that may appear in the main clause of a sentence that will have the subjunctive in its dependent clause. If there are two different subjects in the sentence, a verb in the subjunctive form will be required in the dependent clause.

A. Verbs of will that trigger the subjunctive

1. Wishes and the subjunctive:

agradecer (to be grateful)	*insistir* (to insist)
desear (to wish)	*preferir* (to prefer)
esperar (to hope)	*querer* (to want)

Esperamos que Uds. **traigan** a sus amigos.	We hope that you will bring your friends.
Prefiero que me **llames** temprano.	I would rather that you call me early.

2. Advice and the subjunctive:

aconsejar (to advise)	*rogar* (to beg)
proponer (to suggest)	*sugerir* (to suggest)
recomendar (to recommend)	*suplicar* (to beg)

| Te aconsejo que **compres** el rojo. | I advise you to buy the red one. |
| Nos recomienda que le **paguemos** el alquiler pronto. | He recommends that we pay him the rent soon. |

3. Permission or prohibition and the subjunctive:

aprobar (to approve)	*impedir* (to prevent)
dejar (to permit, to allow)	*oponerse* (to oppose)
desaprobar (to disapprove)	*permitir* (to let, to allow)
estar de acuerdo (to agree)	*prohibir* (to prohibit)

| Papá no nos deja que **salgamos** con ellos. | Dad does not allow us to go out with them. |
| La profesora nos prohíbe que **demos** los resultados. | The teacher does not allow us to give out the results. |

4. Commands and the subjunctive:

decir (to tell)	*ordenar* (to order)
exigir (to demand)	*pedir* (to ask)
instigar (to urge)	*requerir* (to require)
mandar (to command)	*rogar* (to beg)

| El jefe requiere que los empleados **firmen** las tarjetas. | The boss requires the employees to sign the cards. |
| La señora pidió que el mozo le **trajera** más pan. | The lady asked the waiter to bring her more bread. |

NOTES:

Certain verbs, such as *decir* (*to tell* or *to say*), **notificar** (*to notify*), or **mencionar** (*to mention*), do not trigger the subjunctive if they only provide information. The indicative is used in that case:

| El dijo que <u>viene</u> su hermano mañana. (information ➤ indicative) | He said that his brother comes tomorrow. |
| El dijo que **venga** su hermano mañana. (expression of will ➤ subjunctive) | He said for his brother to come tomorrow (that his brother should come tomorrow). |

B. Verbs of emotion that trigger the subjunctive:

alegrarse (to be glad)	*lamentar* (to regret)
encantar (to be delighted)	*sentir* (to be sorry)

esperar (to hope)   sorprenderse (to be surprised)

gustar (to like)   temer (to fear)

¡Me encanta que **vengas** a casa!   I am delighted that you are coming home!

Le sorprende que **digas** eso.   It surprises her that you say that.

C. Verbs of doubt, disbelief, or denial that trigger the subjunctive:

no creer (not to believe)   negar (to deny)

no comprender (not to understand)   no parecerle (not to seem)

dudar (to doubt)   no suponer (not to assume)

no estar seguro (not to be sure)

Dudo que ellos **tengan** su dirección.   I doubt that they have her address.

Negó que ella **hubiera pedido** el divorcio.   He denied that she had asked for the divorce.

No es verdad que ella **tenga** tres hijos.   It is not true that she has three children.

However, in the case of an affirmation, the indicative is used:

Es verdad que Juan <u>estudia</u> abogacía.   It is true that Juan studies law.

No niega que ella <u>ha pedido</u> el divorcio.   He doesn't deny that she has asked for the divorce.

D. Verbs that indicate nonexistence or indefiniteness and that trigger the subjunctive:

buscar (to look for)   necesitar (to need)

no encontrar (not to find)   querer (to want)

no haber (there is/are not)   no tener (not to have)

Necesito una casa que **tenga** tres   I need a house that has three rooms. Do you
habitaciones. ¿Tiene una?   have one?

No hay nadie que **quiera** trabajar el sábado.   There's no one who wants to work on
                                            Saturday.

However, when the sentence indicates existence or affirmation, the indicative is used:

Tengo una casa que <u>tiene</u> tres habitaciones.   I have a house that has three rooms.

Hay alguien que <u>quiere</u> trabajar el sábado.   There is someone who wants to work on
                                            Saturday.

Impersonal expressions that trigger the subjunctive:

1. Some of the most frequently used impersonal expressions that indicate emotions or opinions are the following:

es agradable	it is nice	*es malo*	it is bad
es bueno	it is good	*es necesario*	it is necessary
es curioso	it is unusual	*es raro*	it is unusual
es estupendo	it is great	*es recomendable*	it is advisable
es extraño	it is strange	*es urgente*	it is urgent
es una lástima	it is a pity	*es vergonzoso*	it is a disgrace

2. The verb *ser*, shown in the expressions above in the present tense, may also be used in these same expressions in any of the other tenses, such as the preterit, the imperfect, the conditional, or the future:

*Fue curioso que yo **recibiera** esa nota.* (preterit)	It was unusual for me to get that note.
*Era raro que ellos **llegaran** a tiempo.* (imperfect)	It was unusual for them to arrive on time.
*Sería posible que ellos **tuvieran** tiempo.* (conditional)	It would be posible for them to have time.
*Será estupendo que Jaime **consiga** ese trabajo.* (future)	It will be great if Jaime gets that job.

3. The verb *parecer* (*to seem*) is also used in impersonal expressions with the subjunctive:

*Parece increíble que tú no **quieras** hablarle.*	It seems incredible that you don't want to talk to him.
*Parecía un milagro que todos **estuvieran** juntos allí.*	It seemed like a miracle that everyone was there together.

The Present Subjunctive

The subjunctive has four tenses: present, imperfect or past, past perfect, and pluperfect. The following rules apply for verb endings and stems in the present subjunctive:

Forms of the Present Subjunctive

Present Subjunctive Endings

-ar verbs:	*-e, -es, -e, -emos, -éis, -en* *
-er and *-ir* verbs:	*-a, -as, -a, -amos, -áis, -an* **

Present Subjunctive Stems

The stem of most verbs in the present subjunctive comes from the stem of the *yo* form of the present indicative (without the *o* ending). This holds true for regular and stem-changing verbs and also for verbs in which the first person is irregular. Other verbs change the spelling in the subjunctive form to preserve the pronunciation of the indicative stems.

A. Regular verbs: stems in the present subjunctive

Present Indicative	Present Subjunctive	Present Indicative	Present Subjunctive
cantar		*leer / vivir*	
yo **cant**o	yo cant**e**	yo **le**o / **viv**o	le**a** / viv**a**
	tú cant**es**		le**as** / viv**as**
	él cant**e**		le**a** / viv**a**
	ella cant**e**		le**a** / viv**a**
	Ud. cant**e**		le**a** / viv**a**
	nosotros/as cant**emos**		le**amos** / viv**amos**
	vosotros/as cant**éis**		le**áis** / viv**áis**
	ellos cant**en**		le**an** / viv**an**
	ellas cant**en**		le**an** / viv**an**
	Uds. cant**en**		le**an** / viv**an**

---

* Please note that these are the same endings as for *-er* verbs in the present indicative, except for the *yo* form: (*como*), *comes, come, comemos, coméis, comen*

** Please note that these are the same endings as for *-ar* verbs in the present indicative, except for the *yo* form: (*hablo*), *hablas, habla, hablamos, habláis, hablan*

B. Stem-changing verbs: stems in the present subjunctive

1. *e* ➤ *ie* stem-changing verbs in the present subjunctive

(a) *e* ➤ *ie* stem-changing -*ar* and -*er* verbs change the stem in the subjunctive for all persons except the *nosotros/as* and the *vosotros/as* forms, just as they do in the present indicative (in the *nosotros/as* and *vosotros/as* forms, they revert to the infinitive stem). Remember that in stem-changing verbs, it is the second *e* that changes when there are two *e*s in the stem:

Infinitive	Present Indicative	Present Subjunctive
pensar (to think)	*pien**s**o*	*pien**s**e, pien**ses**, pien**s**e, pen**s**emos, pen**s**éis, pien**s**en*
defender (to defend)	*defiendo*	*defienda, defiendas, defienda, defendamos, defendáis, defiendan*
querer (to want)	*quiero*	*quiera, quieras, quiera, queramos, queráis, quieran*

Present Indicative:
*pensar: pienso, piensas, piensa, **pensamos**, **pensáis**, piensan*
*defender: defiendo, defiendes, defiende, **defendemos**, **defendéis**, defienden*
*querer: quiero, quieres, quiere, **queremos**, **queréis**, quieren*

(b) *e* ➤ *ie* stem-changing -*ir* verbs carry out the stem change in the subjunctive for all persons except for the *nosotros/as* and *vosotros/as* forms; for those forms, there is a different stem change: the single *e* of the stem (or the second *e* if there are two) changes to an *i* (note that this is different from what happens in the present indicative, where the *nosotros/as* and *vosotros/as* forms follow the stem of the infinitive):

Infinitive	Present Indicative	Present Subjunctive
mentir (to lie)	*miento*	*mienta, mientas, mienta, mintamos, mintáis, mientan*
preferir (to prefer)	*prefiero*	*prefiera, prefieras, prefiera, prefiramos, prefiráis, prefieran*

Present Indicative:
*mentir: miento, mientes, miente, **mentimos**, **mentís**, mienten*
*preferir: prefiero, prefieres, prefiere, **preferimos**, **preferís**, prefieren*

NOTES:

(1) If the stem of the infinitive ends in a *z*, the *z* becomes *c* in all the persons of the subjunctive, as in *empezar* (*to begin*):

yo empiezo ➤ *empiece, empieces, empiece, empecemos, empecéis, empiecen*

(2) There is one verb that changes *i* ➤ *ie*: *adquirir* (*to acquire*):

yo adquiero ➤ *adquiera, adquieras, adquiera, adquiramos, adquiráis, adquieran*

Notice that the **nosotros** and **vosotros** forms use the *i* of the infinitive, as they do in the present tense of the indicative:

adquirir: adquiero, adquieres, adquiere, adquirimos, adquirís, adquieren

(3) For practical reasons, only the six basic personal pronouns are used in the examples.

2. *e* ➤ *i* stem-changing verbs in the present subjunctive:

-*ir* verbs only: all persons change *e* to *i*

Infinitive	Present Indicative	Present Subjunctive
pedir (to ask for)	*pido*	*pida, pidas, pida, pidamos, pidáis, pidan*
medir (to measure)	*mido*	*mida, midas, mida, midamos, midáis, midan*

Present Indicative:

*pedir: pido, pides, pide, **pedimos, pedís**, piden*
*medir: mido, mides, mide, **medimos, medís**, miden*

3. *o* ➤ *ue* stem-changing verbs in the present subjunctive

(a) *o* ➤ *ue* stem-changing -*ar* and -*er* verbs change the stem in the subjunctive for all persons except the **nosotros/as** and the **vosotros/as** forms, which follow the infinitive:

Infinitive	Present Indicative	Present Subjunctive
contar (to count)	*cuento*	*cuente, cuentes, cuente, contemos, contéis, cuenten*
poder (to be able)	*puedo*	*pueda, puedas, pueda, podamos, podáis, puedan*

Present Indicative:

*contar: cuento, cuentas, cuenta, **contamos**, **contáis**, cuentan*

*poder: puedo, puedes, puede, **podemos**, **podéis**, pueden*

NOTE:

If the stem of the infinitive ends in a *z*, the *z* becomes *c* in all the persons of the subjunctive:

almorzar   *(to have lunch)*

yo almuerzo ➤ almuerce, almuerces, almuerce, almorcemos, almorcéis, almuercen

(b) *o ➤ ue* stem-changing -ir verbs change the stem in the subjunctive for all persons except the *nosotros/as* and *vosotros/as* forms, which change the *o* of the infinitive into a *u* (not like the present indicative, where the *nosotros/as* and *vosotros/as* stems follow the infinitive):

Infinitive	Present Indicative	Present Subjunctive
morir (to die)	**muer**o	*muera, mueras, muera, muramos, muráis, mueran*
dormir (to sleep)	**duerm**o	*duerma, duermas, duerma, durmamos, durmáis, duerman*

Present Indicative:

*morir: muero, mueres, muere, **morimos**, **morís**, mueren*

*dormir: duermo, duermes, duerme, **dormimos**, **dormís**, duermen*

C. Verbs with irregular first person in the present indicative: stems in the present subjunctive

Some verbs are irregular in the *first person indicative* only (all other persons follow the infinitive). Since the stem of the present subjunctive comes from the *yo* form of the present indicative, this stem change is maintained in all persons of the present subjunctive, as shown in the following examples:

Infinitive	Present Indicative		Present Subjunctive
caber (to fit)	*quepo*	**cab ➤ quep**	*quepa, quepas, quepa, quepamos, quepáis, quepan*
*conocer** (to know)	*conozco*	**add z**	*conozca, conozcas, conozca, conozcamos, conozcáis, conozcan*

---

* One of the exceptions to this pattern for verbs ending in -cer is *mecer* (*to rock*), which is conjugated in the present indicative tense as *yo mezo, tú meces, él mece, nosotros mecemos, vosotros mecéis, ellos mecen*. The present subjunctive, derived from the present indicative *yo* form, is *meza, mezas, meza, mezamos, mezáis, mezan*.

hacer (to do)	*hago*	**c ➤ g**	*haga, hagas, haga,* *hagamos, hagáis, hagan*
lucir (to show off)	*luzco*	**add z**	*luzca, luzcas, luzca,* *luzcamos, luzcáis, luzcan*
poner (to put)	*pongo*	**add g**	*ponga, pongas, ponga,* *pongamos, pongáis, pongan*
salir (to go out)	*salgo*	**add g**	*salga, salgas, salga,* *salgamos, salgáis, salgan*
traer (to bring)	*traigo*	**add ig**	*traiga, traigas, traiga,* *traigamos, traigáis, traigan*

D. Verbs that change the stem to preserve pronunciation in the present subjunctive

In certain verbs, a spelling change is required in the present subjunctive to preserve the pronunciation of the first person indicative. As mentioned before, the spelling of the subjunctive stem originates in the *first person indicative (yo)*. The change affects all persons:

Infinitive	Present Indicative		Present Subjunctive
buscar (to look for)	*busco*	**c ➤ qu**	*busque, busques, busque,* *busquemos, busquéis, busquen*
pagar (to pay)	*pago*	**g ➤ gu**	*pague, pagues, pague,* *paguemos, paguéis, paguen*

NOTE:

If the stem in the first person indicative already has a *u* following the *g*, a diaeresis is placed on the *u* of the subjunctive to preserve the pronunciation of the *u*:

Infinitive	Present Indicative		Present Subjunctive
atestiguar (to witness)	*atestiguo*	**u ➤ ü**	*atestigüe, atestigües, atestigüe,* *atestigüemos, atestigüéis, atestigüen*
averiguar (to find out)	*averiguo*	**u ➤ ü**	*averigüe, averigües, averigüe,* *averigüemos, averigüéis, averigüen*

If there is already a spelling change in the first person indicative to preserve the pronunciation of the infinitive, the change is also kept through all persons of the present subjunctive:

Infinitive	Present Indicative		Present Subjunctive
exigir (to require)	*exijo*	g ➤ j	*exija, exijas, exija, exijamos, exijáis, exijan*
recoger (to collect)	*recojo*	g ➤ j	*recoja, recojas, recoja, recojamos, recojáis, recojan*

All forms for verbs like *exigir* and *recoger* have a *g* in all persons of the present indicative, except the first person *yo*, which has a *j*.

E. Irregular present subjunctive forms

The following verbs are irregular in the present subjunctive since they do not follow the spelling of the first person of the present indicative:

Infinitive	Present Indicative	Present Subjunctive
dar (to give)	*doy*	*dé*, des, dé*, demos, deis, den*
estar (to be)	*estoy*	*esté, estés, esté, estemos, estéis, estén*
haber	*he*	*haya, hayas, haya, hayamos, hayáis, hayan*
ir (to go)	*voy*	*vaya, vayas, vaya, vayamos, vayáis, vayan*
saber (to know)	*sé*	*sepa, sepas, sepa, sepamos, sepáis, sepan*
ser (to be)	*soy*	*sea, seas, sea, seamos, seáis, sean*

---

* The accent mark on **dé** (one-syllable word) is used to distinguish it from the preposition **de** (*of*).

NOTE:

Haber is an auxiliary verb used to form the compound tenses: the present perfect and the past perfect indicative, the present perfect subjunctive, the pluperfect subjunctive, the future perfect, and the conditional perfect. A form of *haber* is also used to express availability as in *there is* and *there are* (*hay*). The other forms for expressing availability are: *hubo* (*there was / there were*), *había* (*there was / there were*), *habrá* (*there will be*), *habría* (*there would be*), and the subjunctive forms *haya* and *hubiera*.

*El recomienda que **haya** un lápiz para cada estudiante.*	He recommends that there be one pencil for each student.
*La maestra espera que **haya** veinte niños en la clase.*	The teacher hopes that there will be twenty children in class.

Uses of the Present Subjunctive

The present subjunctive reflects the following actions or states.

A. An action that is happening in the present

*Quiero que **firmes** el formulario ahora.*	I want you to sign the form now.

B. A state of being

*¡Qué bueno que **seas** mi amigo!*	How nice that you are my friend!
*¡Qué maravilloso que **estés** estudiando!*	How wonderful that you are studying!

C. Habitual actions

*Nos alegra que ellos **se reúnan** siempre con nosotros.*	We are pleased that they always join us.

D. An action that is likely to happen in the future

*Es importante que Ud. **envíe** la carta el viernes.*	It is important that you send the letter on Friday.

NOTE:

In all the cases above, the verb in the main clause is in the present indicative, while the verb in the dependent clause is in the present subjunctive.

There is another case, however, when the verb in the main clause is in the preterit while the verb in the dependent clause is in the present subjunctive. This may happen only when

(1) the preterit verb is a verb of will, such as *decir* (*to say*), *recomendar* (*to recommend*), *aconsejar* (*to advise*), or *sugerir* (*to suggest*), and

(2) what was suggested, advised, recommended, etc., was expected to happen at that particular moment or in the future:

*Ayer le <u>sugerí</u> que **juegue** esta tarde con nosotros.*	Yesterday I suggested to him that he play with us this afternoon.
*Les <u>dije</u> que **vayan** mañana a ver esa película.*	I told them to go tomorrow to see that movie.

However, observe also the following examples where the imperfect (or past) subjunctive—underlined in these examples—must be used after the preterit, because of two different circumstances:

■ The time for the suggested or recommended action has already passed:

Les dije que <u>fueran</u> esa misma tarde a ver la película. Les gustó muchísimo.	I told them to go that afternoon to see the movie. They liked it a lot.

■ The time for the suggested or recommended action is followed by a verb in the past tense:

Ayer le sugerí que <u>jugara</u> esta tarde con nosotros, pero no quiso.	Yesterday I suggested to him that he play with us this afternoon, but (at that particular moment) he didn't want to.

Other Uses of the Present Subjunctive

A. **Suggestions or invitations to do something as a group using the *nosotros/as* (*we*) form of the subjunctive**

Grammatically, the *nosotros/as* (*we*) form of the subjunctive is known as a *let's command*. This form is equivalent to the English *Let's* + verb, as in *Let's go*, *Let's sing*, etc:

***Cenemos** en Casa Mariel esta noche.*	Let's have dinner at Mariel's tonight.

NOTES:

(1) The other standard (and nonsubjunctive) way to express this kind of suggestion or invitation to do something as a group in Spanish is by using *vamos a* + infinitive:

Vamos a cenar en Casa Mariel esta noche.
Let's have dinner at Mariel's tonight.

The *vamos a* + infinitive construction and the *let's commands* (*nosotros* form of the subjunctive) are equally acceptable.

(2) Pronouns are attached to affirmative *let's commands*:

Pongámoslo en la sala.	Let's put it in the living room.

(3) When the pronoun *nos* is attached to a *let's command*, the *s* of the verb is omitted:

Pongámonos los abrigos. ¡Hace mucho frío!	Let's put on our coats. It's very cold!
(Not: *pongámosnos*)	

(4) When both the indirect object and the direct object pronouns are used, and the indirect object pronoun is a *se* form, the *s* of the command form is dropped:

Pongamos el abrigo al chico.
Pongámoselo.
(Not: *pongámosselo*)

(5) Pronouns used in the dependent clause of a subjunctive sentence are placed before the verb (these are not *let's commands*):

Juan quiere que lo pongamos en la sala.	Juan wants us to put it in the living room.
Mamá sugiere que nos pongamos los abrigos.	Mom suggests that we put on our coats.

B. **Indirect commands (*Let's have someone else do it!*) using the subjunctive**

1. To express this command, the main clause is eliminated and the sentence begins with the relative pronoun *que*:

¡Que ella le dé la buena noticia!	Let her give him the good news!

2. Here are some common indirect commands and expressions:

¡Ojalá* que llegue bien!	I hope he will get there safely.
¡Ojalá que no haga frío!	I hope it won't be cold.
Que descanse en paz.	May he rest in peace.
¡Que lo pase bien!	I hope you have a good time!
¡Que regresen pronto!	We hope you come back soon!
¡Que sean muy felices!	May you be very happy!
¡Que te vaya bien!	I hope everything goes well!
¡Que tengan felices vacaciones!	Have a good vacation!

C. The subjunctive in time clauses

1. The subjunctive in the time clause when the main clause indicates future action

When the verb in the main clause indicates a future action (simple future or informal future), the subjunctive is normally used in the time clause. Some of the expressions that trigger the subjunctive are: *cuando* (*when*), *en cuanto* (*as soon as*), *ni bien* (*as soon as*), *tan pronto como* (*as soon as*), *hasta que* (*until*), *mientras* (*while*), *antes* (*de*) *que* (*before*), and *después* (*de*) *que* (*after*) (see notes [a] and [b] below about when *que* can be omitted in *hasta que*, *antes* [*de*] *que*, and *después* [*de*] *que*):

Cuando **llegue** a casa, dormiré una siesta. (future)	When(ever) I arrive home, I will take a nap.
Cuando **llegue** a casa voy a dormir una siesta. (informal future)	When(ever) I arrive home, I'm going to take a nap.
Iremos al banco en cuanto **recibamos** el cheque. (future)	We'll go to the bank as soon as we receive the check.
Va a ir al banco en cuanto **reciba** el cheque. (informal future)	She is going to the bank as soon as she receives the check.

(a) When the subject of the dependent clause is the same as the subject of the main clause, the relative pronoun *que* may be deleted. In this case, the infinitive is used instead of the subjunctive:

---

* Derived from the Arabic language, the expression *ojalá* means *I hope* (*yo espero*) and is widely used by Spanish speakers. It had its origin as praise to Allah; however, it no longer has religious connotations.

*Leeré el libro <u>hasta que</u> (yo) lo **termine**.*
(subjunctive)

Leeré el libro hasta <u>terminar</u>lo. (infinitive)   I will read the book until I finish it.

*Juan traerá el mapa <u>antes de que</u> (él) **salga** para su clase.*

Juan traerá el mapa <u>antes de</u> <u>salir</u> para su clase.   Juan will bring the map before leaving for class.

*El abogado firmará el documento <u>después de que</u> él lo **lea**.*

El abogado firmará el documento <u>después de leer</u>lo.   The lawyer will sign the document after reading it.

(b) When the subject in the dependent clause is different from the subject in the main clause, the relative pronoun *que* must be used:

*Leeré el libro **hasta que** Marta lo necesite.*   I will read the book until Marta needs it.

■ However, the preposition *de* in *antes (de) que*, *después (de) que* may be left out:

*Juan traerá el mapa <u>antes de que</u> Pedro **llegue**.*

*Juan traerá el mapa <u>antes que</u> Pedro **llegue**.*   Juan will bring the map before Pedro arrives.

*El abogado firmará el recibo <u>después de que</u> el cliente lo **lea**.*

*El abogado firmará el recibo <u>después que</u> el cliente lo **lea**.*   The lawyer will sign the document after his client reads it.

2. The subjunctive following *antes de que*

If the main verb indicates an action that is performed habitually, the present indicative is used in the dependent clause after the adverbial conjunction, with the exception of *antes de que* (*before*), which is always followed by the subjunctive:

<u>Cuando</u> Pedro <u>llega</u> a casa, (siempre) duerme una siesta.   When Pedro arrives home, he (always) takes a nap. (indicative)

*Vamos al banco **en cuanto** <u>recibimos</u> el cheque (cada vez).*   We go to the bank as soon as we receive the check (every time). (indicative)

*Siempre hago la tarea <u>antes de que</u> **vengan** mis amigos.*   I always do my homework before my friends come. (subjunctive)

3. The subjunctive with verbs that convey information

Certain verbs, such as *recordar, decir, insistir,* and *repetir,* require the indicative in the dependent clause if they are used to convey information; otherwise, the subjunctive is needed:

Siempre le recuerdo (a ella) que es mi mejor amiga. (indicative)	I always remind her that she is my best friend.
Le recuerdo que alimente al gato por la noche. (subjunctive)	I remind you to feed the cat at night.
Mamá nos repite que tenemos suerte con los niños. (indicative)	Mom keeps telling us that we are lucky with the kids.
Mamá nos repite que volvamos antes de las cinco. (subjunctive)	Mom keeps telling us to come back before five o'clock.

The Imperfect Subjunctive

The imperfect subjunctive, also called past subjunctive, is used in the same cases as the present subjunctive, with the exception that the situation or action indicated in the sentence has already happened. In this case, the verb in the main clause may be in the imperfect tense or in the preterit tense of the indicative. The conditional tense also appears in the main clause when a probability is indicated. Notice the following sentences, in which four different tenses are used in the main clause:

Present:

Mamá quiere que prepare la ensalada. (*prepare*: present subjunctive)	Mom wants me to prepare the salad.

Imperfect:

Mamá siempre quería que preparara la ensalada. (*preparara*: imperfect subjunctive)	Mom always wanted me to prepare the salad.

Preterit:

Mamá quiso que preparara la ensalada ayer. (*preparara*: imperfect subjunctive)	Mom wanted me to prepare the salad yesterday.

Conditional:

Mamá querría que yo preparara la ensalada. (*preparara*: imperfect subjunctive)	Mom would like me to prepare the salad.

Forms of the Imperfect Subjunctive

Imperfect Subjunctive Endings

The imperfect subjunctive may be formed in two different ways.

A. The first way of forming the imperfect subjunctive

The first way of forming the imperfect subjunctive, for *-ar*, *-er*, and *-ir* verbs, is to take the third person plural (*ellos*) preterit form of the verb, eliminate the ending *-on*, and add the following endings:

> *a, as, a, amos, ais, an*
>
> *cantar<u>on</u>* ➤ *cantara, cantaras, cantara, cantáramos, cantarais, cantaran*

These are the same endings as for the present subjunctive of *-er* and *-ir* verbs, as in *veng<u>a</u>; escrib<u>as</u>, teng<u>amos</u>*. However, the stem is different: remember that for the present subjunctive, the stem that the endings are added to is the stem of the first person singular, *yo*, of the present indicative; for the imperfect subjunctive, it is the stem of the third person plural of the preterit.

Some examples of the imperfect subjunctive are:

*yo hicier**a***	*hacer*	to do / to make
*tú fuer**as***	*ir / ser*	to go / to be
*él comier**a***	*comer*	to eat
*nosotros supiér**amos***	*saber*	to know
*vosotros dier**ais***	*dar*	to give
*ellos amar**an***	*amar*	to love

B. The second way of forming the imperfect subjunctive

The second way of forming the imperfect subjunctive, for *-ar*, *-er*, and *-ir* verbs, is to take the third person plural (*ellos*) preterit form of the verb, eliminate the ending *-ron*, and add the following endings:

> *se, ses, se, semos, seis, sen*
>
> *cantar<u>on</u>* ➤ *cantase, cantases, cantase, cantásemos, cantaseis, cantasen*

(These endings are used mostly in Spain, while the endings shown previously in A. are used both in Latin America and Spain.) See the following examples:

yo hicie**se**	hacer	to do / to make
tú fue**ses**	ir / ser	to go / to be
él comie**se**	comer	to eat
nosotros supié**semos**	saber	to know
vosotros die**seis**	dar	to give
ellos ama**sen**	amar	to love

> **NOTE:**
> For reasons of practicality, only the first set of endings (*a, as, a, amos, ais, an*) will be used for the examples in this chapter.

Imperfect Subjunctive Stems

As we have seen, the stem of the imperfect subjunctive comes from the third person plural (*ellos*) of the preterit tense: ***cantaron*** (*they sang*), ***bebieron*** (*they drank*), ***vivieron*** (*they lived*). The preterit ending *-on* is dropped, and new endings are added to form the subjunctive. The forms for all verb categories are as follows:

A. The imperfect subjunctive of regular verbs:

	Preterit	Imperfect Subjunctive
-ar	cantar**on** they sang	cantar**a**, cantar**as**, cantar**a**, cantár**amos**, cantar**ais**, cantar**an**
-er	comier**on** they ate	comier**a**, comier**as**, comier**a**, comiér**amos**, comier**ais**, comier**an**
-ir	vivier**on** they lived	vivier**a**, vivier**as**, vivier**a**, viviér**amos**, vivier**ais**, vivier**an**

B. The imperfect subjunctive of stem-changing verbs

1. *-ar* and *-er* verbs do not change the stem in the preterit; therefore, there is no change in the stem of the imperfect subjunctive:

Infinitive	Preterit third person plural	Imperfect Subjunctive
pensar (to think)	pensaron	pensara, pensaras, pensara, pensáramos, pensarais, pensaran
tender (to hang)	tendieron	tendiera, tendieras, tendiera, tendiéramos, tendierais, tendieran

2. However, since -ir verbs change the stem in the preterit in both the third person singular and the third person plural, the spelling of the imperfect subjunctive form is affected.

(a) The imperfect subjunctive of *e* ➤ *ie* stem-changing -ir verbs

For *e* ➤ *ie* stem-changing -ir verbs, the *e* of the stem changes to an *i* in the third person plural of the preterit. If there are two *e*s in the stem, it is the second *e* that changes:

Infinitive	Preterit third person plural	Imperfect Subjunctive
sentir (to feel)	sintieron	sintiera, sintieras, sintiera, sintiéramos, sintierais, sintieran
preferir (to prefer)	prefirieron	prefiriera, prefirieras, prefiriera, prefiriéramos, prefirierais, prefirieran

(b) The imperfect subjunctive of *e* ➤ *i* stem-changing -ir verbs

The *e* of the stem changes to an *i*. If there are two *e*s in the stem, it is the second *e* that changes:

Infinitive	Preterit third person plural	Imperfect Subjunctive
pedir (to ask for)	pidieron	pidiera, pidieras, pidiera, pidiéramos, pidierais, pidieran
repetir (to repeat)	repitieron	repitiera, repitieras, repitiera, repitiéramos, repitierais, repitieran

(c) The imperfect subjunctive of *o* ➤ *u* stem-changing -ir verbs

The *o* of the stem changes to *u*:

Infinitive	Preterit third person plural	Imperfect Subjunctive
dormir (to sleep)	durmieron	durmiera, durmieras, durmiera, durmiéramos, durmierais, durmieran

NOTE:

There are also irregular verbs whose infinitives end in *-ar*, *-er*, or *-ir*, which have irregular forms in the preterit. The imperfect subjunctive of these verbs follows the spelling of the third person plural of their respective preterit forms. See the section immediately following.

C. The imperfect subjunctive of verbs that have irregular forms in the preterit

Irregularities of the preterit will be carried over to all persons of the imperfect subjunctive, as shown in the following examples:

Infinitive	Preterit third person plural	Imperfect Subjunctive	
caber	cupieron	cupier-	a, as, a, amos, ais, an
dar	dieron	dier-	a, as, a, amos, ais, an
decir	dijeron	dijer-	a, as, a, amos, ais, an
estar	estuvieron	estuvier-	a, as, a, amos, ais, an
haber	hubieron	hubier-	a, as, a, amos, ais, an
hacer	hicieron	hicier-	a, as, a, amos, ais, an
ir	fueron	fuer-	a, as, a, amos, ais, an
leer	leyeron	leyer-	a, as, a, amos, ais, an
tener	tuvieron	tuvier-	a, as, a, amos, ais, an
poder	pudieron	pudier-	a, as, a, amos, ais, an
poner	pusieron	pusier-	a, as, a, amos, ais, an
querer	quisieron	quisier-	a, as, a, amos, ais, an
saber	supieron	supier-	a, as, a, amos, ais, an
ser	fueron	fuer-	a, as, a, amos, ais, an
traducir	tradujeron	tradujer-	a, as, a, amos, ais, an
traer	trajeron	trajer-	a, as, a, amos, ais, an

NOTES:

(1) The *nosotros/as* forms carry an accent mark on the last *e* of the stem:

cupiéramos   diéramos   leyéramos

(2) The imperfect subjunctive of *hay* (*there is* or *there are*) is *hubiera*, and it is always singular:

El recomendó que **hubiera** un lápiz para cada estudiante.

He recommended that a pencil be available for each student.

La profesora esperaba que por lo menos **hubiera** veinte niños en la clase.

The teacher hoped that there would be at least twenty children in the class.

(3) The imperfect subjunctive forms *hubiera, hubieras, hubiera, hubiéramos, hubierais*, and *hubieran* of the verb *haber* are used as the auxiliary form for the pluperfect subjunctive (a compound form covered later in this chapter):

*Era bueno que ellos **hubieran venido** temprano.*	It was good that they had come early.

D. The imperfect subjunctive of verbs that change the stem to preserve pronunciation

-ar verbs that change their spelling in the present subjunctive to preserve the sound of the infinitive (*buscar* ➤ *busque*) do not need to change in the imperfect subjunctive, since the endings in the imperfect subjunctive begin with *a* and not *e*, and there is therefore no change in pronunciation. Besides, the spelling for the imperfect subjunctive derives from the *ellos* form of the preterit, where there is no need to change the spelling to preserve pronunciation to begin with (*buscaron, tocaron, pagaron, llegaron*):

Infinitive	Present Subjunctive	Imperfect Subjunctive
*bus**car*** (to look for)	*bus**que***	*bus**ca**ra, bus**ca**ras, bus**ca**ra, bus**cá**ramos, bus**ca**rais, bus**ca**ran*
*to**car*** (to touch)	*to**que***	*to**ca**ra, to**ca**ras, to**ca**ra, to**cá**ramos, to**ca**rais, to**ca**ran*
*pa**gar*** (to pay)	*pa**gue***	*pa**ga**ra, pa**ga**ras, pa**ga**ra, pa**gá**ramos, pa**ga**rais, pa**ga**ran*
*lle**gar*** (to arrive)	*lle**gue***	*lle**ga**ra, lle**ga**ras, lle**ga**ra, lle**gá**ramos, lle**ga**rais, lle**ga**ran*

Uses of the Imperfect Subjunctive

The imperfect subjunctive is used in the following cases:

A. The imperfect subjunctive is used to indicate an action in the past in the same situations where the subjunctive would be required in the present:

Present Subjunctive	Imperfect Subjunctive
Es interesante que Carlos me <u>cuente</u> las noticias.	*Era interesante que Carlos me **contara** las noticias.*

It is interesting that Carlos tells me about the news.	It was interesting that Carlos would tell me about the news.
Se alegra que llevemos los abrigos.	*Se alegró que lleváramos los abrigos.*
She is glad that we are taking the coats.	She was glad that we took the coats.

NOTE:

When the effects of the past action are still felt in the present, the present perfect subjunctive replaces the imperfect subjunctive:

*Es una pena que lo **despidieran**.*	*Es una pena que lo **hayan despedido**.*
(imperfect subjunctive)	(present perfect subjunctive)
It's a pity that they fired him.	*It's a pity that they have fired him.*

B. The imperfect subjunctive is used after the expression *ojalá* (or *ojalá que*), meaning *I hope*, to indicate contrary-to-fact or unlikely events:

Present Subjunctive	**Imperfect Subjunctive**
(there is hope)	(the possibility is remote)
*Ojalá que **llueva** mañana.*	*Ojalá **lloviera** mañana.*
I hope it rains tomorrow.	I hope it would rain tomorrow.
*Ojalá que me **escriba** pronto.*	*Ojalá me **escribiera** pronto.*
I hope she writes to me soon.	I wish she'd write to me soon.

C. The imperfect subjunctive is used in *if clauses* to indicate contrary-to-fact or unlikely events:

*Si **pudiera**, cambiaría de carrera ahora mismo.*	If I could, I would change careers right now.
*Iríamos en avión **si tuviéramos** que viajar.*	We would go by plane if we had to travel.

D. When the verb in the main clause is in one of the past tenses or in the conditional, the imperfect subjunctive is used in the dependent clause.

Notice that, as always, the pronoun is optional:

Preterit

*Quise que (ella) me **dijera** la verdad.*	I wanted her to tell me the truth. (one-time event)

Imperfect

*Quería que (ella) me **dijera** la verdad.*

I wanted her to tell me the truth, but she always refused. (repeated action)

Present Perfect

*He querido que me **dijera** la verdad.*

I have wanted her to tell me the truth. (recent past)

Past Perfect

*Había querido que me **dijera** la verdad antes de irse.*

I had wanted her to tell me the truth before she left. (two actions in the past)

Conditional

*Querría que me **dijera** la verdad.*

I would like her to tell me the truth. (possibility)

E. The imperfect subjunctive is used when the verb in the main clause is in the present indicative, but refers to a previous occurrence:

*No me parece que (ella) **llegara** con él.*

It doesn't seem to me that she arrived with him.

*Es bueno que (ellos) **vinieran** juntos.*

It's good that they arrived together.

*Es obvio que (ella) **quisiera** haber tenido amigas.*

It's obvious that she would have wanted to have friends.

F. Imperfect subjunctive endings used to indicate politeness

The imperfect subjunctive endings *a, as, a, amos, ais*, and *an* (and not the *se* endings as in *quisiese*) are used with the verbs *querer* (*to want*), *poder* (*to be able*), and *deber* (*should*) to indicate politeness. The conditional tense may also be used:

***Quisiera** venir temprano.*	I would like to come early.
Conditional: *Querría venir temprano.*	
*¿**Pudiera** Ud. firmar aquí?*	Could you sign here?
Conditional: *¿Podría Ud. firmar aquí?*	
*Tú **debieras** ayudarlo a Juan.*	You should help Juan.
Conditional: *Tú deberías ayudarlo a Juan.*	

Other Uses of the Imperfect Subjunctive

If Clauses and the Imperfect Subjunctive

To indicate that a situation is contrary to fact, the imperfect subjunctive is used in the *if clause* while a verb in the conditional form must be used in the main clause of the sentence:

Si tuviera tiempo, te escribiría (conditional) *más seguido.*   If I had time, I would write to you more often.

The *if clause* (*si tuviera tiempo*) may be placed at the beginning of the sentence or after the main clause, as is also the case in English:

Te escribiría más seguido si tuviera tiempo.   I would write to you more often if I had time.

Observe the use of the imperfect subjunctive in another example:

La llevaría (conditional) *a la fiesta si supiera bailar.*   He would take her to the party if he could dance.

Si supiera bailar, la llevaría a la fiesta.   If he could dance, he would take her to the party.

> **NOTE:**
>
> To imply a statement of possibility (likely to happen), both verbs in the sentence take the indicative:
>
> *Si tengo dinero a fin de mes, me compro algo lindo.*   If I have money at the end of the month, I (always) buy something nice for myself. (present/present)
>
> If the possibility is pending, the present and the future are used:
>
> *Si tengo dinero a fin de mes, me compraré algo lindo.*   If I have money at the end of the month, I will buy something nice for myself. (present/future)
>
> To imply the possible occurrence of two future actions, the conditional is used with the imperfect subjunctive:
>
> *Yo lo llamaría* (conditional) *después que ella viniera.*   I would call him after she arrived.
>
> *Comeríamos* (conditional) *cuando tú llegaras.*   We would eat when you arrived.

The Present Perfect Subjunctive

The present perfect subjunctive, just like the present perfect indicative (*I have done, I have witnessed*), is used to indicate an action that was completed before the enunciation of the speaker's statement.

Forms of the Present Perfect Subjunctive

To form the present perfect subjunctive, it is necessary to use the auxiliary verb *haber* and the past participle of the main verb. The only difference is that the auxiliary verb *haber* is in the present subjunctive form.

The forms of *haber* in the present subjunctive (used to make the present perfect) are: *haya, hayas, haya, hayamos, hayáis, hayan*:

Haber	Past Participle	
yo haya	*leído*	I have read
tú hayas	*venido*	you have come
él haya	*roto*	he has broken
nosotros hayamos	*hablado*	we have spoken
vosotros hayáis	*abierto*	you have opened
ellos hayan	*descubierto*	they have discovered

Compare the following sentences in the present perfect indicative and the present perfect subjunctive. The subjunctive sentences are introduced by the verbs *dudar* and *alegrarse*, which require the use of the subjunctive in the dependent clause:

Present Perfect Indicative	Present Perfect Subjunctive
El ha comprado las entradas.	*Dudo que él las haya comprado.*
He has bought the tickets.	I doubt he has bought them.
Papá ha hablado con Juan.	*Me alegro que haya hablado con él.*
Dad has talked to Juan.	I'm glad he has talked to him.

NOTES:

(1) While the verb *to have* indicates possession and is also used as an auxiliary (helping) verb in English, Spanish has two different verbs for these two functions: *tener* for possession and *haber* as an auxiliary verb:

Tiene un buen libro. (She <u>has</u> a good book.) (possession)

Ella ha comprado uno. (She <u>has</u> bought one.) (auxiliary verb)

(2) The present perfect subjunctive form of *hay* (*there is* or *there are*) is **haya habido**:

*¡Qué bueno que **haya habido** tantos programas!*	It's good that there have been so many programs!

Uses of the Present Perfect Subjunctive

The present perfect subjunctive is used with past actions or with future events.

A. The present perfect subjunctive with past actions

The verb in the main clause may be in the present indicative, present perfect indicative, future, or future perfect:

Present:

*Lamento que tú no **hayas podido** venir anoche.*	I regret that you were not able to come last night.

Present Perfect:

*A papá le <u>ha gustado</u> mucho que le **hayas mandado** una postal.*	Dad liked it very much that you sent him a card.

Future:

*Siempre <u>sentiré</u> que él no **haya reconocido** su error.*	I will always regret that he has not recognized his mistake.

Future Perfect:

*Al final de mi carrera creo que <u>me</u> <u>habré</u> <u>lamentado</u> de que tú nunca **hayas querido** estudiar conmigo.*	By the end of my career I think that I will have regretted that you never wanted to study with me.

B. The present perfect subjunctive with future events

The present perfect subjunctive is used to indicate an action to be completed prior to another future event. In this case, the verb in the main clause may be in the present indicative, in the future, or in a command form.

Present:

*<u>Es</u> posible que para el lunes él ya **haya pintado** la casa.*	It is possible that he will have painted the house by Monday.

Present:

*No creo que tú ya **hayas tomado** una decisión para mayo.*

I don't think that you will have made a decision by May.

Future:

*Será bueno que para mayo tú ya **hayas tomado** una decisión.*

It will be good for you to have made a decision by May.

NOTE:

If it is a most unlikely possibility that the event will happen, the conditional is used in the main clause, while the past perfect (or pluperfect) subjunctive (covered in the next section) is used in the dependent clause:

Conditional:

*Sería bueno que para mayo tú ya **hubieras tomado** una decisión.*

It would be good for you to have made a decision by May.

Command (the command form is suggested by the present tense):

*Insisto que para fin de curso Uds. **hayan entregado** el resumen.*

I insist that by the end of the course you have turned in your summary.

The Pluperfect Subjunctive

The pluperfect subjunctive, also called past perfect subjunctive, indicates a completed action that took place prior to another action in the past, in cases where a dependent clause is subordinate to a main clause.

Forms of the Pluperfect (Past Perfect) Subjunctive

The pluperfect subjunctive is equivalent to the past perfect indicative (*yo había hecho / I had done*), but with the difference that the auxiliary verb *haber* is in the imperfect subjunctive form (*hubiera*) rather than in the imperfect indicative (*había*). (Note that there is another imperfect subjunctive form of *haber* (*hubiese*, etc.) which is used mainly in Spain):

Haber	Past Participle	
yo hubiera (hubiese)	*venido*	I had come
tú hubieras (hubieses)	*traído*	you had brought
él hubiera (hubiese)	*regresado*	he had returned
nosotros hubiéramos (hubiésemos)	*dicho*	we had said

vosotros hubierais (hubieseis)	*cantado*	you had sung
ellos hubieran (hubiesen)	*reflexionado*	they had reflected

Notice the following examples:

Past Perfect Indicative	**Pluperfect or Past Perfect Subjunctive**
Tú habías visto las fotos.	*Carlos dudó que tú hubieras visto las fotos.*
You had seen the pictures.	Carlos doubted that you had seen the pictures.
Ud. había perdido el avión.	*Yo no creí que Ud. hubiera perdido el avión.*
You had missed the plane.	I did not believe that you had missed the plane.

NOTES:

(1) As we pointed out in the notes to the section on the present perfect subjunctive, in English, the verb *to have* indicates possession (*I have a dog*) and is also used as an auxiliary (helping) verb (*I have bought a dog*). In Spanish, however, the verb ***tener*** is used for possession (***tengo un perro***), while ***haber*** functions as the auxiliary verb.

(2) The form ***hubiese*** is more common in Spain and in the written, literary form.

(3) The past perfect subjunctive form of ***hay*** (*there is / there are*) is ***hubiera habido***, equivalent to *there had been*, although it is not possible to translate the Spanish verb form literally into English all of the time:

*Fue interesante que **hubiera habido** tanta gente.*	It was interesting that there had been so many people.

Uses of the Pluperfect (Past Perfect) Subjunctive

The pluperfect subjunctive is used in the following cases.

A. The pluperfect subjunctive to describe a prior event in the past

The pluperfect subjunctive is used to describe an action in the past that took place prior to another action, also in the past. The verb in the main clause may appear in the preterit or in the imperfect indicative:

Preterit:

*El no pudo aceptar que sus amigos **hubieran muerto**.*	He could not accept that his friends had died.

Imperfect:

Yo dudaba que Uds. hubieran leído la carta.   I doubted that you had read the letter.

B. The pluperfect subjunctive to indicate an action that is contrary to fact

When the pluperfect subjunctive indicates an action that is contrary to fact, the verb in the main clause is in the conditional tense:

¡Qué triste sería que ellos no hubieran llegado a tiempo!   How sad it would be for them not to have arrived on time!

C. The pluperfect subjunctive or *de* plus infinitive in *if clauses*

1. The pluperfect subjunctive is used in *if clauses* when the verb in the main clause is in the conditional perfect or in the pluperfect subjunctive:

Yo lo habría (or hubiera) comprado si tú me hubieras entregado el dinero.   I would have bought it if you had given me the money.

Yo debería haber estado allí si lo hubiera sabido.   I would have to have been there, if I had known about it.

Si mi hermano hubiera tenido paciencia, yo habría (or hubiera) hecho lo posible por ir a verlo.   If my brother had been patient, I would have done everything possible to go and see him.

   Notice the same sentence when the hypothetical action is pointing toward the future rather than to an event that could have happened in the past, but never did:

Si mi hermano tuviera paciencia, yo haría lo posible por ir a verlo.   If my brother were patient, I would do everything possible to go and see him.

2. Note that in such cases, the expression *de* plus the infinitive (or perfect infinitive) can also be used instead of the pluperfect subjunctive in the *if clause*, underlined below:

Si lo hubiera sabido antes, yo hubiera (or habría) desistido.
De saberlo antes, yo hubiera (or habría) desistido.
De haberlo sabido antes, yo hubiera (or habría) desistido.
If I had known ahead of time, I would have given up.

*Si les **hubieran dado** permiso, ya **hubieran** (or habrían) salido.*

***De darles** permiso, ya **hubieran** (or habrían) salido.*

***De haberles dado** permiso, ya **hubieran** (or habrían) salido.*

If they had been given permission, they would have already left.

*Si **hubiera ido** allá, yo **hubiera** (or habría) visitado el museo.*

***De ir** allá, yo **hubiera** (or habría) visitado el museo.*

***De haber ido** allá, yo **hubiera** (or habría) visitado el museo.*

If I had gone there, I would have visited the museum.

15

The Imperative

Commonly known as *commands*, the imperative is used to give orders that are more direct than the "softened commands" expressed by the subjunctive. The different forms of the imperative include the formal commands for *Ud.* (*usted*); the informal or familiar commands for *tú*; the command forms for *Uds.* (*ustedes*) and *vosotros/ as*; the first person plural commands (*Let's commands* or commands for the *nosotros* form); and the impersonal commands.

The *Ud.* and *Uds.* Formal Commands

These commands are used when addressing people (one person or more) in a formal manner. They are classified as single or plural formal commands.

A. Affirmative formal commands

The forms used for affirmative formal commands (to tell someone to do something) are the subjunctive forms for *Ud.* (*usted*) and *Uds.* (*ustedes*):

(Ud.) **Venga** más temprano.	Come earlier.
(Uds.) **Esperen** el correo.	Wait for the mail.

NOTE:

The equivalent softened commands, expressed with the subjunctive, would be similar to the following examples:

Sugiero que Ud. <u>venga</u> más temprano.	I suggest that you come earlier.
Queremos que Uds. <u>esperen</u> el correo.	We want you to wait for the mail.

Commands can be made more polite by the addition of the personal pronouns *Ud.* and *Uds.* and expressions such as *por favor* (*please*), *se lo ruego* (*I beg you*), *hágame el favor* (*do me the favor*), *si le parece* (*if you like*), *si Ud. quiere* (*if you want*), *si le viene bien* (*if it is convenient for you*), and others:

<u>Venga</u> Ud. más temprano.	Come earlier.
<u>Esperen</u> Uds. el correo.	Wait for the mail.

Pida un taxi, por favor.	Ask for a taxi, please.
Vaya a verlo, se lo ruego.	Go see him, I beg you.
Agregue otra página, si le parece.	Add another page, if you like.

B. Negative formal commands

To express a formal command in the negative, simply place _no_ before the verb:

No ponga (Ud.) su cartera allí.	Don't put your purse there.
No dejen (Uds.) los libros acá.	Don't leave the books here.

> **NOTE:**
>
> The equivalent softened commands, expressed with the subjunctive, would be similar to the following examples:
>
> | | |
> |---|---|
> | _Recomiendo que <u>no ponga</u> (Ud.) su cartera allí._ | I recommend that you not put your purse there. |
> | _Sugerimos que <u>no dejen</u> (Uds.) los libros acá._ | We suggest that you not leave the books here. |

C. Formal commands with reflexive verbs

1. Affirmative formal commands with reflexive verbs

The pronoun _se_ must be attached to both singular and plural command forms of the reflexive verb. Note the _n_ that signals the plural form of the verb:

	Singular	Plural	
sentarse	_Siéntese._	_Siéntense._	Sit down.
levantarse	_Levántese._	_Levántense._	Get up.
vestirse	_Vístase._	_Vístanse._	Get dressed.

> **NOTE:**
>
> If a subjunctive sentence is used to express a softened command, the _se_ is placed before the verb:
>
> | | |
> |---|---|
> | _Le pido que <u>se</u> <u>levante</u> más temprano._ | I ask you to get up earlier. |

2. Negative formal commands with reflexive verbs

In negative commands, the pronoun _se_ must be placed between _no_ and the verb:

No **se** siente (Ud.) en la sala.	Don't sit down in the living room.
No **se** queden (Uds.) aquí.	Don't stay here.

If a subjunctive sentence is used to express a softened command in the negative with a reflexive verb, the word order is the same as the one used for the direct command, above:

Le ruego que <u>no se siente</u> (Ud.) en la sala.	I beg you not to sit in the living room.
Les pido que <u>no se queden</u> (Uds.) aquí.	I ask you not to stay here.

D. **Formal commands with direct and indirect object pronouns**

1. Affirmative formal commands with object pronouns

Attach both direct and indirect object pronouns to the commands:

*Díga**le** (Ud.) la verdad.*	Tell <u>him</u> the truth.
*Mánden**lo** (Uds.) temprano. (el sobre)*	Send <u>it</u> early. (the envelope)
*Envíenos**la** (Ud.) pronto. (la nota)*	Send <u>it</u> to us soon. (the note)
*Llénen**nos** (Uds.) los vasos.*	Fill the glasses <u>for us</u>.

Notice the double *n* in the last example sentence above: ***Llénennos (Uds.) los vasos.*** The first *n* is part of the plural command form ***llenen***; the other *n* is part of the indirect object pronoun ***nos***.

NOTE:

If a subjunctive sentence is used to express a softened command, the object pronouns are placed before the verb in the dependent clause, which is in the subjunctive:

Quiero que <u>le</u> <u>diga</u> la verdad.	I want you to tell him the truth.
Sugiere que <u>lo</u> <u>manden</u> más temprano.	He suggests that you send it earlier.

2. Negative formal commands with object pronouns

Direct and indirect object pronouns are placed between *no* and the verb:

*No **le** diga (Ud.) la verdad.*	Don't tell him the truth.
*No **lo** manden (Uds.) más temprano.*	Don't send it earlier.

If a subjunctive sentence is used to express a softened command, there is no change in the form, and the word order remains the same:

Quiere que Ud. <u>no le diga</u> la verdad.   He wants you not to tell him the truth.

Ellos dicen que <u>no lo manden</u> más temprano.   They say for you not to send it earlier.

E. Formal commands with direct and indirect object pronouns together

1. Affirmative formal commands with double pronouns

    Attach both pronouns to affirmative commands. When using object pronouns together, the indirect object pronoun is always placed before the direct object pronoun. Notice that the indirect object pronoun changes from *le* or *les* to *se* when the direct object pronoun begins with *l* (*lo*, *la*, *los*, *las*). This rule applies to all cases where double objects are used with commands:

    *Vénda**selo** (Ud.).*   Sell it to her.

    el libro (lo); ella (le)

    *Tráigan**nosla** (Uds.).*   Bring it to us.

    NOTE:

    If a subjunctive sentence is used to express a softened command, both pronouns are placed before the verb in the dependent clause, which is in the subjunctive:

    Sugiero que <u>se lo</u> venda.   I suggest that you sell it to her.

    Queremos que <u>nos la</u> traigan.   We want you to bring it to us.

2. Negative formal commands with double pronouns

    The indirect object pronoun is placed before the direct object pronoun, and both are placed between *no* and the verb:

    *No **se lo** venda (Ud.).*   Don't sell it to her.

    *No **nos la** traigan (Uds.)*   Don't bring it to us.

    NOTE:

    If a subjunctive sentence is used to express a softened command, there is no change in the form and the word order remains the same:

    Le pido que <u>no se lo venda</u>.   I ask you not to sell it to her.

    Queremos que (Uds.) <u>no nos la traigan</u>.   We want you not to bring it to us.

F. **Formal commands with reflexive verbs and pronouns**

1. Affirmative formal commands with reflexive verbs and pronouns

   Direct object pronouns are attached to affirmative commands:

ponerse (to put on)	*Aquí está el abrigo. Póngaselo (Ud.).*
	Here's the coat. Put it on.
lavarse (to wash)	*Tienen las manos sucias. Lávenselas (Uds.).*
	Your hands are dirty. Wash your hands. (*Literally: Wash them.*)

   > **NOTE:**
   > If a subjunctive sentence is used to express a softened command, both the reflexive pronoun *se* and the direct object pronoun are placed before the verb:
   >
   > | | |
   > |---|---|
   > | *Pido que **se** lo ponga.* | I ask you to put it on. |
   > | *Queremos que **se** las laven.* | We want you to wash them. |

2. Negative formal commands with reflexive verbs and pronouns

   Both the reflexive pronoun *se* and the direct object pronoun are placed between *no* and the verb, with the reflexive pronoun always before the direct object pronoun:

ponerse	affirmative:	*Pónga**selo** (Ud.).*	Put it on.
	negative:	*No **se** lo ponga.*	Don't put it on.
lavarse	affirmative:	*Láven**selas** (Uds.).*	Wash them (your hands).
	negative:	*No **se las** laven.*	Don't wash them.

   > **NOTE:**
   > If a subjunctive sentence is used to express a softened command, there is no change in the form and the word order remains the same:
   >
   > | | |
   > |---|---|
   > | *Sugiero que <u>no se lo ponga</u>.* | I suggest that you do not put it on. |
   > | *Es malo que <u>no se las laven</u>.* | It's bad for you not to wash them. |

The *tú* Informal or Familiar Commands

This command is used to address a person or a pet in an informal manner. The person could be a friend, a relative, a parent, a child, or a peer.

A. Affirmative *tú* commands

There are two different forms: regular and irregular.

1. Regular affirmative *tú* commands

   This form is the same as the third person singular (*él*, *ella*, *Ud.*) of the present indicative:

	Present indicative	***tú* command**
hablar	El (ella) <u>habla</u> español.	**Habla** español, Tita.
	He speaks Spanish.	Speak Spanish, Tita.
vivir	Ud. <u>vive</u> feliz.	**Vive** feliz, Juan.
	You live happily.	Live happily, Juan.

   > **NOTE:**
   >
   > If a subjunctive sentence is used to express a softened command, the subjunctive form of the verb is used in the dependent clause, instead of the third person singular of the indicative:
   >
   > | | |
   > |---|---|
   > | Quiero que **hables** español. | I want you to speak Spanish. |
   > | Te ruego que **vivas** feliz. | I beg you to live happily. |

2. Irregular affirmative *tú* commands

   These forms are very short and must be memorized.

decir (to say)	**Di** la verdad.	Tell the truth.
hacer (to do)	**Haz** la tarea.	Do the homework.
ir (to go)	**Ve** a casa.	Go home.
poner (to put)	**Pon** la mesa.	Set the table.
salir (to go out)	**Sal** de aquí.	Get out of here.
ser (to be)	**Sé** bueno.	Be good.
tener (to have)	**Ten** paciencia.	Be patient.
venir (to come)	**Ven** pronto.	Come soon.

   > **NOTE:**
   >
   > Another short command is *he*, from the verb *haber* (*He aquí, Henos, Helas,* etc.), when *haber* was a synonym of *tener*. This form is very rare and appears in older manuscripts, literary works, and biblical materials. This form is not to be confused with *heis*, from the auxiliary *haber*, equivalent to *has* (*puesto*), and widely used in the *romances* and literature of the Golden Age.

NOTE:

If a subjunctive sentence is used to express a softened command, the subjunctive form of the verb is used in the dependent clause instead of the irregular form, above:

Quiero que <u>digas</u> la verdad, Miguel.   I want you to tell the truth, Miguel.

Sugiero que <u>hagas</u> la tarea, Lucía.   I suggest you do the homework, Lucía.

B. Negative *tú* commands

These commands use the same form as the second person singular *tú* of the present subjunctive. There are no irregular negative *tú* commands:

	Present subjunctive	**Negative *tú* command**
hablar	Quiero que tú <u>hables</u>.	**No hables.**
	I want you to speak.	Don't speak.
estar	Siento que <u>estés</u> triste.	**No estés triste.**
	I'm sorry that you are sad.	Don't be sad.
decir	Quiero que <u>digas</u> la verdad.	**No digas la verdad**.
	I want you to tell the truth.	Don't tell the truth.
hacer	Quiero que <u>hagas</u> la tarea.	**No hagas la tarea**.
	I want you to do the homework.	Don't do the homework.

C. Informal *tú* commands with reflexive verbs

1. Affirmative *tú* commands with reflexive verbs

The pronoun *te* must be attached to the command form of the verb:

lavarse	Lá**vate** las manos.	Wash your hands.
cambiarse	Cámbia**te** la ropa.	Change your clothes.
ponerse	Pon**te** los zapatos.	Put on your shoes.
irse	Ve**te** de aquí.	Get out of here.

NOTES:

(1) Notice the use of the irregular forms *pon* and *ve*, of the verbs *poner* and *ir*, to express the affirmative command.

(2) If a subjunctive sentence is used to express a softened command with a reflexive verb, the *te* is placed before the subjunctive form of the verb (e.g., *te cambies*) instead of being attached to the end of the command form (*cámbiate*):

Sugiero que **te cambies** la ropa.	I suggest that you change your clothes.

The same rule applies to the irregular forms *pon*, *sal*, etc:

Recomiendo que **te pongas** los zapatos.	I recommend that you put on your shoes.

2. Negative *tú* commands with reflexive verbs

To express a negative command, place *te* between *no* and the second person of the present subjunctive form of the verb, such as *laves*, *pongas*, *hables*, etc:

	Present subjunctive without the *se*	Negative *tú* command
cambiar**se** (cambiar)	(tú) cambies	**No te cambies.**
	Do not change.	
ir**se** (ir)	(tú) vayas	**No te vayas.**
	Do not go.	

NOTE:

If a subjunctive sentence is used to express a softened command, there is no change in the form and the word order stays the same:

Quiero que **no te cambies** la ropa.	I want you not to change your clothes.
Sugerimos que **no te vayas** ahora.	We suggest that you don't go now.

D. **Informal *tú* commands with direct and indirect object pronouns**

1. Affirmative *tú* commands with object pronouns

Direct and indirect object pronouns are attached to regular and irregular affirmative commands:

Escríb**ela**. (la carta)	Write it. (the letter)
Haz**lo** ahora. (el ejercicio)	Do it now. (the exercise)
Mír**alo**. (a Juan)	Look at him.
Llám**anos**.	Call us.

If a subjunctive sentence is used to express a softened command, the object pronouns are placed before the verb, which is conjugated in the subjunctive:

*Quiero que **la** escribas.*	I want you to write it.
*Sugiere que **lo** hagas.*	He suggests that you do it.
*Digo que **lo** mires.*	I tell you to look at him.
*Pedimos que **nos** llames.*	We ask that you call us.

2. Negative *tú* commands with object pronouns

Place the object pronoun between *no* and the second person singular form of the subjunctive:

*No **la** escribas.*	Do not write it.
*No **lo** hagas ahora.*	Do not do it now.
*No **lo** mires.*	Do not look at him.
*No **nos** llames.*	Do not call us.

NOTE:

If a subjunctive sentence is used to express a softened command, there is no change in the form, and the word order stays the same:

*Sugiero que **no la escribas**.*	I suggest that you don't write it.
*Dice que **no lo hagas** ahora.*	She says for you not to do it now.

E. ***Tú* commands with direct and indirect object pronouns together**

1. Affirmative *tú* commands with double object pronouns

Attach both object pronouns to the commands. The indirect object pronoun must always be placed before the direct object pronoun:

escribir	*Escríbe**mela**. (la carta)*	Write it to me. (the letter)
revisar	*Revísa**selos**. (los ejercicios)*	Check them for him. (the exercises)
hacer	*Ház**noslo**. (el trabajo)*	Do it for us. (the work)

If a subjunctive sentence is used to express a softened command, both objects must be placed before the second person singular form of the subjunctive, in the dependent clause:

*Quiero que **me la** escribas.*	I want you to write it for me.
*Sugerimos que **se los** revises.*	We suggest that you check them for him.
*Queremos que **nos lo** hagas.*	We want you to do it for us.

2. Negative *tú* commands with double object pronouns

Object pronouns are placed between *no* and the verb, with the indirect object pronoun always before the direct object pronoun (notice that a softened command with a subjunctive sentence takes the same form):

*No **me la** escribas.*	Don't write it for me.
*Sugiero que no **me la** escribas.*	I suggest that you don't write it for me.
*No **se los** revises.*	Do not check them for him.
*Queremos que no **se los** revises.*	We want you not to check them for him.
*No **nos lo** hagas.*	Don't do it for us.
*Pedimos que no **nos lo** hagas.*	We ask that you not do it for us.

F. ***Tú* commands with reflexive verbs and a direct object pronoun**

1. Affirmative *tú* commands with reflexive verbs and a pronoun

Direct object pronouns are attached to affirmative commands. Notice the reflexive pronoun *te*:

lavarse	*Láva**telas**. (las manos)*	Wash them. (your hands)
ponerse	*Pón**telo**. (el sombrero)*	Put it on. (the hat)

If a subjunctive sentence is used to express a softened command, both the reflexive pronoun *te* and the direct object pronoun are placed before the verb, which is conjugated in the subjunctive form:

*Es bueno que **te las** laves.*	It's good that you wash them.
*No quiero que **te lo** pongas.*	I don't want you to put it on.

2. Negative *tú* commands with reflexive verbs and a pronoun

Both the reflexive pronoun *te* and the direct object pronoun are placed between *no* and the verb, which is conjugated in the second person singular of the present subjunctive form:

No **te las** laves.	Don't wash them.
No **te lo** pongas.	Don't put it on.

NOTE:

If a subjunctive sentence is used to express a softened command, there is no change in the form and the word order remains the same:

Ruego que no **te las** laves.	I beg you not to wash them.
Pido que no **te lo** pongas.	I ask you not to put it on.

The Plural of the *tú* Informal Command

This form is used to give an informal or familiar command to more than one person. The word *ustedes (Uds.)* is used in both Latin America and Spain, while *vosotros/as* is used only in Spain.

A. The *ustedes* command

The informal *ustedes* command follows the same rules as the formal *ustedes* command. A review of the various forms follows.

1. Affirmative *ustedes* commands:

	Lean el capítulo.	Read the chapter.
with direct object	Léan**lo**.	Read it.
with indirect object	Léan**nos**.	Read to us.
with both objects	Léan**noslo**.	Read it to us.
with reflexive verbs	Pónga**nse** el gorro.	Put on your caps.
reflexive and object	Pónga**nselo**.	Put it on.

2. Negative *ustedes* commands:

	No lean el capítulo.	Don't read the chapter.
with direct object	No **lo** lean.	Don't read it.
with indirect object	No **nos** lean.	Don't read to us.

with both objects	No *nos lo* lean.	Don't read it to us.
with reflexive verbs	No *se* pongan el gorro.	Don't put your caps on.
reflexive and object	No *se los* pongan.	Don't put them on.

B. Affirmative and negative *vosotros* commands

This form is used to give a command to more than one person, and is used in Spain.

1. Affirmative *vosotros* commands:

Change the letter *r* of the infinitive to a *d*:

	Vosotros	
Infinitive	**Command**	
cantar	*Cantad.*	Sing.
beber	*Bebed.*	Drink.
reír	*Reíd.*	Laugh.

> **NOTE:**
>
> If a subjunctive sentence is used to express a softened command, the verb in the dependent clause must be in the subjunctive form. The endings for the *vosotros/as* form are *-éis* for *-ar* verbs, and *-áis* for *-er* and *-ir* verbs:
>
> *Queremos que vosotros <u>cantéis</u> en el coro.* (cantar) — We want you to sing in the choir.
>
> *Sugiere que <u>comáis</u> más. (comer)* — She suggests that you eat more.
>
> *Quiero que <u>abráis</u> la correspondencia ahora.* (abrir) — I want you to open the mail now.

2. Negative *vosotros* commands:

Use the present subjunctive *vosotros* form for negative *vosotros* commands:

	Present Subjunctive	**Command**	
cantar	(vosotros) cantéis	No cantéis.	Do not sing.
beber	(vosotros) bebáis	No bebáis.	Do not drink.
reír	(vosotros) riáis	No riáis.	Do not laugh.

> **NOTE:**
>
> If a subjunctive sentence is used to express a softened command, there is no change in the form and the word order remains the same:
>
> *Sugerimos que vosotros <u>no bebáis</u> más.* — We suggest that you do not drink more.
>
> *Es triste que vosotros <u>no cantéis</u> con nosotros.* — It is sad that you don't sing with us.

C. *Vosotros* commands with reflexive verbs

1. Affirmative *vosotros* commands with reflexive verbs

To give a command with a reflexive verb, start with the nonreflexive affirmative command, eliminate the final *d,* and then add the reflexive pronoun *os*:

	Affirmative Command	**Command**	
peinarse	*Peinad.*	*Peinaos.*	Comb your hair.
ponerse	*Poned.*	*Poneos los anillos.*	Put on the rings.
reírse	*Reíd.*	*Reíos.*	Laugh.

NOTES:

(1) The verb *irse* is an exception to the above rule:

irse

Affirmative command of *ir*:	*Id.*	Go away.
Command of *irse*:	*Idos.*	Go away.

(2) If a subjunctive sentence is used to express a softened command, the reflexive pronoun *os* is placed before the verb in the dependent clause, which is in the subjunctive:

Quiero que vosotros os peinéis en el baño.	I want you to comb your hair in the bathroom.
Es bueno que vosotros os riáis del cuento.	It's good that you laugh at the story.

2. Negative *vosotros* commands with reflexive verbs

To give a negative command with a reflexive verb, put the reflexive pronoun *os* between the *no* and the verb, which is in the subjunctive:

	Present Subjunctive	**Command**	
peinarse	*peinéis*	*No os peinéis.*	Don't comb your hair.
ponerse	*pongáis*	*No os pongáis una corbata.*	Don't put on a tie.
reírse	*riáis*	*No os riáis.*	Do not laugh.

If a subjunctive sentence is used to express a softened command, there is no change in the form and the word order remains the same:

Es bueno que vosotros <u>no os pongáis</u> una corbata.	It is good that you don't put on a tie.
Os pido que <u>no os riáis</u> de mí.	I ask you not to laugh at me.

D. Vosotros commands with object pronouns

1. Affirmative *vosotros* commands with object pronouns

Attach both direct and indirect object pronouns to the command form:

Mirad**me**.	Look at me.
Traed**los** (los libros).	Bring them (the books).
Pedid**la** (la cuenta).	Ask for it (the bill).

NOTE:

If a subjunctive sentence is used to express a softened command, the pronoun is placed before the verb in the dependent clause, which must be in the subjunctive form:

Quiero que <u>me miréis</u>.	I want you to look at me.
Es bueno que <u>los traigáis</u>.	It's good that you will bring them.

2. Negative *vosotros* commands with object pronouns

Both direct and indirect object pronouns are placed between *no* and the verb in the subjunctive:

No **nos** pidáis dinero.	Don't ask us for money.
No **los** traigáis.	Don't bring them.
No **lo** reguéis (el jardín).	Don't water it (the garden).

E. Vosotros commands with direct and indirect object pronouns together

1. Affirmative *vosotros* commands with double object pronouns

Both pronouns are attached to the command. When using direct and indirect object pronouns together, the indirect object is placed before the direct object:

Abrídmela (la ventana).	Open it for me (the window).
Firmádselo. (firmar)	Sign it for him.

NOTE:

If a subjunctive sentence is used to express a softened command, both pronouns are placed before the verb in the dependent clause, which is in the subjunctive form:

*Os pido que **me la** <u>abráis</u>.*	I ask you to open it for me.
*Quiere que **se lo** <u>firméis</u>.*	He wants you to sign it for him.

2. Negative *vosotros* commands with double object pronouns

Both direct and indirect object pronouns are placed between *no* and the verb, which is in the subjunctive form:

*No **se lo** digáis.*	Don't say it to him.
*No **nos los** deis.*	Don't give them to us.

NOTE:

If a subjunctive sentence is used to express a softened command, there is no change in the form and the word order remains the same:

*Espero que no **se lo** digáis.*	I hope you won't say it to him.
*Preferimos que no **nos los** deis demasiado tarde.*	We prefer that you not give them to us too late.

F. *Vosotros* commands with reflexive verbs and object pronouns

1. Affirmative *vosotros* commands with reflexive verbs and object pronouns

Attach the object pronouns to the commands:

limpiarse	*Limpiáos**los**. (los zapatos)*	Clean them yourselves.
preguntarse	*Preguntáos**lo** (un asunto).*	Ask it of yourselves.

NOTE:

If a subjunctive sentence is used to express a softened command, both the reflexive pronoun *os* and the direct object pronoun are placed before the verb in the dependent clause, which is in the subjunctive:

*Desea que **os los** limpiéis.*	She wishes you to clean them.
*Espero que **os lo** preguntéis.*	I hope that you will ask it of yourselves.

2. Negative *vosotros* commands with reflexive verbs and object pronouns

Both the reflexive pronoun *os* and the direct object pronoun are placed between *no* and the verb, which is in the subjunctive form:

No ***os los*** *limpiéis.*	Do not clean them yourselves.
No ***os lo*** *preguntéis.*	Don't ask it of yourselves.

NOTE:

If a subjunctive sentence is used to express a softened command, there is no change in the form and the word order remains the same:

Sugiero que no ***os los*** *limpiéis.*	I suggest that you not clean them yourselves.
Es mejor que no ***os lo*** *preguntéis.*	It's better that you not ask it of yourselves.

The First Person Plural *nosotros* Commands (*Let's* Commands)

This command is used when the speaker suggests an action to be performed as a group, where the group includes the speaker.

A. Affirmative and negative *nosotros* commands

1. Affirmative *nosotros* commands may be expressed in two different ways in Spanish.

    (a) The *nosotros* form of *ir* in the present tense, plus an infinitive:

Vamos a tomar un taxi.	Let's take a taxi.
Vamos a sacar las entradas.	Let's buy the tickets.

NOTE:
This form is more common in informal speech.

(b) The *nosotros* form of the present subjunctive:

	Present Subjunctive	Command	
tomar	nosotros tomemos	*Tomemos un taxi.*	Let's take a taxi.
sacar	nosotros saquemos	*Saquemos las entradas.*	Let's buy the tickets.
ir	nosotros vayamos	<u>exception:</u> *Vamos* a su casa.*	Let's go to his house.

---

* The subjunctive form ***vayamos*** is also used, as in: *Vayamos por partes.* (Let's take it step by step.) and *Vayamos a las cifras actuales.* (Let's review the current figures.)

If a subjunctive sentence is used to express a softened command, there are no changes in the form and the word order remains the same:

Es mejor que tomemos un taxi.	It's better for us to take a taxi.
Ella quiere que saquemos las entradas.	She wants us to buy the tickets.
Sugiero que vayamos* a su casa.	I suggest that we go to her house.

2. Negative *nosotros* commands are expressed only with the subjunctive:

No insistamos más.	Let's not insist any more.
No lleguemos tarde.	Let's not arrive late.

NOTE:

If a subjunctive sentence is used to express a softened command, there are no changes in the form, and the word order stays the same:

Él dice que no insistamos más.	He says for us not to insist any more.

B. First person plural *nosotros* commands with reflexive verbs

1. Affirmative *nosotros* commands with reflexive verbs

Drop the final *s* of the subjunctive and add the reflexive pronoun *nos*:

sentarse (to sit)	*sentemos* ➤ *sentemo + nos = sentémonos*
acordarse (to remember)	*acordemos* ➤ *acordemo + nos = acordémonos*

Observe these examples:

Sonriámonos ahora. (sonreírse)	Let's smile now.
Probémonos los zapatos. (probarse)	Let's try on the shoes.

NOTE:

If a subjunctive sentence is used to express a softened command, place the reflexive pronoun *nos* before the verb in the dependent clause, which will be in the subjunctive:

*Quiere que **nos** sonriamos ahora.*	She wants us to smile now.
*Es bueno que **nos** probemos los zapatos.*	It's good for us to try on the shoes.

---

* Notice the normal use of the subjunctive form.

2. Negative *nosotros* commands with reflexive verbs

To express a negative *nosotros* command, place the reflexive pronoun *nos* between *no* and the subjunctive form of the verb:

No **nos** hagamos los tontos.	Let's not clown around.
No **nos** durmamos.	Let's not fall asleep.

> **NOTE:**
>
> If a subjunctive sentence is used to express a softened command, there is no change in the form, and the word order remains the same:
>
> | | |
> |---|---|
> | Dice que no **nos** hagamos los tontos. | She says for us not to clown around. |
> | Quiere que no **nos** durmamos en la conferencia. | He wants us not to fall asleep at the conference. |

C. First person plural *nosotros* commands with object pronouns

1. Affirmative *nosotros* commands with object pronouns

Direct and indirect object pronouns are attached to the affirmative *nosotros* command:

Bañémos**lo** (al perro).	Let's bathe him (the dog).
Corrámos**la** (a la niña).	Let's run after her (the little girl).
Cerrémos**los** (los sobres).	Let's close them (the envelopes).

> **NOTE:**
>
> If a subjunctive sentence is used to express a softened command, place the object pronoun before the verb in the dependent clause, which is in the subjunctive:
>
> | | |
> |---|---|
> | Mamá pide que **lo** bañemos. | Mom asks that we bathe him. |
> | Dijo que **la** corramos. | She said for us to run after her. |
> | Es hora que **los** cerremos. | It's time for us to close them. |

2. Negative *nosotros* commands with object pronouns

Direct and indirect object pronouns are placed between *no* and the verb:

No **los** comamos fríos.	Let's not eat them cold.
No **le** causemos problemas.	Let's not cause her problems.
No **la** abramos hasta mañana.	Let's not open it until tomorrow.

If a subjunctive sentence is used to express a softened command, there is no change in the form, and the word order remains the same:

Carlos dice que no **los** comamos fríos.	Carlos says for us not to eat them cold.
Papá quiere que no **le** causemos problemas.	Dad wants us not to cause him problems.

D. **First person plural *nosotros* commands with direct and indirect object pronouns together**

The indirect object pronoun is always placed before the direct object pronoun. As mentioned before, the indirect object pronoun changes from *le* or *les* to *se* when the direct object pronoun begins with *l* (*lo*, *la*, *los*, *las*). With the *nosotros* commands, the *s* of the verb is dropped before adding *nos* or *se*.

Hagamos una fiesta para Lidia.	Let's have a party for Lidia.
<u>Direct object</u>: *una fiesta* ➤ *la*	
<u>Indirect object</u>: *para Lidia* ➤ *le*	
hacer: hagamos ➤ hagamo + **se** + **la** = Hagámo**sela**.	Let's have it for her.

1. Affirmative *nosotros* commands with double object pronouns

   Both direct and indirect object pronouns are attached to an affirmative command. Always drop the *s* before adding *nos* or *se*:

Comprémo**noslo**.* (un regalo)	Let's buy it for ourselves.
Arreglémos**telas**. (las ventanas)	Let's fix them for you.
Dibujémo**sela**. (la fruta)	Let's draw it for them.

2. Negative *nosotros* commands with double object pronouns

   Direct and indirect object pronouns are placed between *no* and the verb:

No **nos lo** compremos.	Let's not buy it for ourselves.
No **te las** arreglemos.	Let's not fix them for you.
No **se la** dibujemos.	Let's not draw it for them.

---

* The *s* is dropped in the first and third examples above: *Compremo(s) nos lo* ➤ *Comprémonoslo* and *Dibujémo(s) se la* ➤ *Dibujémosela*.

If a subjunctive sentence is used to express a softened command, there is no change in the form, and the word order remains the same:

*Prefiero que no **nos lo** compremos.*	I prefer that we not buy it for ourselves.
*Sugiero que no **te las** arreglemos.*	I suggest that we not fix them for you.
*Es bueno que no **se la** dibujemos.*	It's good that we not draw it for them.

E. First person plural *nosotros* commands with reflexive verbs and pronouns

1. Affirmative *nosotros* commands with reflexive verbs and pronouns

   Attach the pronouns to the commands:

lavarse	*Lavémo**noslas**. (las manos)*	Let's wash our hands.
calentarse	*Calentémo**noslos**. (los pasteles)*	Let's warm them up for ourselves.

   NOTE:

   If a subjunctive sentence is used to express a softened command, place the reflexive pronoun *nos* and the direct object pronoun before the verb in the dependent clause, which must be in the subjunctive form:

*Insiste en que **nos las** lavemos.*	She insists that we wash them.
*Mamá prefiere que **nos los** calentemos.*	Mom prefers that we warm them up for ourselves.

2. Negative *nosotros* commands with reflexive verbs and pronouns

   Direct object pronouns follow the reflexive pronouns:

*No **nos las** lavemos. (las manos)*	Let's not wash our hands.
*No **nos los** calentemos. (los pasteles)*	Let's not warm them up for ourselves.

   NOTE:

   If a subjunctive sentence is used to express a softened command, place the reflexive pronoun *nos* before the object pronoun:

*Quiere que no **nos las** lavemos.*	She wants us not to wash them.
*Sugiere que no **nos los** calentemos.*	He suggests that we not warm them up for ourselves.

The Impersonal Commands

These commands are given in a general sense and may be expressed in two different ways:

A. Impersonal commands using the infinitive:

No *fumar*.	No smoking.
No *pisar* el césped.	Keep off the grass.
Abrocharse los cinturones.	Fasten your seatbelts.

B. Impersonal commands using the subjunctive:

Hágase la luz.	Let there be light.
No *haya* pleitos entre amigos.	Let there not be arguments among friends.
Haya paz en el mundo.	Let there be peace on earth.

Commands Expressed with the Present Tense

It is common to use the present tense to express a command in informal speech.

A. *Ud.* and *Uds.* commands

1. Using the imperative:

Lleve los vasos y *pónga*los en la mesa. (*Ud.*)
Lleven los vasos y *póngan*los en la mesa. (*Uds.*) Take the glasses and put them on the table.

2. Using the present indicative:

Ud. *lleva* los vasos y los *pone* en la mesa.
  (present)
Uds. *llevan* los vasos y los *ponen* en la mesa. You take the glasses and put them on the table.

B. *Tú* commands

1. Using the imperative:

*Escribe la carta y **mándasela**.*   Write the letter and send it to him.

2. Using the present indicative:

*Tú **escribes** la carta y **se la mandas**.* (present)   You write the letter and send it to him.

C. Informal *ustedes* (plural of *tú*) commands

1. Using the imperative:

*Limpien su cuarto y después **hagan** sus tareas.*   Clean your room and then do your homework.

2. Using the present indicative:

*Ustedes **limpian** su cuarto y después **hacen** sus tareas.* (present)   You clean your room and then do your homework.

D. *Vosotros* commands

1. Using the imperative:

*Cerrad la puerta y **marchaos** para casa.*   Close the door and go home.

2. Using the present indicative:

*Vosotros **cerráis** la puerta y **os marcháis** para casa.* (present)   You close the door and go home.

E. First person plural (*nosotros*) commands

1. Using the imperative:

*Salgamos silenciosamente y no **regresemos** más tarde.*   Let's leave silently and not come back later.

2. Using the present indicative:

Nosotros **salimos** silenciosamente y no **regresamos**. (present)

We leave silently and don't come back.

Commands Expressed with the Future Tense

The future tense is also used to express a command in the second person singular and plural.

A. *Ud.* and *Uds.* commands

1. Using the imperative:

Venga mañana y **déselo**. (Ud.)
Vengan mañana y **dénselo**. (Uds.)

Come tomorrow and give it to him.

2. Using the future indicative:

Ud. **vendrá** mañana y **se lo dará**. (future)
Uds. **vendrán** mañana y **se lo darán**.

You will come tomorrow and give it to him.

B. *Tú* commands

1. Using the imperative:

No **esperes** hasta que él llegue.

Don't wait until he comes.

2. Using the future indicative:

No **esperarás** hasta que él llegue. (future)

You will not wait until he comes.

C. Informal *ustedes* (plural of *tú*) commands

1. Using the imperative:

Resérvense el derecho de opinar.

Reserve yourselves the right to express an opinion.

2. Using the future indicative:

Se reservarán el derecho de opinar. (future) You will reserve yourselves the right to express an opinion.

D. *Vosotros* commands

1. Using the imperative:

Comed hasta saciaros. Eat until you are full.

2. Using the future indicative:

Comeréis hasta saciaros. (future) You will eat until you are full.

16

Pronouns

A pronoun is a word that stands in place of a noun or nouns. It is used mainly to avoid repetition of a noun already mentioned in the sentence, or when the noun is clearly understood in context. Nouns replaced by pronouns may belong to different groups, such as persons, things, nonhuman beings, places, abstract nouns, qualities, or events.

Pronouns are divided into the following categories: personal, object (direct and indirect), demonstrative, possessive, relative, interrogative, indefinite, and reflexive pronouns.

Personal (Subject) Pronouns

Personal pronouns (also called subject pronouns) are classified into persons (first, second, and third), both singular and plural. For example, *yo* (*I*) is the first person singular, and *vosotros* (*you*) is the second person plural.

Persons	Singular	Plural
first	*yo* (I)	*nosotros, nosotras* (we)
second	*tú* (you)	*vosotros, vosotras* (you)
third	*él* (he), *ella* (she)	*ellos* (they), *ellas* (they)
	ello (it, neuter)	
	usted (you)	*ustedes* (you)

> **NOTE:**
>
> *tú* and *él* carry accent marks to distinguish them from the possessive adjective *tu* (*tu libro*) and the definite article *el* (*el libro*), respectively.

Special Uses of Some Subject Pronouns

A. *Tú*

You, informal. It is used to address children, relatives, friends, peers, or pets.

B. *Vos*

In some Latin American countries, *vos* is used instead of *tú* in everyday Spanish. This practice is known as *voseo*, as opposed to *tuteo*, which means addressing someone with the *tú* form.* Although widespread in some areas, the usage of *vos* (singular) is considered somewhat incorrect. This form has its origin in the pronoun *vosotros* (plural), brought by the Spaniards during the conquest and colonization of America. It uses a modified *vosotros/as* form of the verb, as follows:

Costa Rica y Argentina

1. *Vos* in the present indicative

(a) In the present tense of *-ar* and *-er* verbs, *vos* forms drop the *i* of the *vosotros* form, and an accent mark is placed on the last vowel:

| Vosotros cantáis bien. ➤ | Vos **cantás** bien. | You sing well. |
| Vosotros coméis mucho. ➤ | Vos **comés** mucho. | You eat a lot. |

(b) In the present tense, *-ir* verbs remain exactly the same for the *vos* form as for the *vosotros* form:

Vosotros salís ahora.
Vos **salís** ahora.   You are going out now.

(c) Here are interrogative sentences using the present-tense *vos* forms of *-ar*, *-er*, and *-ir* verbs:

¿Vos **cantás** bien?	Do you sing well?
¿**Comés** mucho vos?	Do you eat much?
¿**Salís** ahora?	Are you going out now?

(d) Placement of the pronoun and punctuation with *vos* in interrogative sentences.

---

* When in a formal situation one person asks permission to start addressing the other one less formally, the question is: ¿*La puedo tutear?* or ¿*Nos podemos tutear?*, which grammatically means *Can I address you as tú (instead of Ud.)?*, and not ¿*La puedo vosear?* or ¿*Nos podemos vosear?* In the regions where people use the pronoun *vos*, the verb *tutear* indicates addressing someone with the *vos* form.

Notice that the pronoun can be used before or after the verb, and can also be left out. However, there should never be a comma separating the pronoun. If the speaker wishes to attract the attention of the person being asked the question, and this appears in written form (a dialogue in a short story or a novel, for example), a comma may be placed to indicate the emphasis:

Vos, ¿cantás bien?	You (there) . . . ¿Do you sing well?
¿Cantás bien, vos?	Do you sing well? You?

In a spoken situation, the intonation of the voice will determine the desired emphasis.

2. *Vos* in the imperative

In the imperative (commands), the final *d* of the *vosotros* form is dropped to make the *vos* form. An accent mark is used in all three conjugations:

vosotros:	*¡Cantad!* (Sing!)	*¡Comed!* (Eat!)	*¡Salid!* (Go out!)
vos:	*¡Cantá!*	*¡Comé!*	*¡Salí!*

3. *Vos* is also used after prepositions:

Tengo un regalo para vos. (para ti)	I have a gift for you.
Me gustaría ir al cine con vos. (contigo)	I would like to go to the movies with you.
Estaremos muy tristes sin vos. (sin ti)	We will be very sad without you.

NOTE:

See Appendix D, Sample Conjugations with the Pronoun *vos*.

C. *Usted*

You, formal: *usted*, abbreviated *Ud.*, is used to address someone older, a person we do not know, or a superior. It is usually considered a third person pronoun because it takes the same verb forms as *él* (*he*) and *ella* (*she*).

NOTES:

(1) Although the informal pronouns *tú* and *vos* and the formal *Ud.* are each used to address one person, they are not interchangeable. Once the sentence has begun with one of them, the same pronoun must be used again, whenever necessary. Keep in mind that a person who uses *vos* has no problem in communicating

with somebody else who uses *tú*, and vice versa. Notice the agreement between these pronouns and the verb:

tú tienes	**vos tenés**	**Ud. tiene**
you, informal	*you, informal*	*you, formal*

(2) Special forms of address, such as **Vuestra Majestad** (*Your Majesty*), **Vuestra Alteza** (*Your Highness*), and **Vuestra Señoría** (*Your Lordship*), are also considered third person (formal) pronouns.

¿**Vuestra Majestad** <u>desea</u> tomar el té ahora?   Your Majesty wishes to have tea now?

(3) *Ud.* or *Uds.* is usually added to a verb to indicate politeness:

Quiere **Ud.** entrar, por favor.	Would you come in, please.
Siéntense **Uds.**	Sit down, please.
Es claro que **Ud.** lo sabe.	It's clear that you know it.

D. Vosotros/as

This pronoun is used only in Spain, to address more than one person informally. In Latin America, *vosotros* is not usually used, but can be found in some versions of the Bible and in other religious writings.

E. Ustedes

Abbreviated *Uds.*, it is the equivalent of *vosotros/as* in Latin America, but it is also used in Spain. It is both formal and informal.

> **NOTE:**
> In English, the informal *you all* or *you guys* corresponds to the informal *vosotros* and *ustedes*.

F. Nosotros

This is the equivalent of *we*. The form *nos* as a subject pronoun is rarely heard or seen. It used to apply to high-ranking officers, as the beginning of the preamble of the Argentine constitution shows:

Nos, los representantes del pueblo de la Nación Argentina	We, the representatives of the people of the Nation of Argentina

G. Optional personal pronouns

Some personal pronouns that function as the subject of the sentence, or that belong to a dependent clause, are easily understood and may therefore be eliminated. It is not incorrect to use them, however:

(Yo) Quiero ir de compras.	I want to go shopping.
(Tú) Escribes buenos poemas.	You write good poems.
(Nosotros) Tenemos prisa.	We are in a hurry.
(Vosotros) Comeréis aquí.	You will eat here.
(Yo) Pienso que (tú) debes venir.	I think you should come.

NOTES:

(1) If the subject of a sentence is a thing or an animal, the subject pronoun is usually omitted in context:

Los pastores alemanes son inteligentes. *Pueden reunir todas las ovejas con facilidad.*	German shepherds are intelligent. They can gather all the sheep together very easily.
Compré un auto nuevo. Es importado.	I bought a new car. It is imported.

The corresponding object pronoun will be used, however:

Este es mi auto. Quiero pintarlo de rojo.	This is my car. I want to paint it red.

(2) The subject pronoun is used if a nonhuman subject is personified:

El amor es el más preciado de los dones. *Él enriquece el alma de quien lo da.*	Love is the most valuable gift. It enriches the soul of whoever gives it.

H. Required subject pronouns

Subject pronouns should be used in the following cases.

1. Whenever there is ambiguity (some pronouns share the same verb form):

Simple Tenses

Present Indicative	*él, ella, Ud.*	*tiene*
	ellos, ellas, Uds.	*tienen*
Preterit	*él, ella, Ud.*	*fue*
	ellos, ellas, Uds.	*fueron*
Imperfect	*yo, él, ella, Ud.*	*cantaba*
	ellos, ellas, Uds.	*cantaban*

Future	*él, ella, Ud.*	*comerá*
	ellos, ellas, Uds.	*comerán*
Conditional	*yo, él, ella, Ud.*	*leería*
	ellos, ellas, Uds.	*leerían*
Present Subjunctive	*yo, él, ella, Ud.*	*salga*
	ellos, ellas, Uds.	*salgan*
Imperfect Subjunctive	*yo, él, ella, Ud.*	*saliera*
	ellos, ellas, Uds.	*salieran*

Compound Tenses

Past Perfect Indicative	*yo, él, ella, Ud.*	*había comprado*
	ellos, ellas, Uds.	*habían comprado*
Conditional Perfect	*yo, él, ella, Ud.*	*habría dicho*
	ellos, ellas, Uds.	*habrían dicho*
Present Perfect Subjunctive	*yo, él, ella, Ud.*	*haya venido*
	ellos, ellas, Uds.	*hayan venido*
Pluperfect Subjunctive	*yo, él, ella, Ud.*	*hubiera puesto*
	ellos, ellas, Uds.	*hubieran puesto*

2. To give emphasis or to point to someone:

Yo *creo que es una buena idea.*	I think it is a good idea.
Nosotros *lo recomendamos.*	We recommend it.
Tú *haces esto, y* **ella** *hace el resto.*	You do this, and she does the rest.

Agreement of Personal Pronouns

Personal pronouns agree in gender and number with the noun to which they refer, which is called the *antecedent.*

Some of the personal pronouns are obviously masculine or feminine, singular or plural:

él	he
ella	she
nosotras	we (feminine)
vosotras	you (feminine plural, in Spain)
ellas	they (feminine)

Other personal pronouns can have a gender or number given that is made clear by the modifying adjective or adjectives. See the following examples:

yo	I
tú	you (informal, singular)
usted (Ud.)	you (formal, singular)
ustedes (Uds.)	you (formal or informal, plural)

In the following examples, (f) stands for feminine and (m) for masculine:

*Yo soy trabajad**ora**. (f)*	I am a hard worker.
Yo soy español. (m)	I am Spanish.
*Tú eres atractiv**a**. (f)*	You are attractive.
Tú eres bueno. (m)	You are good.
*Ud. es un**a** buen**a** director**a**. (f)*	You are a good principal.
*Ud. está loc**o**. (m)*	You are crazy.
*Uds. están content**as**. (f)*	You are happy.

When the adjective used with the pronouns *nosotros*, *vosotros*, *ellos*, and *ustedes* (*Uds.*) is masculine, it may refer to a group of males only or to a combination of males and females. Since an adjective referring to males only or to males and females together must be in the masculine plural form, further clarification of gender may be necessary in those cases. In the following sentences, each statement could refer to Guillermo and Miguel or to Miguel and Cecilia.

*Nosotros somos simpátic**os**.*	We are nice.
*Vosotros estáis cansad**os**.*	You are tired.
*Ustedes parecen segur**os**.*	You seem to be sure.
*Ellos son alt**os**.*	They are tall.
*Ellos—Miguel y Cecilia—viven sol**os**.*	They—Miguel and Cecilia—live alone.

Form Variations in Personal Pronouns

Personal pronouns change their form when they are used after a preposition (i.e., as objects of prepositions). Here are the forms they take when they are the objects of prepositions:

Pronouns	Variation (Object of Preposition)	
yo	*mí (sin mí, de mí)*	except after *con*, *conmigo*
tú	*ti (ante ti, por ti)*	except after *con*, *contigo*
él, ella, Ud.	*sí (para sí, en sí)*	except after *con*, *consigo*
ellos, ellas, Uds.	*sí (en sí, de sí)*	except after *con*, *consigo*

Marta hizo el trabajo por ti. (not: *por tú*)   Marta did the job for you.

Ella tiene un regalo para mí. (not: *para yo*)   She has a gift for me.

NOTES:

(1) The regional pronoun *vos* does not change after a preposition:

con vos, ante vos, sin vos

(2) *Nosotros, nosotras, vosotros*, and *vosotras* do not change after a preposition:

de nosotros, con nosotras, contra vosotros, sin vosotras

(3) The following pronouns carry an accent to distinguish them from other expressions:

*para **mí*** (for me)	but	***mi** casa* (my house)
*en **sí*** (in himself)	but	***si** puedes* (if you can)

Direct Objects and Direct Object Pronouns

This section begins with an introduction of the direct object prior to discussing the rules that regulate its corresponding pronouns.

The direct object (called **complemento directo** in Spanish) is the word or words that receive directly the action of the verb. It is easy to identify a direct object by asking the question *what? (¿qué?)* or *whom? (¿a quién?)* immediately after the verb in simple sentences:

The maid <u>put</u> flowers on the table.	La mucama <u>puso</u> flores en la mesa.
The maid put (<u>What</u> did she put?) **flowers**.	La mucama puso (<u>¿Qué</u> puso?) ***flores***.

Observe the following sentence, where the expression *my sons (**a mis hijos**)* answers the question *Whom? (¿A quién?)*:

I <u>love</u> my sons.	<u>Quiero</u> a mis hijos.
I love (*Whom?*) **my sons**.	Quiero (*¿A quién?*) ***a mis hijos***.

The word ***flores*** and the expression ***a mis hijos*** in the preceding sentences are direct objects.

NOTE:

The personal *a* is required when the direct object is a person or a pet.

Word Order in Sentences with a Direct Object

In Spanish, the direct object usually follows the verb, unless emphasis is desired:

Quiero una casa con muchas ventanas.	I want a house with many windows.
Una casa con muchas ventanas quiero yo.	A house with many windows (is what) I want.

NOTE:

Sometimes, however, it may be difficult to distinguish between the subject and the direct object. See the following sentences:

Aterrizó el avión.	*El avión aterrizó.*

They could possibly both mean *He landed the plane* or *The plane landed*. Therefore, in order to avoid ambiguity, whether the subject and/or the direct object refers to persons, animals, or things, the preposition *a* (the personal *a*) is placed before the direct object. Observe the sentences now:

Aterrizó el avión.	(Either he or the plane landed.)
Aterrizó al avión.	He landed the plane.
Chocó el auto.	(Either he wrecked the car or his car was involved in a wreck.)
Chocó al auto.	He wrecked the car.
El gato mordió la araña.	(Either the cat or the spider bit.)
El gato mordió a la araña.	The cat bit the spider.

NOTE:

Another level of difficulty is when the subject and the direct object are both inanimate and the personal *a* is not used. See the following sentence:

La tala de los árboles provocó la sequía del suelo.	The cutting down of trees caused the dryness of the soil (soil dryness).

It is possible to ask: What did the cutting down of trees cause? The answer would immediately signal the direct object: the dryness of the soil.

However, the elements of the sentence could be inverted to produce an emphatic effect:

La sequía provocó la tala de los árboles.

In this example, it cannot be assumed that soil dryness is the subject of the sentence and that the cutting of trees is the direct object, for logical reasons. Meaning, therefore, would have to be drawn from context in this kind of sentence.

Uses of the Personal *a* Before a Direct Object

The personal *a* precedes the direct object when the direct object is a specific person or persons:

*Yo veo **a Dawn** en la cocina.*	I see Dawn in the kitchen.
Yo veo (¿A quién?) a Dawn.	I see (Whom?) Dawn.

If the specific person is a single male being referred to with a noun and the article *el*, such as *el profesor, el médico,* or *el cartero*, the contraction of *a + el* must be used:

*Yo respeto **al** médico.*	I respect the doctor.

There are many verbs in Spanish that require the personal *a* before a direct object that refers to persons. Some other such verbs are:

esperar	(to wait for)	*escuchar*	(to listen to)
conocer	(to know)	*comprender*	(to understand)
llevar	(to take)	*querer, amar*	(to love)

NOTES:

(1) The personal *a* is not used if the direct object is an unidentified person or persons. Observe the difference in the following sentences:

Busco un cardiólogo que no cobre mucho.	I am looking for a cardiologist who will not charge much.
*Busco **a** un cardiólogo que me recomendaron.*	I am looking for a cardiologist that they have recommended.
Escucho unos chicos que juegan en la calle.	I listen to some children who are playing in the street.
*Escucho **a** los chicos que viven enfrente.*	I listen to the children who live across the street.

The personal *a* is used, however, before indefinite pronouns and adjectives such as ***nadie*** (*no one*), ***alguien*** (*someone*), ***ninguno/a, ningún*** (*no one*), ***alguno/a, algún*** (*someone*), ***cualquiera, cualquier*** (*anyone, anybody*), ***todos/as*** (*everybody*), ***cada uno/a*** (*each one*):

*No veo **a** nadie.*	I don't see anyone.
*Quiero ver **a** alguien.*	I want to see someone.
*Necesito **a** cualquiera.*	I need anybody.

(2) The verb ***tener*** (*to have*) does not use a personal *a* when the direct object is a person or a pet and the verb is followed by *un, una* (*a, an*), or by numbers:

*Tengo **un** hermano casado.*	I have a brother who is married.
*Tengo **un** hermano y **dos** hermanas.*	I have one brother and two sisters.
*Tengo **una** secretaria.*	I have a secretary.
*Tengo **una** secretaria que habla francés y **tres** que hablan ruso.*	I have one secretary who speaks French and three who speak Russian.
*Tenemos **un** buen mecánico.*	We have a good mechanic.
*Tenemos **un** mecánico, pero hace el trabajo de dos.*	We have one mechanic but he does the work of two.
*Tienen **un** gato negro.*	They have a (one) black cat.

(3) When *tener*, followed by the personal *a*, precedes a direct object (a person or a pet) *tener* becomes equivalent to *estar* (to be). A literal English translation is given for the following examples:

*Tengo **a** mi hermano en el teléfono. (Está en la línea.)*	I have my brother on the phone. (He is on the line).
*Tenemos **a** Juan y **a** Pedro en casa. (Están en casa).*	We have John and Peter at home. (They are at home).
*Tengo **a** mi gato en el jardín. (Está en el jardín).*	I have my cat in the yard. (It is in the yard).

(4) When the direct object is a pet or any personified noun, the personal *a* is also used:

*Llevó **a** Zen al veterinario.*	He took Zen to the vet.
*Veo **al** perro en el jardín.*	I see my dog in the garden.
*Agradezcamos **a** la suerte por darnos la oportunidad.*	Let's thank our lucky stars for giving us the opportunity.

Direct Object Pronouns

Direct objects may be replaced by their corresponding pronouns:

Personal	Direct Object Pronouns	
yo	*me*	me
tú	*te*	you
usted (Ud.)	*lo, la*	you
él	*lo*	him
ella	*la*	her
ello	*lo*	it
nosotros/as	*nos*	us
vosotros/as	*os*	you

ustedes (Uds.)	**los, las**	you
ellos	**los**	them
ellas	**las**	them

NOTE:

In Spain and some regions of Latin America, *le* and *les* are sometimes used instead of *lo* and *los* to replace a masculine noun. This practice is called *leísmo*. The use of these forms (*le* and *les*) is acceptable if the noun is a masculine person. However, it is incorrect to use them for feminine nouns, animals, or masculine objects:

Correct	**Acceptable**	
*Yo **lo** vi (a Juan).*	*Yo **le** vi.*	I saw him.
*Uds. **los** vieron.*	*Uds. **les** vieron.*	You saw them.
(a Juan y a Carlos)		

Correct	**(Incorrect)**	
***La** visito. (a Elena)*	*(**Le** visito.)*	I visit her.
***Lo** veo. (a mi gato)*	*(**Le** veo.)*	I see it (my cat).
***Lo** compré. (el lápiz).*	*(**Le** compré.)*	I bought it.

NOTE:

Direct object pronouns that replace nouns take the following forms:

Feminine singular:	*la pera*	**la**
Feminine plural:	*las peras*	**las**
Masculine singular:	*el árbol*	**lo**
Masculine plural:	*los árboles*	**los**

Word Order with Direct Object Pronouns

To insert a direct object pronoun into a sentence, the following rules apply.

A. The direct object pronoun before a single conjugated verb

The direct object pronoun must always be placed directly before the conjugated verb if there is only one verb. Note the specific rules for the pronoun depending on whether the direct object is human or not.

1. If the direct object is a person

The direct object *pronoun* must always be used for the persons *yo (me)*, *tú (te)*, *Ud. (lo, la)*, *nosotros/as (nos)*, *vosotros/as (os)*, and *Uds. (los, las)*, while the direct object that it stands for may be omitted:

Correct:	**(Incorrect:)**
*El **me** quiere a mí.*	*(El quiere a mí.)*
*El **me** quiere.*	
He loves me.	
*Yo **te** veo a ti.*	*(Yo veo a ti.)*
*Yo **te** veo.*	
I see you.	
***Lo** visitaré a Ud.*	*(Visitaré a Ud.)*
***Lo** visitaré.*	
I will visit you.	
***Nos** aprecia a nosotros.*	*(Aprecia a nosotros.)*
***Nos** aprecia.*	
He appreciates us.	
*No **os** olvida a vosotros.*	*(No olvida a vosotros.)*
*No **os** olvida.*	
She does not forget you.	
***Los** esperaremos a Uds. mañana a las 10.*	*(Esperaremos a Uds. mañana a las 10.)*
***Los** esperaremos mañana a las 10.*	
We will wait for you tomorrow at 10.	

However, the direct object pronouns *lo, la, los,* and *las*, which replace the direct objects equivalent to the third person singular (*él, ella*), and plural (*ellos, ellas*), may be left out when the direct object also appears in the sentence.

All Correct:	
Quiero a Juan.	I love Juan.
***Lo** quiero a Juan.*	
***Lo** quiero.*	
Aprecio a mis primas.	I appreciate my cousins.
***Las** aprecio a mis primas.*	
***Las** aprecio.*	

2. If the direct object is not human, it needs to be left out when the pronoun is used in the sentence:

Nosotros compramos las maletas.	We bought the suitcases.
*Nosotros **las** compramos.*	We bought them.
Vieron el tigre.	They saw the tiger.
***Lo** vieron.*	They saw it.

However, when both the pronoun and the direct object are used in the sentence, the direct object is preceded by *a:*

Nosotros compramos las maletas.	We bought the suitcases.
*Nosotros **las** compramos <u>a las maletas</u>.*	We bought the suitcases.
Vieron el tigre.	They saw the tiger.
***Lo** vieron <u>al tigre</u>.*	They saw the tiger.

B. Placement of the direct object when there are two verbs

If there are two verbs, whether a combination of a conjugated verb before an infinitive or a conjugated verb before a present participle *(-ing: -ando, -iendo)*, there are two possibilities, both entirely correct.

1. The direct object pronoun may be placed immediately before the conjugated verb:

Nosotros preferimos comprar las revistas.	We prefer to buy the magazines.
*Nosotros **las** preferimos comprar.*	We prefer to buy them.
El está escribiendo una carta.	He is writing a letter.
*El **la** está escribiendo.*	He is writing it.
*Yo **te** quiero ver siempre.*	I want to see you always.
*Iolanda **os** quiere ver.*	Iolanda wants to see you.

2. The direct object pronoun may be attached to the infinitive or to the present participle:

*Nosotros preferimos comprar**las**.*	We prefer to buy them.
*El está escribiéndo**la**.*	He is writing it.
*Yo quiero ver**te** siempre.*	I want to see you always.
*Iolanda quiere ver**os**.*	Iolanda wants to see you.

C. The direct object pronoun before the auxiliary *haber*

The direct object pronoun is always placed before the auxiliary verb *haber* in compound tenses. It cannot be attached to the past participle nor placed between the auxiliary verb and the past participle:

Te *he recordado siempre.*	I have always remembered you.
Las *hemos comprado.*	We have bought them.

Direct Objects and Objects of Prepositions

There are some verbs in English which require a following preposition but for which the corresponding verb in Spanish does not require one. Some of these verbs are *to wait for* (*esperar*), *to look for* (*buscar*), and *to look at* (*mirar*):

El espera el tren.	He waits for the train.
Yo busco un lápiz.	I am looking for a pencil.
Ellos miran el agua.	They look at the water.

While in Spanish *el tren, un lápiz*, and *el agua* function as direct objects, the equivalent expressions in English are objects of prepositions (*for, for*, and *at*, respectively).

> **NOTE:**
> If the direct object is a person or a pet, the verb in Spanish requires the personal *a*:
>
> | | |
> |---|---|
> | *El espera **a** su hermana.* | He waits for his sister. |
> | *Yo busco **a** Jill.* | I'm looking for Jill. |
> | *Ken mira **a** Zoe.* | Ken looks at Zoe. |
> | *Mi vecina alimenta **a** Fifi.* | My neighbor feeds Fifi. |

Imperative Form (Commands) and Direct Object Pronouns

Direct object pronouns are attached to affirmative commands and are placed between *no* and the verb in negative commands:

*Estúdia**las**.*	Study them.
*No **los** escuches.*	Do not listen to them.

For other examples and uses of a direct object pronoun with one or two verbs, and together with an indirect object pronoun in the same sentence, see Chapter 15, The Imperative.

Indirect Objects and Indirect Object Pronouns

This section begins with an introduction of the indirect object prior to discussing the rules that regulate its corresponding pronouns.

The Indirect Object

The indirect object is the word on which the action of the verb falls indirectly. It refers to people or things and can be identified by asking the questions *To whom?* and *For whom? (¿A quién? ¿Para quién?)* or *To what?* and *For what? (¿A qué? ¿Para qué?)* after the direct object. The question goes back to the verb, though, as the examples show:

Juana <u>compró</u> unos pasteles para la niña.	Juana <u>bought</u> some pastry for the girl.
Juana <u>compró</u> unos pasteles (¿Para quién?) **para la niña.**	Juana <u>bought</u> some pastry (For whom?) for the girl.
Mi padre <u>consiguió</u> unas patas nuevas para la mesa.	My father <u>got</u> new legs for the table.
Mi padre <u>consiguió</u> unas patas nuevas (¿Para qué?) **para la mesa.**	My father <u>got</u> new legs (For what?) for the table.

Indirect objects may be replaced by their corresponding pronouns:

Personal	Indirect Object Pronouns	
yo	**me, mí**	me
tú	**te, ti**	you
Ud.	**le, se, sí**	you
él	**le, se, sí**	him
ella	**le, se, sí**	her
ello	**le, se**	it
nosotros/as	**nos**	us
vosotros/as	**os**	you
ustedes	**les, se, sí**	you
ellos	**les, se, sí**	them
ellas	**les, se, sí**	them

NOTES:

(1) *Mí*, *ti*, and *sí* are used after *para* to indicate an indirect object:

Tiene una carta para **mí**.   He has a letter for me.

(2) The following pronouns do not change when used after *para* to indicate an indirect object:

vos	usted	vosotros
él	ustedes	vosotras
ella	nosotros	ellos
ello	nosotras	ellas

The regional pronoun *vos*, which is used instead of *tú*, appears as follows:

para vos	con vos	sin vos
for you	with you	without you

(3) In some areas, especially in Spain, *la* and *las* are sometimes used instead of *le* and *les* for females, but these forms (*la* and *las*) are incorrect for the indirect object. This practice is called *laísmo*:

Correct	**(Incorrect)**
Pedro **le** dio un regalo a Carmen.	(Pedro **la** dio un regalo.)
Pedro **le** dio un regalo.	
Pedro gave her a gift.	
Pedro **les** dio un regalo a las niñas.	(Pedro **las** dio un regalo.)
Pedro **les** dio un regalo.	
Pedro gave them a gift.	

Personal *a* and Indirect Objects

In some cases, an expression preceded by a personal *a* may be either an indirect object or a direct object (since direct objects are sometimes preceded by the personal *a*). In order to figure out whether it is a direct or an indirect object, try to place the word *to* in the English translation of the sentence. If the sentence makes sense with *to* in it, the expression is an indirect object.

In the sentence ***Romeo ama a Julieta*** (*Romeo loves Juliet*), for example, it is not possible to insert *to* in the sentence. Observe the following cases:

*Romeo ama **a Julieta**.*	Romeo loves Juliet.
(Romeo loves (To whom?) Juliet.)	
(Incorrect, therefore *Juliet* is a direct object.)	
*Romeo le manda una nota **a Julieta**.*	Romeo sends a note to Juliet.
Romeo sends a note (To whom?) to Juliet.	
Correct, therefore *Juliet* is an indirect object.	

NOTES:

(1) A personal *a* is required in Spanish before indefinite pronouns such as ***alguien, alguno/a, nadie, cualquiera, cada cual, cada uno/a***, and ***todos/as***:

*En la calle no vemos **a** <u>nadie</u>.*	We don't see anybody in the street.
*Le dio **a** <u>cada uno</u> un beso.*	She gave each one a kiss.

(2) The pronouns ***cualquiera, cada cual, cada uno/a***, and ***todos/as*** may refer to people or things:

*Juan les puso una marca **a** <u>todas</u>. (las cajas)*	John put a mark on all of them. (boxes)
*Le echaré fertilizante **a** <u>cada uno</u>. (rosales)*	I will put some fertilizer on each one. (rose bushes)

Word Order in Sentences with an Indirect Object

In Spanish there are several ways in which the indirect object may be used in a sentence.

A. The indirect object after the direct object or before the subject

The indirect object, preceded by the preposition *a*, may be placed either after the direct object or before the subject when emphasis on the indirect object is desired:

*Juana le dio unos pasteles **a la niña**.*	Juana gave some pastry to the girl.
***A la niña** Juana le dio unos pasteles; al niño le dio unas frutas.*	To the girl, Juana gave some pastry; to the boy, she gave some fruit.
*¿Juana les dio unos pasteles **a ustedes**?*	Did Juana give you some pastry?
*¿**A Uds.** Juana les dio unos pasteles?*	Did Juana give <u>you</u> some pastry? (In English, the word *you* may be pronounced with more emphasis.)

B. Placement of the indirect object when the subject is left out

If the subject *(Juana)* is left out, the indirect object [*a la niña*] may be placed either before the indirect object pronoun [*le*] or after the direct object [*unos pasteles*]:

Before:	*A la niña **le** dio unos pasteles.*	She gave some pastry to the girl.
After:	***Le** dio unos pasteles a la niña.*	She gave some pastry to the girl.
Before:	*A Uds. **les** dio unos pasteles.*	She gave you some pastry.
After:	***Les** dio unos pasteles a Uds.*	She gave you some pastry.

C. Use of the indirect object pronoun with specific persons

The indirect object pronoun must always be present when the indirect object (included or left out) refers to specific persons:

Indirect object included:	*Juana **le** dio unos pasteles a la niña.*	Juana gave some pastry to the girl.
Indirect object left out:	*Juana **le** dio unos pasteles.*	Juana gave her some pastry.
Indirect object included:	*Juana **les** dio unos pasteles a Uds.*	Juana gave you some pastry.
Indirect object left out:	*Juana **les** dio unos pasteles.*	Juana gave you some pastry.

> **NOTE:**
>
> If the indirect object refers to individuals in a general way or to inanimate objects, the pronoun may be left out. In the following sentences, the pronoun is not necessary:
>
> | | |
> |---|---|
> | *Él siempre (**les**) escribe cartas a los presos.* | He always writes letters to people in jail. |
> | *Pedro (**le**) dedicó un poema a la geografía de su país.* | Pedro dedicated a poem to the geography of his native country. |

D. When the indirect object is triggered by *para*

If the indirect object is triggered by the preposition *para*, there are two options.

1. To use the indirect object pronoun without the indirect object. The subject may be present or left out:

*Juana **le** compró unos pasteles.*	Juana bought her some pastry.
***Le** compró unos pasteles.*	She bought her some pastry.

2. To use the indirect object without the indirect object pronoun. The subject may be present or left out:

*Juana compró unos pasteles **para** la niña.*	Juana bought some pastry for the girl.
*Compró unos pasteles **para** la niña.*	She bought some pastry for the girl.

NOTES:

(1) If the indirect object pronoun *le* is used <u>with</u> the indirect object, the sentence has a different meaning. In that case, *le* refers to someone else from whom Juana bought pastry for the girl:

*Juana **le** compró unos pasteles <u>para la niña</u>.*	Juana bought (from him) some pastry for the girl.
*Juana **le** compró (<u>al hombre</u>) unos pasteles para la niña.*	Juana bought (from the man) some pastry for the girl.

(2) In Spanish, always use an indirect object pronoun in cases where, in English, a direct object would be introduced by a possessive adjective. The possessive adjective in English is replaced by the definite article in Spanish:

He made up <u>her face</u>.	***Le** maquilló **la** cara (a ella).*
(<u>Not</u>: *[Él] Maquilló su cara.*)	
(*sounds like*: He put makeup on himself.)	
She dressed <u>their wounds</u>.	***Les** curó **las** heridas (a ellos).*
(<u>Not</u>: *[Ella] Curó sus heridas.*)	
(*sounds like*: She dressed her own wounds.)	

The incorrect Spanish sentences shown do not actually mean anything; the English translations given are the closest approximation to what those formulations might mean, but in fact, to be correct and have those meanings, the Spanish sentences would need a reflexive verb: *Él se maquilló la cara*; *Ella se curó las heridas*.

Word Order in Sentences with an Indirect Object Pronoun

When placing an indirect object pronoun in a sentence, the following rules apply.

A. Placement of the indirect object pronoun with a single verb

If there is only one verb in the sentence, the indirect object pronoun is placed directly before the conjugated verb. If the statement is negative, the word *no* precedes the pronoun:

El mozo **nos** sirvió agua.	The waiter served us water.
Raúl **me** mandó una carta.	Raúl sent me a letter.
Pedro **no les** escribió.	Pedro didn't write to them.

B. Placement of the indirect object pronoun with two verbs

If there are two verbs, the first one being a conjugated verb and the second one either an infinitive or a present participle (ending in *-ing: -ando, -iendo*), there are two possibilities, both entirely correct.

1. The indirect object pronoun may be placed immediately before the conjugated verb. The negative *no* precedes the pronoun when the statement is negative:

El mozo **nos** <u>quiere</u> servir agua.	The waiter wants to serve us water.
Raúl **me** <u>vino</u> a dar una carta.	Raúl came to give me a letter.
Ella **te** <u>está</u> haciendo un vestido.	She is making a dress for you.
Juan **no te** <u>tiene</u> que dar nada.	Juan doesn't have to give you anything.

2. The indirect object pronoun may be attached to the infinitive or to the present participle:

El mozo quiere servir**nos** agua.	The waiter wants to serve us water.
Raúl vino a dar**me** una carta.	Raúl came to give me a letter.
Ella está haciéndo**te** un vestido.	She is making you a dress.

In a negative sentence, then, the negative word is placed before the first verb:

Juan **no** tiene que dar**te** nada.	Juan doesn't have to give you anything.

C. Placement of the indirect object pronoun before *haber*

The indirect object pronoun is always placed before the auxiliary verb *haber* in compound tenses, never between the auxiliary verb and the past participle. Also, it cannot be attached to the past participle:

Juan **me** ha dicho la verdad.	Juan has told me the truth.
Ellos **te** han traído dinero.	They have brought you money.
(Incorrect: *Juan ha **me** dicho la verdad*.)	

If there is a negative word, this is placed before the indirect object pronoun:

El **no nos** ha llamado.	He hasn't called us.

Indirect object pronouns are attached to affirmative commands and are placed between *no* and the verb in negative commands:

Da**nos** *el dinero.*	Give us the money.
No nos *des el dinero.*	Do not give us the money.

In Chapter 15, The Imperative, there are examples and uses of indirect object pronouns when the sentences have one or two verbs, and also of indirect object pronouns used together with direct object pronouns in the same sentence.

Indirect Object Pronoun in Place of a Subject

Uses with *gustar* and Similar Verbs

Some verbs in Spanish use an indirect object pronoun instead of the subject that would appear in equivalent English sentences. One of these verbs is *gustar* (*to like*). In a sentence with *gustar*, the thing or person that is liked becomes the subject of the sentence, while the indirect object pronoun signals who is doing the action of liking.

There are two possibilities for placing the indirect object pronoun in this type of sentence.

A. Sentences beginning with the indirect object or indirect object pronoun

The sentence may begin with the indirect object pronoun or with the preposition *a* plus a noun or pronoun, in which case more emphasis is being placed on who is doing the liking:

Me *gustan los días tibios.*	I like warm days.
A mí *me gustan los días tibios.*	I like warm days.
A María *le gustan los días tibios.*	María likes warm days.
Al perro *le gustan los días tibios.*	The dog likes warm days.

B. Sentences ending with the indirect object, or indirect object pronoun, plus verb

The sentence may end with the forms of the indirect object, or the pronoun, and the verb indicated in the preceding sentences. The meaning in English is the same:

*Los días tibios **me** gustan.*	I like warm days.
*Los días tibios me gustan **a mí**.*	I like warm days.
*Los días tibios le gustan **a María**.*	María likes warm days.
*Los días tibios le gustan **al perro**.*	The dog likes warm days.

NOTES:

(1) These sentences literally mean: *Warm days are appealing (or pleasing) to me / María / the dog.*

(2) The verb *gustar* is also used with reflexive/reciprocal pronouns: *yo me gusto* (*I like myself*); *te gustas* (*you like yourself*); *nos gustamos* (*we like each other*). Other forms with indirect objects include:

Le gustamos a Felipe.	Felipe likes us.
Me gustas mucho.	I like you a lot.
¿Te gusto?	Do you like me?

Forms of *gustar*

The verb *gustar*, which belongs in the category of verbs such as *faltar* (*to lack*), *quedar* (*to have left*), *parecer* (*to seem*), etc. (excluding the forms in the second item of the preceding note), uses two forms, singular and plural, regardless of who does the action of the verb. The verb matches in number the things or persons liked. See the section Other Verbs Like *gustar* that follows for examples using these other verbs.

A. Simple tenses of *gustar*

	Singular	Plural
present indicative (*presente indicativo*)	*gusta*	*gustan*
imperfect indicative (*imperfecto indicativo*)	*gustaba*	*gustaban*
preterit (*pretérito*)	*gustó*	*gustaron*
future (*futuro*)	*gustará*	*gustarán*
conditional (*condicional*)	*gustaría*	*gustarían*

present subjunctive	*guste*	*gusten*
(presente subjuntivo)		
imperfect subjunctive	*gustara*	*gustaran*
(imperfecto subjuntivo)		

Examples:

*Me **gusta** la naranja.*	I like the orange.
*Me **gustan** las manzanas.*	I like the apples.
*Nos **gusta** la película.*	We like the movie.
*Nos **gustan** los invitados.*	We like the guests.

B. Compound tenses of *gustar*

1. Compound forms of *gustar* with the auxiliary *haber*

The compound tenses of *gustar* use the corresponding form of the auxiliary verb *haber* (singular or plural) and the past participle of the main verb, *gustado*.

	Singular	Plural
present perfect indicative	*ha gustado*	*han gustado*
(presente perfecto del indicativo)		
past perfect indicative	*había gustado*	*habían gustado*
(pretérito perfecto del indicativo)		
preterit perfect*	*hubo gustado*	*hubieron gustado*
(pretérito anterior)		
future perfect	*habrá gustado*	*habrán gustado*
(futuro perfecto)		
conditional perfect	*habría gustado*	*habrían gustado*
(condicional perfecto)		
present perfect subjunctive	*haya gustado*	*hayan gustado*
(presente perfecto del subjuntivo)		
pluperfect subjunctive	*hubiera gustado*	*hubieran gustado*
(pluscuamperfecto del subjuntivo)		

*Le **ha gustado** la obra hasta ahora.*	He has liked the play so far.
*A Teresa le **han gustado** las clases.*	Teresa has liked the classes.
*No nos **han gustado** los libros.*	We haven't liked the books.

---

* No longer used in oral speech; only found in older writings.

2. Compound forms of *gustar* with the auxiliary *estar*

Another compound form uses the auxiliary verb *estar* (singular and plural) and the present participle (gerund) of the main verb, which is *gustando*.

estar	Singular	Plural
present	*está gustando*	*están gustando*
preterit	*estuvo gustando*	*estuvieron gustando*
imperfect	*estaba gustando*	*estaban gustando*
future	*estará gustando*	*estarán gustando*
conditional	*estaría gustando*	*estarían gustando*
present subjunctive	*esté gustando*	*estén gustando*
past/imperfect subjunctive	*estuviera gustando*	*estuvieran gustando*

Examples:

Me **estaba gustando** la película.	I was liking the movie.
Creo que no le **estará gustando** la casa.	I think he might not be liking the house.

Uses of *gusta* and *gustan*

The following rules apply for the use of the singular or plural forms of *gustar*.

A. The singular form *gusta* is used in the following cases.

1. When the item, person, or nonhuman liked is singular:

Nos **gusta** el verano.	We like the summer.
Le **gusta** su profesor.	He likes his professor.
Me **gusta** el gato Félix.	I like Felix the Cat.
¿Os **gusta** la ópera?	Do you like the opera?

2. When what is liked is indicated by one or more infinitives:

Les **gusta** enseñar.	They like teaching.
Me **gusta** cantar y bailar.	I like to sing and dance.

B. The plural form *gustan* is used when what is liked is plural:

*No me **gustan** mucho* mis tareas.*	I don't like my homework much.
*Le **gustan** los de cuero.*	He likes the leather ones.
*Nos **gustan** los jardines y la casa.*	We like the gardens and the house.

Other Verbs Like *gustar*

Some other verbs conjugated like *gustar* include:

doler (to hurt)	***interesar*** (to interest)
encantar (to be very pleasing)	***parecer*** (to seem)
enfermar (to feel sick)	***quedar*** (to have remaining or left)
faltar (to be lacking)	***resultar*** (to seem)

Just as with *gustar*, if the object liked is plural, an *n* must be added to the singular form of the present tense of the verb:

*Esta obra me **parece** buena.*	This seems like a good play to me.
*Me **faltan** dos capítulos para leer.*	I still have two chapters to read. (Literally, I lack two chapters to be read).
*Nos **quedan** dos hijos en casa.*	We still have two sons at home. (the others are gone).
*Le **duelen** los pies.*	His feet hurt.
*Les **interesa** la película.*	They are interested in the movie.
*Te **resultan** aburridoras.*	They seem boring (to you).
*Nos **encanta** estudiar.*	We like studying very much.
*Le **enferma** ir al dentista.*	Going to the dentist makes her sick.

NOTES:

(1) Some students of the language confuse the verb *parecer* (*to seem*) with *aparecer* (*to appear*). Instead of the first example, they would say erroneously, *Esta obra me aparece buena.*

(2) *Quedar* would also be a good choice for the second sentence, instead of *faltar*. The sentence would then read:

Me quedan dos capítulos para leer.	I still have two chapters remaining (to read).

---

* Words like ***mucho*** (*much*), ***poco***, ***un poco*** (*a little*), ***algo*** (*some*), and ***bastante*** (*quite a bit*) must be placed immediately after the verb.

(3) In the third sentence, *faltar* cannot be used instead of *quedar*, since the meaning of the sentence would change. The statement *Nos faltan dos hijos en casa* means that two of the sons are away from the house or that the family would like to have two sons.

(4) *Resultar* and *parecer* are synonyms; therefore sentences one and six could each use either verb.

(5) These verbs can be conjugated in all the simple and compound tenses specified for the verb *gustar*.

Direct and Indirect Objects Used Together

In Spanish, as well as in English, an indirect object may precede or follow the direct object:

Manuel le dio un auto <u>a su hijo</u>.	Manuel gave a car <u>to his son</u>.
Manuel le dio <u>a su hijo</u> un auto.	Manuel gave <u>his son</u> a car.

NOTES:

(1) In English, the preposition *to* is needed when the indirect object follows the direct object, while in Spanish the objects just change positions in the sentence.

(2) Notice that the indirect object pronoun *le* is needed in both sentences.

In Spanish, the indirect object is preceded by either *a* or *para*. However, a particular word order may be incorrect depending on the preposition used. Observe the following examples:

Correct:

*Manuel compró <u>un auto</u> **para** su hijo.*	Manuel bought a car for his son.
*Manuel le compró <u>un auto</u> **a** su hijo.*	Manuel bought a car for his son.
*Manuel le compró **a** su hijo un auto.*	Manuel bought a car for his son.
*Manuel, **a** su hijo, le compró <u>un auto</u> y **a** su hija (le compró) <u>una muñeca</u>.*	Manuel bought a car for his son and a doll for his daughter.

(<u>Incorrect</u>: *Manuel le compró un auto para su hijo.**)

---

* If the pronoun *le* is eliminated, the same word order may be used if the speaker wants to make a clarification: *Manuel compró un auto para su hijo y una muñeca para su hija.* (Manuel bought a car for his son and a doll for his daughter.) If the pronoun *le* is kept in the sentence, the sentence is correct but the meaning has changed: *Manuel le compró un auto para su hijo.* (Manuel bought [from someone else] a car for his son.)

Direct and Indirect Object Pronouns Together

When both the direct and the indirect object pronouns are used together in a sentence, the position of the pronouns is the same as when direct and indirect object pronouns appear individually.

A. The indirect object pronoun always precedes the direct object pronoun.

B. Both pronouns are placed before a conjugated verb (here IOP stands for Indirect Object Pronoun; DOP for Direct Object Pronoun):

Carlos compra <u>flores</u> <u>para ti</u>.	Carlos buys flowers for you.
*Carlos **te** (IOP) **las** (DOP) compra.*	Carlos buys them for you.

C. Placement of direct and indirect object pronouns together, with two verbs

If there are two verbs, the first being a conjugated verb and the second one an infinitive or a present participle (ending in *-ando* or *-iendo*), both pronouns are placed either <u>before</u> the conjugated verb or <u>attached</u> to the infinitive or to the present participle, whichever the case might be:

Carlos quiere comprar flores para ti.	Carlos wants to buy flowers for you.
*Carlos **te las** quiere comprar.*	Carlos wants to buy them for you.
*Carlos quiere comprár**telas**.*	Carlos wants to buy them for you.
Carlos está comprando flores para ti.	Carlos is buying flowers for you.
*Carlos **te las** está comprando.*	Carlos is buying them for you.
*Carlos está comprándo**telas**.*	Carlos is buying them for you.

D. Placement of direct and indirect object pronouns before *haber*

Both pronouns are placed before the auxiliary verb *haber* in compound tenses. They are never attached to the infinitive in this case, nor placed between *haber* and the past participle:

Carlos ha comprado flores para ti.	Carlos has bought flowers for you.
*Carlos **te las** ha comprado.*	Carlos has bought them for you.
(Incorrect:)	
(*Carlos ha <u>te las</u> comprado.*)	
(*Carlos ha comprádo<u>telas</u>.*)	

E. When the indirect object pronoun changes to *se*

When both the direct object pronoun and the indirect object pronoun begin with the letter *l* (e.g. *les los, les la, le la, le los*, etc.), the indirect object pronoun changes to *se* (*se los, se la, se la,* and *se los*, respectively).

> **NOTE:**
>
> The following section provides clarification and more examples. As a reminder, the following is a list of direct and indirect object pronouns:
>
> Direct Object Pronouns: *me te lo la nos os los las*
>
> Indirect Object Pronouns: *me te le nos os les*

Rules for the Position of Pronouns

A. The indirect object pronoun (IOP) always precedes the direct object pronoun (DOP).

The following rules apply.

1. Only one verb

If there is only one verb in the sentence, the two pronouns must be placed before the verb:

Compré <u>un lápiz para ti</u>.	I bought a pencil for you.

DOP: *lo*; IOP: *te*

Te lo *compré.*	I bought it for you.

2. One verb + infinitive

If there are two verbs and the second one is an infinitive, there are two possible ways of writing a correct sentence: the two pronouns may be placed before the conjugated verb or attached to the infinitive:

Quiero traer <u>un lápiz para ti</u>.	I want to bring you a pencil.
Te lo *quiero traer.*	I want to bring it for you.
*Quiero traér**telo**.*	I want to bring it for you.

There are some exceptions:

(a) The use of two pronouns may alter the meaning of the sentence, especially with verbs such as *hacer*, *mandar*, and *ordenar*. Observe the following examples:

Le *hice traer* <u>la valija</u>.	I made him bring the suitcase.
Se la *hice traer.*	I made him bring the suitcase. *or* I had someone bring it for him.
Les *mandé llenar* <u>los espacios</u>.	I had them fill in the blanks.
Se los *mandé llenar.*	I had them fill in the blanks. *or* I had someone fill them in for them.

(b) If the conjugated verb is reflexive, the reflexive pronoun must go with its corresponding verb. In the following example, this is the only possible way of enunciating this statement:

Me sentaré *a* <u>esperarlo</u>. *(sentarse)*	I will sit down to wait for him.
(<u>Not</u>: *Sentaré a esperármelo.*)	
(<u>Not</u>: *Me lo sentaré a esperar.*)	

3. **One verb + present participle**

   If there are two verbs in the sentence and the second one is a present participle, there are two possible ways to write a correct sentence in Spanish: the pronouns may be placed before the conjugated verb or attached to the present participle:

Estoy trayendo un lápiz para ti.	I'm bringing you a pencil.
Te lo *estoy trayendo.*	I'm bringing it for you.
*Estoy trayéndo***telo**.	I'm bringing it for you.

4. ***Haber* + past participle**

   The only correct way to use two pronouns in a construction with the auxiliary verb ***haber*** and a past participle is to place the pronouns before the auxiliary verb:

He traído un lápiz para ti.	I have brought you a pencil.
Te lo *he traído.*	I have brought it for you.

B. **When the indirect object pronoun changes to *se***

As mentioned before, when both indirect and direct object pronouns begin with the letter *l,* the indirect object pronoun changes from *le* to *se* and from *les* to *se*. Here are some examples and notes about situations that pertain to the use of *se* in each one of the categories.

1. Only one verb

If there is only one verb in the sentence, the two pronouns must be placed before the verb:

Pagué <u>una cuenta para Tom</u>.	I paid a bill for Tom.

DOP: *la*; IOP: *le*

***Se la** pagué.*	I paid it for him.
Compramos <u>libros para ellas</u>.	We bought books for them.

DOP: *los*; IOP: *les*

***Se los** compramos*.*	We bought them for them.

2. One verb + infinitive

If there are two verbs in the sentence and the second verb is an infinitive, there are two possible ways of writing a correct sentence: the two pronouns may be placed before the conjugated verb or attached to the infinitive:

Quiero pagar <u>una cuenta para Tom</u>.	I want to pay a bill for Tom.

DOP: *la*; IOP: *le*

***Se la** quiero pagar.*	I want to pay it for him.
*Quiero pagár**sela**.*	I want to pay it for him.
Puedo comprar <u>un libro para ellas</u>.	I can buy a book for them.

DOP: *lo*; IOP: *les*

***Se lo** puedo comprar.*	I can buy it for them.
*Puedo comprár**selo****.*	I can buy it for them.

---

* This sentence also means: We bought them <u>from</u> him/them. To indicate the difference in Spanish, the two sentences can be written as follows: *Se los compramos a él/ellos.* (We bought them <u>from</u> him/them.) and *Se los compramos para ellas.* (We bought them <u>for</u> them.)

** This sentence also means: I can buy it <u>from</u> him/them. To indicate the difference in Spanish, the two sentences can be written as follows: *Puedo comprárselo a él/ellos.* (I can buy it <u>from</u> him/them.) and *Puedo comprárselo para ellas.* (I can buy it <u>for</u> them.)

3. One verb + present participle

If there are two verbs in the sentence and the second verb is a present participle, there are two possible ways of writing a correct sentence. The two pronouns may be placed before the conjugated verb or attached to the present participle:

Estoy abriendo el negocio para Ud. DOP: *lo*; IOP: *le*	I am opening the store for you.
Se lo *estoy abriendo.*	I am opening it for you.
*Estoy abriéndo**selo**.*	I am opening it for you.

4. *Haber* + past participle

The only correct way to use two pronouns in a construction with the auxiliary verb *haber* and a past participle is to place the pronouns before the auxiliary verb:

He hecho la tarea para Juana. DOP: *la*; IOP: *le*	I have done the task for Juana.
Se la *he hecho.*	I have done it for her.

5. Since the meaning of the pronoun *se* may be ambiguous when the sentence is out of context, clarification such as the following may be added to the sentence:

para él	*a ellos*	*para Tom*
a ella	*para ellas*	*a los estudiantes*
para Ud.	*para Uds.*	*para mi madre*

Se los compré a Ud.	I bought them for you. *or:* I bought them from you.
Se las dimos a ellas.	We gave them to them.
Se la expliqué a los chicos.	I explained it to the kids.
Se lo hicimos a Tom.	We did it for Tom.

> **NOTE:**
>
> The indirect object triggered in Spanish by the prepositions *a* and *para* (*to* and *for*) can also be indicated in English by *from* and *off*.
>
> | | |
> |---|---|
> | *La madre **le** sacó los zapatos mojados*
  (al niño). | His mother took the wet shoes off him
  (the boy). |
> | *Ella **se los** sacó.* | She took them off him. |

*El juez **le** pidió <u>la verdad</u>.*	The judge asked the truth from the man.
*El juez **se la** pidió.*	The judge asked it from him.

Imperative Form (Commands) with Direct and Indirect Object Pronouns Together

For the use of direct and indirect object pronouns together in sentences that express a command, see Chapter 15, The Imperative.

Demonstrative Pronouns

The word *demonstrative* has its origin in the verb *to demonstrate*, or *to show*. Demonstrative pronouns modify a noun or nouns by showing the location of the noun or nouns represented by them.

In Spanish, there are three different categories of demonstrative pronouns that correspond to the same categories of demonstrative adjectives. Each one of these pronouns agrees in gender and number with the noun it replaces. The words *éste*, *ése*, *aquél*, their feminine forms *ésta*, *ésa*, *aquélla*, and the corresponding plural forms represent the Spanish equivalent of the English demonstrative pronouns. Note that the Spanish equivalents to *this one* and *that one* do not include *uno* or *una* to correspond to *one* in English. The written accent that used to be used to distinguish the demonstrative pronouns from the demonstrative adjectives is no longer required.

Categories of Demonstrative Pronouns

There are three categories of demonstrative pronouns.

A. Demonstrative pronouns replacing a noun or nouns near the speaker:

éste (león)	this one (lion)
éstos (leones)	these (lions)
ésta (mentira)	this one (lie)
éstas (mentiras)	these (lies)
Éstos viven en la selva africana. (leones)	These live in the African jungle. (lions)

B. Demonstrative pronouns replacing a noun or nouns near the person spoken to, or near both the speaker and the listener:

ése (amigo)	that one (friend)
ésos (amigos)	those (friends)
ésa (colmena)	that one (beehive)
ésas (colmenas)	those (beehives)
Ése *es el mejor del mundo. (amigo)*	This one is the best in the world. (friend)

C. Demonstrative pronouns replacing a noun or nouns far from both the speaker and the listener:

aquél *(edificio)*	that one (building)
aquéllos *(edificios)*	those (buildings)
aquélla *(planta)*	that one (plant)
aquéllas *(plantas)*	those (plants)
Aquélla *es de la región amazónica. (planta)*	That one (over there) is from the Amazon region. (plant)

> **NOTE:**
>
> In English, expressions such as *over there, in the corner, further down,* etc., are usually added to the pronoun to point to the third location, which is designated in Spanish by *aquél/aquéllos/aquélla/aquéllas*. Additional identification may be used, if desired or needed:
>
> | | |
> |---|---|
> | **Aquélla** que está allá *es de la región amazónica. (planta)* | That one over there is from the Amazon region. (plant) |
> | **Aquélla** que está allá *es de la región amazónica y* **aquélla** en el rincón *es de los Andes.* | That one over there is from the Amazon region, and that one in the corner is from the Andes. |

Neuter Demonstrative Pronouns

There are three neuter demonstrative pronouns: *esto, eso,* and *aquello*. These pronouns refer to abstract or undefined nouns, situations, and ideas. They are always expressed in the singular form, take masculine singular adjectives, and never carry an accent mark:

Esto *es bueno.*	This is good.
Eso *será ridículo.*	That will be ridiculous.
Aquello *era absurdo.*	That was absurd.

They may also stand by themselves:

¿Qué quieres?	What do you want?
Aquello. *Esto no me gusta.*	That. I don't like this.

If the neuter pronoun is used when the gender of the noun is known, the pronoun replaces the idea behind it, rather than the noun. Notice the speaker's surprise denoted by the expression that has a neuter pronoun:

*¡Qué es **esto**! ¿Quién trajo una cartera tan bonita?*	What is this! Who brought such a pretty purse?

(The speaker is looking at the purse; however, there is no specific mention of the gender of the noun; **esto**/*this* refers to the whole situation.)

Fixed Expressions with Neuter Pronouns

Neuter pronouns are used in some idiomatic expressions, such as the following:

¡Eso!	That's it!
Eso es.	That's right.
Eso es todo.	That's all.
Eso mismo.	Exactly.
en eso	at that particular moment
en esto	at that time
todo esto	all of this
***En eso**, se escuchó un ruido enorme.*	At that moment, a loud noise was heard.
***En esto**, llegaron sus amigos.*	At that moment, his friends came.
*"**Eso es**"—dijo Ismael.*	"That's right"—said Ismael.

The Pronoun *lo*

Besides functioning as a neuter article, as in <u>*lo*</u> *bueno es que…* (*the good thing is that . . .*) and as an object pronoun, as in <u>*lo*</u> *vimos* (*we saw it, we saw him*), the word *lo* also functions as a demonstrative pronoun that replaces *esto*, *eso* or *aquello*:

*Me dijo **lo** de costumbre.*	He told me the usual (thing).
*Recibimos **lo** que habíamos pedido.*	We received what we had ordered.

Uses of Demonstrative Pronouns

Demonstrative pronouns are used in the following cases.

A. The demonstrative pronoun as subject:

Ésta es muy elegante. (blusa)   This one is very elegant. (blouse)

B. The demonstrative pronoun to clarify a subject:

Observe the following example. Keep in mind that in sentences with *gustar*, whatever is liked becomes the subject:

A Delia no le gusta mi prima porque es   Delia does not like my cousin because she is
orgullosa.   proud.

In this sentence, it is not entirely clear who is proud, Delia or the speaker's cousin. To make it clear that it is the cousin, without repeating the subject *mi prima*, *ésta* becomes the new subject of the verb *ser* because it refers to *prima*, the most recent noun in the sentence:

*A Delia no le gusta mi prima porque **ésta** (mi prima) es orgullosa.*

The opposite situation would be:

*A Delia no le gusta mi prima porque **aquélla** (o Delia) es orgullosa.*

C. The demonstrative pronoun as object of the verb:

Direct object:
*Quiero **éstas**.*   I want these.
Indirect object:
*Se lo di a **aquéllos**. (estudiantes)*   I gave it to those (students).

D. The demonstrative pronoun by itself:

Ésta. Prefiero la verde. (blusa)   This one. I prefer the green one. (blouse)
Aquélla. La casa que está en la esquina es   That one. The house that is on the corner is
más linda.   nicer.

E. The demonstrative pronoun to indicate a place:

*El grupo teatral se encuentra en **ésta** desde anoche.*

The theater group has been here (*in this city*) since last night.

*Espero que ya hayan llegado a **ésa** sin problemas.*

I hope that you have already arrived there (in the city you were going to) without any problems.

F. The demonstrative pronoun to indicate time:

Demonstrative pronouns (as well as their corresponding adjectives) are used to indicate limitations of time. *Éste*, *ésta*, *éstos*, and *éstas* reflect the present time; *ése*, *ésa*, *ésos*, and *ésas* point to a time which is not very far from the present; *aquél*, *aquélla*, *aquéllos*, and *aquéllas* reflect a time that is long gone:

***Éstas** son las mejores tardes que hemos tenido.*

These are the best afternoons that we have had.

***Ése** fue un año memorable.*

That was a memorable year.

*Claro que **aquéllos** eran los días más activos en la oficina.*

Of course those were the most active days in the office.

G. The demonstrative pronoun to express the equivalent of *the former* and *the latter*:

*Carlos y Juan comenzaron el curso de español el año pasado. Mientras **éste** (Juan) lo hizo en el otoño, **aquél** (Carlos) lo tomó en la primavera. (In Spanish the word order is reversed).*

Carlos and Juan began the Spanish course last year. While the former took it in the spring, the latter did it in the fall.

Possessive Pronouns

Possessive pronouns indicate who (or what) possesses what the noun indicates. These pronouns agree with the noun in gender and number:

*el **mío*** (mi auto)	mine (my car)
*la **mía*** (mi casa)	mine (my house)
*los **míos*** (mis autos)	mine (my cars)
*las **mías*** (mis casas)	mine (my houses)
*Las **mías** son más grandes.* (casas)	Mine are bigger. (houses)
*el **tuyo*** (tu papel)	yours (informal) (your paper)

la **tuya** (tu fiesta)	yours (informal) (your party)
los **tuyos** (tus papeles)	yours (informal) (your papers)
las **tuyas** (tus fiestas)	yours (informal) (your parties)
El **tuyo** no tiene la rima correcta. (poema)	Yours does not have the correct rhyme. (poem)

These forms are equivalent to the English *yours* (formal, in Spanish), *his*, *hers*, and *theirs*, for both singular and plural nouns.

el **suyo** (su perro)	
la **suya** (su idea)	
los **suyos** (sus perros)	
las **suyas** (sus ideas)	
El **suyo** tiene pelo negro. (perro)	Yours/His/Hers/Theirs has black hair. (dog)
Las **suyas** son excelentes. (ideas)	Yours/His/Hers/Theirs are excellent. (ideas)

NOTE:

In order to avoid ambiguity, the following expressions can be used to indicate *yours*, *his*, *hers*, and *theirs*, both singular (s) and plural (pl):

(1) yours/his/hers/yours (pl)/theirs:

el de Ud./él/ella/Uds./ellos/ellas
la de Ud./él/ella/Uds./ellos/ellas

(2) yours/his/hers/yours (pl)/theirs:

las de Ud./él/ella/Uds./ellos/ellas
los de Ud./él/ella/Uds./ellos/ellas

Example:

El **de Ud.** es más moderno. (televisor)	Yours is more modern. (television set)
el **nuestro** (nuestro cuadro)	ours (painting)
la **nuestra** (nuestra mesa)	ours (table)
los **nuestros** (nuestros cuadros)	ours (paintings)
las **nuestras** (nuestras mesas)	ours (tables)
El **nuestro** es importado de Japón. (cuadro)	Ours is imported from Japan. (painting)
el **vuestro** (vuestro país)	yours* (country)
la **vuestra** (vuestra tarea)	yours (chore)

---

* This pronoun indicates one or more things possessed by two or more persons, informal; it is used in Spain.

los **vuestros** (vuestros países)	yours (countries)
las **vuestras** (vuestras tareas)	yours (chores)
El **vuestro** tiene aire acondicionado. (auto)	Yours has air-conditioning. (car)
Las **vuestras** están en la sala. (maletas)	Yours are in the living room. (suitcases)

Neuter Possessive Pronouns

The neuter possessive pronouns *lo mío, lo tuyo, lo suyo, lo nuestro,* and *lo vuestro,* which refer to abstract or undefined nouns, are always expressed in the singular and take masculine singular adjectives:

Lo mío es secreto.	What I have is secret.
Lo tuyo será expuesto.	What you (informal, singular) have will be exposed.
Lo suyo es muy serio.	What you (formal, singular) have is very serious.
	What he or she has . . .
	What they have . . .
Lo nuestro es placentero.	What we have is pleasant.
Lo vuestro no es bueno.	What you (informal, plural) have is not good.

NOTE:

The construction *lo + de +* a subject pronoun* (i.e. *lo de Ud., lo de Uds., lo de ella, lo de nosotros*) to indicate possession also takes masculine singular adjectives:

Lo de Uds. es increíble.	What you have . . . *or* What you have experienced is incredible.
Lo de nosotros es bueno.	What we have is good.

Uses of Possessive Pronouns

A. The possessive pronoun as subject:

La mía es más interesante. (mi novela)	Mine is more interesting. (my novel)

---

* This prepositional phrase cannot be used with the singular forms of the first person (*yo*) and the second person (*tú*) subject pronouns. Instead of *lo de yo* or *lo de tú,* the following forms are used: *Lo mío es apropiado.* (What I have is appropriate.) and *Lo tuyo es irónico.* (Yours [situation] is ironic.)

As in the preceding sentences, when the verb is followed by an adjective, the adjective must be masculine singular. However, if a modified noun follows the verb, the adjective must agree with the noun: *Lo tuyo no es buena idea.* (What you have . . . or What you suggest is not a good idea.) and *Lo nuestro es un caso perdido.* (Ours is a lost cause.)

B. The possessive pronoun as object of the verb:

Direct object:

Quiere conocer **el mío**. *(apartamento)*　　　She wants to see mine. (apartment)

Indirect object:

Quiere darles un regalo a **los míos**. *(parientes)*　　*Literally*: She wants to give a gift to mine (relatives).

C. The possessive pronoun by itself:

Los tuyos. *No traigas los otros. (informes)*　　Yours. Do not bring the other ones. (reports)

D. The possessive pronoun as an indication of respect:

There are a few fixed expressions of respect and courtesy, mainly used to address or refer to royal or high-ranking persons.

1. *Su* is used when talking about the person:

Su Señoría	His Lordship, Ladyship
Su Alteza	His/Her Highness
Su Majestad	His/Her Majesty
Su Excelencia	His/Her Excellency

2. *Vuestra* is used when addressing the person:

Vuestra Señoría	Your Lordship/Ladyship
Vuestra Alteza	Your Highness
Vuestra Majestad	Your Majesty
Vuestra Excelencia	Your Excelency

NOTES:

(1) Gender is shown by the adjectives or nouns that accompany the pronominal expression:

Su Alteza está ocupado.	His Highness is busy.
Su Majestad la reina.	Her Majesty the Queen.
Su Excelencia, el Presidente de la República.	His Excellency, the President of the Republic.

(2) The adjectives included in the title must be feminine:

Su Alteza Ilustrísima, el Rey de Grecia.	His Illustrious Highness, the King of Greece.

(3) When talking to the person, that is, addressing the person as *vuestra*, the singular form of the possessive adjective, *su*, is also used in the sentence if it is necessary to indicate possession:

Vuestra Señoría, **su** *hermano acaba de llegar.*   Your Lordship, your brother has just arrived.

(4) The abbreviation *Usía*, Vuecencia, and Vuecelencia* are shortened forms of *Vuestra Señoría* and *Vuestra Excelencia*, respectively. Students of the language will find these expressions mainly in old works of literature or documents.

E. **The possessive pronoun after the verb *ser* (*to be*)**

1. To indicate possession in a general way, the article is usually omitted:

Esa entrada es **mía***; voy a ir al teatro mañana.*   That ticket is mine; I am going to the theater tomorrow.

2. To indicate possession in a specific way, especially when there is a selection involved, the article is used:

Esa entrada es **la mía***, no la de Juan.*   That ticket is mine, not Juan's.

Relative Pronouns

A relative pronoun refers to a noun (called the *antecedent*), which also appears in the same sentence. In English, *that, who, whom, which, whose,* and *what* are relative pronouns. These pronouns connect two sentences:

The lawyer arrived yesterday. He will be present.	*El abogado llegó ayer. Él estará presente.*
The lawyer, <u>who</u> arrived yesterday, will be present.	*El abogado, <u>quien</u> llegó ayer, estará presente.*
She sent flowers. The flowers are beautiful.	*Ella mandó flores. Las flores son preciosas.*
She sent flowers <u>that</u> are beautiful.	*Ella mandó flores <u>que</u> son preciosas.*

In Spanish there are four basic relative pronouns: *que* (*that, which, who*), *quien* (*who*), *cual* (*which*), and *cuyo* (*whose*).

---

* *Usía* comes from *Useñoría* and *Vuestra Señoría*.

The Relative Pronoun *que* (that, which, who)

This pronoun is invariable and never changes form. It may refer to humans, nonhumans, and things:

*El hombre **que** trajo la carta ya se fue.*	The man that (who) brought the letter has already left.
*Los conejos **que** ellos crían son grises.*	The rabbits that they raise are gray.
*Su generosidad, **que** muestra a menudo, es una de sus cualidades.*	His generosity, which he often shows, is one of his virtues.

Uses of the Relative Pronoun *que*

This pronoun is used in several ways.

A. The relative pronoun distinguished from the conjunction

The relative pronoun *que* must not be confused with the conjunction *que*. This conjunction cannot be replaced by *quien* or by any of the forms of *cual* (*el/la cual, los/las cuales*) as the relative pronoun can. (For uses of *lo cual* and *lo que*, see the subsection Neuter Relative Pronouns at the very end of this section, The Relative Pronoun *que*.)

1. *que* as a relative pronoun

*La mujer **que** abrió la puerta era vieja.*	The woman who opened the door was old.
*La mujer, **quien** abrió la puerta, era vieja.*	The woman, who opened the door, was old.
*La mujer, **la cual** abrió la puerta, era vieja.*	

In the preceding first Spanish sentence, the information that follows the relative *que* is necessary and the clause is called a restrictive clause. Notice that there are no commas around a restrictive clause. In the next two Spanish sentences, the information provided after the relative is not necessary, and the clause is called a nonrestrictive clause, which has commas around it. Other examples are:

*Todos los niños **que** habían esperado en el aula salieron a la misma hora.*	All the children who had waited in the classroom left at the same time.
*Todos los niños, **quienes** habían esperado en el aula...*	All the children, who had waited in the classroom . . .
*Todos los niños, **los cuales** habían esperado en el aula...*	

2. *que* as a conjunction

When *que* is used as a conjunction, it does not replace a noun previously mentioned in the sentence (the antecedent):

*Creo **que** está sentado en la cocina.*	I think (that) he is sitting in the kitchen.
*Nos dijeron **que** el museo abre a las once.*	They told us (that) the museum opens at 11:00 A.M.

B. **The relative pronoun *que* preceded by *el*, *la*, *los*, or *las***

1. The article that precedes *que* agrees in gender and number with the antecedent. This expression may mean *the one(s) who*, *the one(s) that*, or simply *who* or *which*. Verbs used with this expression include *ser* as well as others. In all cases, the noun could be inserted in the sentence without changing the meaning:

*Lola es **la** (chica) **que** me dio el dinero.*	Lola is <u>the one who (who)</u> gave me the money.
*Lola es **quien** me dio el dinero.*	
*Jaime habló con **el** (amigo) **que** lo llamó.*	Jaime talked to the person <u>who</u> called him.
*Jaime habló con **quien** lo llamó.*	
*Estos son **los** (sobres) **que** me trajo mi hermana.*	These are <u>the ones that</u> my sister brought me.
***Los** (guantes) **que** me diste son muy bonitos.*	<u>The ones (that)</u> you gave me are very pretty.
*Éste es el cambio que me sobró, con **el que** me podré comprar el periódico.*	This is the change I have left, with <u>which</u> I'll be able to buy the paper.

2. A preposition may also precede the relative pronoun:

*Estas son las flores **de las que** te hablé.*	These are the flowers I talked to you about.

3. A definite article plus *que* may function as a subject, especially in proverbial usage. *Quien* (*who*) is also used in this case:

***El que** persevera gana.*	The one who (He who) perseveres, wins.
***Quien** persevera gana.*	

C. The relative pronoun *que* in a nonrestrictive clause

When there is a nonrestrictive clause (one which supplies information that is not essential), commas must be placed before *que* and at the end of the clause:

El tren, **que** siempre llega atrasado, viene de San Juan.	The train, <u>which</u> always arrives late, comes from San Juan.
Las lecciones, **que** enseña sin cobrar, son de inglés.	The lessons, <u>which</u> she teaches at no charge, are English lessons.

D. The relative pronoun *que* is not optional

Que cannot be left out of a restrictive clause (one which gives information that is essential), as is commonly done in English:

La derrota **que** sufrieron fue terrible.	The defeat (that) they suffered was terrible.

E. Placement of a preposition before *que*

If a preposition is used, it always precedes the relative pronoun *que* (notice how, in English, the preposition follows the verb when the relative pronoun is absent):

El dolor **con que** tuvo que vivir terminó con su vida.	The pain he had to live **with** ended his life.

F. The relative pronoun *que* as subject of the verb

1. In a restrictive clause, which gives specific information:

El libro **que** salió a la venta es de Jiménez.	The book that went on sale is by Jiménez.
El doctor **que** firmó la receta es un especialista.	The doctor who signed the prescription is a specialist.

> **NOTE:**
> In a restrictive clause, *que* cannot be replaced by *quien,* even when the antecedent is a person. Therefore, it is <u>incorrect</u> to say: (*El doctor quien firmó la receta es un especialista.*)

2. In a nonrestrictive clause (one that supplies additional information and can be left out):

El libro, **que** salió antes de tiempo, es de Jiménez.	The book, *which* came out ahead of time, is by Jiménez.

G. The relative pronoun *que* as object of a preposition

Que combines with the prepositions *a*, *con*, *de*, and *en*. While the definite article may be left out in a restrictive clause, it must be used in nonrestrictive clauses. Observe the following examples, where a form of *cual* may be used instead of *que*:

Restrictive:	*El lío en (el) que (en el cual)* [where] *está metido lo tiene nervioso.*
	The problem in which he is involved makes him nervous.
Nonrestrictive:	*El lío, en el que (en el cual) está metido, lo tiene nervioso.*
Restrictive:	*La simpatía con (la) que (con la cual)* [with which] *me dio el dinero me dejó pensando.*
	The friendliness with which he gave me the money made me think.
Nonrestrictive:	*La simpatía, con la que (con la cual) me dio el dinero, me dejó pensando.*
Restrictive:	*Las tiendas a (las) que (a las cuales)* [to which] *te refieres son muy caras.*
	The stores you are referring to are very expensive.
Nonrestrictive:	*Las tiendas, a las que (a las cuales) te refieres, son muy caras.*
Restrictive:	*Los ejercicios de (los) que (de los cuales) consta cada manual facilitan la comprensión.*
	The exercises that each manual contains facilitate comprehension.
Nonrestrictive:	*Los ejercicios, de los que (de los cuales) consta cada manual, facilitan la comprensión.*

NOTE:

Sometimes the relative pronoun *que* is used after the prepositions *a*, *con*, *de*, and *en t*o refer to people, although this is not considered correct. It is better to use *quien*, *quienes*, or a form of *cual* (*el cual, la cual, los cuales, las cuales*).

H. *Que* as an adverbial relative

Que preceded by some prepositions and/or a definite article becomes an adverbial relative:

*El salón **en (el) que** estudiamos es bien grande.*	The classroom in which (where) we study is very large.
*La fiesta **de la que** llegó era en casa de Irene.*	The party from which she arrived was at Irene's house.
*La oficina **a la cual** nos dirigimos estaba lejos.*	The office to which (where) we went was far away.
*El valor **con el que** sufrió su enfermedad lo hizo un santo.*	The courage with which he suffered his illness made him a saint.

NOTE:

Other adverbial expressions include a combination of *que*, preceded by a definite article, after a word or expression such as *al lado*, *alrededor*, *debajo*, *detrás*, *encima*, *frente*, or others. *Que* may be replaced by *cual* in these cases, although it makes the sentence more literary:

Esa era la casa **frente** <u>a la que</u> (a la cual) estaba la estatua.	That was the house in front of which the statue was located.
Lo puso en la mesa, **alrededor** <u>de la que</u> (de la cual) estaban sentados los invitados.	He put it on the table, around which the guests were sitting.

▪ I. The relative pronoun *qué* as an interrogative

Que carries an accent mark (*qué*) when it is used as an interrogative after verbs of perception such as *comprender*, *decir*, *entender*, *imaginarse*, *pensar*, *preguntar*, *saber*, *tener idea de*, *ver*, and others. It may also be preceded by a preposition:

No me imagino con **qué** excusa vendrá.	I can't imagine with what excuse he is going to come.
No tenemos idea **qué** van a decidir.	We don't have any idea what they are going to decide.

▪ J. The relative pronoun *que* with prepositions other than *a*, *con*, *de*, and *en*

Que combines with other prepositions besides *a*, *con*, *de*, and *en*, but the definite article must then be used in both restrictive and nonrestrictive clauses:

Este es el cuarto **para el que** compré la pintura.	This is the room for which I bought the paint.
El cuarto, **para el que** compré la pintura, está arriba.	The room, for which I bought the paint, is upstairs.

▪ K. The relative pronoun *que* as a direct object

El barco **que** alquilamos ayer tiene un motor japonés.	The boat (that) we rented yesterday has a Japanese engine.
El diario **que** compré trae la noticia.	The newspaper (that) I bought has the news.
La tienda cubana, **que** visito con frecuencia, es buena.	The Cuban store, which I visit frequently, is good.

L. The relative pronoun *que* as an indirect object

*Este es el vestido **al que** le arreglé el ruedo.*	This is the dress whose hem I fixed.
*Se llevó la blusa azul, **a la que** le puse botones.*	She took the blue blouse, which I put buttons on.

M. The relative pronoun *que* and the personal *a*

Before the definite article and *que*, the personal *a* is used when the relative pronoun could be replaced by *at which*, *to which*, or *(to) whom*:

*La estación **a la que** llegamos era Carlos Paz.*	The station where (at which) we arrived was Carlos Paz.
*La estación, **a la que** llegamos temprano, era Carlos Paz.*	The station, where (at which) we arrived early, was Carlos Paz.
But:	
*La estación **que** vimos era Carlos Paz.*	The station we saw was Carlos Paz.
*Esa estación, **que** vimos ayer, era Carlos Paz.*	That station, which we saw yesterday, was Carlos Paz.
*La tienda **a la que** le mandamos el recibo es cara.*	The store to which we sent the receipt is expensive.
*La tienda, **a la que** le mandamos el recibo, es cara.*	The store, to which we sent the receipt, is expensive.
But:	
*La tienda **que** quería el recibo estaba cerrada.*	The store that wanted the receipt was closed.
*La tienda, **que** quería el recibo, estaba cerrada.*	The store, which wanted the receipt, was closed.
*El profesor **al que** nos mandaron es francés.*	The professor to whom they sent us is French.
*El profesor, **al que** nos mandaron, es francés.*	The professor, to whom they sent us, is French.
But:	
*El profesor **que** llegó era francés.*	The professor who arrived was French.
*El profesor, **que** llegó tarde, era francés.*	The professor, who arrived late, was French.
*Las primas **a las que** no había visto nunca estaban allí.*	The cousins whom I had never seen were there.
*Las primas, **a las que** no había visto nunca, estaban allí.*	The cousins, whom I had never seen, were there.
But:	
*Las primas **que** vivían allí estaban presentes.*	The cousins who lived there were present.
*Las primas, **que** vivían allí, estaban presentes.*	The cousins, who lived there, were present.

N. Prepositions used with *que* preceded by an indefinite noun

If an indefinite noun such as *nada* or *algo* precedes the relative pronoun *que*, a preposition is used when the expression can be replaced by <u>that preposition + a form of</u> <u>*cual*</u> (*which*):

No había nada **a que** *(a lo cual) referirse.*	There was nothing to refer to.
Había algo **a que** *(a lo cual) resignarse.*	There was something we could resign ourselves to.
Tiene algo **de que** *(de lo cual) preocuparse.*	She has something to worry about.
Encontramos algo **en que** *(en lo cual) tener fe.*	We found something to have faith in.

In the following sentences, *que* is used without a preposition and the substitution is not possible. The verb may appear conjugated or in the infinitive form:

No había <u>nada</u> **que** *pudiéramos hacer.*	There was nothing that we could do.
No hubo <u>nada</u> **que** *hacer.*	There was nothing to be done (that we could do).
Había <u>algo</u> **que** *podíamos hacer.*	There was something that we could do.
Me dieron <u>algo</u> **que** *(tenía que) revisar.*	They gave me something (that I had) to check.

NOTE:

The *que* in *tener que* (*to have to*) and *haber que* (*must*) before an infinitive does not fit into the category of a relative pronoun:

<u>Tenemos que</u> *pedirle dinero a Papá.*	We have to ask Dad for money.
<u>Hay que</u> *decirle que no venga.*	We must tell him not to come.

O. Substitution of *lo cual* or *lo que* for *que*

When the antecedent is an indefinite noun such as *algo* or *nada*, and the relative pronoun is preceded by a preposition, *lo cual* or *lo que* must be used instead of *que* if the verb is conjugated.

No hay nada **de lo cual** *(de lo que) pueda arrepentirse.*	There is nothing she can repent of.
(<u>Incorrect</u>: No hay nada <u>de que</u> pueda arrepentirse.)	
Hay algunos **con los cuales** *(con los que) hablo a menudo.*	There are some with whom I talk often.
(<u>Incorrect</u>: Hay algunos <u>con que</u> hablo a menudo.)	

Lo que and *lo cual* are called neuter relative pronouns because of the neuter article *lo*. (Remember that definite articles are *el, la, los,* and *las*.)

1. The Neuter Relative Pronoun *lo que* (that, which, whatever)

The relative pronoun *lo que* is the neuter equivalent of *el que* and corresponds to the English pronouns *what, which*, and *whatever*. It may refer to a concept or an idea, as well as to a noun previously mentioned. Notice that the neuter definite article *lo* must precede *que*. This pronoun is invariable.

2. Uses of the Neuter Relative Pronoun *lo que*

(a) *Lo que* with a clause as an antecedent:

*El informe no se envió a tiempo, **lo que** nos preocupa.*	The report was not sent on time, which worries us.

When *lo que* is followed by the subjunctive, it takes the meaning of *whatever* in English:

***Lo que** <u>sea</u>, será bienvenido.*	Whatever it is, it will be welcome.
*Déjalo que haga **lo que** <u>quiera</u>.*	Let him do whatever he wants.

NOTES:

(1) *Lo cual* may replace *lo que* when it functions as a clause:

*Todos los miembros estaban presentes, **lo cual** era de esperar.*	All the members were present, which was expected.

(2) The expression *cosa que* may sometimes be used instead of *lo cual* or *lo que*:

*Llegó ayer por la tarde, **cosa que** me sorprendió.*	He arrived yesterday afternoon, which surprised me.

(b) *Lo que* to replace an undefined noun:

*No puedo creer **lo que** me has dicho.*	I cannot believe what you have told me.
*Te compré **lo que** me pediste.*	I bought you what you asked for.

(c) *Lo que* as a subject

Sometimes *lo que* functions as a subject, and is translated into English as *what*. As opposed to English, however, the neuter article must be used in Spanish:

***Lo que** pasa es inexplicable.*	What is going on is beyond words.

However, the English interrogative or exclamatory *what* is rendered into Spanish as *que*, without the article:

¡**Qué** buena película!	What a good movie!
¿**Qué** dice al pie de la página?	What does it say at the bottom of the page?

3. **Different Meanings of *lo que***

cuánto

Yo sé muy bien **lo que (cuánto)** ha trabajado.	I know <u>how much</u> she has worked.

cómo

Es increíble **lo que (cómo)** te extraña.	It's incredible <u>how</u> she misses you.

eso que, or **aquello que**

Guardaré el secreto de **lo que (eso que)** dijiste.	I will keep the secret of <u>what</u> you said.

lo cual

Nos llamó, **lo que (lo cual)** nos sorprendió.	He called us, <u>which</u> surprised us.

según

Firmaron el contrato, **lo que (según)** se dice.	They signed the contract, <u>according to</u> what they say.

> **NOTE:**
>
> The equivalent of the idiomatic expression *lo que es* is *as for* or *with regard to*:
>
> | | |
> |---|---|
> | **Lo que es** su trabajo, no lo satisface. | As for his job, he is not satisfied. |

4. ***Lo cual*** (which)

The neuter relative *lo cual* refers to an entire clause, rather than to a noun, in which case it is equivalent to *lo que*:

<u>Decidió cambiar la alfombra</u>, **lo cual** (lo que) me pareció una buena idea.	She decided to change the carpet, which I thought was a good idea.

Compare the following sentence, where the definite article *la*, used instead of *lo*, changes entirely the meaning of the sentence, since the relative pronoun is now used to make reference only to the noun, not to the whole idea, as indicated by *lo cual*, in the preceding example.

Decidió cambiar <u>la alfombra</u>, **la cual** ya estaba muy gastada.	She decided to change the carpet, which was already worn out.

The Relative Pronoun *quien* (who)

This pronoun has a plural form, *quienes*, but has no gender. It refers to persons only. Commas must enclose the relative clause when the pronoun is not preceded by a preposition:

*Esta señora, **quien** vive lejos, es su hermana.*	This lady, who lives far away, is his sister.
*Aquellos niños, **quienes** tienen hambre, comerán aquí.*	Those children, who are hungry, will eat here.

If there is a preposition, the commas are used when the information between the commas may be left out without altering what the speaker wants to convey:

*La secretaria con **quien** trabajo se llama Amalia.*	The secretary with whom I work is called Amalia.
*Los médicos, de **quienes** te hablé, son italianos.*	The doctors, whom I talked to you about, are Italian.

In English, the relative pronouns in expressions such as *to whom* (*a quien*), *with whom* (*con quien*), or *for whom* (*para quien*), may be omitted. These relative pronouns, along with the prepositions, must always be expressed in Spanish:

*Esa es la chica **a quien** le dimos la muñeca.*	That is the girl to whom we gave the doll.
	That is the girl we gave the doll to.
*El muchacho **con quien** salgo estudia negocios.*	The boy with whom I go out studies business.
	The boy I go out with studies business.
*El hombre **para quien** trabajo es muy joven.*	The man for whom I work is very young.
	The man I work for is very young.

Uses of the Relative Pronoun *quien*

A. The relative pronoun *quien* as a subject

When there is no antecedent preceding *quien*, the relative pronoun functions as a subject. In this case, *quien* is equivalent to *el que*, but cannot be replaced by *el cual*:

***Quien** (**El que**) te hizo semejante regalo merece un aplauso.*	Whoever (He who) gave you such a gift deserves applause.
***Quien** (**El que**) lo dice, lo hace.*	Whoever (He who) says it, does it.

B. The relative pronoun *quien* as a direct object

When *quien* functions as a direct object, it must be preceded by the preposition *a*:

El cartero, **a quien** vi en el correo, no dejó el sobre.	The mailman, whom I saw in the post office, did not leave the envelope.

C. The relative pronoun *quien* as an indirect object

When *quien* functions as an indirect object, it must be preceded by the preposition *a*:

El cartero, **a quien** le di la carta, ya pasó.	The mailman, to whom I gave the letter, has already gone by.

D. The relative pronoun *quien* to mean *somebody* (*someone*) or *nobody* (*no one*)

Tenía **quien** lo fuera a buscar.	He had someone to pick him up.
No hay **quien** lo pueda aprobar.	There is no one who can approve it.

> **NOTE:**
>
> However, if the word *alguien* (*someone*) or *nadie* (*no one*) appears in the sentence, *que* is used instead of *quien*:
>
> | | |
> |---|---|
> | Tenía <u>alguien que</u> lo fuera a buscar. | He had someone to pick him up. |
> | No hay <u>nadie que</u> lo pueda aprobar. | There is no one who can approve it. |

E. The relative pronoun *quien* and the prepositions

With the exception of *cabe* (*near*) and *entre* (*between*), all prepositions may precede *quien*. *Entre* may, however, precede the <u>plural</u> form *quienes*:

Estos son los hombres entre **quienes** se mantuvo el secreto.	These are the men among whom the secret was kept.

> **NOTE:**
> *Cabe* is a form that appears in older literary pieces.

F. *Quién(es)* as an interrogative

Quien(es), with an accent mark (*quién/quiénes*), is used as an interrogative word after verbs of perception such as *comprender, decir, entender, imaginarse, pensar, preguntar, saber, tener idea de, ver*, and others. It may also be preceded by a preposition:

| No sé **quién** llegó. | I don't know who arrived. |
| No comprendió con **quiénes** había salido. | She didn't understand with whom he had gone out. |

The Relative Pronoun *cual* (which)

This pronoun is used only in nonrestrictive clauses and may refer to persons, animals, or things. It has a plural form, *cuales*, while gender is determined by the definite article:

el cual, la cual, las cuales, los cuales

Since all the clauses used in the following examples are nonrestrictive, the relative pronoun may be replaced by *que* (with or without the definite article) or by *quien*. The use of *cual* makes the sentence sound too formal or elaborate:

Las armas, **las cuales** (que, las que) estaban escondidas, serán vendidas.	The guns, which were hidden, will be sold.
Los animales, a **los cuales** (a los que) alimentaron, eran salvajes.	The animals, which they fed, were wild.
Ese farmacéutico, **el cual** (quien) me dio la receta, es alemán.	That pharmacist, who gave me the prescription, is German.

In a restrictive clause, however, it is incorrect to use a form of *cual*:

| Juan escribió en la hoja **que** estaba en la mesa. | Juan wrote on the sheet that was on the table. |
| (Incorrect: *Juan escribió en la hoja <u>la cual</u> estaba en la mesa*.) | |

NOTES:

(1) To clarify the antecedent when there is more than one noun (*fruta* and *plato* in the following example), a form of *cual* or *que*, preceded by the definite article, must be used:

| La fruta de ese plato, **que** trajo Luis, no alcanza. | The fruit on that plate, which Luis brought, is not enough. |

Here, it is not clear whether Luis brought the fruit or the plate. To indicate that the fruit (feminine in Spanish), rather than the plate (masculine), is what Luis brought, the article must be used:

*La fruta de ese plato, **la cual** (la que) trajo Luis, no alcanza.*

However, to show that what he brought was the plate, *el cual* or *el que* should be used.

(2) *Lo cual* has the same meaning as *lo que:*

Nos quedaban dos, **lo cual (lo que)** nos alegró.	We had two left, which made us happy.

Uses of the Relative Pronoun *cual(es)*

The relative pronoun *cual(es)* is used in the following cases:

A. The relative pronoun *cual* instead of *quien*

Cual, preceded by the definite article, is used instead of *quien* to better identify the antecedent, that is, the noun to which the pronoun refers:

Éste es el profesor para **quien** hice el trabajo.
Éste es el profesor para **el cual** hice el trabajo.　　This is the professor for whom I did the job.

B. The relative pronoun *cual* after prepositional phrases

Cual is used after prepositional phrases such as *cerca de*, *detrás de*, *en medio de*, and *por arriba de*:

El jardín estaba lleno de flores, <u>en medio de</u> **las cuales** caminábamos.	The garden was full of flowers, among which we were walking.
El cielo tenía un enorme nubarrón negro, <u>por arriba d**el** cual</u> se veía el sol.	The sky had a huge dark cloud, on top of which the sun could be seen.

Notice the contraction in *por arriba de* + *el cual* in the preceding sentence.

C. The relative pronoun *cual* after longer prepositions

Cual is used after prepositions of more than one syllable, such as *desde*, *entre*, *para*, and *sobre*:

Hay dos habitaciones <u>entre</u> **las cuales** tienen un pequeño baño.	There are two rooms, with a small bathroom in between.
Me gustó la torre, <u>desde</u> **la cual** se puede ver toda la ciudad.	I liked the tower, from which one can see the whole city.

D. The relative pronoun *cual* after *por*, *sin*, and *tras*

Cual is used after the prepositions *por*, *sin*, and *tras*, since the expressions *por que*, *sin que*, and *tras que* have a different meaning:

El camino **por el cual** fuimos a Madrid tenía muchos autos.	The road by which we went to Madrid had a lot of cars.
(<u>Incorrect</u>: El camino *por que* fuimos a Madrid...)	
El libro **sin el cual** no puedo estudiar es muy caro.	The book without which I cannot study is very expensive.
(<u>Incorrect</u>: El libro *sin que* no puedo estudiar...)	
Esa fue la idea **tras la cual** orienté mis esfuerzos.	That was the idea according to which I oriented my efforts.
(<u>Incorrect</u>: Esa fue la idea *tras que* orienté...)	

E. The relative pronoun *cual* replaced by *quien*

Preceded by *a* + a definite article, a form of *cual* may be replaced by *quien*:

Éste es mi primo peruano, **al cual (a quien)** Ud. vio en la biblioteca.	This is my Peruvian cousin, whom you saw in the library.

F. *Cual* as an interrogative

Cual and its derivatives, with an accent mark, functions as an interrogative after verbs of perception such as *comprender*, *decir*, *entender*, *imaginarse*, *pensar*, *preguntar*, *saber*, *tener idea de*, *ver*, and others. It may be preceded by a preposition:

No entiendo **cuál** es la broma.	I don't understand what the joke is.
No sabe con **cuáles** se va a quedar.	She doesn't know which ones she is going to keep.

G. *A cuál más*

The expression *a cuál más* has a specific meaning:

Había flores, **a cuál más** linda.	There were flowers, each one nicer than the others.

> **NOTE:**
>
> *Each one*, otherwise, translates as *cada cual*:
>
> | | |
> |---|---|
> | **Cada cual** recibirá una medalla en la ceremonia. | Each one will receive a medal in the ceremony. |

The Relative Pronoun *cuyo* (whose)

This form is a possessive relative pronoun that functions as an adjective and has gender and number: *cuyo, cuya, cuyos, cuyas*. As an adjective, *cuyo* (and its derivatives) agrees with the noun that follows it, rather than with the antecedent:

El hombre, **cuyo** hijo ganó el concurso, vive aquí.	The man, whose son won the contest, lives here.
Estos árboles, **cuyas** <u>hojas</u> se cayeron, florecerán en la primavera.	These trees, whose leaves have fallen, will bloom in the spring.

As a pronoun, the use of *cuyo* (and all its forms) is obsolete; it may be found in works of literature and old documents. Its use is very limited, since it applies solely to people and can be used only with *ser*. In modern Spanish, it is replaced by *de quien(es)*, *a quien(es)*, or a combination of *de* plus a form of *cual:*

<u>(Obsolete:</u> El hombre, **cuyo** <u>es</u> este portafolio, es muy joven.)
<u>Correct:</u> El hombre, **de quien** <u>es</u> este portafolio, es muy joven.
El hombre, **a quien** <u>pertenece</u> este portafolio, es muy joven.
The man, to whom this briefcase belongs, is very young.

<u>(Obsolete:</u> La autora, **cuyos** <u>son</u> estos artículos, es alemana.)
<u>Correct:</u> La autora, **de la cual** <u>son</u> estos artículos, es alemana.
The author, to whom these articles belong, is German.

NOTES:

(1) The forms *cuyo, cuya, cuyos,* and *cuyas,* never take an article.

(2) If the antecedent is an indirect object, *a quien(es)* replaces a form of *cuyo*. Observe the following cases where English uses *whose* (*de quien*):

Manuela, **a quien** le queda bien la chaqueta, está feliz.	Manuela, <u>whose</u> jacket fits her well, is happy.
El soldado, **a quien** le recortaron el pelo, es nuevo.	The soldier, <u>whose</u> hair was trimmed, is new.

(3) The English *whose,* used as an interrogative pronoun, becomes *de quién(es)* in Spanish, not *cuyo*. It carries an accent:

¿Tú sabes **de quién** es esa obra maestra?	Do you know whose that masterpiece is?
¿**De quién** es esta mochila?	Whose is this backpack?

(4) In indirect discourse, *de quién(es)* is used in Spanish instead of a form of *cuyo*. It carries an accent:

Le pregunté *de quiénes* eran esas gafas.   I asked him whose those glasses were.

(5) The expression *in which case* is translated into Spanish as *en cuyo caso*:

La conferencia puede ser cancelada, *en cuyo*   The conference might be canceled, in which
   caso nos avisarán.   case they will let us know.

The Use of the Personal *a* Before Relative Pronouns

The forms *el/la que*, *los/las que*, *quien*, and *quienes* are preceded by the personal *a* in the following cases.

A. The personal *a* is used when the verb requires it, as in *agradecer a*, *visitar a*, *recordar a*:

Recuerda *a la que* te escribe.   Remember who writes to you.
Agradeció *a los que* la ayudaron.   She thanked those who helped her.
No visitará *a quien* no lo quiera.   He will not visit those who don't want it.

B. The personal *a* is used whenever a relative pronoun acts as an indirect object:

Tu jefe es la persona *a quien* debes enviar   Your boss is the person to whom you must
   el memo.   send the memo.
Esa es la tienda *a la que* podemos devolver   That is the store to which we can return
   la caja.   the box.

The Use of Relative Adverbs Instead of Relative Pronouns

Relative adverbs may replace relative pronouns:

como
La manera *en que* (*como*) lo dijo dejó a todos   The way in which he said it left everybody
   preocupados.   worried. (adverb of manner)
cuando
La hora *a la que* (*cuando*) llegó no es   The time when he arrived is none of my
   asunto mío.   business. (adverb of time)

cuanto

Puse en el informe todo **lo que (cuanto)** me dijo.

I put in the report everything she told me. (adverb of quantity)

donde

El estante **en que (donde)** estaba el florero era de pino.

The shelf where the vase was standing was made of pine. (adverb of place)

Summary of the Uses of Relative Pronouns

Relative pronouns are used in restrictive and nonrestrictive clauses in the following functions. The English sentence is presented in the restrictive form only.

A. The relative pronoun as subject

Restrictive: *La mujer **que** me hizo el vestido cobra mucho.*
Nonrestrictive: *La mujer, **que (quien, la cual)** me hizo el vestido, cobra mucho.*
The woman who made the dress for me charges a lot.

Restrictive: *El hombre **que** vino hace poco está afuera.*
Nonrestrictive: *El hombre, **que (quien, el cual)** vino hace poco, está afuera.*
The man who came not long ago is outside.

Restrictive: *Los chicos **que** vinieron ayer son sus hijos.*
Nonrestrictive: *Los chicos, **que (quienes, los cuales)** vinieron ayer, son sus hijos.*
The children who came yesterday are his sons.

Restrictive: *El perro **que** le mordió en la pierna estaba rabioso.*
Nonrestrictive: *El perro, **que (el cual)** le mordió en la pierna, estaba rabioso.*
The dog that bit her leg was mad.

Restrictive: *Las nubes **que** se aproximaban eran de lluvia.*
Nonrestrictive: *Las nubes, **que (las cuales)** se aproximaban, eran de lluvia.*
The clouds that were approaching were rain clouds.

B. The relative pronoun as direct object

Restrictive: *Ese es el estudiante **que (a quien)** vi en la biblioteca.*
Nonrestrictive: *Ese estudiante, **a quien (al cual, al que)** vi en la biblioteca, estaba estudiando.*
That is the student (whom) I saw in the library.

Restrictive: *Las señoras **que** Juan entrevistó en su casa son maestras.*

Nonrestrictive: *Las señoras, **que (a quienes, a las cuales, a las que)** Juan entrevistó en su casa, son maestras.*

The ladies that Juan interviewed in their house are teachers.

Restrictive: *Me encantó el regalo **que** me compraste.*

Nonrestrictive: *El regalo, **que (el cual)** me compraste ayer, me encantó.*

*Los regalos, **que (los cuales)** me compraste ayer, me encantaron.*

I very much liked the gift(s) that you bought me.

C. The relative pronoun as indirect object

Restrictive: *Este es el informe **al que (al cual)** le agregué un párrafo.*

Nonrestrictive: *El informe, **al que (al cual)** le agregué un párrafo, es éste.*

This is the report to which I added a paragraph.

Restrictive: *Esta es la chica **a quien (a la cual, a la que)** le di la dirección.*

Nonrestrictive: *Esta chica, **a quien (a la cual, a la que)** le di la dirección, irá a visitarte.*

This is the girl to whom I gave the address.

Restrictive: *Veo a los alumnos **a quienes (a los cuales, a los que)** les mostré el video.*

Nonrestrictive: *Esos alumnos, **a quienes (a los cuales, a los que)** les mostré el video, faltaron a clase.*

I see the students to whom I showed the video.

D. The relative pronoun after the prepositions *a*, *con*, *de*, and *en*

Restrictive: *Esa es la situación **a que (a la que, a la cual)** nos vamos a referir.*

Nonrestrictive: *Esa situación, **a la que (a la cual)** nos vamos a referir, es muy importante.*

That is the situation to which we are going to refer.

Restrictive: *Ya tiene una muchacha **con quien (con la cual, con la que)** puede ir al baile.*

Nonrestrictive: *La muchacha, **con quien (con la cual, con la que)** irá al baile, vive cerca de su casa.*

He already has a girl with whom he is going to the dance.

Restrictive: *Este es el tema **de que (del cual, del que)** conversamos.*

Nonrestrictive: *El tema, **del cual (del que)** conversamos, es interesante.*

This is the subject which we talked about.

Restrictive: *Me contó el problema **en que (en el que, en el cual)** está metido.*
Nonrestrictive: *El problema, **en el que (en el cual)** está metido, es muy serio.*
He told me about the problem in which he is involved.

E. The relative pronoun after other prepositions

Restrictive: *Esta es la orden **por la cual (por la que)** lucharemos.*
Nonrestrictive: *Esta orden, **por la cual (por la que)** lucharemos, es estricta.*
This is the ordinance for which we are going to fight.

Restrictive: *Este es el candidato **por quien (por el cual, por el que)** votaremos.*
Nonrestrictive: *El candidato, **por quien (por el cual, por el que)** votaremos, ganará.*
This is the candidate for whom we are going to vote.

F. Relative pronouns and adjectives: *cuyo/a, cuyos/as*

Restrictive: *Los libros **cuyos** capítulos son largos costarán más.*
Nonrestrictive: *Los libros, **cuyos** capítulos son largos, costarán más.*
The books whose chapters are long will cost more.

Interrogative Pronouns

The following basic pronouns are used to formulate questions: *qué, cuál, quién, de quién(es)* (which now replaces the obsolete pronoun *cuyo*), and *cuánto*, with their variations of gender and number. If followed by a noun, these interrogative words function as adjectives.

Singular	Plural
qué	(invariable)
cuál	*cuáles*
quién	*quiénes*
cuyo, cuya	*cuyos, cuyas*
cuánto, cuánta	*cuántos, cuántas*

Uses of Interrogative Pronouns

The Interrogative Pronoun *qué*

A. *Qué* used to ask for a definition

When used to ask for a definition, *qué* is the subject of the verb *ser*, and is not interchangeable with *cuál*:

¿Qué es un mendigo?	What is a beggar?
¿Qué son las flores secas?	What are dried flowers?
¿Qué es esto?	What is this?

B. *Qué* used to secure information about an object or situation

Qué may be the object of any verb. In this case, it is not interchangeable with *cuál*:

¿Qué pasa aquí?	What is going on here?
¿Qué traes en la bolsa?	What are you carrying in your bag?
¿Qué piensan tus padres?	What do your parents think?

C. *Qué* used in place of *cuál* or *cuáles*

Qué can be used in place of *cuál* or *cuáles* to ask for clarification regarding the noun, or if the question involves a selection:

¿Qué te gusta más, el papel blanco o el azul?	Which do you like better, the white paper or the blue one?
¿Cuál te gusta más, el papel blanco?	Which one do you like better, the white paper?

D. *Qué* functioning as an adjective

Qué functions as an adjective when it precedes a noun. When asking for specific information it is better to use *qué* than *cuál*, even when the questions may involve a selection:

¿Qué barco se usa para pescar trucha?	What boat is used for trout fishing?
¿Qué libro recomienda?	What book do you recommend?
¿Qué música te gusta?	What music do you like?

NOTE:

If the noun is left out, *cuál* is used whenever the idea is understood in context. It functions as a pronoun:

¿Cuál se usa para pescar trucha?	Which one is used for trout fishing?
¿Cuál recomienda?	Which one do you recommend?
¿Cuál te gusta?	Which one do you like?

E. Prepositions before *qué*

The identification implied in the question may require the use of a preposition before the interrogative pronoun.

1. Not involving a selection; merely asking for information:

¿De qué está hecha la mesa?	What material is the table made of?
¿Con qué vas a escribir?	What are you going to write with?
¿Contra qué estaba recostado el policía?	What was the policeman leaning against?
¿A qué le recuerda esta música?	What does this music remind you of?
¿Para qué sirve esto?*	What is this good for?
¿Por qué usas eso?*	Why do you use that?

2. If the question involves a selection, *cuál* is used after the preposition:

*¿De **cuál** (de esas maderas) estaba hecha la mesa?*	Which one (of all those types of wood) was the table made of?
*¿Con **cuál** (de estos lápices) vas a escribir?*	Which one (of these pencils) are you going to write with?
*¿Contra **cuál** (de esas paredes) estaba recostado el policía?*	Which one (of those walls) was the policeman leaning against?

F. *Que* after verbs of perception

Que, with an accent mark (*qué*), functions as an interrogative after verbs of perception such as ***comprender***, ***decir***, ***entender***, ***imaginarse***, ***pensar***, ***preguntar***, ***saber***, ***tener idea de***, ***ver***, and others:

No sé qué problemas tiene con la compañía.	I don't know what problems he has with the company.

---

* While ***para qué*** means *for what purpose*, ***por qué*** asks *for what reason*. *¿Para qué vamos allá?* (For what purpose [why] are we going there?); *Vamos para comprar unos sobres.* (To buy some envelopes.); *¿Por qué vamos allá?* (For what reason are we going there?); *Porque Irma no está bien.* (Because Irma is not doing well.)

The Interrogative Pronoun *cuál, cuáles*

Cuál has a plural form, *cuáles*, and both words can refer to either one of the genders. They are used to inquire about something that involves a selection among two or more options.

A. *Cuál* as object of a verb

Cuál may be the object of any verb. The preposition *de* plus an article or demonstrative may be added to emphasize the selection:

¿***Cuál*** *fue la primera de la independencia?* (batalla)	Which one was the first one of Independence? (battle)
¿***Cuál*** *es tu preferido?* (corredor)	Which one is your favorite one? (driver)
¿***Cuál*** *(de ellos) se necesita para mañana?* (informes)	Which one (of them) is needed for tomorrow? (reports)
¿***Cuáles*** *(de éstos) son los más caros?* (autos)	Which ones (of these) are the most expensive? (cars)
¿***Cuáles*** *(de éstos) te gustan más?* (guantes)	Which ones (of these) do you like better? (gloves)

B. *Cuál* as a subject of *ser*

Cuál is not interchangeable with *qué* when the question involves a selection, even when English may use *what*:

¿***Cuál*** *(de éstas) es la última canción de ese grupo?*	What is the last song of that group?
¿***Cuáles*** *fueron las opciones que pudo considerar Emilia?*	What were the options that Emilia could have considered?
¿***Cuáles*** *son los temas que encuentras interesantes?*	What are the subjects that you find interesting?

Notice that in some fixed expressions, *cuál* is used as the subject of *ser*, regardless of what English uses:

¿***Cuál*** *es su dirección?*	What is your address?
¿***Cuál*** *es su número de teléfono?*	What is your phone number?
¿***Cuál*** *es la fecha de hoy?*	What is today's date?
¿***Cuál*** *es tu color preferido?*	What is your favorite color?

C. *Cuál(es)* replaced by *quién(es)*

When the selection refers to human beings, *quién(es)* may be used instead of *cuál(es):*

*¿**Quién** es el mejor alumno?*	Who is the best student?
*¿**Quiénes** son los mejores?*	Which ones are the best?

D. Prepositions before *cuál(es)*

The selection implied in the question may require the use of a preposition before the interrogative pronoun, when referring to either human beings or inanimate objects. *Who* or *which* may be used in English. See earlier section E. 2. under The Interrogative Pronoun *qué:*

*¿Con **cuál** te quedas? Me quedo con el perro negro.*	Which one of these are you going to keep? I'll keep the black dog.
*¿Para **cuáles** es la carta? Es para los que trabajan de noche.*	For whom is the letter? It's for the night shift workers.
*¿A **cuáles** les darán el premio?*	To whom will they give the prize?
*¿Para **cuál** sirve esto?*	Which one is this good for?
*¿En **cuál** estás pensando?*	Who are you thinking about?

E. *Cuál(es)* after verbs of perception

Cuál and *cuáles,* with an accent mark, function as an interrogative after verbs of perception such as *comprender, decir, entender, imaginarse, pensar, preguntar, saber, tener idea de, ver,* and others:

No se imagina cuál es la causa de esa demora.	She cannot imagine what the cause for that delay might be.

The Interrogative Pronoun *quién, quiénes*

A. *Quién(es)* used for human beings

When the identification refers to human beings, *quién* and *quiénes* are used. Spanish gives information on number (singular or plural) and gender (masculine or feminine) with the use of specific forms that are invariable in English:

*¿**Quién** vino ayer?*	Who came yesterday?
*¿**Quiénes** vinieron hoy?* (pl.)	Who came today?

¿Quién es ese? (m.s.)	Who is that?
¿Quiénes son aquéllas? (f.pl.)	Who are they?

The forms *cuál* and *cuáles* may also be used, especially when the question involves a selection:

¿Cuáles están en huelga, los obreros del vidrio o los metalúrgicos?	Which ones are on strike, the glass craftsmen or the metalworkers?
¿Cuál es tu hermano, el que tiene barba?	Which one is your brother, the one with a beard?

B. *Quién(es)* with prepositions

Prepositions may precede *quién* and *quiénes*. This may not necessarily be the case in English:

¿En quién confías?	Whom do you trust?
¿Hacia quiénes corrieron?	Towards whom did they run?
¿Con quién saldrás hoy?	With whom will you go out today?

C. *Quién(es)* after verbs of perception

Quién and *quiénes*, with an accent mark, function as an interrogative after verbs of perception such as *comprender*, *decir*, *entender*, *imaginarse*, *pensar*, *preguntar*, *saber*, *tener idea de*, *ver*, and others:

Carlos me dijo quién había llegado con la noticia.	Carlos told me who had arrived with the news.

Cuyo, cuya, cuyos, cuyas replaced by *de quién, de quiénes*

Cuyo (and its derivatives) is no longer used as a pronoun. It has been replaced by *de quién* and *de quiénes*, which translates in English as *whose*. (As a relative adjective, *cuyo* precedes the noun and agrees with it in gender and number, as in *cuya casa*):

¿De quién es este marco?	Whose is this frame?
¿De quiénes son estos sobres?	Whose are these envelopes?
¿De quién es esta carta?	Whose is this letter?
¿De quién son estas hojas?	Whose are these sheets?

It is possible to use *qué*, preceded or not by a preposition, to imply possession in cases when English uses *whose*:

*¿**Qué** marco es éste? ¿Es el de Pedro?*	Whose frame is this? Pedro's?
*¿Con **qué** auto fueron? ¿Con el tuyo?*	Whose car did you take? Yours? (What car did you take? Yours?)

> **NOTE:**
>
> In these Spanish sentences, there is more emphasis on the item in question (*marco*, *auto*) than on the owner of the object. To emphasize the owner, *de quién*(*es*) should be used:
>
> | | |
> |---|---|
> | *¿**De quién** es este marco?* | Whose frame is this? |
> | *¿**De quién** era el auto?* | Whose car was it? |

The Interrogative Pronoun *cuánto, cuánta, cuántos, cuántas*

This pronoun changes gender and number according to the noun that it replaces in the question:

*¿**Cuánto** (café) necesitas?*	How much (coffee) do you need?
*¿**Cuánta** (nieve) cayó?*	How much (snow) came down?
*¿**Cuántos** (chicos) se quedaron?*	How many (children) stayed?
*¿**Cuántas** (hijas) tienen?*	How many (daughters) do they have?

A. *Cuánto* and its variants with prepositions

Prepositions may precede *cuánto* and its derivatives:

*¿A **cuánto** lo dejamos?*	At how much will you let me have it? (talking about a price)
*¿Con **cuántas** (naranjas) se puede hacer la mermelada?*	With how many (oranges) can we make the marmalade?

B. *Cuánto* and its variants after verbs of perception

Any of the forms of *cuánto*, with an accent mark, function as an interrogative after verbs of perception such as *comprender*, *decir*, *entender*, *imaginarse*, *pensar*, *preguntar*, *saber*, *tener idea de*, and *ver*. These forms may also be preceded by a preposition:

*No sabemos **cuántos** hay.*	We don't know how many there are.
*No me imagino a **cuántas** les dijo lo mismo Don Juan. (mujeres)*	I can't imagine to how many of them Don Juan said the same thing. (women)

Exclamation Words

Many of the interrogative words can be used as exclamative forms.

Qué as an Exclamation

A. *Qué* as an exclamation may be followed by a noun, a modifier or an adverb.

Notice the use of the indefinite article in the English version:

*¡**Qué** problema!*	What a problem!
*¡**Qué** linda casa!*	What a nice house!
*¡**Qué** lejos queda!*	How far it is!

> **NOTE:**
>
> In order to give emphasis, observe the following uses in which the English version is not affected.
>
> **(1)** The adjective may be placed before the noun:
>
> | | |
> |---|---|
> | *¡**Qué** buen programa!* | What a good program! |
>
> **(2)** *Más* (*more*) or *tan* (*so*) may precede the adjective, but only when the adjective follows the noun:
>
> | | |
> |---|---|
> | *¡**Qué** casa **más** linda!* | What a nice house! |
> | *¡**Qué** casa **tan** linda!* | What a nice house! |

B. *Qué* as an exclamation may be preceded by a preposition:

*¡En **qué** situación estaba! No me quiero ni acordar.*	What a situation he was in! I don't even want to remember.
*¡Con **qué** amigos se fue! Ninguno es bueno.*	What friends he left with! None of them is (any) good.
*¡A **qué** abogado fue a consultar!*	What a lawyer he consulted!

C. *Qué* as an exclamation may be followed by the preposition *de* to mean *how many*:

¡Qué de gente había ayer en el concierto!	How many people there were in the concert yesterday!
¡Qué de tragedias sufrió en su vida!	How many tragedies he suffered in his life!

NOTE:

If adjectives are added, they must be placed after the noun:

¡Qué de gente joven había en la fiesta!	How many young people there were at the party!

D. *Qué* as an exclamation may be replaced by *cuán* in literary pieces, with the meaning of *how*:

¡Cuán bellas están las olas!	How beautiful the waves are!

Quién as an Exclamation

This word is used mainly to convey hopes or wishes, and wonder.

A. *Quién* to convey *hope* or *wish*:

¡Quién fuera suertudo!	I wish I were lucky!
¡Quién pudiera ir!	I wish I could go!

B. *Quién* to convey wonder:

¡Quién diría!	Can you imagine?
¡Quién iba a pensar!	Can you imagine? / Who would have thought it?

Indefinite Pronouns

These pronouns replace persons, nonhuman beings, and things, in a general or imprecise manner. In Spanish they are called *indefinidos* or *indeterminados*. They can be categorized as follows.

A. Invariable indefinite pronouns

1. Used only in the singular form:

algo	*Compró algo.*	She bought something.
alguien	*Alguien viene.*	Someone comes.
cada cual	*Cada cual lo hace.*	Each one does it.
cada uno	*Cada uno está en su lugar.*	Each one is in its place.
nada	*No tiene nada.*	He has nothing.
nadie	*Nadie está aquí.*	No one is here.
otro tanto	*Yo hago otro tanto.*	I do likewise.

2. Used also with variations, indicated by the article:

más (lo más, los más)	*more, the most, the majority*
*Quiero **más**.*	I want more.
***Más** vienen los sábados.*	More come on Saturdays.
*Dijeron **lo más** que pueden.*	They said the most they can.
***Los más** están de acuerdo.*	Most of them agree.
*Quiere algunos **más**.*	He wants some more.

menos (lo menos, los menos)	*less (fewer), the least*
*Quiero **menos**.*	I want less.
***Menos** vienen los sábados.*	Fewer come on Saturdays.
*Dijeron **lo menos** que pueden.*	They said the least they can.
***Los menos** están de acuerdo.*	Few of them agree.
*Quiere algunos **menos**.*	He wants a few less.

demás (lo demás, los demás)	*other things, the rest, the others*
*Tiene libros y **demás**.*	She has books and other things.
***Lo demás** es fácil.*	The rest is easy.
*Llegaron **los demás**.*	The others arrived.
<u>Also</u>: *Llegaron los otros.*	The others arrived.

B. Variable indefinite pronouns

1. With variations in number:

bastante(s)	*enough*
Tiene bastante / bastantes.	She has enough.

cual(es)	some, someone
Cual quiere café, cual quiere té.	Someone wants coffee, the other one (wants) tea.
Cuales quieren café, cuales quieren té.	Some want coffee, some tea.

cualquiera / cualesquiera	anybody, whoever
Quiero que venga cualquiera.	I want anybody to come.
Cualquiera que sea.	Whoever it is.
Cualesquiera que sean.	Whoever they are.

quien(es)	some, someone
Quien más, quien menos, todos quieren ir.	Some more, some less, everybody wants to go.
Quienes más, quienes menos, todos quieren salir.	Some more, some less, everybody wants to go out.

quien(es)quiera	whomever
Vendrá con quienquiera.	She will come with whomever she wants (one person).
Vendrá con quienesquiera.	She will come with whomever she wants (more than one person).

suficiente(s)	enough
Tienen lo suficiente.	They have enough.
Gracias. Tengo lo suficiente.	Thank you. I have enough.
No hay suficientes. (platos)	There are not enough. (plates)

tal(es)	someone, some
Tal habrá que no querrá quedarse.	There will be someone who will not want to stay.
Tales habrá que no podrán venir.	There will be some who will not be able to come.

2. Used only in the singular, in both genders:

cada uno/cada una	each one
Cada uno/a lo traerá.	Each one will bring it.

C. Indefinite pronouns used only in the plural, in both genders:

ambos/as	both
Los vi a ambos.	I saw both of them.

Hablaré con ambas.	I will speak to both of them.
<u>or:</u> *Los vi a los dos.*	
Hablaré con las dos.	

otros tantos/otras tantas	*other ones*
Otros/as tantos/as llegarán	Other ones will arrive in the
por la mañana.	morning.
(as many as before)	

unos/unas	*some*
Unos/as vieron la película.	Some saw the movie.

unos cuantos/unas cuantas	*a good number*
Unos/as cuantos/as vieron	A good number (of them) saw
la película.	the movie.

unos pocos/unas pocas	*a few*
Unos/as pocos/as lo saben.	A few know it.

varios/varias	*several, different*
Varios/as cantan bien.	Several sing well.
En cuanto a modelos, hay varios.	As for models, there are different ones.

D. Indefinite pronouns with all the variations of gender and number:

alguno	*some, someone*
Algunos lo pidieron.	Some asked for it.

alguno que otro	*a few, some*
Alguna que otra tendrá la nota.	A few will have the note.

cuanto	*as much, as many*
Recibió cuanta quiso.	He received as much as he wanted.

demasiado	*too much, too many*
Tenía demasiado.	He had too much.
Demasiadas (chicas) tenían esperanzas de conseguir el trabajo.	Too many (girls) hoped to get the job.

mismo (with an article)	*same*
No son las mismas.	They are not the same.

mucho	*much, many*
Mucha (manteca) no es aconsejable.	Much (butter) is not advisable.
Lo oyeron de muchos.	They heard it from many (people).
ninguno*	*no one, none, not . . . any*
No vino ninguno.	No one came.
No compró ninguna.	He didn't buy any.
otro (with or without an article)	*another one, the others, the other one(s)*
(El) Otro lo pintó.	Another one painted it.
Las otras no quisieron escucharlo.	The others did not want to hear it.
poco	*a little, a few*
Me dejó con poca (mostaza).	She left me a little (mustard).
Compró pocas.	He bought a few.
todo	*everything, all*
Todo está bien.	Everything is fine.
Se vino con todo (su poder).	He came with all of it (his power).
uno	*one*
Siempre le dice la verdad a uno.	He always tells one (you) the truth.

Reflexive Pronouns

Reflexive pronouns are used when the direct or indirect object is the same as the subject of the sentence. Reflexive pronouns have the same forms as indirect object pronouns with the exception that *se* is used instead of *le* or *les* in the third persons singular and plural (*él, ella, Ud., ellos, ellas, Uds.*).

The infinitive form of reflexive verbs always ends in *se*, as in the verbs *alegrarse, to be glad; **ponerse**, to put on; **reírse**, to laugh.* When the verb is conjugated, this pronoun changes according to the subject.

---

* The plural, ***ningunos/as***, is rarely seen. It may be used to replace nouns that indicate a plural word, such as ***tenazas*** (*pliers*), ***exequias*** (*funeral rites*), or ***pantalones*** (*pants*).

Forms of the Reflexive Pronouns

The personal pronouns appear in parentheses, for clarification only:

(yo)	**me**	myself	to, for, from, or off myself
(tú)	**te**	yourself	to, for, from, or off yourself
(él)	**se**	himself	to, for, from, or off himself
(ella)	**se**	herself	to, for, from, or off herself
(el / ella)	**se**	itself	to, for, from, or off itself
(Ud.)	**se**	yourself	to, for, from, or off yourself
(nosotros/as)	**nos**	ourselves	to, for, from, or off ourselves
(vosotros/as)	**os**	yourselves	to, for, from, or off yourselves
(ellos /as)	**se**	themselves	to, for, from, or off themselves
(Uds.)	**se**	yourselves	to, for, from, or off yourselves

escribirse	*Yo me escribo notitas.*	I write little notes to myself.
hacerse	*Tú te hiciste un vestido.*	You made a dress for yourself.

Position of Reflexive Pronouns

A. Reflexive pronouns can be placed before a conjugated verb:

*Yo **me** <u>saco</u> el sombrero. (sacarse)*   I take off my hat.

> **NOTE:**
> To make the sentence negative, place *no* before the reflexive pronoun:
> *Yo <u>no</u> me saco el sombrero.*

B. Reflexive pronouns can be placed between the negative and the verb in a negative command:

*No **te** <u>saques</u> el sombrero. (sacarse)*   Do not take off your hat.

C. Reflexive pronouns can be attached to an affirmative command:

<u>Acuésta</u>**te** *temprano. (acostarse)*   Go to bed early.

D. **In the case of two verbs, when there is either an infinitive or a present participle, reflexive pronouns may be:**

1. Placed before the conjugated verb:

Yo **me** <u>quiero</u> sacar el sombrero.   I want to take off my hat.

El **se** <u>está</u> cambiando la ropa.   He is changing his clothes.

2. Attached to the infinitive or to the present participle:

Yo quiero <u>sacar**me**</u> el sombrero.   I want to take off my hat.

El está <u>cambiándo**se**</u> la ropa.   He is changing his clothes.

E. **If there is a direct object pronoun, there are three possible scenarios.**

1. The reflexive pronoun precedes the direct object pronoun when there is only one verb:

Ella **se** <u>lo</u> pone.   She puts it on.

2. If there is a conjugated verb and an infinitive, the reflexive pronoun and the direct object pronoun precede either the conjugated verb or are attached to the infinitive. Observe the use of the pronouns in the second and third examples that follow:

Ella **se** quiere comprar <u>un vestido</u>.   She wants to buy <u>a dress</u> for herself.

Ella **se** <u>lo</u> quiere comprar.   She wants to buy <u>it</u> for herself.

Ella quiere comprár**se**<u>lo</u>.

If the verb is in the progressive tense (endings -*ando* and -*iendo* in Spanish; -*ing* in English), both the reflexive pronoun and the direct object pronoun either precede the verb *estar* or are attached to the present participle:

Yo **me** estoy arreglando <u>la casa</u>.   I am fixing <u>the house</u> for myself.

Yo **me** <u>la</u> estoy arreglando.   I am fixing <u>it</u> for myself.

Yo estoy arreglándo**me**<u>la</u>.

3. If the verb is in one of the perfect tenses, the reflexive pronoun and the direct object pronoun always precede the auxiliary *haber*. They cannot be placed between the auxiliary and the main verb nor be attached to the past participle:

Yo *me* he arreglado <u>la casa</u>.	I have fixed <u>the house</u> for myself.
Yo *me* <u>la</u> he arreglado.	I have fixed <u>it</u> for myself.

F. *Se* and the indirect object pronoun with passive reflexive verbs

When the verb is a passive reflexive (see the section The Passive *se*, under Constructions with *se* at the end of this chapter), the indirect object pronoun follows the pronoun *se*. This form is used to indicate unplanned occurrences. The verb agrees with the direct object in number. In this type of sentence the direct object (*fruta*, *suerte* in the following examples) cannot be replaced by a direct object pronoun:

acabarse:	Se acabó la fruta.	There's no more fruit.
	Se me acabó la fruta.	I ran out of fruit.
terminarse:	Se terminó la suerte.	There's no more luck.
	Se les terminó la suerte.	They ran out of luck.
ponerse:	*Se nos* pusieron los pelos de punta.	Our hair stood on end.

G. In the case of impersonal sentences, the indirect object pronoun follows the pronoun *se*:

Se le dieron todas las oportunidades.	They gave him/her/you (singular/plural)/them all the opportunities.
Se nos entregó el contrato.	They gave us the contract.

Functions of Reflexive Pronouns

Reflexive pronouns may function as either direct or indirect objects.

A. Reflexive pronouns as direct objects

When the action of the verb goes back to the subject of the sentence, a reflexive pronoun is always used in Spanish (in English, expressions such as *myself*, *herself*, etc. may be omitted if the identity of the subject is obvious):

Yo me peiné.	I combed my hair.
José se afeita de mañana.	José shaves in the morning.

Some verbs, such as the following, are reflexive in Spanish but not in English:

reírse	*Yo me reí.*	I laughed.
irse	*Ella se fue.*	She left.
quedarse	*Él se quedó.*	He stayed.
equivocarse	*Nos equivocamos.*	We made a mistake.
sentarse	*Me sentaré aquí.*	I will sit here.
darse	*Se dio cuenta.*	He realized.

B. Reflexive pronouns as indirect objects

When there is a direct object (or a direct object pronoun) in the sentence, the reflexive pronoun functions as the indirect object. In English, this is indicated by expressions such as *to (for, from, off) himself, herself*, etc:

*Ella **se** lo hizo (a ella misma).*	She did it to herself.
*Él **se** buscó una secretaria (para él).*	He looked for a secretary for himself.
*Nosotros **nos** la compramos.*	We bought it for ourselves.
Julia se quitó ese peso de encima.	Julia took that load off her mind.
*Ellos **se** sacan los zapatos.*	They take off their shoes (off themselves).

NOTE:

With parts of the body or personal possessions such as clothing, Spanish does not use possessive adjectives; therefore, the reflexive pronoun functions as an indirect object:

cortarse:	***Me** corté un dedo.*	I cut my finger.
romperse:	*Raúl **se** rompió un brazo.*	Raúl broke his arm.
ponerse:	***Se** puso el sombrero.*	He put on his hat.

Reflexive and Reciprocal Pronouns

The pronouns that precede the first, second, and third persons plural (*nosotros/as, vosotros/as, ellos/as, ustedes*) can function as either reflexive or reciprocal pronouns. This ambiguity does not present itself in English since there are specific words used in each instance. The sentence *Ana y Luisa se ayudan cuando tienen problemas* may mean either:

Ana and Luisa help themselves when they have problems.

(Ana helps herself and Luisa helps herself.)

(or) Ana and Luisa help each other when they have problems.

If it is necessary to clarify the meaning of the sentence in Spanish, the following expressions may be used:

Reflexive:

Ellas se ayudan a sí mismas.   They help themselves. (Each one helps herself.)

Reciprocal:

Ellas se ayudan entre sí.   They help each other.

(also, *mutuamente, recíprocamente, la una a la otra,* or *unas a otras*)

NOTE:

If the verb indicates reciprocity but is not a reflexive verb, the words *uno/a* and *otro/a* are used with prepositions such as the following:

Viven el uno <u>para</u> el otro.	They live for each other.
No salen el uno <u>sin</u> el otro.	They don't go out without each other.
Trabajarán la una <u>por</u> la otra.	They will work for each other.
No pueden trabajar la una <u>sin</u> la otra.	They cannot work without each other.
Siempre están uno <u>con</u> el otro.	They are always with each other.
Cocinan una <u>para</u> la otra.	They cook for each other.

The masculine form *uno para (por, sin,* etc.*) el otro* is used for males only or for mixed-gender pairs or groups. The feminine form *una para (por, sin,* etc.*) la otra* is used for females only.

The Intransitive Character of Spanish Reflexive Verbs

Several verbs in Spanish take on an intransitive meaning when the action stays with the subject; that is, they adopt the reflexive form whenever the subject is also the recipient of the action.

	Transitive	Intransitive Meaning (reflexive form)	
bañar	*Bañé al niño.*	*bañarse*	*Me bañé.*
to bathe	I bathed the child.	to bathe	I bathed (myself).

mirar	*El mira la calle.*	*mirarse*	*El se mira en el espejo.*
to look	He looks at the street.	to look	He looks at himself in the mirror.

Spanish Reflexive Verbs Versus Equivalent Nonreflexive Forms in English

Several verbs that are reflexive in Spanish and are conjugated with reflexive pronouns do not necessarily use expressions like *myself, oneself, themselves,* etc. in English. The English verbs may be one-word verbs, or else an auxiliary verb such as *to get, to be, to feel,* or *to become* combined with a past participle. Some examples follow:

aburrirse	to get bored
divertirse	to have fun
enojarse	to get mad
entristecerse	to get sad
hacerse	to become
morirse	to die
ofenderse	to feel offended
olvidarse	to forget
portarse	to behave
preocuparse	to be worried
sentarse	to sit down

Semantic Changes in Reflexive Verbs

Several Spanish verbs change their meaning in the reflexive form:

ir	*Voy a la escuela.*	***irse***	*Me voy mañana.*
to go, to go out	I go to school.	to leave	I leave tomorrow.
volver	*Volvió temprano.*	***volverse***	*Se volvió loco.*
to return	He returned early.	to become, go	He went crazy.
probar	*Probaron el jugo.*	***probarse***	*Se probaron la gorra.*
to taste	They tasted the juice.	to try on	They tried on the cap.

Ir and other verbs may also be used in their nonreflexive or reflexive forms without altering significantly their basic meaning. In that case, the reflexive form only emphasizes the participation of the subject in the action indicated by the verb, with a slight indication of involvement or enjoyment:

ir	*Ayer fui al cine.*
irse	*Ayer me fui al cine.*
I went to the movies yesterday.	
comer	*Comí un sandwich delicioso.*
comerse	*Me comí un sandwich delicioso.*
I ate a delicious sandwich.	
dormir	*Dormimos una siesta de dos horas.*
dormirse*	*Nos dormimos una siesta de dos horas.*
We took a two-hour nap.	
ver	*Juan vio un partido de fútbol el domingo.*
verse	*Juan se vio un partido de fútbol el domingo.*
Juan watched a football game on Sunday.	

Constructions with *se*

The Passive *se*

Se is used in Spanish in a construction known as the passive reflexive (*voz pasiva refleja*) when the subject is inanimate and there is no specified agent of the action. The verb appears in the third person, singular or plural, according to the subject. Although the pronoun *se* makes the verb appear to be a reflexive verb, it only indicates a passive construction and it does not function as a reflexive pronoun. This construction does not carry a direct object but a passive subject.

Different verb tenses have been selected for the following examples where the passive subject precedes the verb.

Present

passive voice:	*La basura es tirada en el cesto.*
passive *se*:	*La basura se tira en el cesto.*
The trash is thrown into the basket.	

Preterit

passive voice:	*El francés fue usado como idioma diplomático.*
passive *se*:	*El francés se usó como idioma diplomático.*
French was used as a language of diplomacy.	

---

* An additional meaning for ***dormirse*** is *to fall asleep.*

Future

passive voice:	*El almuerzo será servido en el jardín.*
passive *se*:	*Se servirá el almuerzo en el jardín.*
Lunch will be served in the garden.	

Present perfect

passive voice:	*Muchas solicitudes han sido aceptadas.*
passive *se*:	*Se han aceptado muchas solicitudes.*
Many applications have been accepted.	

Present progressive

passive voice:	*Los pedidos están siendo considerados.*
passive *se*:	*Los pedidos se están considerando.*
Requests are being considered.	

> **NOTE:**
>
> The verb(s) may also precede the passive subject:
>
> *Se están considerando los pedidos.*   Requests are being considered.

The Use of *se* in Unexpected Actions

The pronoun *se* precedes the indirect object (*me, te, le, nos, os, les*) in a construction used to emphasize an event as being unexpected, sudden, or just the fact that it happened to us, to him, and so on. The verb appears in the third person, singular or plural, according to the subject:

Se me perdieron los documentos.	I lost the documents.
Se te olvidó el número.	You forgot the number.
Se le quebraron las botellas.	He cracked the bottles.
Se nos cayó el paquete.	We dropped the package.
Se os rompieron los platos.	You broke the plates.
Se les terminó el pan.	They ran out of bread.

The active voice is used when the action is viewed as merely an occurrence. There is almost no change in the English translation:

Perdí los documentos.	I lost the documents.
Te olvidaste el número.	You forgot the number.
Quebró las botellas.	He cracked the bottles.

Dejamos* caer el paquete.	We dropped the package.
Rompisteis los platos.	You broke the plates.
Terminaron el pan.	They finished the bread.

NOTES:

(1) The preposition *a* + a noun or pronoun is usually added for clarification or emphasis:

A mí se me perdieron los documentos.
A Juan se le quebraron las botellas.
A mis padres se les terminó el pan.

(2) This form is also used in cases of possession, particularly with parts of the body, or to indicate personal or emotional attachment:

Se nos ensuciaron los pies.	Our feet got dirty.
Se me arruinó la garganta.	My throat got ruined.
Se te secó la piel.	Your skin dried up.
Se les murió el perro.	Their dog died.
Se le quemó la casa.	Her house burned.
Se me fueron los hijos.	My children moved out.

(3) Reflexive verbs may be used in the command form to express personal or emotional attachment. Some forms are only correct in the negative:

¡No se nos escapen!	Do not flee from us!
¡No se me ponga triste!	Do not get sad!
¡No se nos desaliente!	Do not get discouraged!
Aparézcansele temprano.	Show up early (in his house).

   If the command is informal and singular, the same construction may be used, but se must be changed to *te*:

¡No te me desalientes!	Do not get discouraged!
¡No te nos vayas!	Do not leave us!

(4) If the verb is not in the preterit, there is no indication of an unexpected occurrence:

Se me pierden los papeles	I lose my papers because I do not
porque no los pongo en su lugar.	put them where they belong.
Se les morirá el perro si no	Their dog will die if they do not
lo llevan al veterinario.	take it to the vet.

---

* Notice the use of the verb *dejar* in this sentence, which may be translated into English as *We let the package fall.*

Impersonal Expressions with *se*

Impersonal expressions are formed with the pronoun *se* when the subject is human, but unspecified. Verbs are always in the singular, and are frequently followed by a direct object:

Se espera lluvia.	Rain is expected.
Aquí se habla italiano.	Italian is spoken here.
Se escucha mal por este teléfono.	It is not possible to hear well on this phone.

Uses of *se* in Impersonal Expressions

There are several ways in which *se* is used.

A. *Se* **is used to replace the impersonal** *uno/una* **(one) when this is the subject of the verb.**

All impersonal verbs appear in the third person singular in this case:

Uno nunca sabe lo que está pasando.	
Nunca se sabe lo que está pasando.	One never knows what is going on.
¿Cuándo puede uno venir a la fiesta?	
¿Cuándo se puede venir a la fiesta?	When may one come to the party?
Una es trabajadora aunque no quiera.	
Se es trabajadora aunque no se quiera.	One is a hard worker even when one does not want to be.

> **NOTES:**
>
> (1) The use of *uno* or *una* depends on whether the speaker is male or female.
>
> (2) If the verb is inherently reflexive, such as *sentarse* (*to sit down*), *uno/una* must be used to avoid the repetition of *se*:
>
> | | |
> |---|---|
> | *Uno puede sentarse en el piso.* | |
> | *Uno se puede sentar en el piso.* | One can sit down on the floor. |
> | (Incorrect: *Se puede sentarse en el piso.*) | |
>
> | | |
> |---|---|
> | *Una puede probarse la ropa aquí.* | |
> | *Una se puede probar la ropa aquí.* | One can try on clothes here. |
> | (Incorrect: *Se puede probarse la ropa aquí.*) | |

B. *Se* is used to indicate an undefined subject.

The third person plural that is used in English to indicate an undefined subject, e.g. *They (People) say that it will rain tonight*, is rendered in Spanish in two different ways.

1. *Se* and the singular form of the verb:

   Se dice que va a llover esta noche.

2. The plural form of the verb, without *se*:

   Dicen que va a llover esta noche.

C. *Se* and the personal *a*

When the recipient of the action is animate, including *alguien* and *nadie*, the object is preceded by the preposition *a* and the verb appears in the singular:

Se recibe a todos.	Everybody is welcome.
Se respeta a los ancianos.	Seniors are respected.
Se respeta a la abuela.	The grandmother is respected.
Se cuida a los animales.	The animals are taken care of.
No se respeta a nadie.	No one is respected.

NOTES:

(1) In informal speech, and when the object is human, it is more common to use the verb in the plural (without *se*) with an unspecified subject:

Reciben a todos.	Everybody is welcome.
Respetan a los ancianos.	Seniors are respected.
Respetan a la abuela.	The grandmother is respected.

(2) It is wrong to use the verb in the plural with *se*, since that has no meaning in Spanish:

(Incorrect: *Se reciben a todos.*)
(Incorrect: *Se respetan a los ancianos.*)

(3) If *a* is not used and the verb agrees with the noun, the verb becomes reflexive or reciprocal:

Se respeta a la abuela. (impersonal **se**)	The grandmother is respected.
Se respeta la abuela. (reflexive)	The grandmother respects herself.
Se respeta a los ancianos. (impersonal **se**)	Seniors are respected.

Se respetan los ancianos. (reciprocal)	Seniors respect each other.
Se respetan los ancianos. (reflexive)	Seniors respect themselves.

(4) If the animate object refers to people as categories, rather than to a specific person, the verb is plural and is not preceded by *a*:

*Se nombró **al** secretario.*	The secretary was designated.
Se nombraron secretarios.	Secretaries were designated.

(5) It is possible to replace the direct object with a pronoun:

Se vistió <u>al rey</u> con elegancia.	
Se <u>lo</u> vistió con elegancia.	They dressed up the king with elegance.

Se amó <u>a los enemigos</u> en ese mundo ideal.	
Se <u>los</u> amó.	Enemies were loved in that ideal world.

(6) It is correct to replace the indirect object with a pronoun when the indirect object is preceded by the preposition *para*. Both sentences are correct:

Se abrió una excepción <u>para Pablo</u>.	
Se <u>le</u> abrió una excepción.	They made an exception for Pablo.

However, when the indirect object is preceded by the preposition *a*, it is better to use the form with the pronoun:

(Se dio un premio <u>a Pablo</u>.)	
Se <u>le</u> dio un premio.	Pablo was given an award.

(7) It is not possible to replace both the direct object and the indirect object in the third person, singular or plural. The repetition of *se* must be avoided:

<u>Correct</u>: *Se <u>le(s)</u> perdonó <u>el error</u>.*	They forgave his/their mistake.
(<u>Incorrect</u>: *Se <u>se</u>* <u>lo</u> perdonó.*)	

D. *Se* **is used to express orders, rules, or simply to post a notice:**

Se prohibe escupir en el suelo.	Spitting on the floor is forbidden.
Se paga en la caja.	Pay at the cashier's.
Se abre a las dos de la tarde.	We open at 2:00 P.M.

---

* The indirect object pronoun *le* has to be changed to *se* when it precedes a direct object pronoun that begins with the letter *l* (*lo, la, los, las*), and so this combination must be avoided because it involves the repetition of *se*. However, combinations of the other first or second person pronouns are correct: *Se me otorgó <u>un premio</u> con honores.* or *Se me <u>lo</u> otorgó con honores.* (They gave me an award with honors.); and *Se nos aplazó <u>la entrega</u> por dos meses.* or *Se nos <u>la</u> aplazó por dos meses.* (They delayed delivery to us for two months.)

Summary of the Different Types of *se*

The pronoun *se* may indicate that the construction is reflexive, reciprocal, impersonal, or passive:

Reflexive

El libro se cayó.	caerse
The book fell.	
La niña se sentó.	sentarse
The girl sat down.	
Los hombres se murieron.	morirse
The men died.	

Reciprocal

Las mujeres se pegaron.	pegarse
The women hit each other.	
Los chicos se escriben.	escribirse
The kids write to each other.	

Impersonal

Se visitó la escuela.	visitar
They visited the school.	
Se visitó a los profesores.	
They visited the professors.	
Se visitó a los estudiantes.	
They visited the students.	

Passive

Se visitó la escuela.	visitar
The school was visited.	
Se visitaron las escuelas.	
The schools were visited.	

NOTES:

When the inanimate noun is in the singular form, it is not possible to distinguish the impersonal construction from the passive form. The sentence *Se visitó la escuela* could be expressing the impersonal *se* or the passive voice.

If the inanimate noun is in the plural, the impersonal *se* cannot be used with it. A *se* in this context can only be the passive construction.

<u>Correct</u>: *Aquí se venden manzanas.* (passive)
    Apples for sale here.
(<u>Incorrect</u>: *Se vende manzanas.*) (impersonal)
    Apples for sale here.

If the subject of the verb is the impersonal ***uno/una***, the verb agrees with the subject in the singular:

Uno pide mariscos si no hay pescado.   One orders seafood if there is no fish.

However, if ***uno/una*** is replaced by *se*, the verb must be changed to the plural:

Se piden mariscos si no hay pescado.   People order seafood if there is no fish.

17

Prepositions

Prepositions are invariable words that establish a relationship between two words within a sentence:

almohada **de** plumas	feather pillow
bote **sin** remos	boat without oars
programas **para** los jóvenes	programs for young people

The word *preposition* signals the place of this word in the sentence. A *preposition* precedes the word or words that complement the main word or idea. In the phrase ***almohada de plumas***, the noun ***plumas*** complements the word ***almohada*** by pointing to specific characteristics of this particular pillow (it is *made of feathers*).

A preposition may be represented as a single word (called ***preposición simple***), as two or more words grouped together (***preposición compuesta***), or as part of a compound word.

Simple Prepositions

There are not many simple prepositions in Spanish, and each one has a basic meaning in English:

a	to, at	**desde**	from	**según**	according to
ante	before	**en**	in, on, at	**sin**	without
bajo	under	**entre**	between	**so**	under
cabe*	near	**hacia**	towards	**sobre**	about, on
con	with	**hasta**	until	**tras**	after
contra	against	**para**	for		
de	of, from	**por**	for		

---

* This preposition is obsolete, but is found in old documents and literary works.

Other Equivalent Uses in English

The following list contains the simple Spanish prepositions and their corresponding prepositions, prepositional phrases, or expressions used in English, as well as examples of their use. Please note that the Spanish prepositions are listed in alphabetical order. Their English equivalent prepositions also appear in alphabetical order and not according to the preponderance of their usage. Also note that, in cases where an equivalent preposition is not used in English, it is indicated as (*no preposition*):

Spanish	English	Uses	Examples
a	at	place; verbs of motion	*Llegué temprano al teatro.* I arrived early <u>at</u> the theater.
		place	*Se sentaron a la mesa para almorzar.* They sat <u>at</u> the table to have lunch.
		price/rate	*La harina está a un dólar la libra.* Flour is <u>at</u> one dollar the pound.
		measure	*Maneja a cien millas por hora.* She drives <u>at</u> a hundred miles per hour.
		direction	*El miró a los niños.* He looked <u>at</u> the children.
	by	manner	*Lo haremos poco a poco.* We'll do it little <u>by</u> little.
			Esta blusa está hecha a mano. This blouse was made <u>by</u> hand.
	for	indirect object	*Le compré un regalo a Juan.* I bought a gift <u>for</u> Juan.
	from		*Le compraré los boletos a Inés.* I'll buy the tickets <u>from</u> Inés.
			Le oí decir a Luisa que vendrá. I heard it <u>from</u> Luisa that she'll come.
			Le quitaron los chicos a la madre borracha. They took the children <u>from</u> the drunk mother.

Spanish	English	Uses	Examples
	in	place; verbs of motion	*Mañana llegará **a** Miami.* He'll arrive <u>in</u> Miami tomorrow.
	like		*Este pastel sabe **a** chocolate.* This pie tastes <u>like</u> chocolate.
	of		*Había olor **a** pino.* There was a smell <u>of</u> pine.
	on	location	*El baño está **a** la izquierda.* The bathroom is <u>on</u> the left.
		manner	*Iré **a** pie.* I'll go <u>on</u> foot.
		time	*Te espero **a** la salida.* I'll wait for you <u>on</u> the way out.
			***A**l llegar lo vi leyendo.* <u>On</u> arriving, I saw him reading.
	to	indirect object	*Le daré uno **a** mi jefe.* I will give one <u>to</u> my boss.
		direction	*Vamos **a** la clase.* We go <u>to</u> class.
			*Se fueron **a**l campo.* They went <u>to</u> the countryside.
		reason; purpose	*Se fueron **a** vivir al campo.* They went <u>to</u> live in the countryside.
			*Él vino **a** comprar uvas.* He came <u>to</u> buy grapes.
			*Iré **a** que me den el resultado.* I'll go <u>to</u> get the results.
	upon		***A**l entrar lo vi allí.* <u>Upon</u> entering, I saw him there.
	up to		*La maleza le llegaba **a** la cintura.* The underbrush reached <u>up to</u> his waist.

Spanish	English	Uses	Examples
ante	before		*Se presentará **ante** los testigos.* She will appear <u>before</u> the witnesses.
	confronted with		***Ante** el peligro no sabía qué hacer.* <u>Confronted</u> <u>with</u> the danger, he did not know what to do.
	in front of		*El cura hizo una reverencia **ante** el altar.* The priest bowed <u>in front of</u> the altar.
	in the presence of		*Se rindió **ante** sus enemigos.* He surrendered <u>in the presence of</u> his enemies.
bajo	behind		*Se escondió **bajo** una falsa identidad.* He hid <u>behind</u> a false identity.
	below		*Hacía dos grados **bajo** cero ese día.* It was two degrees <u>below</u> zero that day.
	under		*Estaba fresco **bajo** las ramas.* It was cool <u>under</u> the branches.
cabe	near, close to		*Se paró **cabe** la puerta.* (Found only in old literary works and documents). He stood up <u>near</u> the door.
con	about		*Estoy feliz **con** la noticia.* I am happy <u>about</u> the news.
	in		*Lo marcó **con** lápiz.* He marked it <u>in</u> pencil.
			*La mujer **con** pantalones es mi tía.* (If the subject is omitted, this should read *La **de** pantalones es mi tía.*) The woman <u>in</u> pants is my aunt (the one <u>in</u> pants).
	of		*Sueño **con** hacer un viaje largo.* I dream <u>of</u> making a long trip.

Spanish	English	Uses	Examples
			*Trajo una jarra **con** leche.* She brought a jug <u>of</u> milk.
	on		*Contamos **con**tigo esta noche.* We count **on** you tonight.
	with		*Llegó **con** él.* She arrived <u>with</u> him.
contra	against	position	*Estaba **contra** la puerta.* It was <u>against</u> the door.
		contrary to, in opposition to	*Reveló sus ideas **contra** el uso de armas.* He revealed his ideas <u>against</u> the use of weapons.
	at		*Disparó el revólver **contra** el animal furioso.* He fired <u>at</u> the furious animal.
	into		*Chocó **contra** un poste.* He crashed <u>into</u> a pole.
de	about		*Hablamos **de** sus clases.* We talked <u>about</u> his classes.
			*No sabe **de** qué se trata.* She doesn't know what it is <u>about</u>.
	as; as a		*Los pusieron **de** guías.* They assigned them <u>as</u> guides.
			*María trabaja **de** enfermera.* María works <u>as</u> a nurse.
			***De** niño estudiaba piano.* <u>As</u> a child, he studied the piano.
	at		*Vino **de** noche.* He came <u>at</u> night.
			*Se fue **de** madrugada.* He left <u>at</u> dawn.

Spanish	English	Uses	Examples
	by		*Lo sabemos **de** memoria.* We know it <u>by</u> heart.
			*Leímos dos obras **de** Cela.* We read two plays <u>by</u> Cela.
			*Carlos la tomó **de**l brazo.* Carlos took her <u>by</u> the arm.
			*Vino acompañada **de** Carlos.* She came accompanied <u>by</u> Carlos.
	during		*Trabaja **de** día.* She works <u>during</u> the day.
	from	distance	*Hay cinco cuadras **de** mi casa al banco.* There are five blocks <u>from</u> my house to the bank.
			*Enseña **de** agosto a mayo.* She teaches <u>from</u> August to May.
			*Los aztecas vinieron **de**l norte.* The Aztecs came <u>from</u> the north.
		origin	*Remigio es **de** Asunción.* Remigio is <u>from</u> Asuncion.
			*Recibí una carta **de** Eduardo.* I got a letter <u>from</u> Eduardo.
		out of	*Sacó el conejo **de** una galera.* He took the rabbit <u>from</u> the tall hat.
		manner	*Dijo el poema **de** memoria.* She recited the poem <u>from</u> memory.
	if		***De** salir temprano, lo veré.* <u>If</u> I leave early, I will see him.
	in	clothing	*La chica **de** verde es Elena.* The girl <u>in</u> green is Helen.

Spanish	English	Uses	Examples
			*La chica **de** blusa amarilla es mi prima.* The girl <u>in</u> the yellow blouse is my cousin.
		place	*Es el parque más bonito **de**l estado.* It's the nicest park <u>in</u> the state.
			*Las aulas **de** la escuela son grandes.* The classrooms <u>in</u> the school are large.
		manner	*Lo hicieron **de** prisa.* They made it <u>in</u> haste. (quickly)
			*Leyó el artículo **de** corrido.* He read the article <u>in</u> a continuous manner. (without stopping)
		reason	*Lloró **de** pena.* She cried <u>in</u> grief.
		time	*Estudia **de** tarde.* She studies <u>in</u> the afternoon.
	of	possession, ownership	*Esa es la casa **de** mi tía.* That one is my aunt's house. (the house <u>of</u> my aunt)
			*el evangelio **de**l apóstol* the book <u>of</u> the apostle
			*una obra **de** Lorca* one of Lorca's plays
		category	*Son prisioneros **de** guerra.* They are prisoners <u>of</u> war.
			*Es estudiante **de** primer año.* He is a first-year student. (no preposition)
			*Tengo dolor **de** muelas.* I have a toothache. (no preposition)
			*Tenemos una cama **de** dos plazas.* We have a double bed. (no preposition)

Spanish	English	Uses	Examples
		material, made of	*Quiere un vestido de seda.* She wants a silk dress. (a dress made of silk)
			Me gusta el dulce de pera. (jam made of pears) I like pear jam.
		contents	*No quiero té. Deme una taza de café.* I don't want tea; give me a cup of coffee.
			Un vaso de leche, por favor. A glass of milk, please.
			La botella está llena de vino. The bottle is full of wine.
		identification	*el presidente de la compañia* the president of the company
			Los maestros de la escuela priMaría tuvieron un aumento. The elementary school teachers got a raise. (no preposition)
		partitive	*Quiero un poco de azúcar.* I want some sugar. (a little bit of sugar)
			No dijo nada de nada. She didn't say anything at all. (no preposition)
			Tenemos un poco de todo. We have a little bit of everything.
		pejorative	*El generoso de mi tío no me dio nada para mi cumpleaños.* My generous uncle didn't give me anything for my birthday. (no preposition)
		compassion	*El pobrecito del niño hacía dos días que no comía.*

Spanish	English	Uses	Examples
			The poor little child had not eaten for two days. (no preposition)
		purpose, use	*Compré tazas **de** café.* I bought coffee cups. (no preposition)
			*Estaba en la sala **de** espera.* She was in the waiting room. (no preposition)
			*Trajo las pelotas **de** tennis.* She brought the tennis balls. (no preposition)
			*Tiene una pelota **de** fútbol.* He has a soccer ball. (no preposition)
		age	*Tienen una hija **de** doce años.* They have a twelve-year-old daughter. (no preposition)
	off		*Fueron sacados **de** la lista.* They were taken off the list.
	out of, because of		*Se escondió **de** miedo.* She hid out of fear.
			*Lloró **de** felicidad.* She cried out of happiness.
	than		*Recibí más **de** veinte cartas.* I got more than twenty letters.
			*Tengo más **de** las que tú me diste.* I have more than those you gave me.
	to		*Es hora **de** dormir.* It is time to sleep.
			*El jeroglífico es imposible **de** descifrar.* It is impossible to decipher the hieroglyphics.
	with		*Leandro es el niño **de** ojos azules.* Leandro is the boy with blue eyes.

Spanish	English	Uses	Examples
			*Estaba cubierto **de** sudor.* He was covered <u>with</u> sweat.
			*Está enamorada **de** Julio.* She is in love <u>with</u> Julio.
		price	*Fueron a una cena **de** treinta dólares por persona.* They attended a dinner <u>with</u> a thirty-dollar fixed price.
desde	from	distance	*José caminó **desde** el parque.* Joe walked <u>from</u> the park.
		point of reference	*Se veían las casas **desde** la ventanilla del avión.* One could see the houses <u>from</u> the airplane window.
			***Desde** aquí hasta el hotel hay dos cuadras.* The hotel is two city blocks <u>from</u> here.
		starting point in time	*Estaré en casa **desde** las ocho en adelante.* I'll be home <u>from</u> 8:00 o'clock on.
			***Desde** ahora en adelante deben entregar la tarea.* <u>From</u> now on, you must turn in your homework.
	since	length of time	*Estoy estudiando **desde** las cinco.* I have been studying <u>since</u> five.
en	at	place	*Los chicos están **en** la escuela.* The children are <u>at</u> school.
			*Dennis estudió **en** la universidad.* Dennis studied <u>at</u> the university.
			*La ceremonia será **en** la iglesia.* The ceremony will be <u>at</u> the church.

Spanish	English	Uses	Examples
			*Vamos a comer (estudiar) **en** la mesa de la cocina.*
			We are going to eat (study) <u>at</u> the kitchen table.
			*Papá está **en** casa.*
			Dad is <u>at</u> home.
			*Estaré **en** la salida.*
			I'll be <u>at</u> the exit door.
			*Está **en** una encrucijada.*
			He is <u>at</u> a crossroads.
		figures, numbers	*El alquiler se fijó **en** cien dólares por semana.*
			The rent was fixed <u>at</u> one hundred dollars per week.
by		means	*Me fui **en** coche.*
			I went <u>by</u> car.
			*Vinieron **en** avión.*
			They came <u>by</u> plane.
		based on	***En** sus notas se puede apreciar qué clase de estudiante es.*
			<u>By</u> his grades one can appreciate the kind of student he is.
for			*La casa está **en** venta.*
			The house is <u>for</u> sale.
in		way	*Me llevó **en** su auto nuevo.*
			He took me <u>in</u> his new car.
		location	*Las damas están **en** la iglesia.*
			The ladies are <u>in</u> church.
			*Me gusta vivir **en** el campo.*
			I like to live <u>in</u> the country.

Spanish	English	Uses	Examples
			Se fueron a vivir en el campo. They left (in order) to live in the countryside.
			Roy estudia en su cuarto. Roy studies in his room.
			Pedro se metió en un brete. Pedro is in difficulties.
		length of time	*Volveremos en una semana.* We will return in a week.
		reason	*Lo hicieron en venganza.* They did it in retaliation.
	into		*Empujó la pelota en el agujero.* He pushed the ball into the hole.
	on	condition, state	*Los muebles están en liquidación.* The furniture is on sale.
			Los obreros están en huelga. The workers are on strike.
		location	*La estatua está en el estante.* The statue is on the shelf.
		on top	*El niño se sentó en la mesa.* The child sat on the table.
entre	among		*Había mujeres entre ellos.* There were women among them.
			Entre nosotros no hay nadie que pueda hacerlo. Among us there is no one who could do it.
			Guardaremos el secreto entre nosotros. We'll keep the secret among ourselves.
		each other	*Cuando salen de vacaciones se comunican entre sí.*

Spanish	English	Uses	Examples
			When they go on vacation, they get in touch with <u>each other</u>.
	between		*El pasillo está **entre** los dos cuartos.* The hallway is <u>between</u> the two rooms.
			*Trabajo **entre** las ocho y las cinco.* I work <u>between</u> eight and five.
			***Entre** tú y yo, es una buena idea.* <u>Between</u> you and me, it's a good idea.
			***Entre** nosotros, esto es muy difícil.* <u>Between</u> us, this is very difficult.
	by	cooperation	*Al trabajo lo hicieron **entre** cinco.* The work was done <u>by</u> five persons.
			***Entre** María y Carla se terminó la limpieza.* The cleaning was done <u>by</u> María and Carla.
	in, into		*El venado se perdió **entre** el bosque.* The deer disappeared <u>in(to)</u> the woods.
	to self		*Lo dije **entre** mí para que no se enteraran.* I said it <u>to myself</u> so they wouldn't find out.
			*Lo dijo **entre** sí.* She said it <u>to herself</u>.
	through		***Entre** las cortinas se podía ver la casa de enfrente.* <u>Through</u> the curtains one could see the house across the street.
	what with		***Entre** el trabajo y la casa, no tiene tiempo para estudiar.* <u>What with</u> the job and the house, she does not have time to study.

Spanish	English	Uses	Examples
	within		*Se veía el emblema **entre** los pliegues de la bandera.* One could see the emblem <u>within</u> the folds of the flag.
			*Lo guardé **entre** mí antes de revelarlo.* I kept it <u>within</u> myself before I revealed it.
hacia	around		*Vendrán **hacia** la una.* They will come <u>around</u> one o'clock.
			*Va a decidir **hacia** mayo.* He is going to decide <u>around</u> May.
	for		*Hoy partieron **hacia** Madrid.* They left <u>for</u> Madrid today.
			*Sentía un gran amor **hacia** sus abuelos.* She felt a deep love <u>for</u> her grandparents.
	towards		*Fueron **hacia** el centro.* They went <u>towards</u> downtown.
			*Mostró compasión **hacia** sus enemigos.* He showed compassion <u>towards</u> his enemies.
hasta	as far as		*Manejamos **hasta** Austin.* We drove <u>as far as</u> Austin.
	even		***Hasta** mi hermana lo creyó.* <u>Even</u> my sister believed it.
	until		*Se quedó **hasta** las cinco.* He stayed <u>until</u> five.
	up to		*No han llamado **hasta** ahora.* They have not called <u>up to</u> now.
			*Leí **hasta** el tercer capítulo.* I read <u>up to</u> the third chapter.

Spanish	English	Uses	Examples
			*Subimos **hasta** la cima.* We went <u>up to</u> the top.
para	around		*La conferencia será **para** mediados de abril.* The conference will be <u>around</u> the middle of April.
	by		*Tendré los documentos **para** las cinco.* I will have the documents <u>by</u> five o'clock.
			***Para** entonces habremos recibido el pedido.* <u>By</u> then, we will have received the order.
	for	destination	*Tengo algo **para** ti.* I have something <u>for</u> you.
		duration	*Tengo trabajo **para** dos meses.* I have work <u>for</u> two months.
		deadline	*El ejercicio es **para** el lunes.* The exercise is <u>for</u> Monday.
		use	*Me dio una alfombra **para** la sala.* She gave me a carpet <u>for</u> the living room.
		direction	*Salió **para** Boulder anoche.* He left <u>for</u> Boulder last night.
		considering	*Es humilde **para** su posición.* She is humble <u>for</u> her position.
		purpose	*Traje esto **para** que lo veas.* I brought this <u>for</u> you to see.
			*Necesito aceite **para** freír.* I need oil <u>for</u> frying.
		inquiry	*¿**Para** qué sirve esta herramienta?* What is this tool good <u>for</u>?

Spanish	English	Uses	Examples
		comparison	*Para principiante tiene bastante talento.* For a beginner, he has lots of talent.
			Estoy muy cansada para ese trabajo. I'm too tired for that job.
			Para un buen café, el de Brasil. As for good coffee, the best is from Brazil.
	to	destination	*Manda saludos para ti.* He sends regards to you.
		direction	*Iremos para Florida mañana.* We'll go to Florida tomorrow.
		in order to, purpose	*Fui a casa para estudiar.* I went home to study.
			Llamé para hablar contigo. I called to talk to you.
		objective	*Estudia para maestra.* She's studying to be a teacher.
		opinion	*Para él, esto es una ganga.* To him, this is a bargain.
	to self		*Se lo dijo para sí.* He said it to himself.
			Siempre me lo repetía para mí misma. I always repeated it to myself.
por	about		*Me preocupo por el resultado.* I worry about the results.
		imminence	*La revolución está por estallar.* The revolution is about to break out.
	according to		*Por lo que dijo, lo van a considerar.* According to what he said, they are going to consider it.

Spanish	English	Uses	Examples
	along		*Corrían **por** la playa.* They ran <u>along</u> the beach.
	around		*Caminábamos **por** la ciudad.* We walked <u>around</u> town.
		indefinite location	*El vive **por** allá.* He lives <u>around</u> there.
			*El trabaja **por** California ahora.* He works <u>around</u> California now.
		indefinite time	***Por** aquellos tiempos vivíamos en una casa grande.* <u>Around</u> that time we lived in a large house.
	at		*Trabaja **por** la noche.* He works <u>at</u> night.
	because		*A Luis lo suspendieron **por** venir tarde.* They suspended Luis <u>because</u> he came late.
			*Se ganó el premio **por** buena alumna.* She won the prize <u>because</u> she is a good student.
	because of	reason	*Tengo dos trabajos **por** mis hijos.* I have two jobs <u>because of</u> my kids.
			*Chocaron **por** la lluvia.* They got into a wreck <u>because of</u> the rain.
			*Se casó **por** su dinero.* He got married <u>because of</u> her money.
	by	location, passage	*Fui **por** la oficina de Jeff pero no estaba allí.* I went <u>by</u> Jeff's office but he wasn't there.
		means	*Viajamos **por** avión.* We traveled <u>by</u> plane.

Spanish	English	Uses	Examples
		manner	*Lo mandé **por** correo.* I sent it <u>by</u> mail.
		agent; passive voice	*La cena fue preparada **por** mi mamá.* Dinner was prepared <u>by</u> my mother.
			*Yerma es una obra de teatro escrita **por** García Lorca.* *Yerma* is a play written <u>by</u> García Lorca.
	for	duration	*Me quedé allí **por** un mes.* I stayed there <u>for</u> a month.
			*Lo pensó **por** unos minutos.* He thought about it <u>for</u> a few minutes.
		exchange	*Pagué diez pesos **por** él.* I paid ten pesos <u>for</u> it.
			*Lo venderé **por** lo que me den.* I'll sell it <u>for</u> whatever they give me.
			*Compramos el bote **por** diez mil dólares.* We bought the boat <u>for</u> ten thousand dollars.
		in the amount of	*Les di un cheque **por** diez dólares.* I gave them a check <u>for</u> ten dollars.
		instead of	*Yo trabajé **por** él cuando estuvo enfermo.* I worked <u>for</u> him when he was sick.
		on behalf of	*Lo ha hecho **por** su madre.* She did it <u>for</u> her mother.
		to get	*Volvió **por** su cartera.* She came back <u>for</u> her purse.
		to pick up	*Iré **por** mi amiga primero.* I'll go <u>for</u> my friend first.
		for the sake of	*Hazlo **por** piedad.* Do it <u>for</u> mercy's <u>sake</u>.

Spanish	English	Uses	Examples
			*No lo niegue, **por** Dios.* Do not deny it, <u>for</u> God's <u>sake</u>.
			*Se casaron **por** amor.* They got married <u>for</u> love.
			*Continúa trabajando en esa compañía **por** conveniencia propia.* She continues working at that company <u>for</u> her own convenience.
		towards	*Sentimos pena **por** ellos.* We feel sorry <u>for</u> them.
	in		*Estaré en casa **por** la mañana.* I will be home <u>in</u> the morning.
			*Lo necesita **por** escrito.* He needs it <u>in</u> writing.
		necessity	*Hay problemas **por** resolver.* There are problems <u>to be</u> resolved. (no preposition)
	on	manner	*Está hablando **por** teléfono.* He is talking <u>on</u> the phone.
			*Lo dijeron **por** radio.* They said it <u>on</u> the radio.
			*Lo pasaron **por** televisión.* They showed it <u>on</u> TV.
	out of		*Lo llamó **por** compasión.* She called him <u>out of</u> compassion.
			*Pedro lo hizo **por** vanidad.* Pedro did it <u>out of</u> vanity.
	over		*El camión pasó **por** el puente.* The truck went <u>over</u> the bridge.
	per	measure, rate	*Gana siete pesos **por** hora.* He makes seven pesos <u>per</u> hour.
	regardless of		***Por** más bonita que sea, no creo que merezca el premio.*

Spanish	English	Uses	Examples
			<u>Regardless</u> of how beautiful she is, I don't think she deserves the award.
	through		*El tren va **por** un túnel.* The train goes <u>through</u> a tunnel.
			*Saltó **por** la ventana.* He jumped <u>through</u> the window.
			*Se internaron **por** el río.* They went in <u>through</u> the river.
			*Es muy conocido **por** sus artículos periodísticos.* He is very well known <u>through</u> his newspaper articles.
	throughout		*Se sabe **por** toda la ciudad.* It is known <u>throughout</u> the city.
	to	purpose, in order to	*Se esmeró **por** darle un hogar.* He did his best <u>to</u> give her a home.
			*Llamé **por** compartir algo contigo.* I called you (in order) <u>to</u> share something with you.
	up to, down to		*Cuando se inundó la casa, el agua les llegaba **por** las rodillas.* When the house got flooded, the water went <u>up to</u> their knees.
			*El pelo lo tiene **por** los hombros.* Her hair comes <u>down to</u> her shoulders.
según	according to		***Según** él, está claro.* <u>According to</u> him, it's clear.
			*el evangelio **según** San Marcos* the gospel <u>according to</u> Mark
	as		***Según** parece, nos mudaremos.* <u>As</u> it seems, we'll move out.

Spanish	English	Uses	Examples
			*La empleada archivaba las cartas **según** iban llegando.* The employee was filing the letters <u>as</u> they arrived.
	depending on		*Actuaremos **según** lo que pase.* We'll act <u>depending on</u> what happens.
sin	without		*Lo hizo **sin** pensar.* He did it <u>without</u> thinking.
			*Había personas **sin** electricidad.* There were people <u>without</u> power.
so	under		*Habló **so** pena de muerte.* (*bajo*) He spoke <u>under</u> punishment of death.
			*Consiguió el puesto **so** pretexto de experto.* He got the job <u>under</u> the pretext of being an expert.
sobre	about		*El presidente habló **sobre** el presupuesto.* The president spoke <u>about</u> the budget.
	above		*Se levantaba el sol **sobre** las montañas.* The sun was rising <u>above</u> the mountains.
	around time		*Iremos **sobre** las cinco.* We'll go <u>around</u> five.
	on		*El papel está **sobre** la mesa.* The paper is <u>on</u> the table.
			*La luna se reflejaba **sobre** el agua.* The moonlight was reflected <u>on</u> the water.

Spanish	English	Uses	Examples
			*Los charcos **sobre** la tierra parecían lagunitas.* The puddles <u>on</u> the ground resembled little ponds.
	on top of		*Un pájaro grande se posó **sobre** la chimenea.* A big bird was perched <u>on top of</u> the chimney.
	over		*El avión voló **sobre** la ciudad.* The plane flew <u>over</u> the city.
	upon		*El sol brilla **sobre** las nubes.* The sun shines <u>upon</u> the clouds.
tras	after		***Tras** (de) esperar, salió.* <u>After</u> waiting, he left. *Las cartas llegaron una **tras** otra.* The letters arrived one <u>after</u> another. *Reanudaron su amistad año **tras** año.* They renewed their friendship year <u>after</u> year.
	behind		*Jaime corría **tras** (de) la madre.* James ran <u>behind</u> his mother. *Se veía un lindo jardín **tras** (de) la cerca.* One could see a pretty garden <u>behind</u> the fence.
	beyond		*La aldea comenzaba **tras** (de) la pradera.* The village began <u>beyond</u> the prairie.

Simple Prepositions in Compound Words

Almost all the simple Spanish prepositions can be joined to other words as prefixes to form compound words. Some examples follow:

*a*cortar	to shorten
*a*valuar	to value
*ante*dicho	aforesaid
*ante*mano	with anticipation
*ante*sala	antechamber
*bajor*relieve	bas-relief
*con*llevar	to bear
*contra*decir	to contradict
*contra*peso	counterweight
*de*caer	to decay, languish
*en*caminar	to guide, to direct
*entre*ver	to see imperfectly
*para*frasear	to paraphrase
*por*venir	future
*sin*verguenza	rascal
*so*cavar	to undermine
*so*liviantar	to rise up
*sobre*humano	superhuman
*tras*papelar	to misplace papers
*tras*tornar	to disturb

Compound Prepositions

Compound prepositions are made up of two or more words. They are also called prepositional phrases (*frases preposicionales*). Some of the compound prepositions in Spanish are equivalent to simple Spanish prepositions, while others are not. Compound prepositions may also be translated into English as one or more words. Some examples follow in each category.

A. Compound prepositions corresponding to an equivalent simple preposition in Spanish:

ante	*al frente de*	in front of
	delante de	in front of, before
	enfrente de	in front of
	en presencia de	before, in the presence of
	frente a	in front of
bajo	*debajo de*	under, below
	por debajo de	

con	en compañía de	with
contra	al contrario de	contrary to
	en contra de	contrary to, in opposition
en	dentro de	inside
	en el interior de	
entre	en medio de	among, in between
hacia	con destino a	toward
	con rumbo a	
	a camino a	
para	a fin de	in order to
	con el propósito de	with the purpose of
	con intención de	with the intention of
por	a causa de	because of
	a través de	through
	a cambio de	for, in exchange for
	en favor de	for
	en virtud de	because of, by virtue of
	en vista de	because of
	por efecto de	because of, as a result of
	por medio de	through
según	conforme a	according to
	en cuanto a	as for, in regard to
sobre	acerca de	about
	arriba de	on top of, above
	encima de	on top of, above, on
	por encima de	above
	respecto a	about
tras	después de	after
	detrás de	behind
	en pos de	after, behind
	tras que	besides

B. Compound prepositions with no equivalent simple preposition:

a excepción de	with the exception of
a fuerza de	with perseverance
a pesar de	in spite of

alrededor de	around
ante todo	above all, first of all
antes de	before
de por fuerza	necessarily
en lugar de	instead of
en vez de	instead of
fuera de	outside of
junto a	close to, next to
lejos de	far from
más allá de	beyond

C. Two prepositions together

In some cases, two prepositions are grouped together to indicate a specific meaning:

*Llegó **hasta con** sombrero.*	He even came wearing a hat.
*Fue fácil porque Diego estaba **de por** medio.*	It was easy because Diego acted as a mediator.
*Sólo tenía billetes **de a** diez en la cartera.*	She only had ten-dollar bills in her wallet.
*Era muy generoso **para con** todos sus amigos.*	He was very generous toward all of his friends.
*Tuvo que declarar **por ante** el juez.*	He had to declare before the judge.
*El gato vino **de entre** las plantas.*	The cat came out from the bushes.
***Tras de** llegar tarde, no trajo la llave.*	Besides coming late, she did not bring the key.

Functions of Prepositions

Prepositions point out the grammatical cases that exist in a sentence, that is, their specific functions within the sentence.

Prepositions	Cases		
de	genitive case (used to indicate possession)	*el libro **de** Juan*	Juan's book
a and *para*	dative case (used to indicate indirect object)	*Le di el papel **a** Carlos.*	I gave the paper to Carlos.
		*El libro es **para** Miguel.*	The book is for Miguel.
a	accusative case (used to indicate direct object)	*Veo **a** María.* *Quiere **a** sus hijos.*	I see María. He loves his children.

all of the prepositions	ablative case (used to indicate a particular circumstance)	*Vino **sin** llamar.*	He came without calling.
		*Está **contra** la puerta.*	It is against the door.
		*Lo mandó **por** correo aéreo.*	He sent it via airmail.

General Notes on Preposition Usage

For the correct use of prepositions, the following rules must be taken into consideration.

A. Prepositions are placed before the noun:

*Estudio **con** mi amiga.*	I study with my friend.
*Viajamos **hasta** Chicago.*	We traveled to Chicago.

B. Prepositions that are linked to a relative pronoun follow the noun to which they refer:

*El jardín, **en** el cual había rosas, era pequeño.*	The garden, in which there were roses, was small.
*La posada **a** la que llegamos estaba llena.*	The inn at which we arrived was full.
*El hombre **con** quien hablé trabaja en esa oficina.*	The man to whom I spoke works in that office.

C. Prepositions cannot be joined by conjunctions:

con/sin	Correct: *Me gusta el pastel **con** sal o **sin** ella.*	I like the pie with or without salt.
	(Incorrect: *Me gusta el pastel **con** o **sin** sal.*)	
de/para	Correct: *Empaquetan artículos **de** Perú y **para** ese país.*	They pack articles from and to Perú.
	(Incorrect: *Empaquetan artículos **de** y **para** Perú.*)	
a/de	Correct: *Le pidió dinero **al** jefe y lo recibió **de** él.*	He asked for and received money from the boss.
	(Incorrect: *Le pidió dinero **al** y recibió dinero **del** jefe.*)	
sobre/debajo	Correct: *Deja el almohadón **sobre** la mesa o **debajo** de ella.*	Leave the pillow on or under the table.
	(Incorrect: *Deja el almohadón **sobre** o **debajo** de la mesa.*)	

Uses of Specific Prepositions

The Preposition *a*

A. **The preposition *a* to introduce the accusative case (the direct object)**

Also called *personal a* (*la **a** personal*) when it appears before the direct object, the preposition *a* is used in the following cases.

1. Use *a* with a proper name that refers to a human being, a fictional character, or a personified animal, including pets:

*Ella ama **a** Juan.*	She loves Juan.
*Los niños admiraban **a** Caperucita.*	The children admired Little Red Riding Hood.
*Me gustaba verlo **a** Tonto en las películas del oeste.*	I liked to see Tonto in the movies of the Far West.
*Yo quiero **a** Pelusa, mi gato siamés.*	I love Pelusa, my Siamese cat.
*Yo quiero **a** mi caballo.*	I love my horse.

> **NOTE:**
>
> The preposition *a* is not used with the verb ***gustar*** or similar verbs. However, when these verbs are followed by an infinitive, the preposition *a* must follow the infinitive:
>
> | | |
> |---|---|
> | *Me gusta mi perro.* | I like my dog. |
> | *Me gusta alimentar **a** mi perro.* | I like to feed my dog. |
> | *Nos molesta Carlos. Es muy aburridor.* | Carlos bothers us. He is very boring. |
> | *Nos molesta escuchar **a** Carlos.* | It bothers us to listen to Carlos. |

2. Use *a* with wildlife, to indicate that the subject has a preference for specific animals:

*Me gusta alimentar **a** los pájaros que vienen al jardín trasero.*	I like to feed the birds that come to the backyard.

But:

No me gusta ver las ardillas cerca de la casa.	I don't like to see the squirrels near the house.

*El guardián del zoológico alimentó **al** elefante.*	The zookeeper fed the elephant.

But:

El domador del circo tuvo que encerrar el tigre que se escapó.	The circus tamer had to lock up the tiger that escaped.

NOTE:

The preposition *a* is also added when it is not clear which element is the direct object. In the following case, the subject's likes and dislikes are not taken into consideration, as in the preceding examples. The following sentence may have two meanings:

El guardián mató el elefante que se enloqueció.	The zookeeper killed the elephant that went mad.
	(or) The elephant that went mad killed the zookeeper.

By adding the personal *a*, it becomes clear that it was the zookeeper who killed the animal:

*El guardián mató **al** elefante que se escapó.*	The zookeeper killed the elephant that escaped.

Although this action may be expressed in English with the passive voice (*The elephant was killed by the zookeeper*), the active voice is preferred in Spanish for this type of sentence. Also see item 6 that follows.

3. Use *a* with a direct object that represents a person:

When the human direct object is not particularly singled out, the personal *a* is not used. Compare *Quiero **a** mi abuelo* with the following sentences:

Quiero una secretaria que sepa inglés.	I want a secretary that knows English.
Nunca encuentro un amigo cuando lo necesito.	I never find a friend when I need one.

4. Use *a* before each noun when the direct object is multiple:

*Reconozco **a** María y **a** Elena en la foto.*	I recognize María and Elena in the picture.
*Vi **a** mi primo y **a** mi tío en el mercado.*	I saw my cousin and my uncle in the market.

5. Use *a* before a collective noun that represents human beings:

*El actor oía **al** público que lo aplaudía.*	The actor heard the audience applauding him.
*El político juntó **a** los adversarios.*	The politician gathered his adversaries.

6. Use *a* before animate or inanimate direct objects, whenever it is not clear which one is the object (see note under preceding item 2):

El niño corre el ratón.	The boy runs after the mouse.
	The mouse runs after the boy.
But: *El niño corre **al** ratón.*	The boy runs after the mouse.
El gato mordió el perro.	The cat bit the dog.
	The dog bit the cat.
But: *El gato mordió **al** perro.*	The cat bit the dog.
La colina tapa la iglesia.	The hill hides the church.
	The church hides the hill.
But: *La colina tapa **a** la iglesia.*	The hill hides the church.

7. Use *a* after the verb *ir*, whether the verb is followed by an infinitive or a noun:

*Voy **a** ver a Juan mañana.*	I'm going to see Juan tomorrow.
*Iremos **a** Ohio en avión.*	We'll go to Ohio by plane.

8. Use *a* after verbs of motion when a place is mentioned:

*Ayer llegó **a** Dallas.*	He arrived in Dallas yesterday.
*El avión se acercaba **al** aeropuerto en la niebla.*	The plane was approaching the airport in the fog.

9. Use *a* after certain verbs, to change their meaning:

faltar (to be lacking)	*faltar **a** (to miss)*
Faltan dos sillas.	*Jaime faltó **a** la reunión.*
Two chairs are lacking.	Jaime missed the meeting.
darse (to give to oneself)	*darse **a** (to devote oneself to)*
Me di un golpe en el pie.	*Se dio **a** la investigación.*
I hit my foot.	He devoted himself to research.

10. Use *a* in the contraction of *a + el* and an infinitive, to indicate a precise moment, as in *on/upon going, entering,* etc.:

***Al salir** de la oficina, me caí en la calle.*	Upon leaving the office, I fell down in the street.

11. Use *a* before the indefinite pronouns *alguien* and *nadie*, which always refer to people:

Vi *a* alguien entrar.	I saw someone coming in.
No reconozco *a* nadie aquí.	I don't recognize anybody here.

12. Use *a* before the indefinite pronouns *alguno/a/os/as* and *ninguno/a*, when these refer to human beings:

Vi *a* algunos que entraron.	I saw some people entering.
No queremos oír *a* ninguno.	We don't want to hear anybody.

13. Use *a* before the adjectives *alguno/a/os/as* and *ninguno/a*, when these refer to people:

Oyó *a* algunos chicos que estaban jugando.	She heard some children that were playing.
No respeta *a* ningún colega.	He doesn't respect any colleagues.

14. Use *a* to indicate a price, except after the verbs *costar* (*to cost*) and *valer* (*to be worth*):

El sillón está *a* dos mil pesos.	The sofa costs two thousand pesos.
Se vendió *a* diez pesos.	They sold it at ten pesos.
But:	
El sillón cuesta dos mil.	The sofa costs two thousand.
El plato vale diez pesos.	The dish is worth ten pesos.

15. Use *a* to indicate a specific time:

Tengo que tomar la pastilla *a* las tres.	I have to take the pill at three o'clock.

NOTES:

Besides the limitations pointed out in items 1, 2, 3, and 14, the preposition *a* is also not used in the following cases.

(1) The preposition *a* is not used after verbs such as *dejar* or *abandonar*, when the direct object is a place:

Dejé Caracas la semana pasada.	I left Caracas last week.
Abandonaron la ciudad cuando empezó la guerra.	They abandoned the city when the war began.

(2) The preposition *a* is not used after *ir* and other verbs of motion, when these verbs are followed by the adverbs *ahí*, *acá*, *allí*, or *allá*:

Fuimos allí el año pasado.	We went there last year.
Llegó allá el martes.	He arrived there on Tuesday.
Vine aquí para verte.	I came here to see you.

(3) The preposition *a* is not used when the direct object is a place, unless the verb requires the proposition:

Juan de Garay fundó Buenos Aires.	Juan de Garay founded Buenos Aires.
Vimos el estadio desde la carretera.	We saw the stadium from the highway.
Nosotros visitamos Paraguay.	We visited Paraguay.
Recuerdo Madrid.	I remember Madrid.
Recorrió Valencia.	He toured Valencia.

<u>But</u>:

Viajamos a Colombia.	We traveled to Colombia.
Tú fuiste a la ciudad.	You went to the city.

B. **The preposition *a* to introduce the dative case (the indirect object)**

In the dative case (the indirect object), the preposition *a* is used with animate and inanimate objects:

*Le mandé una carta **a** Tito.*	I sent a letter to Tito.
*Le puso el collar **al** perro.*	He put the collar on the dog.
*Le agregué huevos **a** la masa.*	I added eggs to the dough.
*Me mandó flores **a** mí, lo que me sorprendió mucho.*	He sent flowers to me, which surprised me a lot.

NOTE:

The indirect object preceded by *a* may be replaced entirely by the indirect object pronoun when it is understood in context:

Le mandé una carta.	I sent him a letter.
Me mandó flores.	He sent me flowers.

The Preposition *con*

The preposition *con* is used in the following cases:

A. *Con* is used when **with** is used in English followed by animate, inanimate, and abstract nouns:

Iré **con** *José.*	I'll go with José.
Camina **con** *su perro.*	She walks with her dog.
Se fue **con** *esperanzas.*	He left with hopes.

B. *Con* is used to indicate a health problem:

Estoy **con** *dolor de cabeza.*	I have a headache.
Está **con** *un resfrío bárbaro.*	He has a terrible cold.

C. *Con* is used to signal a state of mind:

Está **con** *pena de él.*	She feels sorry for him.
Dio el regalo **con** *alegría.*	She gave the gift gladly.

D. *Con* is used in adverbial phrases, instead of adding *-mente* (*-ly*) to the adverb:

Habló **con claridad**. *(claramente)*	He spoke clearly.
Lo escuchó **con paciencia**. *(pacientemente)*	She listened to him patiently.

The Preposition *de*

The preposition *de* is used in the following cases.

A. *De* is used to indicate possession:

el trabajo **de** *Pedro*	Pedro's job
la hoja **del** *árbol*	the leaf of the tree

B. *De* is used to specify the author of a book, painting, etc.:

Don Quijote es una novela **de** *Cervantes.*	Don Quixote is a novel by Cervantes.
Vimos dos cuadros **de** *Goya.*	We saw two paintings by Goya.

C. ***De*** is used with or without the verb *ser* (*to be*), to show origin or nationality:

*La profesora es **de** Perú.*	The teacher is from Perú.
*Sus padres son **de** Alabama.*	Their parents are from Alabama.
*las uvas **de** Mendoza*	the grapes from Mendoza

D. ***De*** is used with verbs of movement, to show where the action originated:

*Llegaron **de** Jamaica.*	They arrived from Jamaica.
*Partió **de** Miami.*	He left Miami.
*Me mudé **del** departamento.*	I moved out of the apartment.

E. ***De*** is used in a phrase used to qualify the noun (adjectival phrase):

*Las flores **de**l jardín tienen mucha luz para crecer.*	The flowers in the garden have a lot of sunlight for growing.
*Las fotos **de**l libro son en blanco y negro.*	The photos in the book are in black and white.
*Tienen una casa **de** campo.*	They have a country house.
*La chica **de** pelo crespo es su hija.*	The girl with curly hair is her daughter.

F. ***De*** is used to show of what material an object is made:

*Le dio un anillo **de** oro.*	He gave her a gold ring.
*Compré un cinturón **de** cuero.*	I bought a leather belt.

G. ***De*** is used as an equivalent of ***than*** when making a comparison that involves numbers:

*Hay más **de** cuarenta sillas en esta clase.*	There are more than forty chairs in this classroom.
*Tengo menos **de** un mes para hacerlo.*	I have less than a month to do it.

H. ***De*** is used in the ***de*** + infinitive combination as an equivalent of the English ***if clause***:

***De** saberlo, hubiera comprado una entrada para mañana.*	If I had known, I would have bought a ticket for tomorrow.

I. ***De*** is used to show what a container holds or for what it is used:

*una taza **de** té*	a cup of tea
*una caja **de** chocolates*	a box of chocolates
*un vaso **de** vino*	a glass of wine

J. *De* is used to tell the time or the part of the day when something takes place:

A las dos *de* la mañana.	At two in the morning.
Es la una *de* la tarde.	It's one in the afternoon.
Vamos a ir *de* mañana.	We'll go in the morning.
Llegaron *de* noche.	They arrived at night.

K. *De* is used to indicate measurements:

La torre mide cincuenta metros *de* alto.	The tower is fifty meters tall.
La barra tiene dos centímetros *de* espesor.	The bar is two centimeters thick.

L. *De* is used to indicate the purpose of an object:

gorra *de* baño	shower cap
reloj *de* bolsillo	pocket watch
broche *de* la ropa	clothes pin
sombrero *de* playa	beach hat

M. *De* is used as part of an adverbial expression of manner:

lleno *de* deudas	full of debts
cargado *de* regalos	loaded with gifts
muerto *de* risa	dying with laughter

N. *De* is used before a noun or a verb, to indicate the cause of an action:

Se murió *de* pena.	She died of grief.
Adelgazó *de* caminar mucho.	She lost weight from walking so much.
Nos cansamos *de* escuchar esa música todo el día.	We got tired of listening to that music all day.

O. *De* is used to show a portion or quantity:

un kilo *de* cebollas	a kilogram of onions
un poco *de* leche	some milk

P. *De* is used after an adjective, to describe someone:

el bueno *de* mi hermano	my good brother
la modesta *de* Juana	that modest Juana
el sabio *de* su profesor	his wise professor

18

Adverbs

Adverbs are parts of a sentence that modify verbs, adjectives, and other adverbs. In Spanish, an adverb that modifies a verb is called a *complemento circunstancial*.

While adjectives agree in gender and number with the noun they modify, adverbs are invariable:

*Dos niños llegaron **tarde**.*	Two boys came late.
*Una chica también llegó **tarde**.*	A girl also came late.

Classification of Adverbs

Adverbs in Spanish are classified into two main groups: qualifying adverbs (*calificativos*) and determinative adverbs (*determinativos*). This last group includes the demonstrative, interrogative, relative, and indefinite adverbs. Some examples follow.

A. Qualifying adverbs:

mejor (better)   *peor* (worse)   *bien* (well)   *mal* (badly)   *claro* (clearly)

B. Determinative adverbs:

1. Demonstrative adverbs:

aquí (here)   *acá* (here)   *allí* (there)   *así* (so, this way)

2. Interrogative adverbs:

¿cuándo? (when?)   *¿dónde?* (where?)   *¿cuánto?* (how much?)   *¿cómo?* (how?)

3. Relative adverbs:

cuando (when)   *donde* (where)   *como* (how)   *cuanto* (how much)   *cual* (which)

4. Indefinite adverbs:

quizá (perhaps)   *tal vez* (maybe)   *dondequiera* (wherever)   *nada* (nothing)

Other Categories for Classifying Adverbs

Adverbs are further classified according to their meaning, formation, and origin. Any given adverb may belong to two or more categories at the same time:

Allá en aquella época salía con mis amigos. *(adverbio de tiempo)*	At that time, I used to go out with my friends. (adverb of time)
Me gustaba estar allá con ellos. (adverbio de lugar)	I liked to be there with them. (adverb of place)

The following lists illustrate how some adverbs are classified according to these three categories.

A. Adverbs classified according to their meaning:

Since adverbs indicate *place* (**lugar**), *time* (**tiempo**), *manner* (**modo**), *quantity* (**cantidad**), etc., they can be classified as adverbs of place, time, manner, quantity, and so on.

1. Adverbs of place (*adverbios de lugar*)

These adverbs answer the question *¿dónde?*

aquí, acá, ahí, allí, allá, fuera, arriba, abajo, delante, detrás

> **NOTES:**
>
> **(1)** While *aquí* and *acá* both mean *here*, *aquí* refers to a place which is more specifically defined. *Acá* is also used in expressions like *por acá* (*around here*), *más acá* (*closer*), *un poco más acá* (*a little closer*):
>
> | | |
> |---|---|
> | *Ponlo aquí.* | Put it (over) here. |
> | *Déjalo por acá.* | Leave it around here. |
>
> **(2)** Although *allí* and *allá* are both equivalent to the English *there*, *allí* points to a more definite location. *Allá* is used in expressions like *un poco más allá* (*a little further*), *más allá* (*further away*), or *no tan allá* (*not that far*). (The expression *el más allá* has the meaning of *life after death*.):

*Ella vive **allí**, en esa casa.*	She lives over there, in that house.
*Un poco **más allá** está la iglesia.*	A little further down is the church.

(3) *Aquí, acá, allí*, and *allá* may be followed by *mismo* to indicate an exact point within that location:

*Estaba **aquí mismo**.*	It was right here.
*Se sentó **allá mismo**.*	She sat down right over there.

(4) Adverbs of place which, in English, are preceded by *up* or *down*, are expressed in Spanish as follows:

up here	*aquí arriba, acá arriba*
up there	*ahí arriba, allí arriba, allá arriba*
down here	*aquí abajo, acá abajo*
down there	*allí abajo, allá abajo*

(5) The English suffix *-ward(s),* which conveys movement towards a specific direction, is rendered in Spanish by the preposition *hacia* or *para*:

upward	*hacia arriba, para arriba*
downward	*hacia abajo, para abajo*
backward	*hacia atrás, para atrás*
forward	*hacia adelante, para adelante*

(6) There are no Spanish equivalents for the English suffix *-where* that refers to an unidentified area. Prepositions or phrases are used instead:

somewhere	*en alguna parte*
	en algún lugar
	en algún sitio
	en algún lado
somewhere here	*por acá, por aquí*
somewhere there	*por allá, por allí, por ahí*
nowhere	*en ninguna parte*
	en ningún lugar
	en ningún sitio
	en ningún lado
anywhere	*en cualquier parte*
	en cualquier lugar
	en cualquier sitio
	en cualquier lado

2. Adverbs of time (*adverbios de tiempo*)

These adverbs answer the question *¿cuándo?*

hoy, ayer, mañana, tarde, aún, temprano, anoche, nunca, siempre, ya

NOTE:

(1) When *aún* carries an accent mark, it means *still* or *yet*, depending on context. *Todavía* is a synonym of *aún* in this case. When the verb is negative, it is translated into English as *yet*; when the verb is affirmative, it is rendered into English as *still*. Notice that the verb in Spanish can be affirmative or negative when using *aún* or *todavía*. (See Note 2 for the use of *aun* with no accent mark):

*No lo he leído **aún** (todavía).*	I haven't read it <u>yet</u>.
***Aún** (todavía) está comiendo.*	She's <u>still</u> eating.
***Todavía** (aún) no llamó.*	He hasn't called <u>yet</u>.
***Todavía** (aún) estoy aquí.*	I'm <u>still</u> here.

With compound tenses in the <u>negative</u>, *aún* and *todavía* (*yet*) may be placed either before the negative or after the past or present participle, but never between the auxiliary and the main verb:

*No ha firmado **aún**.*	He has not signed yet.
***Aún** no lo habían dicho.*	They hadn't said it yet.
***Todavía** no han terminado.*	They have not finished yet.
*No he ido **todavía**.*	I haven't gone yet.
*No están comiendo **aún**.*	They are not eating yet.
***Todavía** no está hablando.*	He is not speaking yet.

With progressive tenses in the <u>affirmative</u>, *aún* and *todavía* (*still*) may be placed as indicated below:

- Before the auxiliary verb:

***Aún** estaban durmiendo cuando Juan llegó.*	They were still sleeping when Juan arrived.

- After the present participle:

*Cuando me fui ella estaba trabajando **todavía**.*	When I left, she was still working.

- Between the auxiliary and the present participle, for emphasis:

*El niño se quedó **todavía** jugando después que la madre lo llamó.*	The boy still continued playing after his mother called him.

(2) Without an accent mark, *aun* means *even, including,* or *also. Hasta, incluso,* and *también* are synonyms of *aun* in this case:

***Aun** Juan lo ha leído.*	Even Juan has read it.
*Juan **aun** lo ha leído.*	Juan has even read it.
***Hasta** Pedro vino tarde.*	Even Pedro arrived late.
*Pedro no trajo nada y **hasta** vino tarde.*	Pedro didn't bring anything and he even came late.
***Incluso** Isabel lo está diciendo.*	Even Isabel is saying it.
*Isabel **incluso** lo está diciendo.*	Isabel is even saying it.

The use of *también* is flexible, since it may be placed before or after the subject, and after the main verb. The meaning of the sentence will change depending on the positioning of these adverbs:

***También** Andrés lo ha leído.*	Also Andrés has read it. (Even Andrés.)
*Juan **también** lo ha leído.*	Juan has also read it. (He not only bought it, he also read it.)
*Juan lo ha leído **también**.*	Juan has read it also. (Either one of the above meanings.)

(3) The negative *not even* is rendered in Spanish as *ni aun* or *ni siquiera*. These expressions are placed before the subject when the emphasis is on the subject alone.

***Ni aun** Juan lo ha leído.*	Not even Juan has read it. (Nobody has read it.)
***Ni siquiera** él sabe.*	Not even he knows.

If the emphasis is on the action, *ni aun* (or *ni siquiera*) is placed before the verb and it carries a strong negative connotation:

*Juan **ni aun** lo ha leído.*	Juan has not even read it.
*Él **ni siquiera** lo sabe.*	He doesn't even know it.

It is also possible to split these expressions before and after the verb, but they definitely cannot be used as a whole expression after the verb. However, when *aún* is placed after the verb, it becomes a synonym of *todavía* (*yet*) and must carry an accent mark:

*Él **ni** lo sabe **siquiera**.*	He doesn't even know it.
*Juan **ni** lo ha leído **aún**.*	Juan has not even read it.

(4) *Ya* is translated into English as *already* when the verb is affirmative:

*Nosotros **ya** fuimos allá.*	We already went there.
***Ya** lo habría visto.*	I would have already seen it.
*Lo he visto **ya**.*	I have already seen it.
*Ellos se mudaron **ya**.*	They have moved already.

Notice that *ya* is not placed between *haber* and the past participle in the perfect tenses (as in the second and third sentences). However, in the progressive forms, it may be placed before or after the auxiliary verb, after the present participle, or at the end of the sentence:

*Ella **ya** está diciéndoselo a todo el mundo.*	She is already saying it to everybody.
*Ella está **ya** diciéndoselo a todo el mundo.*	
*Ella está diciéndoselo **ya** a todo el mundo.*	
*Ella está diciéndoselo a todo el mundo **ya**.*	

(5) With a negative verb, *ya* takes the meaning of *no longer* or *not anymore* in English. It may also be used with *más*, for emphasis:

***Ya** no lo veo (más) por aquí.*	I no longer see him around here.
***Ya** no vamos (más) allá.*	We don't go there anymore.
*No se acordaba **ya** de eso.*	She didn't remember that any longer (anymore).
***Ya** no lo había visto más por el barrio cuando me mudé.*	I had no longer seen him around the neighborhood when I moved out.

(6) *Nunca* and *jamás* mean *never* and are considered indefinite adverbs. They may be used together for emphasis as *nunca jamás*, which is equivalent to *never ever*. Observe the use of *nunca más* in the third sentence:

***Nunca jamás** volvió a casa.*	He never ever came back home.
*No lo dijo **nunca jamás**.*	She never ever said it.
*No lo dijo **nunca más**.*	She no longer said it.

However, a combination of *jamás* (*ya más*) and *más* does not exist in Spanish.

3. Adverbs of manner (*adverbios de modo*)

These adverbs answer the question *¿cómo?*

bien, mal, mejor, peor, alto, bajo, rápido, lento, suavemente

4. Adverbs of quantity (*adverbios de cantidad*)

   These adverbs answer the question *¿cuánto?*

   mucho, poco, más, menos, muy, demasiado

5. Sequencing adverbs (*adverbios de orden*)

   These adverbs answer the question *¿antes o después?*

   primero, últimamente, luego, al final, antes, después

6. Affirmative adverbs (*adverbios de afirmación*)

   These adverbs answer the question *¿sí o no?* in the affirmative:

   sí, seguro, cierto, claro, también

7. Negative adverbs (*adverbios de negación*)

   These adverbs answer the question *¿sí o no?* in the negative:

   no, ni, jamás, nunca, tampoco, nunca jamás

8. Adverbs of doubt (*adverbios de duda*)

   These adverbs answer the question *¿sí o no?* with doubt:

   quizás, probablemente, tal vez, posiblemente

B. Adverbs classified according to their formation:

Adverbs are classified into simple and compound, according to whether they are formed by one or more words. Examples follow:

1. Simple adverbs:

   hoy (today)   *así* (this way)   *bien* (well)

2. Compound adverbs:

   anteanoche (the night   *cuando quiera* (whenever)   *también* (also)
   before last)

Adverbs are also classified into primitive and derivative, depending on whether they derive from another word or not.

1. Primitive adverbs:

   bajo (low)   *tarde* (late)   *lejos* (far)

2. Derivative adverbs:

   bajito (low)   *tardísimo* (very late)   *felizmente* (happily)

   NOTES:

   (1) Adverbs may be expressed with a diminutive or a superlative form:

cerca	*Su casa está **cerquita**.*	Her house is close.
poco	*Compré **poquísimo**.*	I bought very little.
bajo	*Habló **bajísimo**.*	He spoke in a low voice.
mucho	*Estudié **muchísimo**.*	I studied very much.

   The forms *cerquísima*, from *cerca* (*near*), and *lejísimos*, from *lejos* (*far*), are used within a familiar setting. It is also very common to hear the word *lejísimo* without the final *s* to refer to something that is far away.

   (2) An accent mark must be placed on an adverb to make a distinction between the adverb and another part of the sentence:

*El habló **más** esa noche.*	He spoke more that night.
*El habló, **mas** esa noche estaba cansado.*	He spoke, although that night he was tired.
*María dijo que **sí**.*	María said yes.
*María dijo que **si** viene lo traerá.*	María said that if she comes, she will bring it.

   (3) The adverbs *tanto* (*much, so*) and *cuanto* (*how*) are shortened to *tan* and *cuán* respectively before adjectives or another adverb. Note that *cuán* takes an accent mark. The adjectives *mejor* and *peor*, however, take the complete form *tanto:*

*Es **tan** bonita que ganó el contrato enseguida.*	She is so beautiful that she got the contract right away.
*Nunca cantó **tan** bien como hoy.*	He never sang as well as today.
*Siempre recuerdo **cuán*** bueno era su padre.*	I always remember how good his father was.
*Se notó **cuán*** sencillamente aceptó el premio.*	It was noticeable how humbly she received the award.

---

* In spoken Spanish, *cuán* is replaced by *qué*.

*Si no quiere venir, **tanto** mejor (peor).*	If he doesn't want to come, so much the better (worse).

(4) The neuter article *lo* placed before an adverb is equivalent to *how* plus an adverb in English:

*Mencionaron **lo pronto** que respondió al llamado.*	They mentioned how soon he responded to the call.

D. Adverbs ending in *-mente* (*-ly* in English)

These are mostly adverbs of manner that derive from adjectives. The suffix *-mente* can be added to the following types of adjectives.

1. *-mente* can be added to the feminine form of many adjectives, including some past participles used as adjectives:

blando	➤	*blanda*	➤	*blanda**mente***	softly
tierno	➤	*tierna*	➤	*tierna**mente***	tenderly
acertado	➤	*acertada*	➤	*acerta**damente***	wisely

2. *-mente* can be added to an adjective that ends in *-e*:

breve	➤	*breve**mente***	briefly
suave	➤	*suave**mente***	softly

3. *-mente* can be added to an adjective that ends in a consonant:

fácil	➤	*fácil**mente***	easily
cortés	➤	*cortés**mente***	politely

Uses of Adverbs

A. An adjective or adverbial phrase used instead of an adverb

In some instances, an adjective or an adverbial phrase is used in Spanish instead of an adverb. An adverbial phrase is a noun preceded by *con,* as in *con generosidad,* or an adjective preceded by the phrase *de una manera/de un modo*:

La miró <u>triste</u> y después se fue.	
La miró <u>con tristeza</u> y después se fue.	
La miró <u>de una manera triste</u> y después se fue.	He looked at her sadly and then he left.

Laura lo esperó <u>ansiosa</u> para saber el resultado.

Laura lo esperó <u>con ansiedad</u> para saber el resultado.

Laura lo esperó <u>de un modo ansioso</u> para saber el resultado.

Laura waited for him anxiously to find out the result.

Lo hicieron <u>rápido</u>.

Lo hicieron <u>con rapidez</u>.

Lo hicieron <u>de un modo rápido</u> y eficiente.

<u>Literally</u>: They did it in a rapid and efficient manner. (fast and efficiently).

B. Accents on adverbs

If the adjective carries a written accent, the accent is maintained in the resulting adverb:

débil ➤ *débilmente*   weakly

C. A past participle used as an adjective may also function as an adverb:

Llegó preocupado.   He was worried when he arrived.

D. When two adverbs modify the same verb

If two adverbs ending in *-mente* modify the same verb, and the adverbs are joined by a conjunction, the suffix *-mente* only appears on the second one. This is usually seen in the written form. In spoken Spanish, the form *con* plus an adjective is more commonly used:

*El hombre se expresó sabia y clara**mente**.*

*El hombre se expresó **con sabiduría** y (con) **claridad**.*

The man expressed himself wisely and clearly.

E. When more than two adverbs modify the same verb

If more than two adverbs are used with the same verb, the last adverb in the series is the only one that may end in *-mente*. The other adverbs use the feminine form of the adjective. Of the two examples that follow, the second sentence is considered better style:

> *El hombre se expresó clara, sabia y elocuente**mente**.*

> *El hombre se expresó **con** claridad, sabiduría*   The man expressed himself clearly, wisely, and
>   *y elocuencia.*   eloquently.

F. When multiple adverbs are separated by a comma

It is also common practice in literary works to use the suffix *-mente* in more than one adverb when they are separated by a comma:

> *Después de oírlo, él salió lenta**mente**,*   After hearing it, he left slowly, secretly.
>   *sigilosa**mente**.*

G. When each adverb modifies a different verb

When each adverb modifies a different verb, repetition of the suffix *-mente* must be avoided:

> *La dama se sentó **con** elegancia y escribió*
>   *lenta**mente**.*

> *La dama se sentó elegante**mente** y escribió*   The lady sat down elegantly and wrote slowly.
>   *despacio.*

H. Adverbs that modify verbs in the perfect and progressive tenses

1. Adverbs that modify verbs in the perfect tenses

Adverbs that end in *-mente* cannot be placed between an auxiliary and the main verb in the perfect tenses:

> *Ellas lo han dicho sincera**mente** y van a*   They have sincerely said it, and are going
>   *hacerlo.*   to do it.

2. Adverbs that modify verbs in the progressive tenses

However, adverbs ending in *-mente* may be used between the auxiliary and the main verb in progressive tenses, especially in literary style:

> *Juana iba silenciosa**mente** caminando*   Juana was silently walking towards the river.
>   *hacia el río.*

Notice the following example, where the phrase *en silencio* is used instead of *silenciosamente*, in a very delicate style:

Juana iba <u>en silencio</u> caminando hacia el río.

▪ I. Adverbs for numbers and sequencing

The only ordinal numbers that end in *-mente* are *primeramente* (*first, firstly*) and *últimamente* (*last, lastly*). In all other cases, phrases such as *en segundo lugar* and *en tercer lugar* are used; the phrases *en primer lugar* and *en último lugar* are possible for *first* and *last*, as well. *First* and *last* can also be expressed as *primero* and *por último*, respectively:

***Primeramente** tenemos que hacer una lista.*	
***En primer lugar** tenemos que hacer una lista.*	
***Primero** tenemos que hacer una lista.*	First (Firstly), we have to make a list.

The adverb *últimamente* is generally used as a synonym of *lately* or *recently*:

***Últimamente** no se han oído más rumores.*	We haven't heard any more rumors lately.
*Ha habido algunos accidentes **últimamente**.*	There have been some accidents recently.

To indicate something that happens *last in a sequence*, *por último* is used instead:

***Por último**, debes darle la fecha de salida.*	Finally, you must give him the date of departure.

Notice the uses of *al fin*, *por fin*, *finalmente* (*finally, at last*), and *al final* (*at the end*), in the following examples:

*¡**Al fin** (¡**Por fin**) llegaron los invitados!*	
*¡**Finalmente** llegaron los invitados!*	Finally the guests arrived!
***Al final** todos se fueron contentos.*	At the end, everybody left happy.

> NOTE:
> *Al final* also has the connotation of *after all*, as in this sentence:
>
> | | |
> |---|---|
> | ***Al final**, después de tanto quejarse ella vino también.* | She came too, after all, in spite of all that complaining. |

Position of Adverbs

A. Adverbs usually follow the verbs they modify:

*El viejo camina **despacio**.*   The old man walks slowly.

B. If formed by a combination of words, adverbs may be placed before or after the word or words they modify:

*Lo abrió **con todo cuidado**.*   She opened it carefully.
***Con todo cuidado** lo abrió.*

C. Adverbs usually precede an adjective or another adverb:

*El hombre es **muy** viejo.*   The man is very old.
*El viejo camina **bastante** despacio.*   The old man walks rather slowly.

NOTES:

(1) *Muy* (*very*), a short form of *mucho* (*much*), is used before some adverbs and adjectives:

muy grande	very large
muy bien	very well
muy bueno	very good
muy generosamente	very generously
muy violentamente	very violently
mucho mejor	a lot (or much) better
mucho peor	a lot (or much) worse
mucho menos	a lot (or much) less
mucho más	a lot (or much) more
mucho mayor	a lot (or much) older
mucho menor	a lot (or much) younger

(2) *Bien* is used instead of *muy* to indicate emphasis:

*Está **bien** interesante esta película.*   This film is very interesting.
*Llegó **bien** temprano ayer.*   She came very early yesterday.

(3) The complete form *mucho* (or the superlative *muchísimo*) is used when the modified word is not stated in the sentence:

*Elena está **muy** <u>nerviosa</u> ¿no?*	Elena is very nervous, don't you think?
*Sí, **mucho** (**muchísimo**).*	Yes, very much (so).

(4) The expression *Muy señor mío* (the equivalent of *Dear Sir*) is used as a polite form for addressing a letter.

(5) In some regions, *muy* is sometimes used before *sin* (*without*) when this preposition is part of an adjectival or adverbial expression:

*No me gusta ese traje. Es **muy sin** gracia.*	I don't like that outfit. It's not appealing (graceful).
*Lo hizo **muy sin** interés.*	He did it without much interest.

Adverbial Complements

Several parts of the sentence may function as adverbial complements:

A verb as adverbial complement

después de <u>comer</u>	*antes de <u>salir</u>*
(after eating)	(before going out)

An adverb as adverbial complement

muy <u>poco</u>	*demasiado <u>bien</u>*
(very little)	(well enough)

A noun as adverbial complement

cerca del <u>patio</u>	*atrás del <u>libro</u>*
(near the patio)	(behind the book)

A pronoun as adverbial complement

atrás del <u>mío</u>	*dentro de <u>sí</u>*
(behind mine)	(inside himself)

A sentence as adverbial complement

Ahora que <u>ella vino.</u>	*Después que <u>Ud. lo lea</u>.*
(Now that she has come.)	(After you read it.)

Adverbial Phrases

Adverbial phrases (*frases* or *modos adverbiales*) are groups of two or more words that function as adverbs. Here are some examples:

de vez en cuando	every once in a while
sin más ni menos	without any to-do
de repente	suddenly
a ciegas	blindly
más adelante	further on
a más y mejor	greatly
a lo mejor	maybe
cuanto antes	as soon as possible
por poco	almost
antes que cante el gallo	very early
más viejo que Matusalén	very old
más largo que esperanza de pobre	very long
a paso de tortuga	very slowly
como quien no quiere la cosa	on the sly
donde el diablo perdió el poncho	very far
como escupida de músico	very fast

Functions of Adverbs

Adverbs may perform different functions in the sentence.

A. Adverbs can function as nouns:

Nunca es un término que no existe en su vocabulario.

Never is a term that doesn't exist in her vocabulary.

B. Adverbs can function as adjectives:

Quiere mucha atención.

She wants a lot of attention.

C. Adverbs can function as pronouns:

No gana mucho (dinero, sueldo).

He doesn't make much (money).

D. Adverbs can function as interjections:

¡Abajo! (Down!)   *¡Bien!* (Well done!)   *¡Adentro!* (Go inside!)

E. Adverbs can function as relative pronouns:

donde:	*Esa es el aula **donde (en la que)** cursé el primer grado.*	That is the classroom where I attend first grade.
como:	*Lo hice **como (de la manera en que)** Ud. me lo indicó.*	I did it as (the way) you showed me.
cuando:	*Esa era la hora **cuando (en que)** llegó.*	That was the time when he arrived.

Comparative and Superlative Forms

Adverbs modify verbs and other adverbs to intensify or diminish their intrinsic qualities. In English, in some cases, adverbs are used by themselves; in other cases, they are followed by *than*. They also help to compare adjectives and nouns (see Chapter 4, Adjectives). Some examples are:

He ate less than Peter.
He ate more slowly than Peter.
I studied a lot.
She sang very nicely.

In Spanish, too, as we have seen, adverbs can be made up of only one word, but they can also appear as an adverbial phrase:

*Él comió **menos que** Pedro.*
*Él comió **más despacio que** Pedro.*
*Yo estudié **mucho**.*
*Ella cantó **muy bien**.*

Comparison of Inequality Involving Verbs

In Spanish, the action indicated by a verb can be moved to a higher or a lower degree of intensity by inserting *más que* or *menos que* right after the verb:

*El perro come **más que** el gato.*	The dog eats more than the cat.
*El secretario viaja **menos que** el jefe.*	The secretary travels less than his boss.

The meanings of the previous sentences shown can be expressed in different ways, as follows.

(1) The meaning stays the same when the order of each sentence is inverted and the comparative expression is changed:

*El gato come **menos que** el perro.*	The cat eats less than the dog.
*El jefe viaja **más que** el secretario.*	The boss travels more than his secretary.

(2) The meaning stays the same when the sentences are expressed in the negative, using the formula *no* + verb + *tanto como*:

*El gato **no** come **tanto como** el perro.*	The cat doesn't eat as much as the dog.
*El secretario **no** viaja **tanto como** el jefe.*	The secretary doesn't travel as much as his boss.

Comparison Involving Numbers

When the comparison involves a number, the preposition *de* follows *más* or *menos*:

*Compraré **más de** <u>dos</u> paquetes.*	I will buy more than two packages.
*Tienen **menos de** <u>ocho</u> vuelos semanales al Uruguay.*	They have fewer than eight flights a week to Uruguay.

Comparison of Equality Involving Verbs

The intrinsic value of a verb which affects more than one subject in the sentence can be equally compared by inserting the adverbial expression *tanto como* right after the verb:

*Este departamento trabaja **tanto como** el de finanzas.*	This department works as hard as the finance department.
*En Puerto Rico llueve **tanto como** en Florida.*	In Puerto Rico it rains as much as in Florida.

NOTES:

(1) The meaning stays the same even when the word order is inverted:

*El de finanzas trabaja **tanto como** este departamento.*	The finance department works as hard as this one.
*En Florida llueve **tanto como** en Puerto Rico.*	In Florida it rains as much as in Puerto Rico.

(2) To negate these sentences, the word *no* is placed in front of the verb, in which case the sentence becomes a comparison of inequality:

*El de finanzas **no** trabaja **tanto como** este departamento.*	The finance department doesn't work as hard as this one.
*En Florida **no** llueve **tanto como** en Puerto Rico.*	In Florida it doesn't rain as much as in Puerto Rico.

Comparison of Inequality Involving Other Adverbs

Adverbs are placed in front of other adverbs to intensify or diminish their inherent value. In Spanish, adverbs and adverbial forms such as *más, menos, mucho más, mucho menos, un poco más, un poco menos, casi tan*, and others, are generally placed before another adverb for this purpose:

*La directora habló **más** claro que la maestra de segundo grado.*	The principal spoke more clearly than the second grade teacher.
*La entrevista fue hecha **menos eficientemente** que la conferencia.*	The interview was conducted less efficiently than the conference.
*El funcionario presentó el problema **mucho más abiertamente** que su superior.*	The official presented the problem much more openly than his superior.
*La chica escribió **un poco más detalladamente** que su novio.*	The girl wrote in a little more detail than her boyfriend.
*Mi amiga lo hizo **casi tan bien como** tú.*	My friend did it almost as well as you.
*Pedro lo sugirió **un poco menos agresivamente** que el entrenador.*	Pedro suggested it a little less forcefully than the coach.

NOTES:

The meanings of the sentences previously shown can be expressed in different ways, as follows.

(1) The meaning stays the same when the order of each sentence is inverted and the comparative expression is changed:

*La maestra de segundo grado habló **menos claro** que la directora.*	The second grade teacher spoke less clearly than the principal.
*El entrenador lo sugirió **un poco más agresivamente** que Pedro.*	The coach suggested it a little more forcefully than Pedro.

(2) The meaning stays the same when the sentences are expressed in the negative, using the formula *no* + verb + *tan* + adverb + *como*:

| La maestra de segundo grado **no** hablÃ³ **tan** <u>claro</u> **como** la directora. | The second grade teacher did not speak as clearly as the principal. |
| Pedro **no** lo <u>sugiriÃ³</u> **tan** <u>agresivamente</u> **como** el entrenador. | Pedro did not suggest it as forcefully as the coach. |

Comparison of Equality Involving Other Adverbs

Another way to express that a verb's function is performed equally by more than one subject in the sentence, insert the formula *tan* + adverb + *como* right after the verb.

| La bailarina baila **tan delicadamente como** su acompaÃ±ante. | The ballerina dances as delicately as her companion. |
| Luisa reza **tan piadosamente como** sus hermanas. | Luisa prays as piously as her sisters. |

NOTES:

(1) The meaning of the sentences previously shown stays the same even when the order of each sentence is inverted:

| Su acompaÃ±ante baila **tan delicadamente como** la bailarina. | Her companion dances as delicately as the ballerina. |
| Sus hermanas rezan **tan piadosamente como** Luisa. | Her sisters pray as piously as Luisa. |

(2) To negate these sentences, the word *no* is placed in front of the verb, in which case the sentence becomes a comparison of inequality:

| Su acompaÃ±ante **no** baila **tan delicadamente como** la bailarina. | Her companion does not dance as delicately as the ballerina. |
| Sus hermanas **no** rezan **tan piadosamente como** Luisa. | Her sisters do not pray as piously as Luisa. |

Superlatives

The superlative forms of adverbs are generally formed with expressions such as *sumamente* (*exceedingly*), *extremadamente* (*extremely*), *inmensamente* (*immensely*), *mÃ¡s* (*most*), *menos* (*least*), *muy* (*very*), and a few that end in -Ãsimo, among others:

| NicolÃ¡s toca el piano **sumamente bien**. | NicolÃ¡s plays the piano exceedingly well. |
| Ella debe estudiar mÃ¡s. Sabe **poquÃsimo**. | She has to study more. She knows very, very little. |

*La casa queda **lejísimos**.*	The house is far, far away.
*Cuanto **menos** tiene Juan, más feliz se siente.*	The less Juan has, the happier he feels.
*Teresa hace lo **más que** puede para satisfacer a su familia.*	Teresa does the most she can to satisfy her family.
*Felipe iba manejando **extremadamente rápido** cuando chocó el auto.*	Felipe was driving extremely fast when he wrecked his car.
*José terminó el trabajo **muy ingeniosamente**.*	José finished the job very cleverly.
*Los saludé **muy atentamente**.*	I sent my regards very sincerely.

19

Conjunctions

Conjunctions are words or phrases that join different parts of a sentence. Simple conjunctions (*conjunciones simples*) are formed by one word (such as *pero*); compound conjunctions (*conjunciones compuestas*) are a combination of two words together (such as *aunque, siquiera*); and conjunctive phrases have two or more words (*si bien, con tal de que*).

Conjunctions are classified according to their function, into coordinating and subordinating conjunctions. Each one of these groups is divided into subgroups. Simple and compound conjunctions and conjunctive phrases can fall into any of these groups and subgroups.

Coordinating Conjunctions

These conjunctions link independent parts of the sentence. They are divided into five subgroups. Examples are provided for each conjunction.

A. Adversative conjunctions (*adversativas*) indicate an opposition:

a pesar de (que)	in spite of
ahora	however; but; now
antes	rather
antes bien	on the contrary; rather
aun cuando	even if; notwithstanding
*Iba a venir; **ahora**, ni vino ni llamó.*	He was going to come; however, he neither came nor called.
*Tiene buena salud **a pesar de** su edad.*	He is in good health in spite of his age.
*No es fácil; **antes (bien)**, lleva mucho tiempo.*	It is not easy; rather, it takes a long time.
*No lo haré **aun cuando** tú lo digas.*	I won't do it, even if you say so.
aunque	although; even if
bien que	although

mas	but
ni siquiera	not even
*No saldré **aunque** vengas.*	I won't go out even if you come along.
*No lo creo, **bien que** lo haya dicho.*	I don't believe it, although she has said it.
*No le gusta, **mas** lo hará.*	He doesn't like it, but he'll do it.
*No vino nadie, **ni siquiera** tu hermano.*	No one came, not even your brother.

pero	but; yet
por más que	even if
si bien	although
*No vino, **pero** llamó.*	He didn't come, but he called.
*No me gusta el jamón, **pero** lo como igual.*	I don't like ham, but I eat it just the same.
*No lo usaré, **por más que** me lo regale.*	I won't wear it, even if he gives it to me.
*No es posible, **si bien** lo hayas sugerido.*	It's not possible, although you have suggested it.

sino	but (rather)
siquiera	even if
*No quiero el vestido **sino** la falda.*	I don't want the dress, but rather the skirt.
*Dile esto, **siquiera** no le digas nada más.*	Tell her this, even if you don't tell her anything else.

B. Continuative conjunctions *(continuativas)* provide a continuation of the discourse:

ahora bien	now then
ahora pues	now then
pues	so
***Ahora bien**, iremos todos.*	Now then, everybody will go.
***Ahora pues**, ¿qué comemos?*	Now then, what do we eat?
*Las compró, **pues**, las comeremos.*	He bought them, so we are going to eat them.

C. Copulative conjunctions *(copulativas)* join simple words or phrases:

y	and (used before a consonant and also before a word that begins with *hie*)
e	and (used before *i* or *hi*)
ni	neither; nor
que	that; than

Juan *y* Pedro	John and Peter
lana *y* hierro	wool and iron
notas *e* ilustraciones	notes and illustrations
aguja *e* hilo	needle and thread
Ni lo veo *ni* lo oigo.	I neither see him nor hear him.
No tengo *ni* pan *ni* vino.	I have neither bread nor wine.
Quiere *que* lo visite.	He wants me to visit him.

D. Disjunctive conjunctions (*disyuntivas* or *distributivas*) imply an exclusion or an alternative.

1. Exclusion:

o	or
u	or (used before *o* or *ho*)
o bien	or
Quiero un libro *o* una revista.	I want a book or a magazine.
O lo comes *o* lo guardo.	Either you eat it or I'll put it away.
leones *u* osos	lions or bears
mujeres *u* hombres	women or men
Iremos en auto *o bien* en autobús.	We'll go either by car or by bus.

2. Alternative:

ahora... ahora...	now . . . now . . .
ora... ora...	now . . . now . . .
bien... bien...	either . . . or . . .
que... que...	either . . . or . . .
ya... ya...	either . . . or . . .
Se pasa el tiempo, *ahora* leyendo, *ahora* trabajando.	He spends his time now reading, now working.
Vive *ora* en el campo, *ora* en la ciudad.	He lives now in the country, now in the city.
Trabaja, *bien* en la casa, *bien* en el jardín.	She works either in the house or in the garden.
Siempre se queja, *que* esto, *que* lo otro.	She always complains, either about this, or about something else.
Los domingos le gusta hacer algo, *ya* coser, *ya* cocinar.	On Sundays she likes to do something, either sewing or cooking.

E. Illative conjunctions (*ilativas*) show a consequence:

así que	so
conque	so; so then; now then
luego	therefore
por consiguiente	therefore
No me gusta, **así que** ya lo sabes.	I don't like it, so now you know.
La maestra lo sugirió, **conque** lo estudiarán.	The teacher suggested it, so they will study it.
Se lo pedimos, **luego** lo hizo.	We asked him; therefore, he did it.
El jefe lo dijo, **por consiguiente** todos fueron.	The boss said so; therefore, everybody went.
por lo tanto	therefore
por tanto	therefore
pues	so
que	so
Nos gusta viajar, **por lo tanto** iremos a Europa.	We like to travel, therefore we'll go to Europe.
No ahorró, **por tanto** se quedó pobre.	He didn't save, therefore he became poor.
No trabajó, **pues**, se quedó sin nada.	He didn't work, so he was left with nothing.
Ponlo ahí, **que** lo veamos.	Put it over there, so that we can see it.

Subordinating Conjunctions

These conjunctions join a dependent clause to the main clause. There are six sub-groups. Examples are provided for each conjunction.

A. Causal conjunctions (*causales*) point to a reason or cause:

como que	because
cuando	since; although
porque	because
Los tengo, **como que** los compré.	I have them, because I bought them.
Cuando tú lo recomiendas debe ser bueno.	Since you recommend it, it must be good.
Aun **cuando** no lo hiciera por él, lo haría por ti.	Although I wouldn't do it for him, I would do it for you.
No te lo repito **porque** ya lo sabes.	I do not repeat it because you already know it.
pues	because; since
pues que	since

puesto que	although; since
que	because; that
*Lo compré **pues** era lindo.*	I bought it because it was pretty.
*No probamos el pastel, **pues que** no lo trajo.*	We didn't taste the pie, since he didn't bring it.
***Puesto que** estudié los verbos, ahora los sé.*	Since I studied the verbs, now I know them.
***Que** es muy habilidoso, todos lo saben.*	Everybody knows that he is very skillful.

supuesto que	since; supposing that
una vez que	since; inasmuch as
*Vamos a ir con ellos, **supuesto que** han llegado.*	We'll go with them, supposing that they have arrived.
*Va a cumplir su promesa **una vez que** lo ha dicho.*	She will fulfill her promise since she has said it.

B. Comparative conjunctions (*comparativas*) show a comparison:

a modo de	like; as
así como	just as
como	as; like
igual que	as; the same as; like
más que	although; even if
*Se puso el pañuelo **a modo de** un cinturón.*	She put the scarf on like a belt.
*Escribe el inglés **así como** lo habla.*	He writes English just as he speaks it.
*Roscoe se porta **como** un niño.*	Roscoe behaves like a child.
*Habla **igual que** un viejo.*	He speaks like an old man.
*No iremos al cine **más que** tú insistas.*	We won't go to the movies even if you insist.

C. Conditional conjunctions (*condicionales*) establish a condition:

como	if
con tal que	provided
cuando	when
dado que	provided; as long as
***Como** no estudies, no aprenderás nada.*	If you don't study, you will not learn anything.
*Ahorraré el dinero **con tal que** tenga suficiente para gastos diarios.*	I'll save the money, provided I have some left over for daily expenses.
*Te daré las llaves **cuando** me las pidas.*	I'll give you the keys when you ask me for them.
***Dado que** él lo dice, lo creeré.*	As long as he says it, I'll believe it.

o bien	otherwise
si	if
si no	otherwise
siempre que	provided
ya que	since

Préstame el libro, **o bien** no te ayudaré.	Lend me the book, otherwise I will not help you.
Comeremos allí **si** tú quieres.	We'll eat there if you like.
No voy a darle la noticia, **si no** se pondrá triste.	I won't give her the news, otherwise she will be sad.
Estaremos listos, **siempre que** lo tengamos que hacer.	We'll be ready, provided we have to do it.
Lo hice **ya que** me lo pediste.	I did it since you asked me.

D. Conclusive conjunctions (*finales*) point to a purpose:

a fin de que	so that
a que	so that
con objeto de que	in order to
para que	in order that; so that

Voy a estudiar **a fin de que** pueda trabajar allí.	I'm going to study so that I can work there.
Vino **a que** se lo reparara.	He came so that I would repair it for him.
Mandó una carta **con objeto de** solicitar trabajo.	He sent a letter in order to apply for a job.
Trajo a su novio **para que** fuera con nosotros.	She brought her boyfriend so that he could come with us.

E. Modal conjunctions (*modales*) indicate a way or manner:

así como	just as
como	as
como si	as if
conforme a	according to; consistent with

Lo haremos **así como** ellos sugieren.	We'll do it just as they suggest.
Será **como** Ud. quiera.	It will be as you want.
Actúa **como si** estuviera cansado.	He behaves as if he were tired.
Lo hizo **conforme a** las especificaciones.	She did it according to specifications.

de manera que	so as to; so that
de modo que	so that

según	according to
según que	as
sin que	without
Lo pondremos aquí **de manera que** lo vean.	We'll put it here so that they will see it.
Vamos a explicarlo, **de modo que** todos lo sepan.	We are going to explain it so that everybody will know it.
Según Pedro, lloverá.	According to Pedro, it will rain.
Voy a responder **según que** vaya recibiendo noticias.	I'll respond as I start receiving the news.
Me lo dio **sin que** se lo pidiera.	He gave it to me without my asking for it.

F. Temporal conjunctions (*temporales*) show a time limit:

apenas	as soon as
así que	as soon as; after
como	as soon as
cuando	when
Hablamos **apenas** vino.	We spoke as soon as he came.
Se fue a dormir **así que** se fueron los huéspedes.	She went to sleep as soon as the guests were gone.
Como su padre llegó, se pusieron a jugar.	They started playing as soon as their father arrived.
Hazlo **cuando** quieras.	Do it whenever you want.

cuanto antes	as soon as possible
en cuanto	as soon as
luego que	after; as soon as
mientras	while
Hazlo **cuanto antes**.	Do it as soon as possible.
Dámelo **en cuanto** esté listo.	Give it to me as soon as it's ready.
Lo haré **luego que** lo aprueben.	I'll do it as soon as they approve it.
Puedo vivir así **mientras** se queden conmigo.	I can live like this while they stay with me.

no bien	as soon as
siempre que	whenever; provided
tan luego	as soon as
Te llamaré **no bien** termine el trabajo.	I'll call you as soon as I finish the job.
Iremos todos **siempre que** vuelvas temprano.	All of us will go provided you come back early.
Saldremos de compras **tan luego** me den el cheque.	We'll go shopping as soon as they give me the check.

NOTES:

(1) Many adverbs and adverbial phrases function as conjunctions.

(2) One conjunction may belong to different subgroups.

(3) *Que* is both a relative pronoun and a conjunction. If it can be replaced by *which*, it is a relative pronoun.

(4) There is another use of *tan luego*, as in the following sentence: *¡Tan luego a mí me lo dice!* In this case, the expression has an ironic connotation, meaning: *And to me she says that!*

20

Interjections

Interjections (*interjecciones*) are expressions of feelings that a speaker produces suddenly. *"Hey!" "Aha!" "Oh!"* and *"Come on!"* are some of the most common interjections used by English speakers. In Spanish, interjections are enclosed in exclamation points, one at the beginning and one at the end of the word or expression, just like all other exclamations in this language.

Categories of Interjections

A. **Interjections classified according to their form**

There are five subdivisions. Several examples are provided for each category.

1. Proper interjections (*propias*)

These are words that have no other function in the sentence but the sudden expression of feelings:

¡Ah!   ¡Ay!   ¡Bah!   ¡Oh!   ¡Uf!   ¡Upa!   ¡Zape!

2. Improper interjections (*impropias*)

These interjections include nouns, adjectives, verbs, and other expressions that are used as interjections:

¡Caracoles!	¡Bueno!	¡Viva!
¡Hola!	¡Dale!	¡Qué macana!

3. Single interjections (*simples*)

These are one-word expressions:

¡Ea!   ¡Anda!   ¡Vale!   ¡Puf!

4. Double interjections (*dobles*)

These are expressions consisting of a repeated word:

¡Hurra! ¡Hurra!   ¡Bien! ¡Bien!   ¡Uy! ¡Uy!   ¡Vamos! ¡Vamos!

5. Exclamative expressions (*modos interjectivos*)

These are two or more words that function as interjections:

¡Madre mía!	¡Válgame Dios!	¡Qué desastre!
¡Ay de mí!	¡Ojalá que sí!	¡Vaya sorpresa!

B. Interjections classified according to the feelings denoted

Some of the most common proper and improper interjections, which vary regionally in the Hispanic world, belong to groups such as the following:

1. Pain:

¡Ay!   ¡Ah!   ¡Uy!   ¡Aya!   ¡Ayayay!

2. Happiness:

¡Ay!   ¡Aleluya!

3. Surprise:

¡Ay!   ¡Ah!   ¡Epa!   ¡Guay!   ¡Uy!   ¡Oh!

4. Admiration:

¡Ah!   ¡Pardiez!   ¡Ha!   ¡Ay!   ¡Ayayay!

5. Cheering:

¡Arre!   ¡Ea!   ¡Upa!   ¡Sus!   ¡Ce!   ¡Vamos!   ¡Olé!

6. Attention:

¡Ea!   ¡Mira!   ¡So!   ¡Ta!   ¡To!   ¡Aquí!

7. Approval:

¡Ajá!   ¡Bis!   ¡Bravo!   ¡Viva!   ¡Arriba!   ¡Amén!   ¡Olé!

8. Bother:

¡Quiá!   *¡Rayos!*   *¡Uf!*   *¡Za!*   *¡Zape!*   *¡Fuera!*

9. Disapproval:

¡Abajo!   *¡Ca!*   *¡Dale!*   *¡Fuera!*

Accents

Depending on how the syllables of a word are emphasized when the word is pronounced, a syllable in Spanish is considered either accented (*tónica* or *acentuada*), when the stress falls on that particular syllable, or else unaccented (*átona* or *inacentuada*), when the stress does not fall on that syllable.

The stress may appear in a word in four different ways.

A. Stress on the last syllable, in which case the word is called *aguda*:

canción, compás, café, barril, feliz

B. Stress on the next-to-last syllable, in which case the word is called *grave* or *llana*:

lápiz, come, lunes, fácil, mártir

C. Stress on the third-to-last syllable, in which case the word is called *esdrújula*:

exámenes, cálido, próxima, geográfico, matemáticas

D. Stress on later syllables, in which case the word is called *sobresdrújula*:

perdóneselo, cántemelas, constrúyanoslo, repítaselos, devotísimamente

NOTES:

(1) All words in the preceding third and fourth categories (C., *esdrújulas*, and D., *sobresdrújulas*) carry an accent mark on the stressed syllable.

(2) Monosyllabic words do not carry accent marks unless they are homonyms needing clarification. See examples in the section headed Monosyllables, at the end of Appendix A.

Rules

The following rules determine whether to place a written accent mark on the stressed syllable of words in each category previously mentioned.

A. Words with stress on the last syllable (*agudas*)

All words in this category that end in *n*, *s*, or in any vowel (*a, e, i, o, u*) carry an accent mark:

> *latón, gruñón, París, salís, bebé, mamá, alelí*

If the word ends in any other consonant, no written accent mark is needed:

> *barril, cantad, feliz, alud, amor.*

> **NOTES:**
>
> **(1)** If the *s* at the end of a word is preceded by a consonant, no written accent mark is needed:
>
> *tictacs, mamuts, robots*
>
> **(2)** The letter *y* is considered a vowel when it sounds like *i* and appears at the end of a word such as:
>
> *ley* and *carey* (diphthongs)
> *Paraguay, Uruguay, buey* (triphthongs)
>
> These words do not have written accent marks.

B. Words with stress on the next-to-last syllable (*graves* or *llanas*)

All words in this category that <u>do not</u> end in the letters *n*, *s*, or a vowel carry an accent mark:

> *difícil, frágil, Ramírez, revólver, carácter, ultimátum*

> **NOTE:**
>
> If a word in this category ends in *n*, *s*, or a vowel, no accent mark is needed, as in:
>
> *examen, joven, martes, saltas, rosa, corre*
>
> This rule is the inverse of rule A.

C. Words with stress on the third-to-last syllable (*esdrújulas*)

All words in this category carry an accent mark, regardless of their final letter:

sílaba, mayúscula, minúscula, físico, Nápoles, mínimo, bellísima

D. Words with stress on earlier syllables (*sobresdrújulas*)

All words in this category carry an accent mark, regardless of their final letter. Many of the words in this category are verbal forms to which pronouns have been added:

cómetelo, termínaselas, recíclanoslos, dibújatelas.

Other words are adverbs formed by the addition of the suffix *-mente* (*-ly* in English) to adjectives that already carry an accent mark, as in:

fácilmente, esporádicamente, entusiásticamente

E. When a word is modified

When the base form of a word is modified in any way, each different modified form takes accent marks according to the rules that apply to that particular modified form:

Él da.	He gives.	(monosyllable, no accent)
Dame.	Give me.	(rule B)
Dámelo.	Give it to me.	(rule C)
Dándomelo.	Giving it to me.	(rule D)
canción	song	(rule A)
canciones	songs	(rule B)
examen	exam	(rule B)
exámenes	exams	(rule C)

F. Capital letters

Every letter that carries an accent mark shows the accent, even if the letter is capitalized:

Él escribió una carta.
LOS ARTÍCULOS
BENITO PÉREZ GALDÓS
ÁREAS INHÓSPITAS DE LA PATAGONIA
JOSÉ MARTÍNEZ RUIZ (AZORÍN)

G. Interrogative and exclamatory words

All interrogative and exclamatory words carry accent marks, as in the following examples:

> *¿Cuál?, ¿Qué?, ¿Cuántos?, ¿Quiénes?, ¿Dónde?, ¿Cómo?*
> *¡Cuántos!, ¡Quién será!, ¡Dónde lo puso!, ¡Qué sorpresa!*

H. Compound words

Compound words are words formed by two or more words. The accent mark is placed only on the last word, and only if an accent mark is necessary according to the preceding rules. Some examples are:

- *puntapié*: The word *pie* does not carry an accent mark, but as part of the compound word, it belongs to rule A.

- *asimismo*: The word *así* loses its accent mark to adjust to the newly formed word: rule B applies and there is no written accent mark.

- *decimoséptimo*: The word *décimo* loses its accent mark; the new word takes its accent mark according to rule C.

However, if the compound word includes a hyphen between the two words that constitute it, each word keeps its original accent, as in *económico-político*.

Diphthongs

The preceding rules also apply when the stressed syllable has a diphthong, which is a gliding combination of two vowels, either a strong vowel (*a, e, o*) followed by a weak one (*i, u*), or vice versa. Here are some examples of words that contain diphthongs, as well as some exceptions to the rules.

A. When the stress is on the last syllable

1. When a word in this category requires a written accent mark because it ends in *n*, *s*, or a vowel (preceding rule A), and the last syllable contains a diphthong, the accent is placed over the strong vowel (*a, e, o*)

   versión, exclamación, permitió, caráu, cantáis, bebéis

2. If the word ends in any other consonant, there is no accent mark:

   la*bial*, flu*vial*, de*sear*

3. Words like *vio*, *dio*, *fue*, *fui*, *pie*, and *fiel* are monosyllabic words and do not carry an accent mark. The word *infiel*, however, has two syllables, but does not have a written accent because it ends in a consonant other than *n* or *s*. *Dios* is also monosyllabic and carries no accent mark, but for *adiós*, which has two syllables, the last one carries an accent mark because it ends in *s*.

4. The words *ciudad* and *fluidez* each have a diphthong formed by two weak vowels. The diphthong is not affected by the stress, which falls on the last syllables, *dad* and *dez*, respectively. These words do not carry an accent mark because they follow rule A. Other examples are *enviudar* and *triunfar*.

5. If in a combination of a strong vowel and a weak one, the weak vowel is stressed, as in *maíz* or *baúl*, the accent mark falls on the weak vowel to preserve pronunciation and the diphthong disappears, becoming a hiatus (see the section Hiatuses that follows). Notice that now the word has become a two-syllable word.

6. The letter *h* between a strong vowel and a weak one does not destroy the diphthong, as in the word *rehusar*, when the diphthong is in the unaccented syllable. When the verb is conjugated, however, an accent mark is needed to preserve pronunciation: *rehúso*; in this case the accent falls on the next-to-last syllable. If the two vowels that appear next to each other are both strong, as in *rehén*, the diphthong disappears and the vowels are pronounced separately.

7. If the two vowels that appear next to each other are weak, as in *construí*, the stress falls on the second vowel. This word carries an accent mark because it follows rule A. However, *construimos* and *construido* have the stress on the second vowel, but no accent mark is required because the words follow rule B. Other words that obey the same rules are *huí* (rule A), and *huiste* (rule B).

B. When the stress is on the next-to-last syllable

1. If the stressed syllable contains a diphthong, the stress falls on the strong vowel: *peine*, *deuda*, *caigo*, *cuartos*, *caucho*.

   These words do not carry an accent mark because they agree with rule B. Some words with diphthongs that do need an accent mark according to the same rule are:

   huésped, káiser, béisbol

2. If, in a combination of a strong vowel and a weak one, the weak vowel is stressed, as in *oído*, the accent mark falls on the weak vowel and the diphthong disappears, becoming a hiatus. Other examples are *continúo*, *continúas*. However, *continuamos* does not carry an accent mark because the stress falls on the strong vowel and the word follows rule B.

3. The letter *h* between a strong vowel and a weak one destroys the diphthong when the stress falls on the diphthong. Examples are *búho* and *vahído*. Both words carry an accent mark on the weak vowel to preserve pronunciation. They are an exception to rule B. However, if two vowels that appear on either side of an *h* are both strong, as in *moho*, the word does not carry an accent mark because it follows rule B.

4. When two vowels that appear next to each other are both strong, there is no diphthong and the syllables are separated:

   lees, caen, paella, saeta

   None of these words are accented because they follow rule B.

5. When two vowels next to each other are both weak, the stress falls on the second vowel:

   viuda, cuita, buitre, jesuita, diurno, cuiden

These words follow the general rules of pronunciation, so a word like *cuídense* becomes a three-syllable word, and must carry an accent mark according to rule C. Words like *construido* and *fluido* do not form a diphthong since the stress falls on the second vowel to preserve pronunciation. An accent is not needed because the word follows rule B. Sometimes the word *fluido* is pronounced *flúido*, in which case it carries an accent mark because it becomes a three-syllable word.

C. When the stress is on earlier syllables

All words in this category carry an accent mark on the stressed syllable. Some examples are:

> archipiélago, averiguándolo, reponiéndomelas, entusiásticamente

Other words with diphthongs not affected by the accent mark are:

> diurético, cuidándolo.

Triphthongs

If the syllable contains a triphthong, which is a gliding combination of three vowels—two weak ones and a strong one in the middle—the accent is placed over the second vowel:

> licuáis, renunciáis, pronunciéis, Vieira, acentuéis.

All these words follow the general rules for the placing of accent marks. However, in the *vosotros* form of the conditional tense, such as *devolveríais*, *pediríais*, and *habríais*, the accent is placed on the first weak vowel to preserve pronunciation, and the triphthong disappears, forming a hiatus.

> NOTES:
>
> (1) The combination of vowels in words like *guión* and *guiar* does not constitute a triphthong since the letter *u* is silent. The syllable *gui* is pronounced as in the English word *guitar*. Besides, in both words there is a hiatus because the diphthong is eliminated by the stress on the strong vowels. They follow rule A.
>
> (2) The accent on the first weak vowel in the combination of four vowels that appears in the *vosotros* form of the conditional tense—as in *leíais* and *veíais*—divides the words into three syllables. There is a diphthong in the last syllable, however.

Hiatuses

The hiatus is a combination of two or more vowels that belong to different syllables. A hiatus may happen in a combination of words or inside one word. Accents are placed according to the rules of pronunciation. Some examples follow.

A. **Hiatuses in a combination of words:**

Está allí inerte.
Llamó u oyó todo.
Peleé en la batalla.
Va a Alabama.

C. **Hiatuses inside a word:**

Rule A: *peón, león, país, engreir, construir*
Rule B: *sentía, poema, poesías, canoa*
Rule C: *poético, paradisíaco, caótico, período*
Rule D: *poéticamente, feísimamente, críenoslo*

Monosyllables

Monosyllabic words do not carry accent marks. In some words of only one syllable where the exact same spelling and pronunciation can have different meanings (homonyms), the distinction between the meanings is made by placing an accent mark on one of them:

aún	yet, still	*aun*	even
dé	give (subjunctive)	*de*	of, from, letter "d"
él	he	*el*	the
más	more	*mas*	but
mí	me	*mi*	my, musical note
sé	I know	*se*	(pronoun)
sí	yes, him/herself	*si*	if, musical note
té	tea	*te*	(pronoun) and letter "t"
tú	you	*tu*	your
qué	what	*que*	that

Some exceptions are:

di	tell (command)		*di*	gave (past tense)

> **NOTE:**
>
> When the command **di** is used in a word that becomes a three-syllable word with the addition of pronouns, as in **dímelo**, the accent mark is used to agree with the general rules for written accent marks (rule C):

ve	go (command)		*ve*	see (command)

Optional Accent Marks

The following pronouns now require an accent mark only in cases when the meaning may be ambiguous; otherwise, the use of the accent mark is optional:

éste	this one (pronoun)		*este*	this (adjective)
ése	that one (pronoun)		*ese*	that (adjective)
aquél	that one there (pronoun)		*aquel*	that (adjective)
sólo	only		*solo*	alone, single

Classification of Words

Homonyms

Homonyms are words that are spelled and pronounced the same way, but have different meanings. Some examples are

aún ➤ *aun; té* ➤ *te; dé* ➤ *de*

More information is provided in Appendix A, Accents, under the heading Monosyllables.

Antonyms

These are words of opposite meaning. Some examples are:

cómodo	comfortable	*molesto*	uncomfortable
exterior	exterior	*interior*	interior
fuerte	strong	*débil*	weak
idéntico	identical	*distinto*	different
mentira	lie	*verdad*	truth
obediente	obedient	*rebelde*	rebellious

Synonyms

These are words that have the same or nearly the same meaning as another word in the same language. Some examples are:

inesperado	sudden	*imprevisto*	unforeseen
inferior	inferior	*subordinado*	subordinate
modificación	modification	*reforma*	reform
mudar	to alter	*cambiar*	to change

nación	nation	*patria*	fatherland
pesado	heavy	*insoportable*	unbearable
precioso	precious	*valioso*	valuable

Paronyms

These are words that are similar because of their etymology or form, but that have different meanings. Some examples are:

abertura	opening	*obertura*	overture
abrazar	to hug	*abrasar*	to burn
acto	act	*apto*	apt
extracto	extract	*estrato*	stratum
lesión	injury	*lección*	lesson
prescindir	to do without	*presidir*	to preside
rayar	to scratch	*rallar*	to grate

Division of Words into Syllables

Words are divided in Spanish according to the following rules.

A. One consonant between two vowels

If there is one consonant between two vowels, the consonant joins the following vowel:

*co-**mi-do**; Pe-**pi-t**a; pa-**ja-ri-t**o.*

At the end of a line, words are separated accordingly:

*Le dije que nosotros siempre hemos **comi-do** en ese restaurante.*

I told him that we have always eaten in that restaurant.

*En su casa tiene muchos **pa-jaritos** cantores.*

At her house, she has many singing birds.

B. Consonant groups

The following consonants grouped together are considered as one consonant and begin a syllable with the next vowel:

bl   br   ch   cl   cr   dr   fl   fr   gl   gr   ll   pl   pr   rr   tr

Examples:

*p**r**o-ce-so; re-**cl**a-mo; re-**tr**a-to; se-**ll**a-do; co-**rr**i-da; mu-**ch**o*

> **NOTES:**
>
> **(1)** These consonants remain together when the syllables are separated at the end of the line, for example in a handwritten note:
>
> *En el museo tenían estatuas y muchos re-**tr**atos de los reyes.*
>
> At the museum they had statues and many portraits of the kings.

Todos los documentos estaban se-   All the documents were sealed and signed.
  llados y firmados.

(2) If the combination *rr* appears in a compound word, as in **contrarreforma**, the double *rr* is not used if the compound word is divided with a hyphen after the first word at the end of the line:

contra-reforma

The word **interrelacionar** is divided into **inter-relacionar** at the end of the line. (Derivatives of this word also keep both words when divided at the end of a line.)

(3) The letter *x* is the equivalent of two consonants in a row, either *gs* or *cs*. In its written form, this letter is grouped with the following vowel:

*e-**xa**-men; pró-**xi**-mo; ta-**xi***

However, when pronounced, it is attached to the previous vowel:

***ex**/amen; **próx**/imo; **tax**/i.*

C. Other consonant combinations

In the case of a combination of consonants not included in rule B, the consonants are separated and each one is grouped with the vowel next to it:

*Car-los; son-**da**; pan-ta-no*

D. Three consonants between two vowels

If there are three consonants between two vowels, the following rules apply.

1. If two of the consonants constitute one of the pairs listed in rule B, those consonants stay together:

*com-**pli**-ca-do; res-**trin**-gi-do; es-**plén**-di-do*

2. If none of the combinations listed in rule B are present, the first two consonants are joined to the vowel before them and the third consonant is joined to the following vowel:

ist-mo; cons-tan-te.

E. Combinations of four consonants

If there is a combination of four consonants, the word is divided as follows:

mons-truo	The *tr* stays together, as specified in rule B. The combination *ns* follows the rule given for the first two consonants in rule D, point 2.
trans-plan-tar	The *pl* stays together, as specified in rule B. The combination *ns* follows the rule given for the first two consonants in rule D, point 2.
subs-tra-er	The *tr* stays together, as specified in rule B. The combination *bs* follows the rule given for the first two consonants in rule D, point 2.

F. Hiatuses

Vowels that follow each other and are not part of a diphthong or a triphthong are separated as part of other syllables and form a hiatus. For more details, consult Appendix A, under the headings Diphthongs, Triphthongs, and Hiatuses. Some examples are:

a-zo-te-a; car-dí-a-co; le-í-a-mos; cre-í-as.

> **NOTE:**
>
> The vowels that form a diphthong or a triphthong stay together when the word is separated into syllables:
>
> *cau-sa; pia-no; a-nun-ciéis*

G. Word division: single vowels should not stand alone

When it is necessary to separate a word at the end of the line, and the first or the last syllable is a vowel, the vowel should not stand alone, and should be attached to the following or previous syllable, depending on the case:

a-con-se-ja-ble	➤	***acon**-sejable* (<u>Not:</u> *a-consejable*)
a-sam-ble-a	➤	*asam-**blea*** (<u>Not:</u> *asamble-**a**)*

H. Word division: *nn* and *cc*

In words with the combinations *nn* and *cc*, these letters are separated into different syllables:

*in-**n**o-va-dor; in-**n**o-ble; lec-**c**ión; re-dac-**c**ión*

I. Word division: foreign words

Foreign words are divided according to the rules in use in the original language, as in *Ten-nes-see*. The user may consult a dictionary of the foreign language in order to divide the word appropriately; otherwise, it is possible to separate the syllables according to the rules in the user's own language.

J. Word division: prefixes

If a word has a prefix, and the word needs to be divided at the end of the line, it is best to separate the prefix from the rest of the word, as in ***pre-decir*** and ***des-unión***.

K. Word division: *h* after a consonant

When a word has an *h* preceded by a consonant, these two letters get divided:

> *al-ha-ja, al-he-lí, des-hie-lo, des-hi-lar, in-hu-ma-no, in-hós-pi-to*

L. Word division: the combination *tl*

In words that contain the combination *tl*, which are very few, these letters stay together:

> *A-tlán-ti-co, a-tlas, a-tle-ta*

Sample Conjugations with the Pronoun *vos*

The pronoun *vos* is widely used throughout Latin America. It can be said that at least in some part of each country, *vos* is used by itself or in combination with *tú*. Argentina and Uruguay are two of the countries where it is used the most, while in Puerto Rico and the Dominican Republic the influence of this pronoun is minimal or nonexistent.

Below are all the conjugations of Spanish verbs in three of the persons: *yo*, *tú*, and *vos*. Just as with any other personal pronoun, the pronoun *vos* itself need not be present when conjugating a verb; its use is optional in both the oral and the written forms.

A. **The present indicative tense**

1. Regular verbs

hablar	*yo hablo*	*tú hablas*	*vos hablás*
beber	*yo bebo*	*tú bebes*	*vos bebés*
vivir	*yo vivo*	*tú vives*	*vos vivís*

2. Irregular verbs

(a) Stem-changing verbs:

e ➤ i pedir	*yo pido*	*tú pides*	*vos pedís*
e ➤ ie pensar	*yo pienso*	*tú piensas*	*vos pensás*
i ➤ ie adquirir	*yo adquiero*	*tú adquieres*	*vos adquirís*
o ➤ ue poder	*yo puedo*	*tú puedes*	*vos podés*
oler	*yo huelo*	*tú hueles*	*vos olés*
u ➤ ue jugar	*yo juego*	*tú juegas*	*vos jugás*

(b) First-person irregular verbs:

add -g tener	yo tengo	tú tienes	**vos tenés**
add -ig caer	yo caigo	tú caes	**vos caés**
c ➤ g hacer	yo hago	tú haces	**vos hacés**
g ➤ j dirigir	yo dirijo	tú diriges	**vos dirigís**
gu ➤ g conseguir	yo consigo	tú consigues	**vos conseguís**
c ➤ z ejercer	yo ejerzo	tú ejerces	**vos ejercés**
c ➤ zc crecer	yo crezco	tú creces	**vos crecés**

(c) Other irregular forms

■ Changes in the stem:

caber	yo quepo	tú cabes	**vos cabés**

■ Changes in the ending:

dar	yo doy	tú das	**vos das**
estar	yo estoy	tú estás	**vos estás**
saber	yo sé	tú sabes	**vos sabés**
ver	yo veo	tú ves	**vos ves**

(d) Irregular forms in more than one person:

ir	yo voy	tú vas	**vos vas**
ser	yo soy	tú eres	**vos sos**
haber	yo he	tú has	**vos has***

■ add -*y*:

oír	yo oigo	tú oyes	**vos oís**
huir	yo huyo	tú huyes	**vos huís**

■ add an accent on *i* or *u*:

esquiar	yo esquío	tú esquías	**vos esquiás**
continuar	yo continúo	tú continúas	**vos continuás**

---

* Although this is the correct form, speakers generally do not use the present perfect, as in *vos has hablado*. Instead, they use the preterit tense: *vos hablaste*.

3. Reflexive verbs

(a) Regular verbs:

lavarse	*me lavo*	*te lavas*	*(vos) te lavás*

(b) Irregular verbs:

dormirse	*me duermo*	*te duermes*	*(vos) te dormís*
ponerse	*me pongo*	*te pones*	*(vos) te ponés*

4. The verb *gustar* and similar verbs:

gustar	*me gusta/n*	*te gusta/n*	*te gusta/n*
faltar	*me falta/n*	*te falta/n*	*te falta/n*

When the verb form is preceded by *A mí, A tí*, etc., as in *A mí me gusta* and *A ti te gustan*, the *vos* form is *A vos te gusta/n*.

B. **The future tense**

1. The informal future

This tense is formed with the present indicative of *ir,* the personal *a*, and the infinitive of the main verb, which is invariable:

cantar	*yo voy a cantar*	*tú vas a cantar*	*vos vas a cantar*
pedir	*yo voy a pedir*	*tú vas a pedir*	*vos vas a pedir*

Direct and indirect object pronouns are used according to the general rules:

vos lo vas a cantar	or	*vos vas a cantarlo*
vos me lo vas a dar	or	*vos vas a dármelo*

2. The simple future

Speakers who use the pronoun *vos* prefer the informal future instead of the simple future.

3. Regular verbs:

-ar	*besar*	*yo besaré*	*tú besarás*	*vos besarás*
-er	*comer*	*yo comeré*	*tú comerás*	*vos comerás*
-ir	*escribir*	*yo escribiré*	*tú escribirás*	*vos escribirás*

4. Irregular verbs:

poner	yo pondré	tú pondrás	**vos pondrás**
decir	yo diré	tú dirás	**vos dirás**

C. The future perfect tense

This form uses the future of the auxiliary verb *haber* and the past participle of the main verb. The *vos* form follows the normal pattern:

restar	yo habré restado	tú habrás restado	**vos habrás restado**
perder	yo habré perdido	tú habrás perdido	**vos habrás perdido**
salir	yo habré salido	tú habrás salido	**vos habrás salido**

D. The imperfect indicative tense

1. Regular verbs:

-ar	andar	yo andaba	tú andabas	**vos andabas**
-er	volver	yo volvía	tú volvías	**vos volvías**
-ir	vivir	yo vivía	tú vivías	**vos vivías**

2. Irregular verbs:

ser	yo era	tú eras	**vos eras**
ir	yo iba	tú ibas	**vos ibas**
ver	yo veía	tú veías	**vos veías**

E. The preterit tense

1. Regular verbs:

-ar	bailar	yo bailé	tú bailaste	**vos bailaste**
-er	barrer	yo barrí	tú barriste	**vos barriste**
-ir	abrir	yo abrí	tú abriste	**vos abriste**

2. Irregular verbs

(a) Irregular in all the forms

ser	yo fui	tú fuiste	**vos fuiste**
ir	yo fui	tú fuiste	**vos fuiste**

dar	yo di	tú diste	**vos diste**
andar	yo anduve	tú anduviste	**vos anduviste**
hacer	yo hice	tú hiciste	**vos hiciste**
caber	yo cupe	tú cupiste	**vos cupiste**
saber	yo supe	tú supiste	**vos supiste**

(b) First-personal irregular

| buscar | yo busqué | tú buscaste | **vos buscaste** |
| pagar | yo pagué | tú pagaste | **vos pagaste** |

(c) Stem-changing verbs

almorzar	yo almorcé	tú almorzaste	**vos almorzaste**
volver	yo volví	tú volviste	**vos volviste**
pedir	yo pedí	tú pediste	**vos pediste**
preferir	yo preferí	tú preferiste	**vos preferiste**
dormir	yo dormí	tú dormiste	**vos dormiste**

F. The conditional tense

1. Regular verbs:

-ar	besar	yo besaría	tú besarías	**vos besarías**
-er	comer	yo comería	tú comerías	**vos comerías**
-ir	escribir	yo escribiría	tú escribirías	**vos escribirías**

2. Irregular verbs:

| tener | yo tendría | tú tendrías | **vos tendrías** |
| salir | yo saldría | tú saldrías | **vos saldrías** |

G. The conditional perfect tense

This tense uses the conditional of the auxiliary verb *haber* and the past participle of the main verb, which is invariable:

pensar	yo habría pensado	tú habrías pensado	**vos habrías pensado**
tender	yo habría tendido	tú habrías tendido	**vos habrías tendido**
ir	yo habría ido	tú habrías ido	**vos habrías ido**

H. The progressive tenses (using the present participle)

1. The present progressive

This tense uses the present indicative of the verb *estar* and the present participle (gerund) of the main verb, which is invariable:

cocinar	yo estoy cocinando	tú estás cocinando	**vos estás cocinando**
ver	yo estoy viendo	tú estás viendo	**vos estás viendo**
decir	yo estoy diciendo	tú estás diciendo	**vos estás diciendo**

2. The past progressive

This tense uses the imperfect indicative of *estar* and the present participle (gerund) of the main verb, which is invariable:

andar	yo estaba andando	tú estabas andando	**vos estabas andando**
coser	yo estaba cosiendo	tú estabas cosiendo	**vos estabas cosiendo**
sentir	yo estaba sintiendo	tú estabas sintiendo	**vos estabas sintiendo**

I. The present perfect indicative

This tense uses the present tense of the auxiliary verb *haber* and the past participle of the main verb, which is invariable:

avisar	yo he avisado	tú has avisado	**vos has avisado***
leer	yo he leído	tú has leído	**vos has leído**
abrir	yo he abierto	tú has abierto	**vos has abierto**

J. The past perfect indicative

This tense uses the imperfect indicative of the auxiliary verb *haber* and the past participle of the main verb, which is invariable:

mirar	yo había mirado	tú habías mirado	**vos habías mirado**
poner	yo había puesto	tú habías puesto	**vos habías puesto**
reñir	yo había reñido	tú habías reñido	**vos habías reñido**

---

* Although this is the correct form, according to the informal rule speakers generally use the preterit tense instead of the present perfect: *vos avisaste.*

K. The subjunctive

1. The present subjunctive

This tense is derived from the *yo* form of the present indicative:

-ar	usar	yo use	tú uses	**vos uses**
-er	vender	yo venda	tú vendas	**vos vendas**
-ir	venir	yo venga	tú vengas	**vos vengas**

2. The imperfect subjunctive

This tense is derived from the *ellos* form of the preterit tense:

-ar	mostrar	yo mostrara	tú mostraras	**vos mostraras**
-er	hacer	yo hiciera	tú hicieras	**vos hicieras**
-ir	ir	yo fuera	tú fueras	**vos fueras**

3. The present perfect subjunctive

This tense uses the present subjunctive form of the auxiliary verb *haber* and the past participle of the main verb, which is invariable:

dibujar	yo haya dibujado	tú hayas dibujado	**vos hayas dibujado**
tener	yo haya tenido	tú hayas tenido	**vos hayas tenido**
escribir	yo haya escrito	tú hayas escrito	**vos hayas escrito**

4. The pluperfect (or past) subjunctive

This tense uses the imperfect subjunctive form of the auxiliary verb *haber* and the past participle of the main verb, which is invariable:

atar	yo hubiera atado	tú hubieras atado	**vos hubieras atado**
mover	yo hubiera movido	tú hubieras movido	**vos hubieras movido**
morir	yo hubiera muerto	tú hubieras muerto	**vos hubieras muerto**

L. The imperative (commands)

1. Affirmative commands

The final *d* of the *vosotros* form is dropped. An accent mark is used in the three conjugations:

vosotros:	¡Sacad!	¡Recorred!	¡Permitid!
vos:	**¡Sacá!**	**¡Recorré!**	**¡Permití!**

2. Negative commands

The letter *i* of the **vosotros** form of the present subjunctive is dropped:

vosotros:	¡No saquéis!	¡No recorráis!	¡No permitáis!
vos:	**¡No saques!**	**¡No recorras!**	**¡No permitas!***

> **NOTE:**
>
> Pronouns are attached to affirmative commands: *¡Sacálo!* In negative commands, *no* and the pronoun are placed before the verb: *¡No lo saques!*
>
> When pronouns are attached to the irregular, affirmative, short command forms, such as *di*, *pon*, *haz*, and *ten*, the whole word is used: *decime* (tell me) instead of *dime*; *decímelo* (say it to me) instead of *dímelo*; *ponelo* (put it) instead of *ponlo*; *ponéselo* (put it on him) instead of *pónselo*; *hacelo* (do it) instead of *hazlo*; *tenelo* (have it, hold it) instead of *tenlo*; etc.

---

* In the lyrics of some Argentine tangos, the negative command carries an accent mark, as in *¡No saqués!*, *¡No recorrás!*, *¡No permitás!*

Punctuation

A. The period (*el punto*)

1. At the end of a complete sentence, the period in Spanish is called *punto*. If the sentence is followed by another sentence, it is no longer called just *punto,* but rather *punto y seguido*. At the end of a paragraph, it becomes *punto y aparte* if the paragraph is followed by another paragraph. The final period in a text is called *punto final*. In the example that follows, the name of each mark is spelled out for clarification purposes:

> *Con el Neoclasicismo no había tantos temas religiosos (punto y seguido). Los españoles esta-ban interesados en sus retratos y en su inmortalidad (punto y seguido). Había muchos encargos de la nueva burguesía (punto y aparte).*
>
> *La escultura española no produjo escultores buenos como los franceses (punto y seguido). José Álvarez Cubero se destacó como escultor (punto y seguido). Estudió en la Academia de Bellas Artes de San Fernando (punto y seguido). Una de sus obras más conocidas es «La defensa de Zaragoza» (punto final).*

2. To express *thousands* and *millions*, the period is used in Spanish; however, decimals are separated by a comma:

   7.345   22.972   667.009   1.447.723   567,98

3. Abbreviations are followed by a period (***punto***):

   Ud.   *Sr.*   *prov.* (province)   *p. ej.* (for example)

B. The comma (*la coma*)

The comma is used in Spanish in the following contexts.

1. The comma is used with vocatives, to address someone:

   Mire, María, aquí están las tazas.   Look, María, here are the cups.

2. The comma is used with appositives, to identify a noun:

La Sra. Velez, maestra de primer grado, ganó el premio.

Mrs. Velez, the first grade teacher, won the prize.

3. The comma is used to separate nouns in a series; however, no comma is placed before the *y* (*and*):

Compré lápices, cuadernos, etiquetas y lapiceras.

I bought pencils, notebooks, labels, and pens.

4. The comma is used when a subordinate sentence precedes the main sentence:

Pensando que Juan iba a venir, preparé una ensalada.

Thinking that Juan was coming, I prepared a salad.

5. The comma is used after expressions such as *sin embargo, no obstante, por ejemplo, es decir*:

Vendimos la casa, es decir, nos vamos a mudar.

We sold the house, that is to say, we are moving.

C. The colon (*los dos puntos*)

The colon is used in Spanish in the following contexts.

1. The colon is used before a literal reproduction of a text:

Carlos respondió: «Más vale tarde que nunca».

Carlos answered, "Better late than never."

2. The colon is used to introduce a list:

Debes recordar tres cosas: salud, dinero y amor.

You must remember three things: health, money, and love.

3. The colon is used after a salutation in letters:

Estimado Sr. Ruiz:
Querido Pedro:

Dear Mr. Ruiz:
Dear Pedro,

4. The colon is used to introduce a clause that explains the one before it:

Los celulares han cambiado el mundo: ahora Cellular phones have changed the world: now
no se puede vivir sin un teléfono celular. nobody can live without one.

D. The semicolon (*el punto y coma*)

The semicolon is used in Spanish in the following contexts.

1. The semicolon is used to connect two sentences that are related to each other:

Ayer me llamó Carmen; las cosas andan muy Carmen called me yesterday; things are going
bien ahora. well now.

2. The semicolon is used to connect a series of sentences that contain commas:

El Sr. Gómez dijo que no hicieran el trabajo, Mr. Gómez said not to do the work, since he
pues ya lo tenía terminado; que no se had already finished it; not to forget to
olvidaran de echar las cartas, porque hoy mail the letters, because today was the
se vencía el plazo; que no faltaran a la expiration date; not to miss the meeting,
reunión, porque el asunto era importante. because the subject was important.

3. The semicolon is used before conjunctions such as *sin embargo*, *aunque*, *pero*, *mas*, etc., if there is already a comma in the sentence:

Los aficionados, que estaban juntos en una The fans, who were together in one section
sección del estadio, mostraban pancartas; of the stadium, were showing banners;
sin embargo, se quedaron tristes cuando however, they became sad when the
perdió el equipo. team lost.

E. Ellipsis points (*los puntos suspensivos*)

Ellipsis points in Spanish are represented by three periods without spaces in between. No period is added to the ellipsis points at the end of the sentence. They are used as follows.

1. Ellipsis points to indicate an omission, which does not change the meaning of the sentence, and intends to make the reader think or imagine the scene. The first example that follows shows a complete sentence; however, no period is used after the ellipsis points:

El jardín estaba precioso... Había rosas y The garden was beautiful . . . . There were
jazmines. roses and jasmine.

In the next example, the ellipsis points are inserted in the middle of the sentence. They indicate a hesitation by the speaker:

Empezó diciendo que... el viaje será en junio.	She began saying that . . . the trip will be in June.

2. Ellipsis points to indicate an omission within material that has been reproduced literally:

«Durante la sesión del jurado (...) se notificó de la nueva fecha».
"During the session of the jury . . . they were notified of the new date."
«El presidente anunció [...] la reforma de la constitución».
"The president announced . . . the amendment of the constitution."

Notice in the preceding examples that the ellipsis points may be placed between either parentheses or brackets (*corchetes*).

3. Ellipsis points to indicate feelings of doubt or surprise:

Ellos vinieron a las... 5 de la tarde, más o menos.	They came at around . . . 5 in the afternoon.
Abrí el sobre... ¡y encontré un cheque adentro!	I opened the envelope . . . and I found a check inside!

4. Ellipsis points to leave open an enumeration:

En la feria había peras, manzanas, naranjas...	In the market, there were pears, apples, oranges . . . .

F. Quotation marks (*las comillas*)

Quotation marks are used in Spanish as follows.

1. Quotation marks before and after a literal quote:

El senador se lamentó: «La crisis económica produce caos y violencia».	The senator lamented: "The economic crisis is producing chaos and violence."

2. Quotation marks to emphasize a word that is used with a different meaning:

Felipe era un «león» cuando se trataba de defender a sus hijos.	Felipe was a "lion" when it came to defending his children.

3. The English quotation marks (" ") can also be used in Spanish.

4. Single quotation marks are used, for any of the previous reasons given, in a sentence that is already within (double) quotation marks:

Raúl asintió: "Creo que todos los 'menores' deben asistir".

Raúl agreed: "I believe that all the 'minors' have to attend."

G. The dash (*el guión, la raya*)

There are two types of dashes in Spanish.

1. The short dash, or hyphen, called *guión*, is used to separate syllables of a word at the end of a line.

2. The long dash, called *raya*, is used to introduce the speakers in a dialogue:

—Juan, ¿cuándo van a entregarte el documento?

—No lo sé. Posiblemente mañana.

—¿Crees que de veras lo tendrás?

—¡Ya te lo dije! ¡No lo sé!

"Juan, when are they going to give you the document?"

"I don't know. Possibly tomorrow."

"Do you think that you will have it for sure?

"I already told you! I don't know!"

3. The *raya* is also used to show direct speech:

—Juan, ¿cuándo van a entregarte el documento? —dijo Alberto— ¿mañana?

"Juan, when are they going to give you the document?"—Alberto said—"tomorrow?"

4. The *raya* is also used to insert text to clarify or to give emphasis:

El salón principal—alfombrado en rojo— mostraba el carácter de su dueña.

The main room—covered with red carpet— showed its owner's character.

H. Parentheses

Parentheses are used in Spanish to clarify a statement:

La calle Florida (la más tradicional) está llena de tiendas lindas.

Florida Street (the most traditional) is full of pretty stores.

I. The apostrophe (*el apóstrofe*)

Apostrophes are not used in modern Spanish. In the oldest literary works, an apostrophe was sometimes used instead of a letter, but this is no longer the case nowadays.

J. Question marks and exclamation points *(signos de interrogación y de admiración)*

All questions and exclamatory sentences in Spanish begin with upside-down marks and end with normal punctuation marks:

¿Cuántas materias vas a tomar el semestre próximo?	How many subjects are you going to take next semester?
¡Qué buena era la clase de anatomía!	How good the anatomy class was!z

Index

manner (by + gerund in
English), 232–33
regular endings, 226
replacements for, 231–32
stems, 227–28
use of infinitive as the object of
a verb, 233
with direct and indirect objects,
233–34
with reflexive or reciprocal
verbs, 234
Present perfect indicative, 241–43
Present perfect subjunctive,
285–87
Present subjunctive
irregular forms, 270–71
regular verbs, conjugations for
-ar, -er, and -ir verbs, 265
stem-changing verbs, 266–68
uses, 271–76
verbs that change the stem to
preserve pronunciation,
269–70
verbs with irregular first persons
in the present indicative,
268–69
Preterit perfect, 246, 247
Preterit tense
action in the past viewed as a
whole, 206
action that extends into the
present, 206
change expressed by a reflexive
or reciprocal verb, 208
completed action in the past,
206
completed action of specific
length, 208
contrast with imperfect,
210–12
event prior to another event in
the past, 207
event that had a specific
beginning or end, 207
irregular forms, 201–2
obligation or duty with *deber* +
infinitive, 208
progression of an event with
irse + the gerund, 208

regular verbs, 200
series of events within a
segment of time, 207
sudden change in time or
condition, 208
verbs that change their meaning
in, 209
with verbs of action or
movement, 207
Prices, with *estar*, 81
primero, 154, 155, 156, 157
Primitive adverbs, 442
Probability, 221, 225
Professions
gender of, 32, 34
nouns with no plural form, 39
with indefinite article, 22
with *ser*, 76–77
Progressive tenses
adverbs that modify verbs in,
445–46
present progressive, 75
use of present participle,
228–30
with gerund and present
participle, 234
Pronouns, 315–400. *See also*
Direct object pronouns;
Indirect object pronouns;
Personal pronouns
acting as a noun, 48
adverbs functioning as, 449
and nouns, 51–52
complemented by adverb, 448
lo as a demonstrative pronoun,
349
propio/a, 114, 171
Proverbs, with direct article, 15
próximo, with direct article, 15
Punctuation
apostrophe, 493–94
colon, 490–91
comma, 489–90
dash, 493
ellipsis points, 491–92
parentheses, 493
period, 489
question marks and
exclamation points, 495

quotation marks, 492–93
semicolon, 491

Qualifying adverbs, 435
Quantity, adverbs of, 441
que, 55–56, 58–59, 254–55,
356–64
qué (interrogative pronoun),
375–76, 381–82
¡Qué…! with indefinite article, 26
quedar, 230
quedarse, 82
querer, 195, 196, 209, 223
Question marks, 495
quien, quienes, 365–67
quién, quiénes (interrogative
pronoun), 378–79, 382
quien, relative pronoun, 56
Quotation marks , 492–93

Reciprocal pronouns, 234,
390–93
Reflexive pronouns
and reciprocal pronouns,
390–91
forms, 386, 387
functions, 389–90
position, 387–89
Reflexive verbs
in the present tense, 72
in simple future, 193
intransitive character of,
391–92
semantic changes in, 392–93
verbs that change meaning,
392
vs. equivalent nonreflexive
forms in English, 391–92
with present participle, 234
Relative adverb, 435
Relative clause, as replacement for
present participle, 231
Relative pronouns
adverbs functioning as, 450
after other prepositions, 374
after prepositions *a, de, con, en*,
373–74
and adjectives, 374
as direct object, 372–73